AF521795

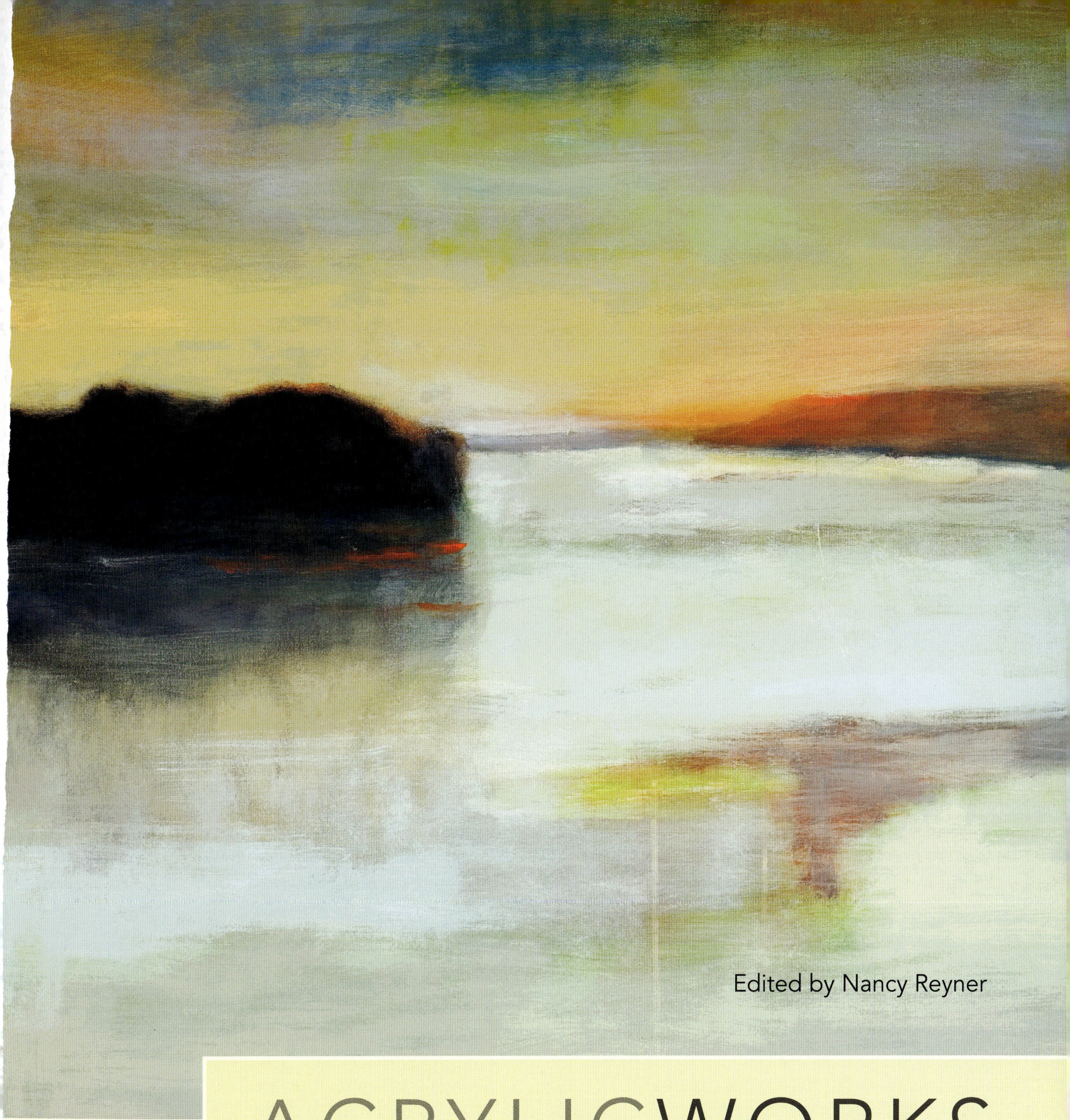

Edited by Nancy Reyner

ACRYLICWORKS

THE BEST OF ACRYLIC PAINTING

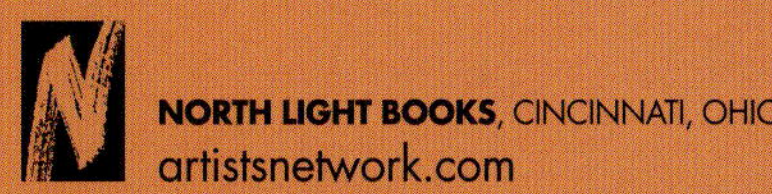
NORTH LIGHT BOOKS, CINCINNATI, OHIO
artistsnetwork.com

CONTENTS

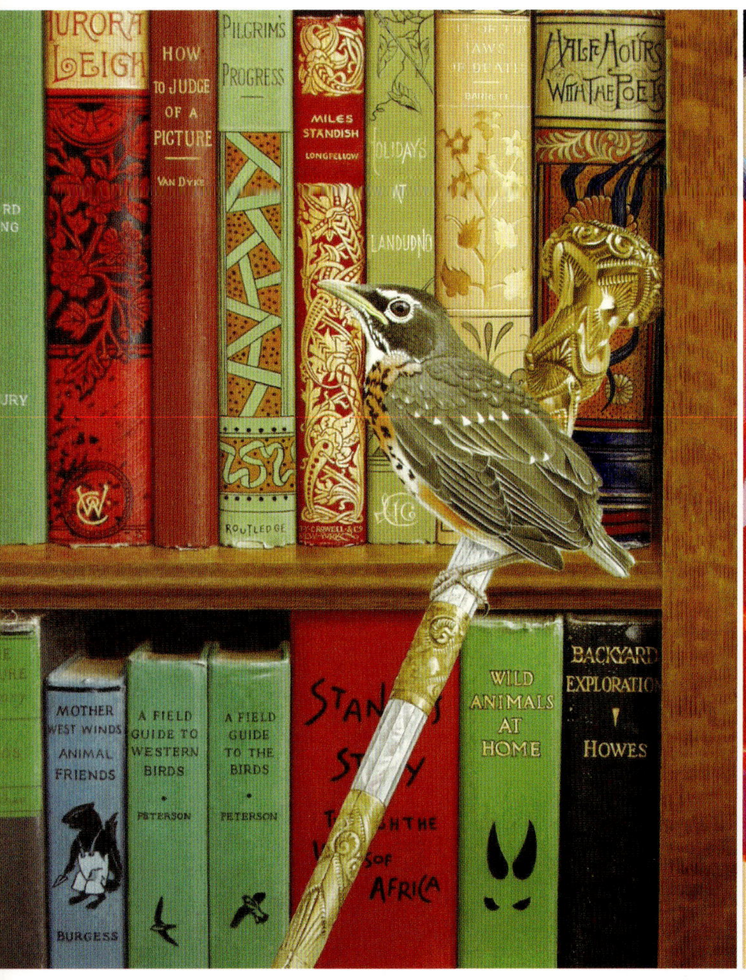
HOW TO JUDGE OF A PICTURE
VAN DYKE
PILGRIMS PROGRESS
ROUTLEDGE
MILES STANDISH
LONGFELLOW
HALF-HOURS WITH THE POETS
MOTHER WEST WINDS ANIMAL FRIENDS
BURGESS
A FIELD GUIDE TO WESTERN BIRDS
PETERSON
A FIELD GUIDE TO THE BIRDS
PETERSON
WILD ANIMALS AT HOME
BACKYARD EXPLORATION
HOWES

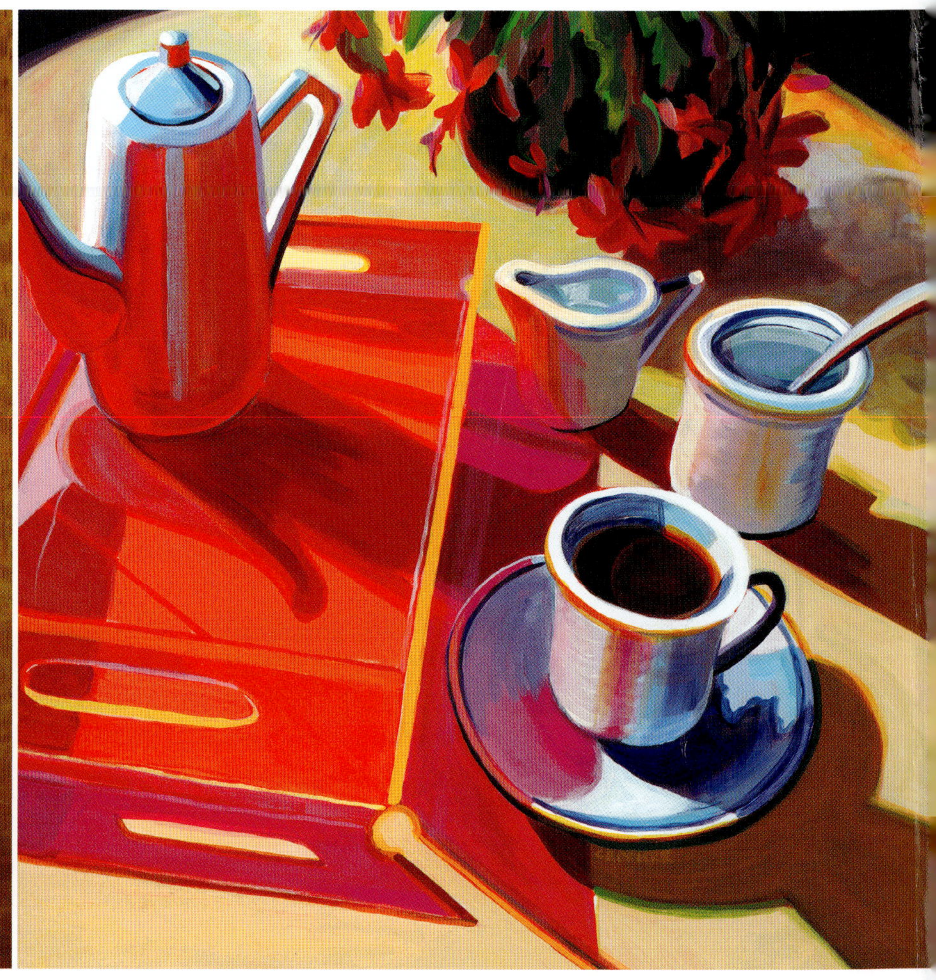

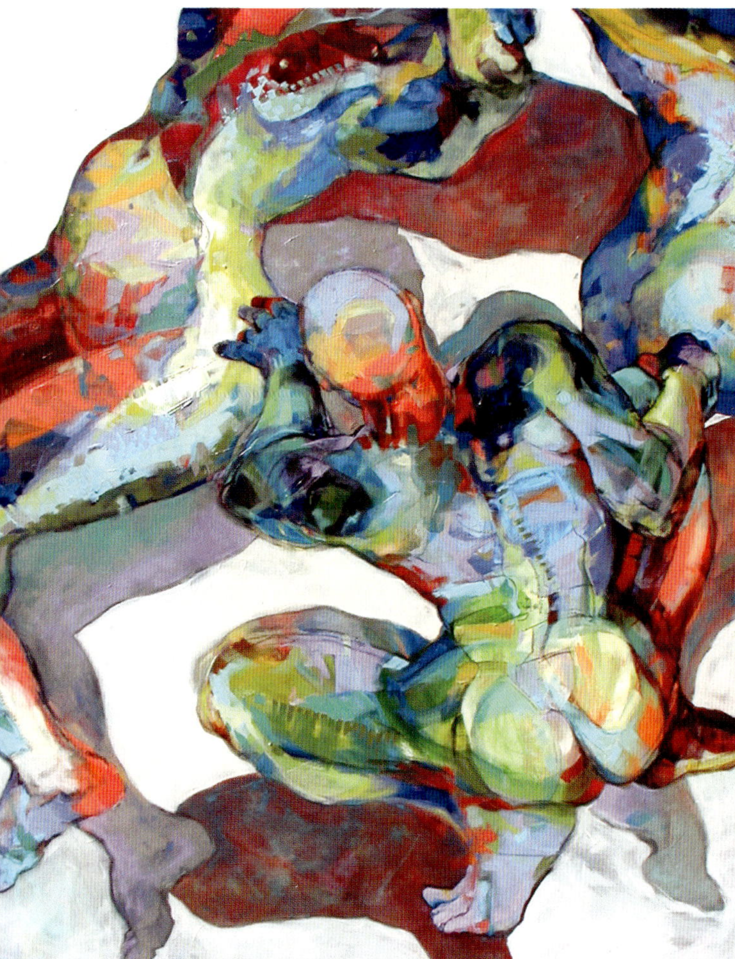

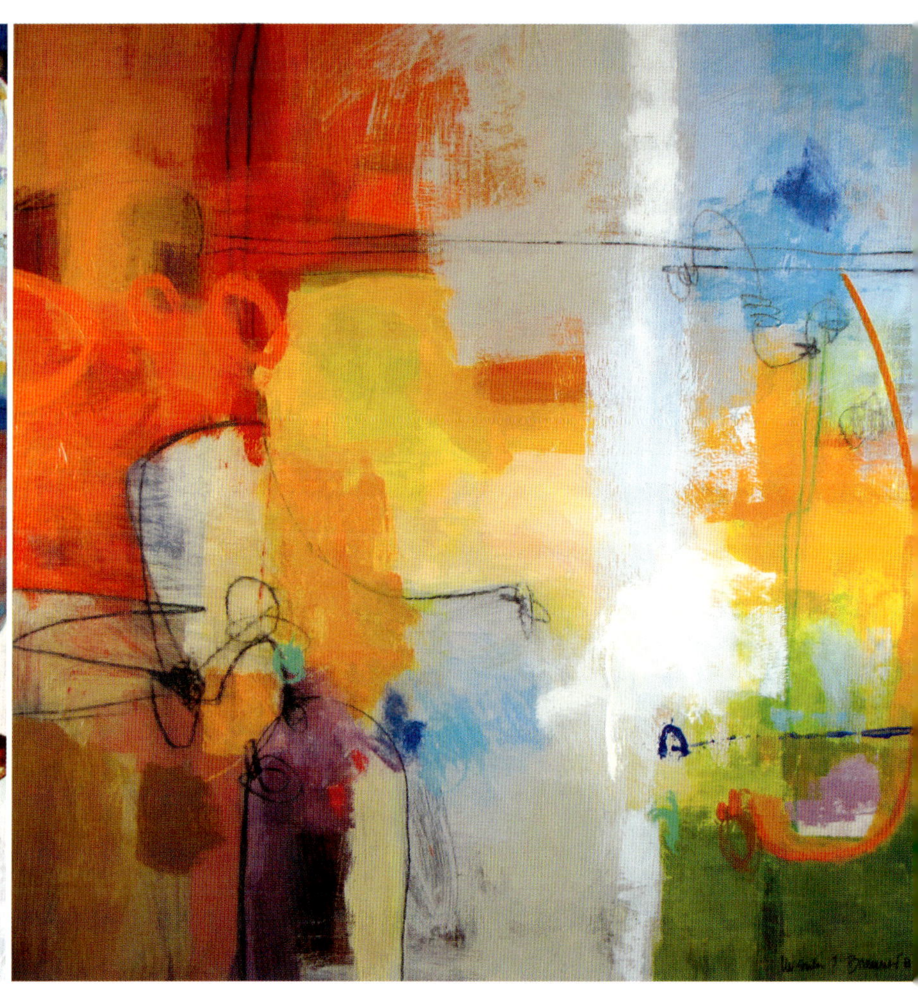

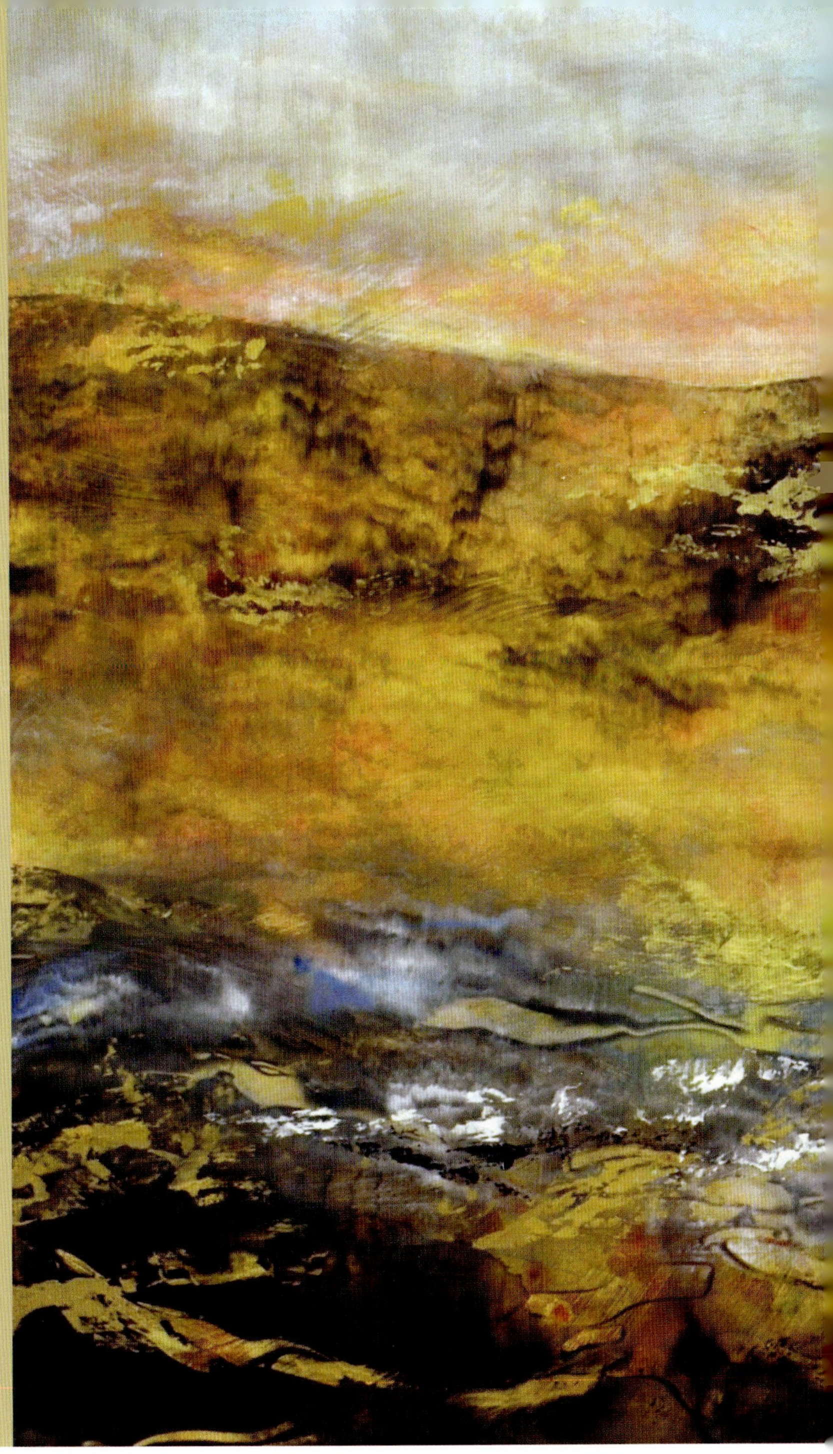

INTRODUCTION

Each of us has the ability to bring creativity to all we do. I am grateful for those who choose to express themselves through making art. Powerful art allows us to feel a connection to others, to humanity and our culture. Art adds a great deal to my life experience – both viewing and making it. So I was pleased and honored to jury artwork for this book.

While some art books focus on a specific subject matter or style (e.g. still life, landscape, abstraction, etc.), this book focuses on a single medium – acrylic. And what a medium! Acrylic is extremely versatile and capable of an incredible spectrum of effects and techniques. An appropriate analogy is to compare acrylic paint to all other mediums just as Photoshop compares to a typewriter. Even though acrylic can imitate other art mediums such as oil, watercolor and encaustic (wax), it goes way beyond by offering unique effects only possible with acrylic.

And so I embarked on this jurying journey, hopeful that the submissions would enable a diverse selection, fitting for this "king of mediums." My prayers were answered at first sight of the submitted artworks. How delighted I was to view the impressive variety of styles, techniques and subject matter! In selecting works for this book I was foremost interested in demonstrating this diversity, convinced that this could help dispel a myth that working in acrylic also means the work must be abstract. Both realism and abstraction are represented here along with a wide window of hybrid and experimental styles.

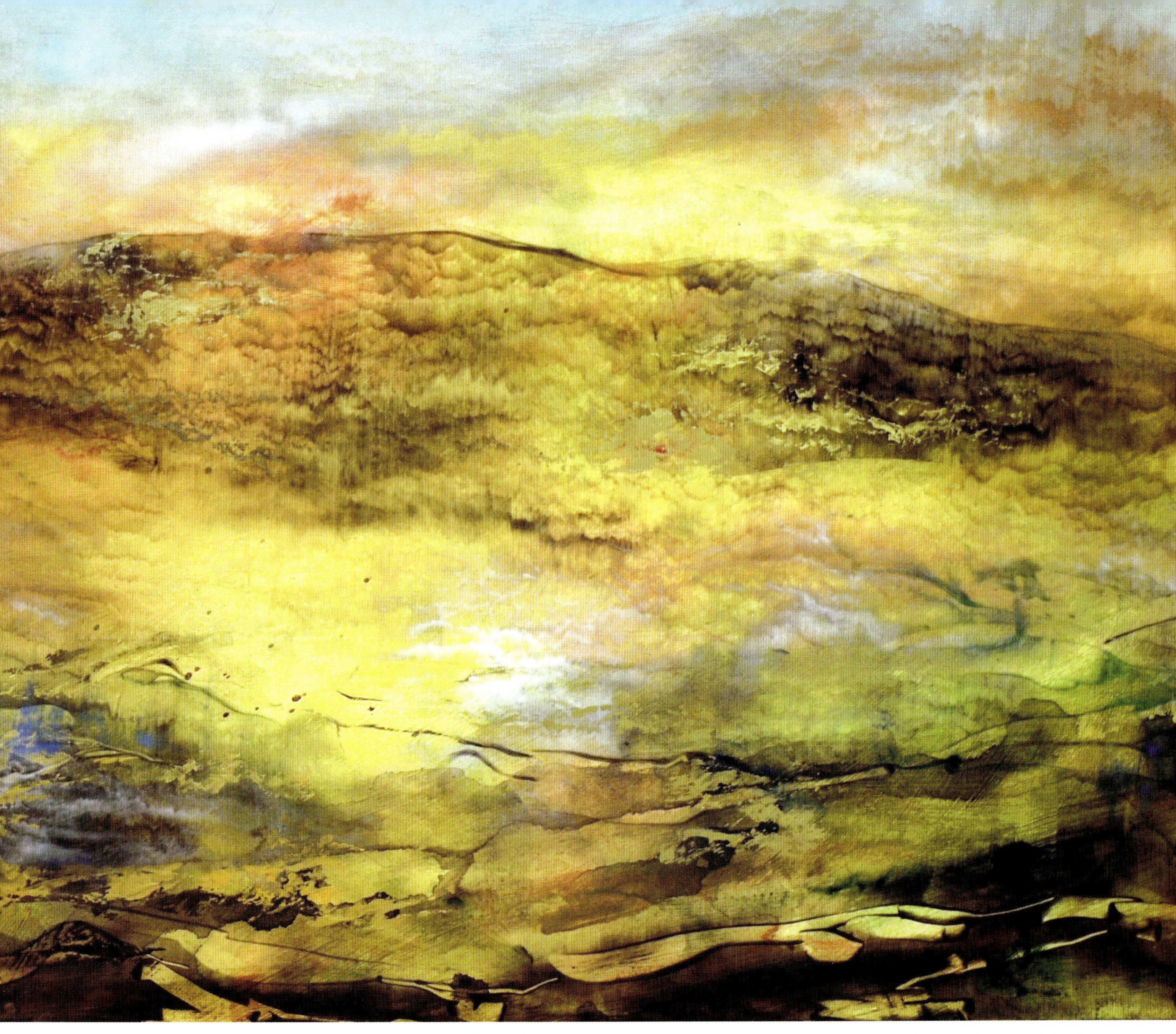

STONES OF FIRE II, Nancy Reyner, Acrylic and gold leaf on panel, 23" × 41" (58cm × 104cm)

I approached this assignment with excitement and curiosity along with a touch of sentiment as I realized that not all of the deserving works will be able to be included. First I arranged the works into groups representing the wide diversity. The two main categories of style, realism and abstraction, were not enough for this task. Instead I broke these down into subgroups such as color field and non-objective abstraction, abstraction with recognizable imagery, realism with a specific focus (e.g. people, landscapes, animals, still life and objects, architecture). There was an abundance of fabulous images in every category to choose from. In all cases I favored a visible collaboration between artist and medium allowing the medium to show through the imagery. Additionally I looked for a combination of technical skill, unique viewpoint, well-composed arrangement, distinctive spatial qualities and interesting subject matter.

Art enhances our lives. Whether we view it for pleasure or create as artists, art can serve us in so many ways. My hope is that this book will bring to artists and art appreciators inspiration and enjoyment for years to come.

Nancy Reyner

—Nancy Reyner

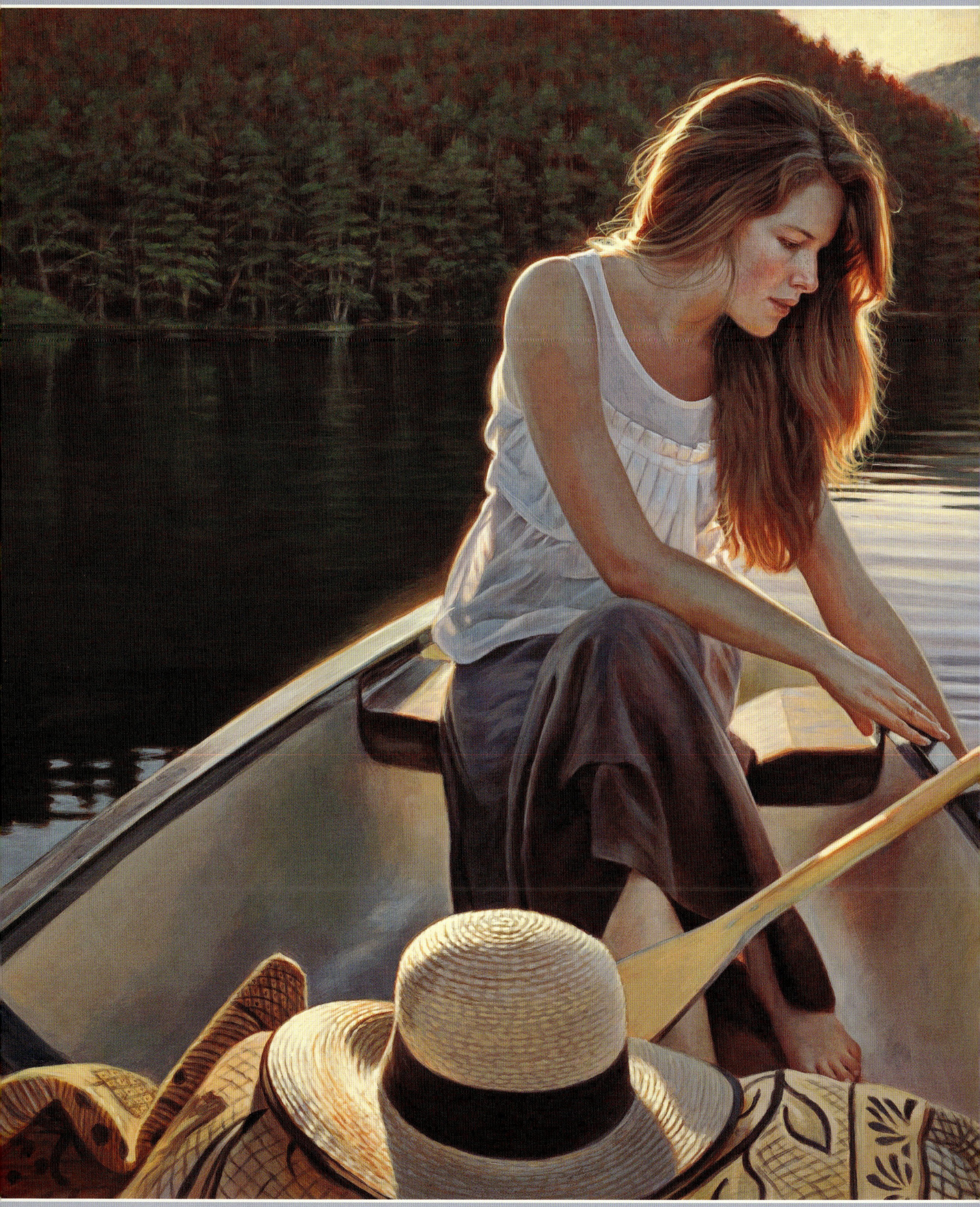

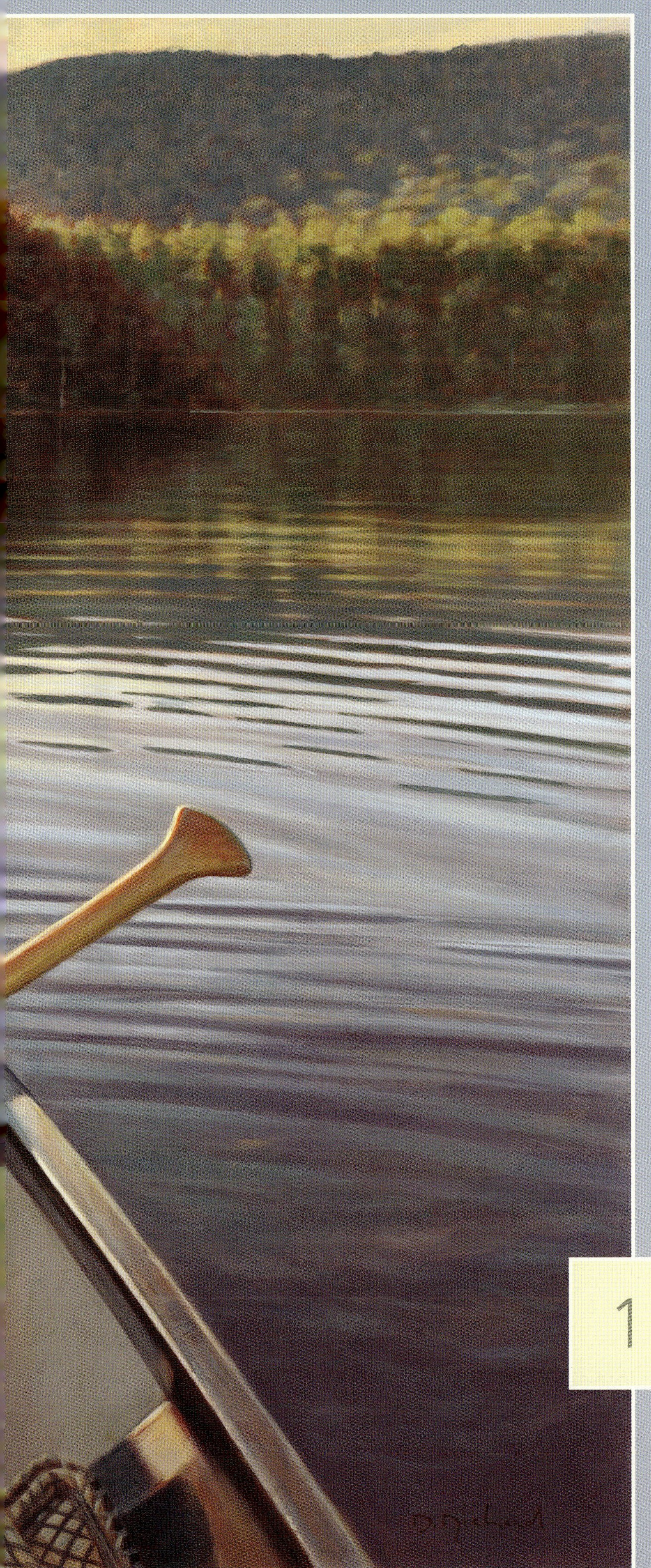

FOREVER HERE | Danielle Richard
Acrylic on linen, 36" × 48" (91cm × 122cm)

I completed this painting in the theme of remembering. I find that water scenes are great for it. I mostly work with the light coming from behind, probably for the mystery that it brings. It's not always easy because there is often a lack of information in the face, but through the years I have developed some tricks with reflection. I prefer to watch and follow my model, trying to catch the best light in the best angles. Then, an idea comes to life. I know exactly what I want, where I will go and how I will proceed. This painting was born the minute I saw the composition made with her hair, arms and rowing paddle perpendicular with the side of the canoe. I found that the sides of the canoe were like the sides of a shell in which you are secure and predisposed to introversion. My palette was limited to a few colors to keep the image pure and simplified.

1 | REALISTIC

"When painting underwater art, use a coarse brush to lightly splatter the suggestion of sediment in the water. It really adds to that underwater feel."

—MARCO ANTONIO AGUILAR

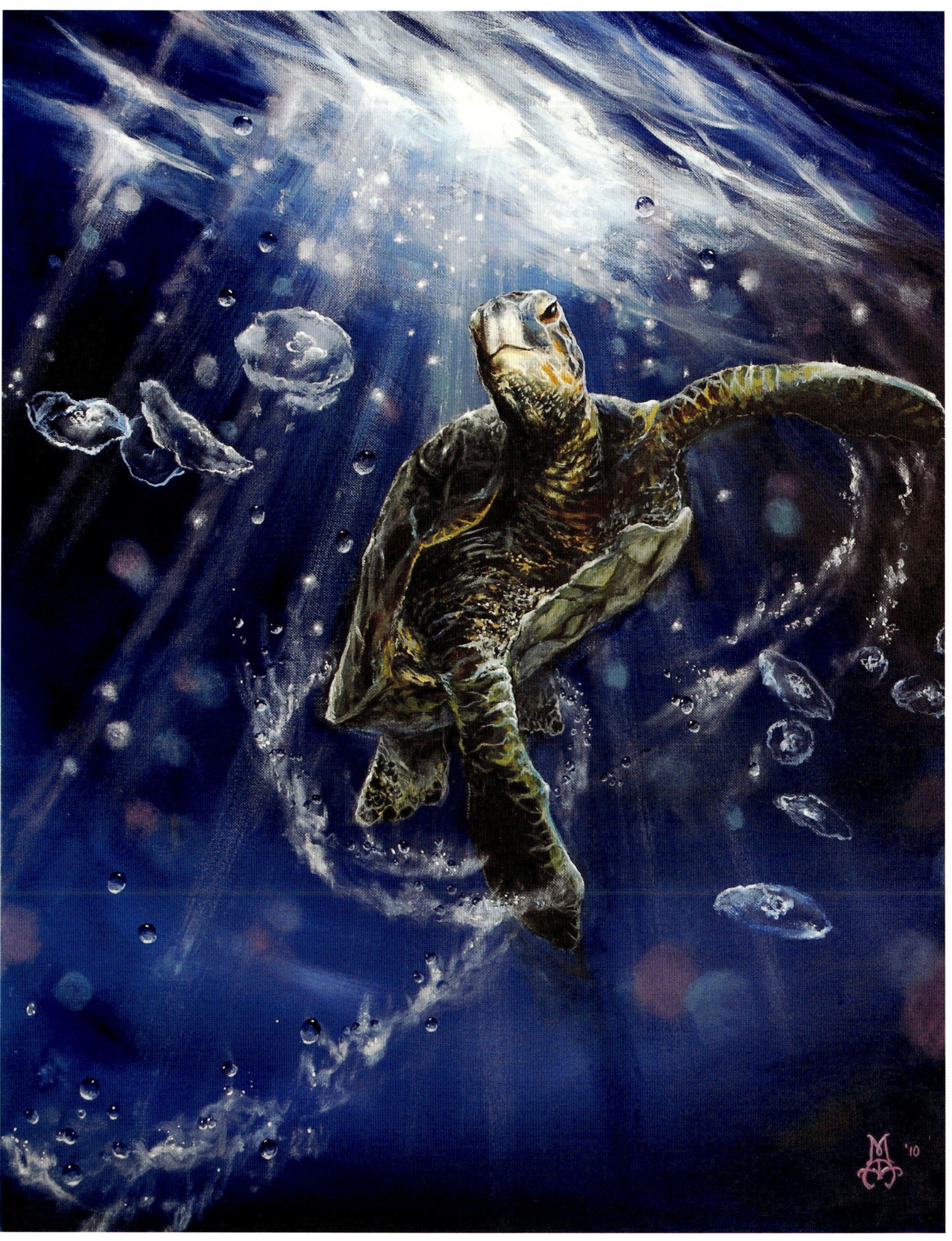

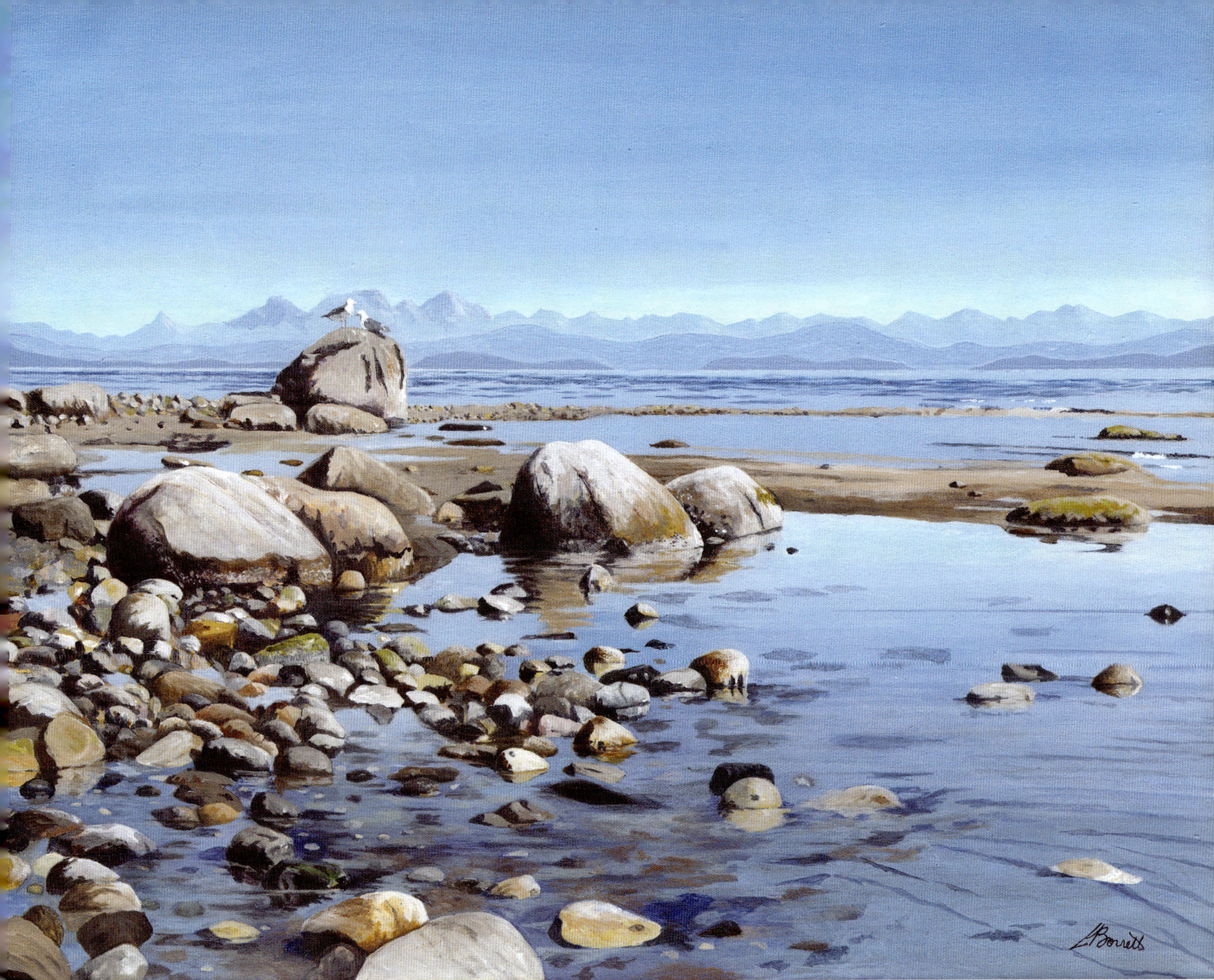

HONU'S DANCE | Marco Antonio Aguilar
Acrylic on canvas, 30" × 24" (76cm × 61cm)

I have developed a deep connection to the endangered green sea turtle, and I love the symbolism that this creature holds in Hawaiian culture. This image is my personal ode to joy and love of the sea. I wanted to express the Honu (as the Hawaiians call him) in a state of joy, basking in the sunlit Pacific Ocean surrounded by moon jellies, one of his favorite foods. I included several bubbles to add the sense of movement. To add to the magical quality of this image, I added lens flare that you would see from refracted light on a camera. This was achieved by placing circle stencils of varying sizes all over the painting and lightly drybrushing color over them.

MEETING PLACE | Carol Borrett
Acrylic on canvas, 22" × 28" (56cm × 71cm)

Water and shorescapes, where the varied textures of land meet the reflections and many colors of water, have long been my theme of choice. After years of exploration with watercolor, I finally broke into the world of acrylics. My work became more bold and vibrant.

Acrylics offer freedom—freedom to rework a piece by adding layers, freedom to use retardants and have more time to work the paint, freedom to experiment with the many other complementary mediums (gels, pastes, glazes, et al).

My process involves taking many photos of a subject to create a composition in my home studio. I often embellish the landscape. In the case of *Meeting Placc*, I was drawn to the familiar relationship of seagulls. They were like two friends meeting over coffee to review the events of the day.

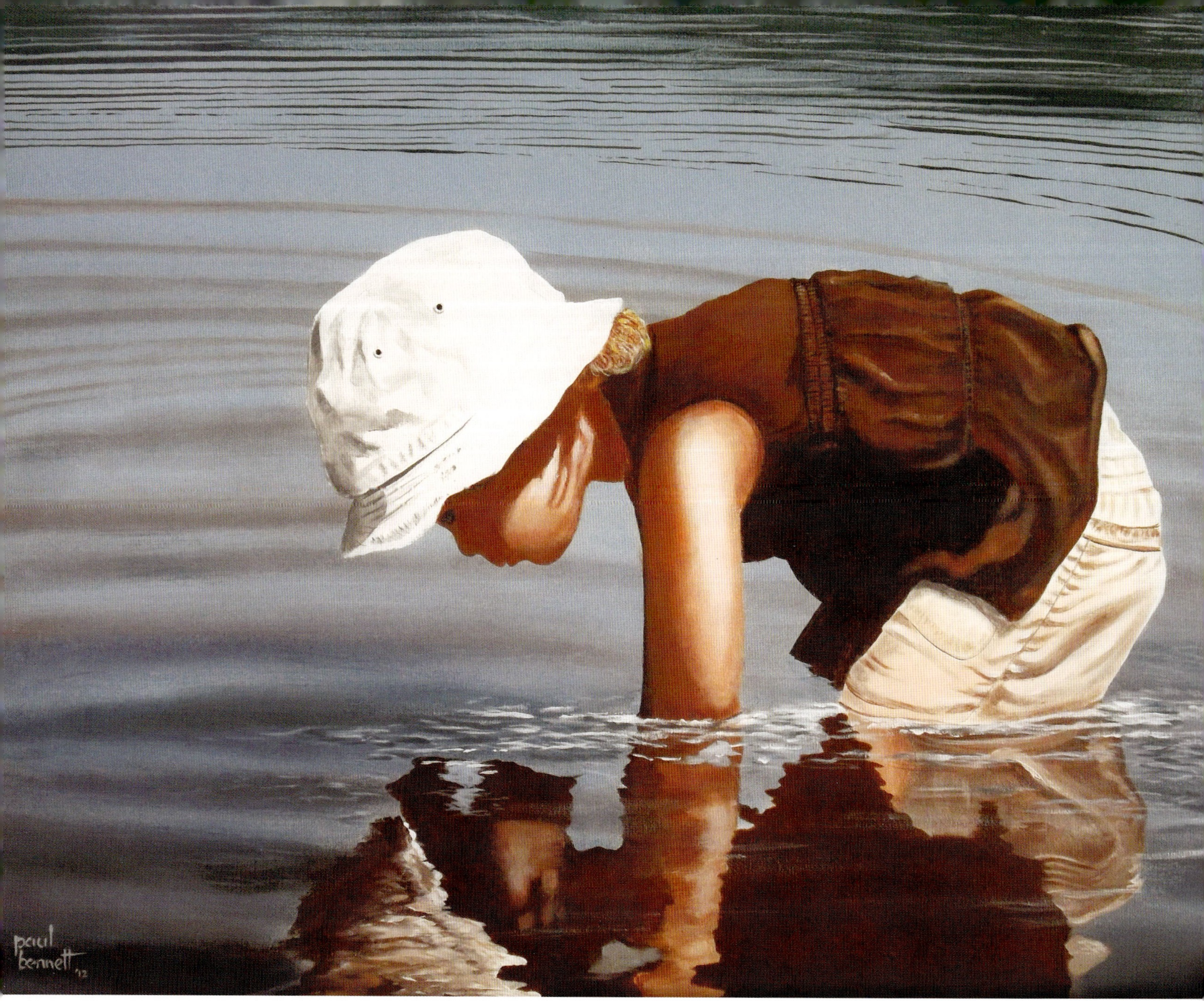

OUTSIDE LOOKING IN | Paul Bennett
Acrylic on stretched canvas, 24" × 30" (61cm × 76cm)

When I first saw this photo I had to paint the scene. The innocence and curiosity of children always seems to give me pleasure. Only two years of painting exclusively with acrylics after a lifetime painting with every other medium at some stage or another, I have found my place. Acrylics allow me to work at a fast pace and to blend or glaze without waiting for paint to dry. I strive for realism in my painting and work always from photos although it may take two or three photos to arrange the desired composition. This does not mean that I paint exactly to the photo but use it as a reference for size and correct shape dimensions. I prefer variety in my painting so all genres such as nature, seascape, landscape, still life and portraiture are targets in my endeavor to improve my skills and achieve a higher standard.

DON'T BE AFRAID TO TAKE CHANCES | Angela Bandurka
Acrylic on canvas, 24" × 24" (61cm × 61cm)

Don't Be Afraid to Take Chances was painted in my studio from life. Placing a bright light behind the scene made for a more dramatic setting and heightened the contrasts. I prefer painting on canvas because of the gentle give of the textile, but I don't enjoy the uniform weave it has, so a thin coat of modeling paste goes under my favorite red gesso before painting. The first and most important step, once the canvas is prepped, is the drawing, which I created with a light pastel pencil. The darkest values are the first to go down in thin applications with the lighter values building up thicker with each subsequent value range. The final step before signing is adding chunky, bright white highlights with my favorite white, Titanium Buff by Golden Acrylics. It allows the light areas of the painting to be warm without the chalkiness of mixing with white.

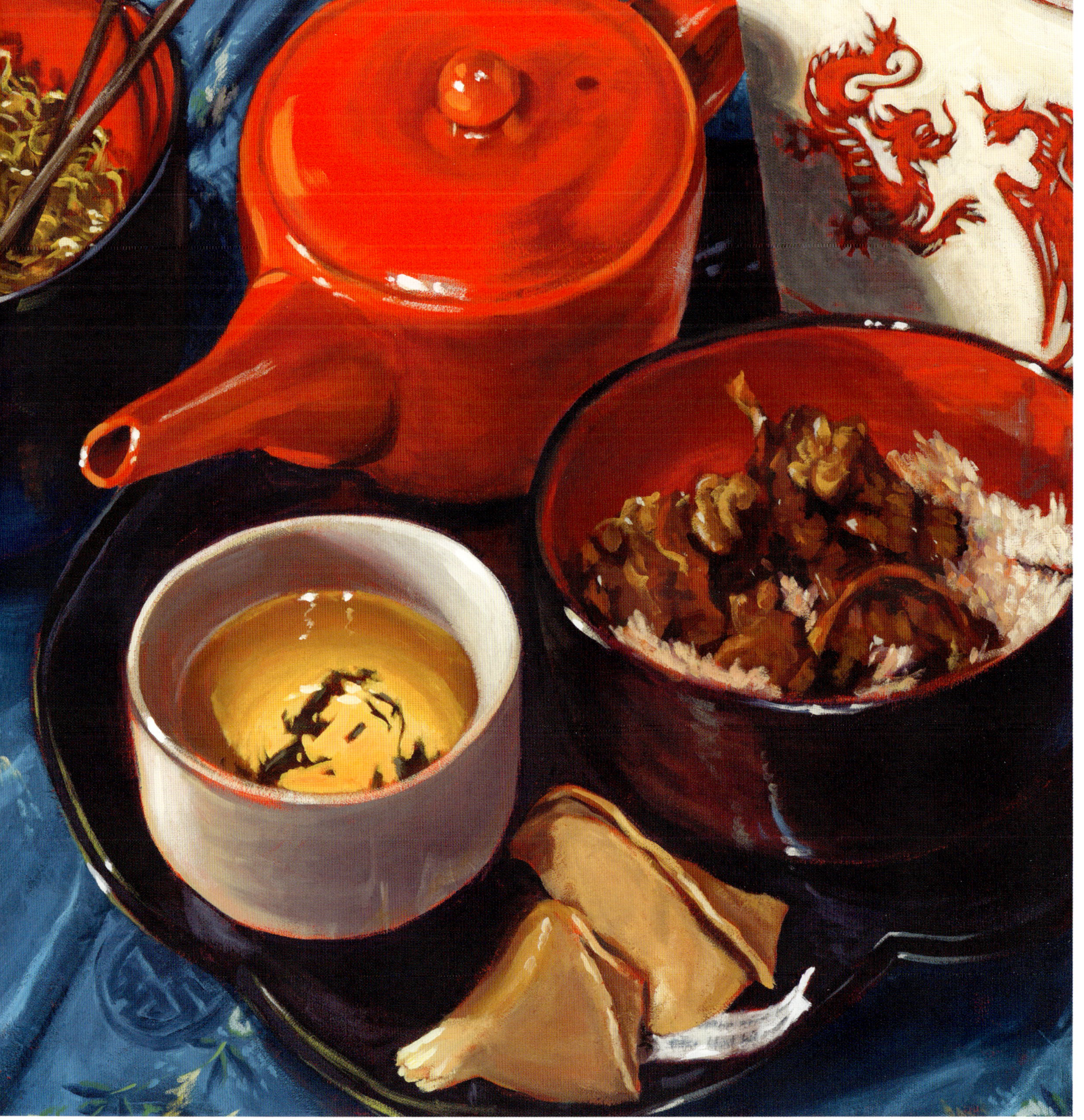

BACK HOME | Richard Belanger
Acrylic on wood, 36" × 48" (91cm × 122cm)

This is kind of my playground right in back of my house. It is filled with subject ideas for my paintings: a discarded car, an old panel truck, old farm tools and even a fox leaving its den. Over the years I did multiple pencil sketches, watercolor sketches of this piece of land. I also did a lot of final works using mediums as different as watercolor, oil and acrylic. After jotting down ideas with preliminary sketches I use my camera to record the scene, as in this case for a moving character in action. I used to paint with the egg tempera medium where there was a lot of scumbling and glazing involved in the process, also splatters of paint to create textures needed to create realistic impressions. I find acrylic imitates to perfection this age-old medium. One clear advantage is that acrylic almost dries to the touch, making it easy to add finishing touches without having to wait long periods of drying time.

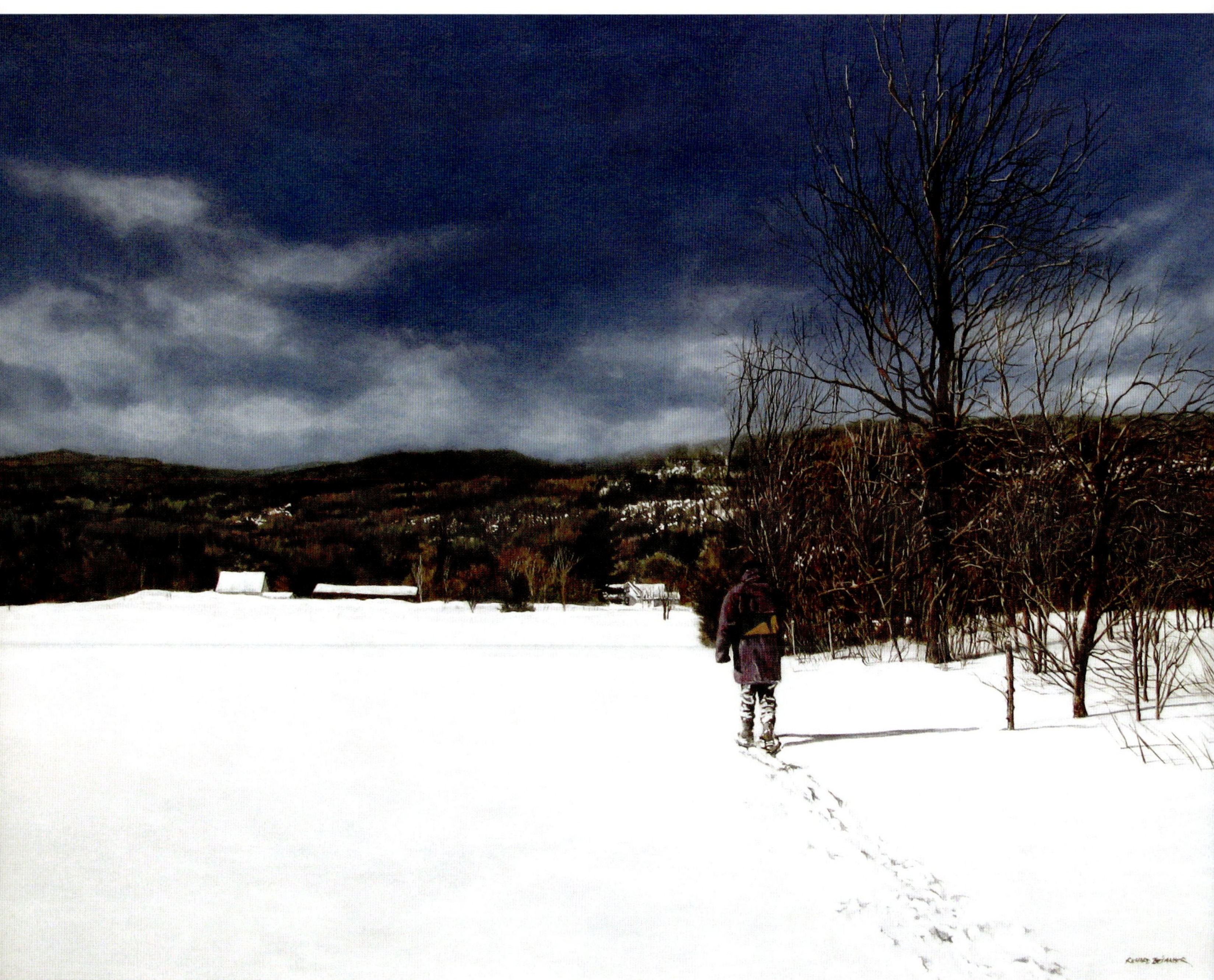

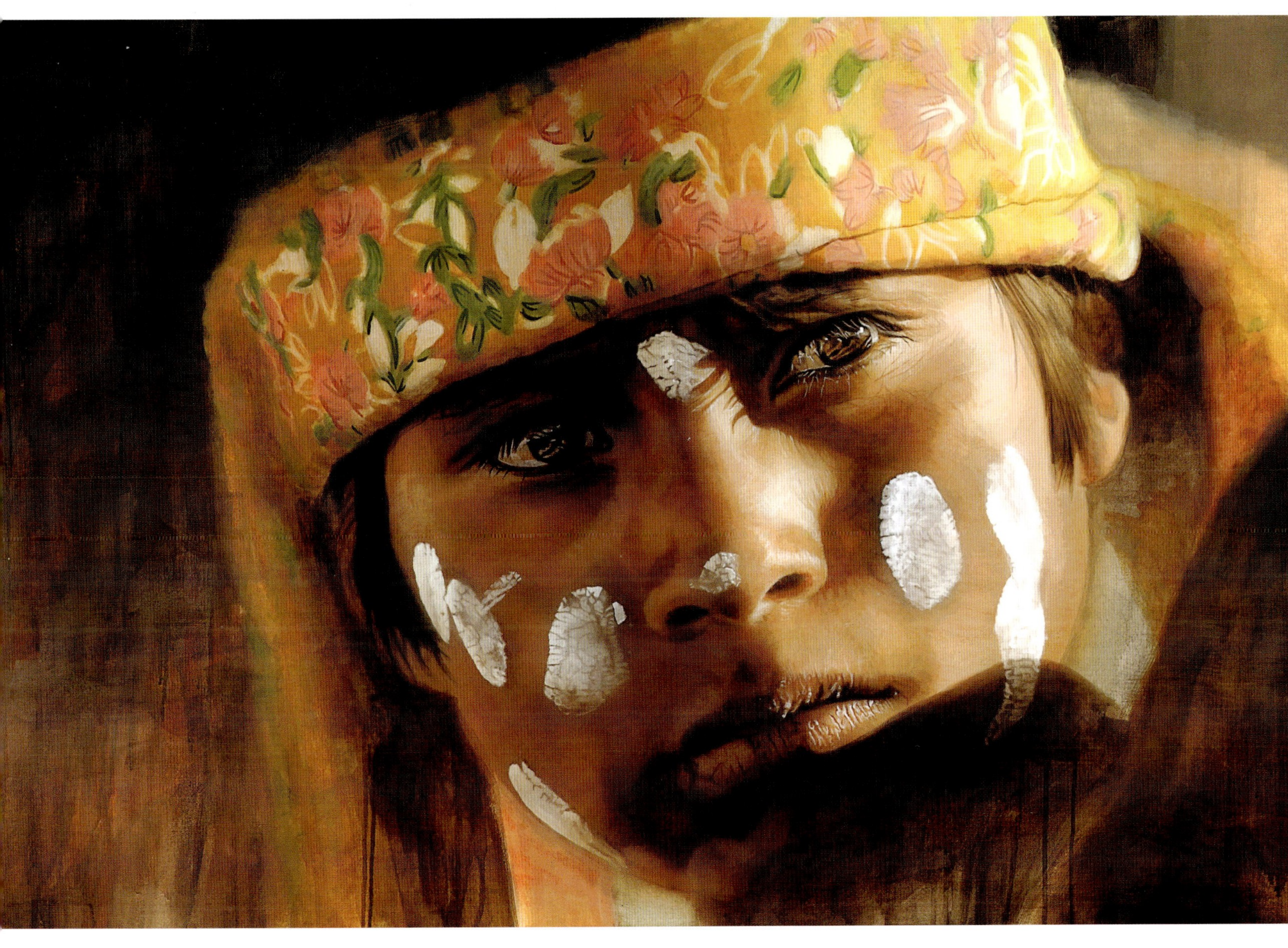

PURIFICACIÓN | Patricia Guzmán
Acrylic on canvas, 31" × 47" (79cm × 119cm)

My aim is to dignify, to honor Mexican indigenous groups. To paint their truth, honor and beauty through aesthetics and realism. Their presence is magnificent, their gaze is filled with joy and sadness, strength and fragility, their identity and harsh reality, all of which I wanted to express in the painting. I wanted the viewer to focus on the eyes; therefore, there is much detail around that area and so the background starts losing focus. I like painting acrylics in thin layers, both with brushes and airbrush; this allows me to give the skin a more real, tactile effect.

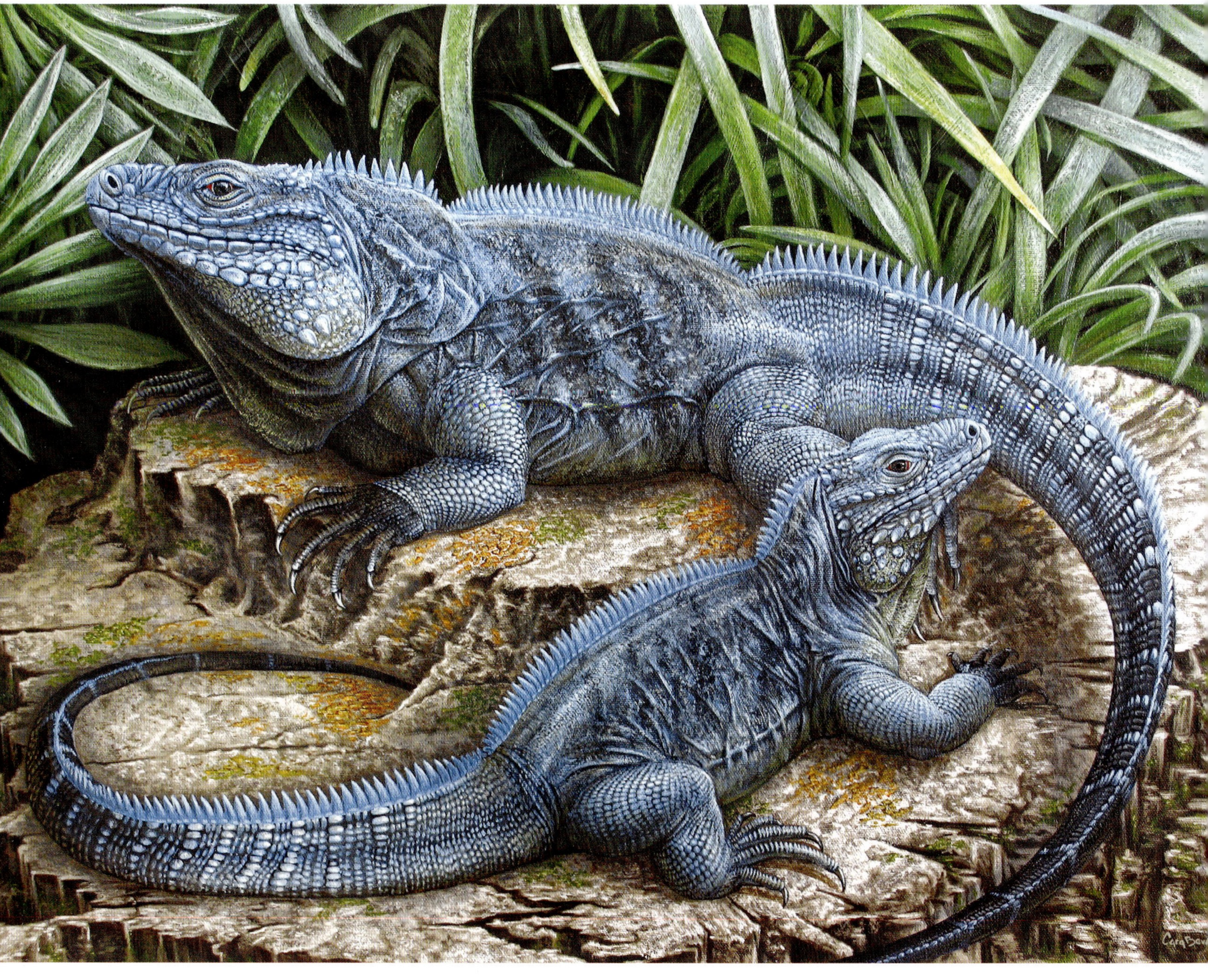

▲ THE GRAND CAYMAN BLUE IGUANAS | Cara Bevan
Acrylic on gallery-edged canvas, 18" × 24" (46cm × 61cm)

I've always been a photorealist, striving for the tiny details with whatever medium I choose. I love acrylics for their versatility and ease of use. I paint with a method that I've developed over time and experimentation. I start with solid, dark blocky colors, similar to an Impressionist's painting. With rocks and scenery, I use a large brush to create a basic texture. But with my favorite subject—animals—I'm more controlled. I'll break out my 0 liner brush and paint every scale, speck, shadow and highlight by hand. I use at least six layers of color, each layer still painted bit by bit. It seems tedious, but the seemingly insignificant details make them so real, and that's what makes it so enjoyable for me.

▶ IVY | Cara Bevan
Acrylic on birch panel, routered edges, 14¼" × 9½" (36cm × 24cm)

It's the most enigmatic creatures that catch your eye. You admire their prowess and are humbled to be in their presence. I felt this way toward Ivy, our beautiful tiny cat. Ivy was born in 1994 with five siblings. Her paws were the width of quarters, her head fit in your palm. Because of her size, her sisters drove her away. She lived in a vehicle shed and became a wild barn cat. Unless you had food, you couldn't get near her—and touching her was out of the question. She spent her days hunting mice, birds and bugs among the farm animals. She could be admired from a distance, and her mysterious life still captivates me.

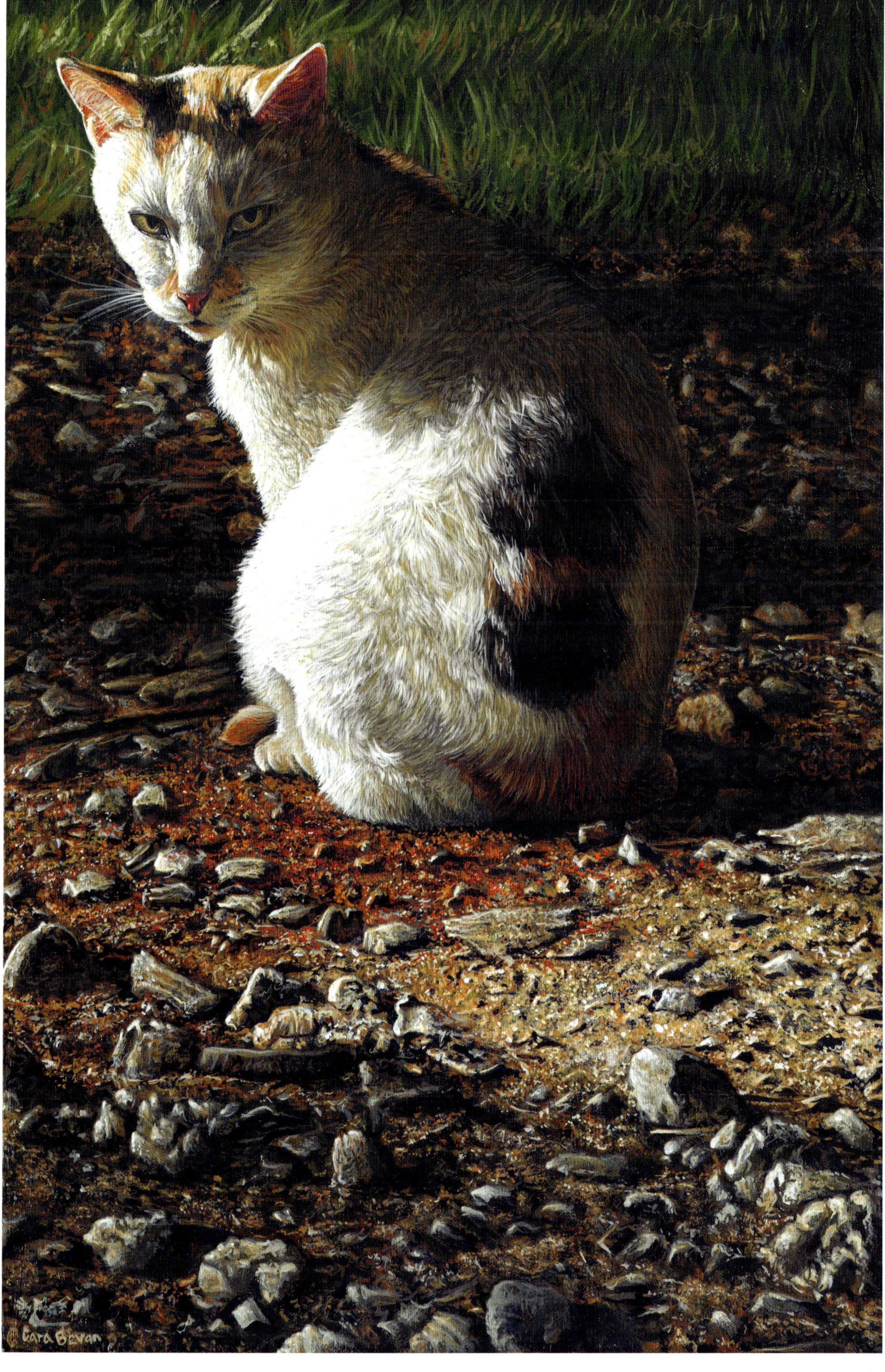
© Cara Bevan

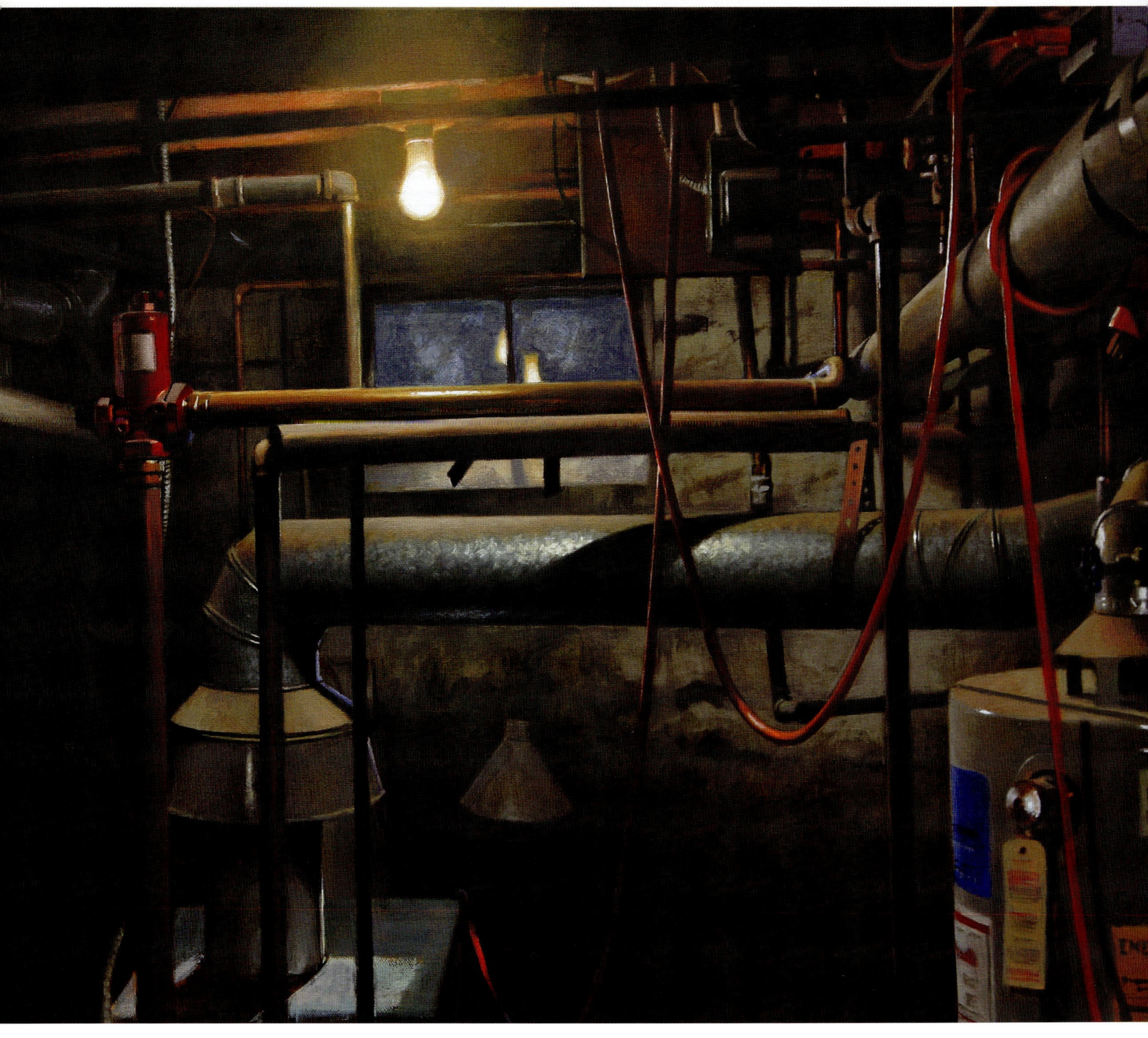

▲ BASEMENT DE STIJL | Hank Buffington
Acrylic on canvas, 20" × 24" (51cm × 61cm)

The basement painting was done from observation in my house. The setting allowed me to have consistent lighting no matter when I painted, and being in the basement allowed me to leave my easel set up for months without fear of my children disturbing it.

I originally chose the scene because I felt it was nearly unpaintable for me. My initial intention was to abstract the scene and interpret it much like I would a plein air landscape, but as I worked on it elements just got tighter and tighter and it became very literal. I expected it to take a couple of days, but I ended up working on it for several months.

▶ ME | Harry Burman
Acrylic on canvas mounted on board, 15¼" × 9½" (39cm × 24cm)

To me the human face is the most fascinating subject an artist can attempt. I am moved more deeply by a great portrait than by any other type of painting. My self-portrait *Me* was my first attempt at using acrylics. I had a preconceived belief that acrylics dried too quickly, had a plastic look and were the wrong medium for my kind of work. I like to paint directly—no gimmicks. You should analyze the color with regards to hue, value and intensity before you apply the paint. Don't count on accidents, but if one occurs that helps your painting use it. Golden's OPEN Acrylic is my favorite medium.

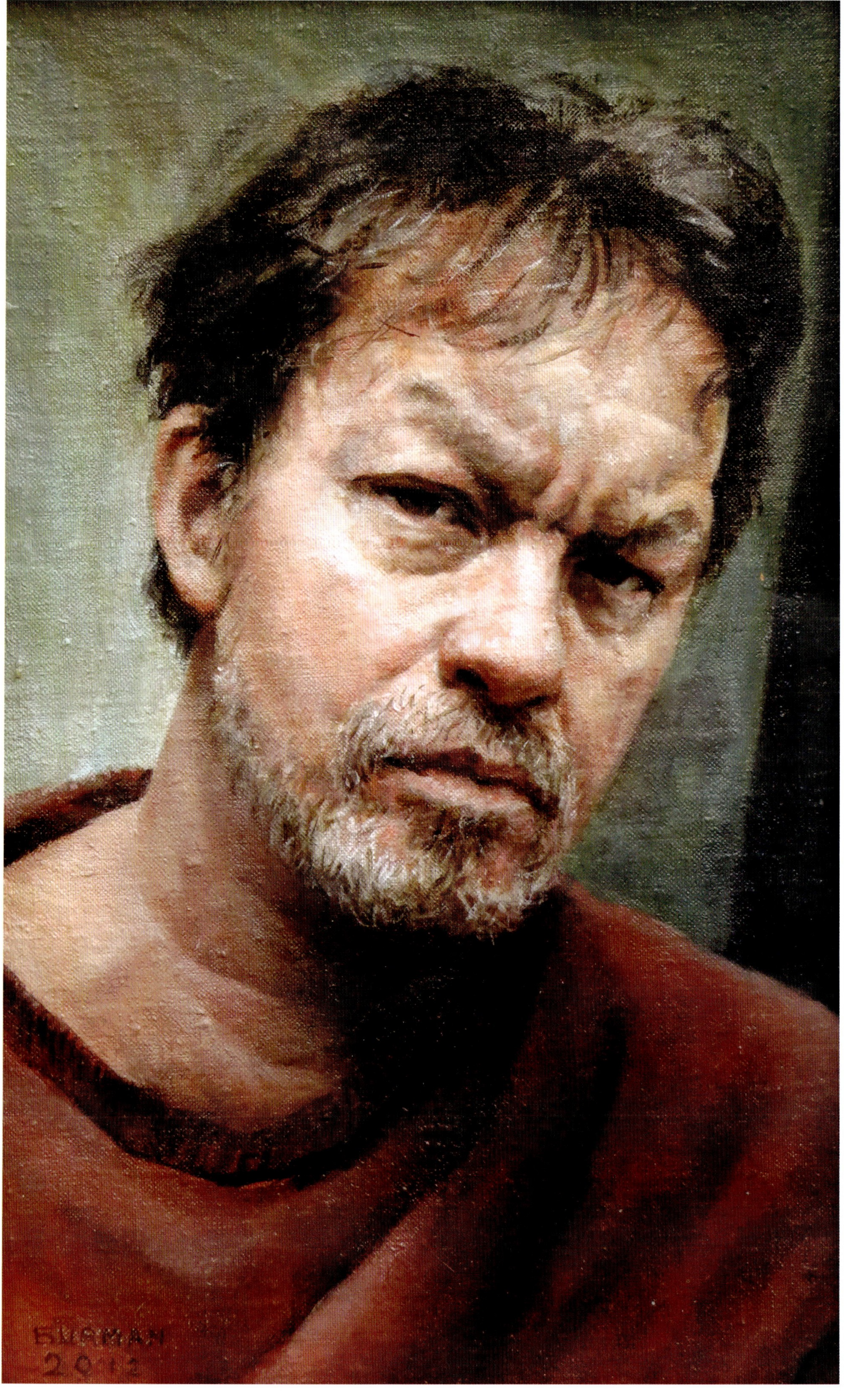

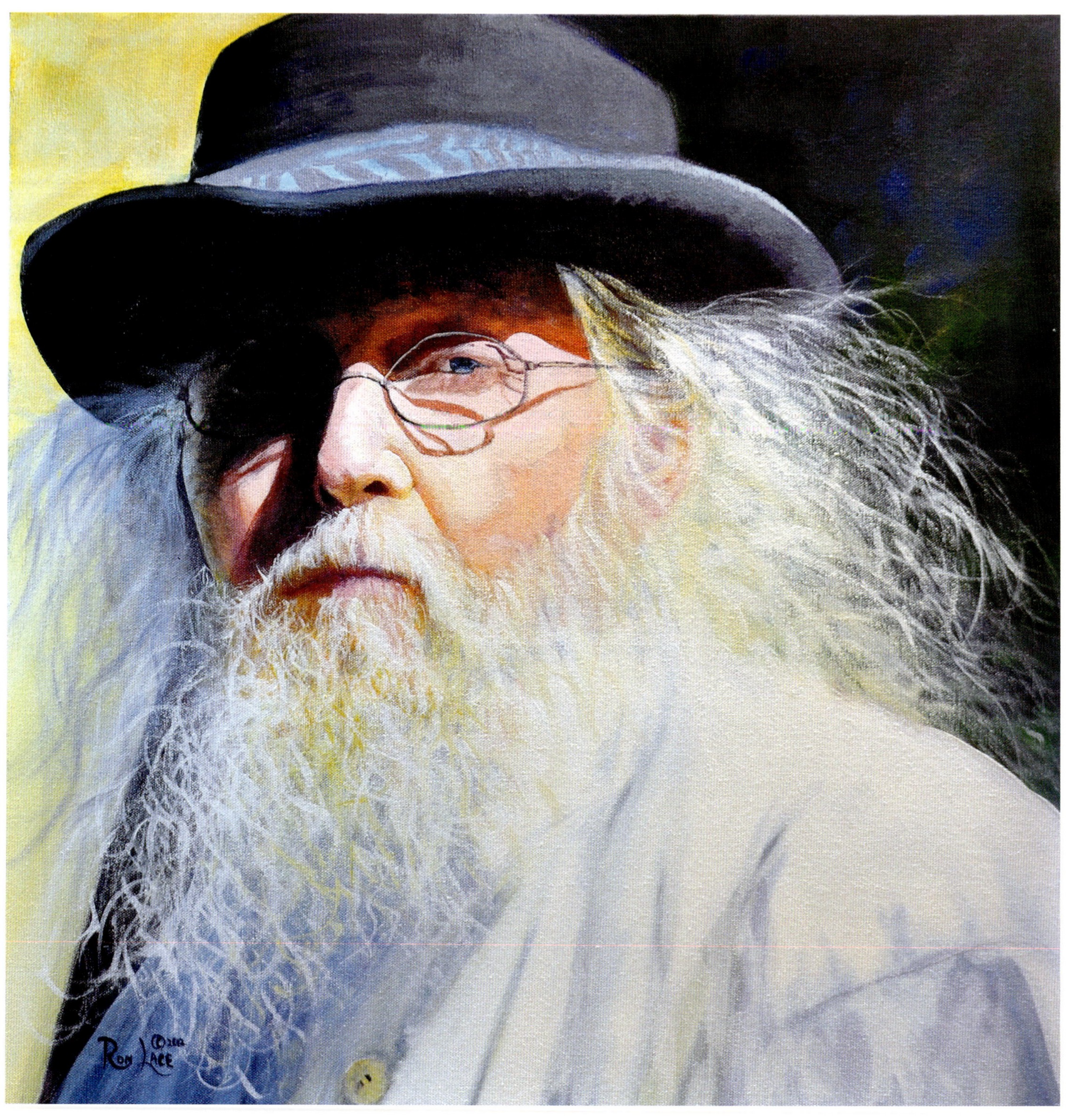

THE PROPHET | Ron Lace
Acrylic on gallery-wrapped cotton canvas, 24" × 24" (61cm × 61cm)

This painting was created from a photograph taken at an outdoor festival celebrating America's diverse heritage. The subject was a Civil War reenactor standing in the midst of a living history encampment. While I was snapping photos, the subject looked up at me with an intense gaze, the light flooding his face and flowing white beard. It was one of those moments when your heart rate increases and you think as you look through the lens, *this has to be painted!*

In the studio I cropped the photo to create interesting shapes on both sides of the figure and then transferred the drawing to the canvas before beginning the application of acrylic paint. My goal was to capture the contrast of darks and lights and the character of the face in a realistic style, manipulating and blending the medium like oil to achieve a luminous quality. After blocking in the basic shapes of the background and figure, I painted the face with thin layers of paint and glazes to achieve the desired effect. The final details were then added including the glasses and the fun part, the beautiful flowing hair and beard. Acrylic is such a versatile medium; it inspires me with confidence, knowing I can use thin washes, glazes or impasto to achieve my desired end without having to wait long periods for the paint to dry.

FIRST ICE | Garry Kaye
Acrylic on canvas, 36" × 48" (91cm × 122cm)

I enjoy documenting our six acres and immediate surroundings in my paintings. This particular painting is painted from a multitude of photos that I feel make it unique as we experience the first ice on our little pond. The timing is of great importance as in two hours the sun will have melted the ice and an opportunity lost. Rather than working from a photograph I put the image on Photoshop where I can study the composition and the color in detail.

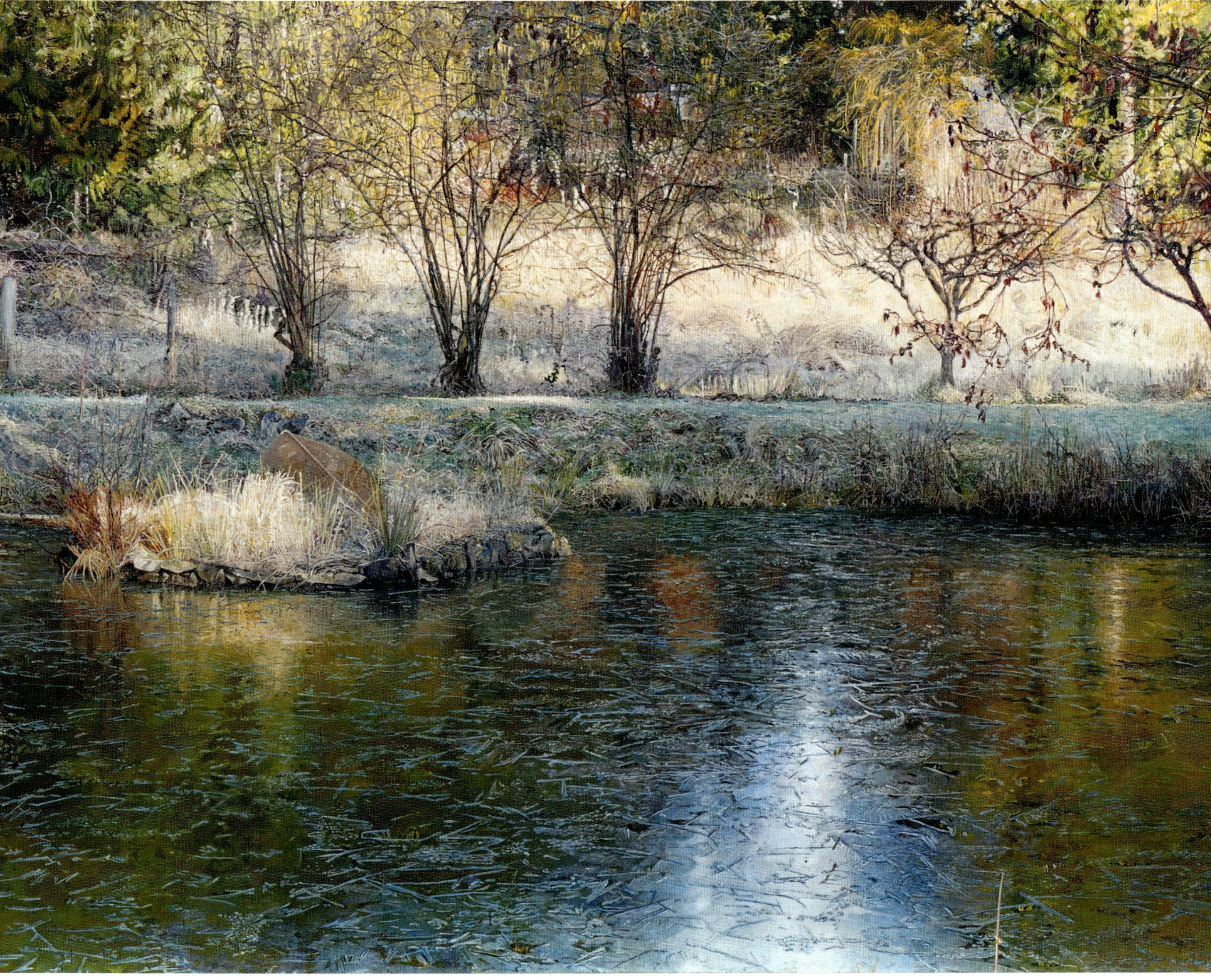

"Paint with passion, enjoy the process. It's painting that really matters, everything else will follow!"

—RON LACE

"In today's technologically mad world, my vision must embody aged remnants of simpler times."

—STEVE WILDA

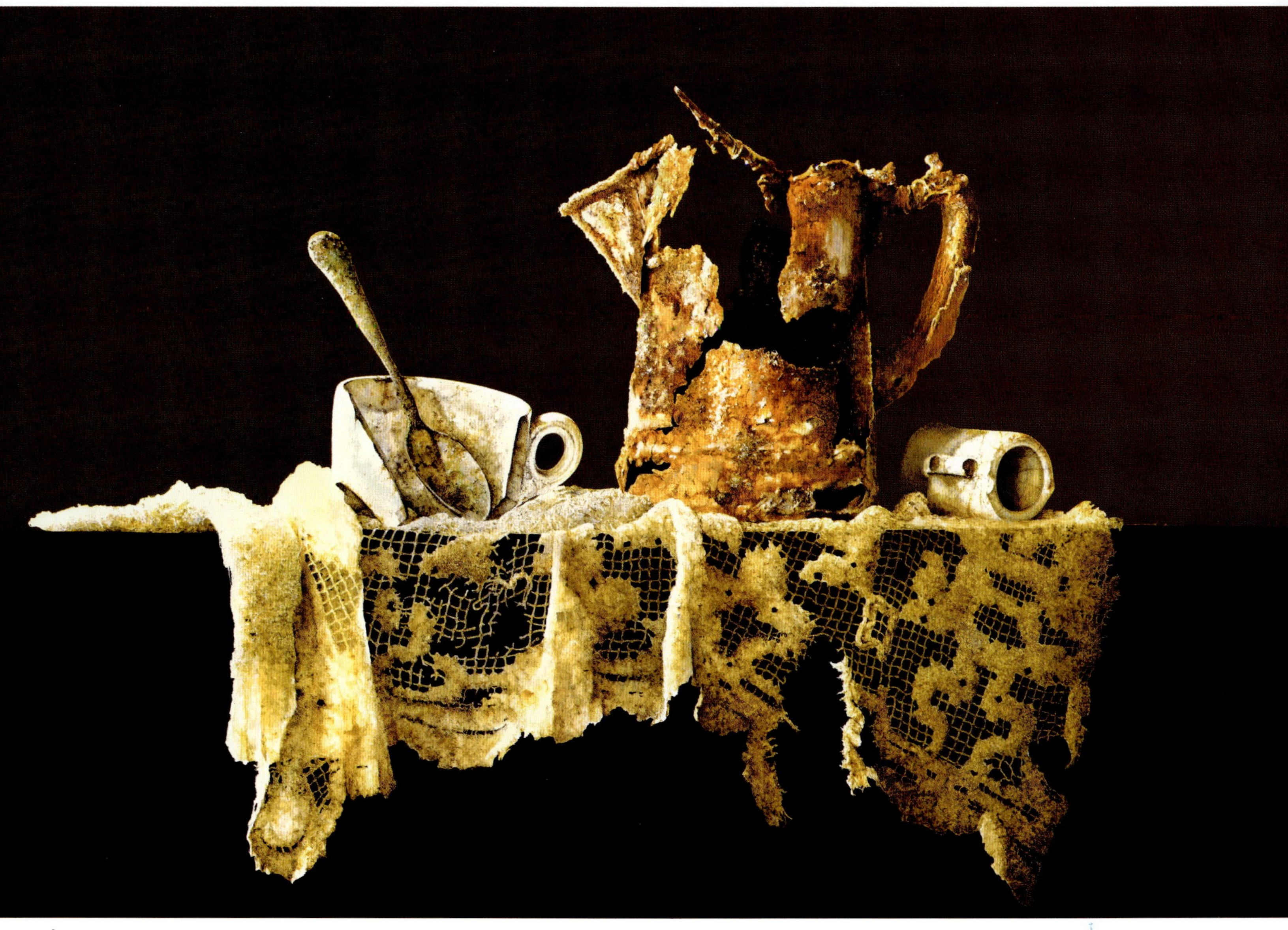

▲ COFFEE BREAK | Steve Wilda
Acrylic on panel, 16½" × 24" (42cm × 61cm)

Finding unique objects in disrepair that relate together for a particular theme is the most invigorating part of the creative process. The main elements in the painting were discovered at a century-old trash site. The draped, worn lace doily not only evokes grace, but also contrasts against the stark base. *Coffee Break* being its title, I intentionally left the table unfinished, implying that the artist had also taken a break. Rarely are alterations made from my own reference photographs. Multiple glazes were used throughout, except on the coffeepot. With heavily corroded objects, opaque paint is additionally applied.

▶ STANDING EGRET | Sheryl Hughes
Acrylic and gouache on board, 12" × 9" (30cm × 23cm)

Standing Egret was painted from a photo taken at Flamingo Gardens in Davie, Florida. I have spent a lot of time taking photos at zoos, parks, gardens, during underwater dives and in the Everglades. My photographs not only help with creative details but also inspire ideas for future paintings. My artistic joy lies in bringing life to the eyes of my wildlife subjects and capturing the intricate details that make a viewer want to reach out and touch the painting. My goal is to bring the unique impact of my subjects to the viewer by using full, bold color for both land and underwater scenes. As an artist I focus on photorealism, bold colors, details and eyes. I spend hours taking photos above and below the water looking for just the right inspiration that can be shared on canvas for others to enjoy.

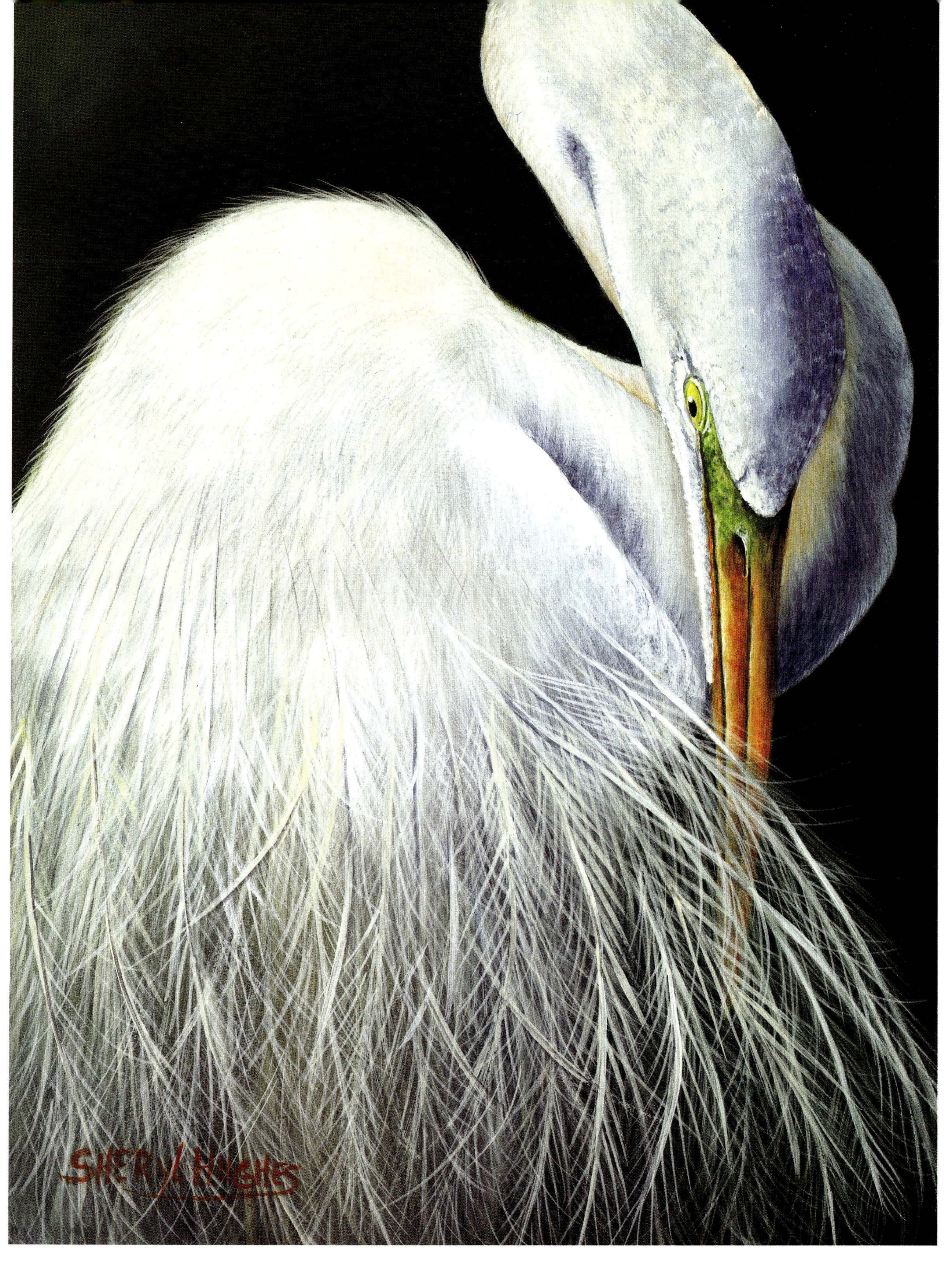

"Practice, practice, practice. Practice is an investment in your skills."

—SHERYL HUGHES

ALONG FAIRWAY 1 – SALEM GLEN, NC | Ray Hill
Acrylic on canvas panel, 8" × 10" (20cm × 25cm)

On our daily walks my wife, Charlene, and I always pass by this massive oak tree that's been growing along the first fairway for well over a hundred years. Its asymmetrical and stately appearance always attracts my attention. I'm fascinated by the image it presents from different viewpoints, under varying lighting and weather conditions as well as the time of year. I primarily paint with acrylics to take advantage of their drying time and versatility of application. In this painting, to get the light effect as seen on the clouds and tree, I used acrylics with like watercolor glazes, opaque oil passages and scumbling. To promote color harmony I used four colors plus white: Burnt Sienna, Yellow Oxide, Hooker's Green and Ultramarine Blue.

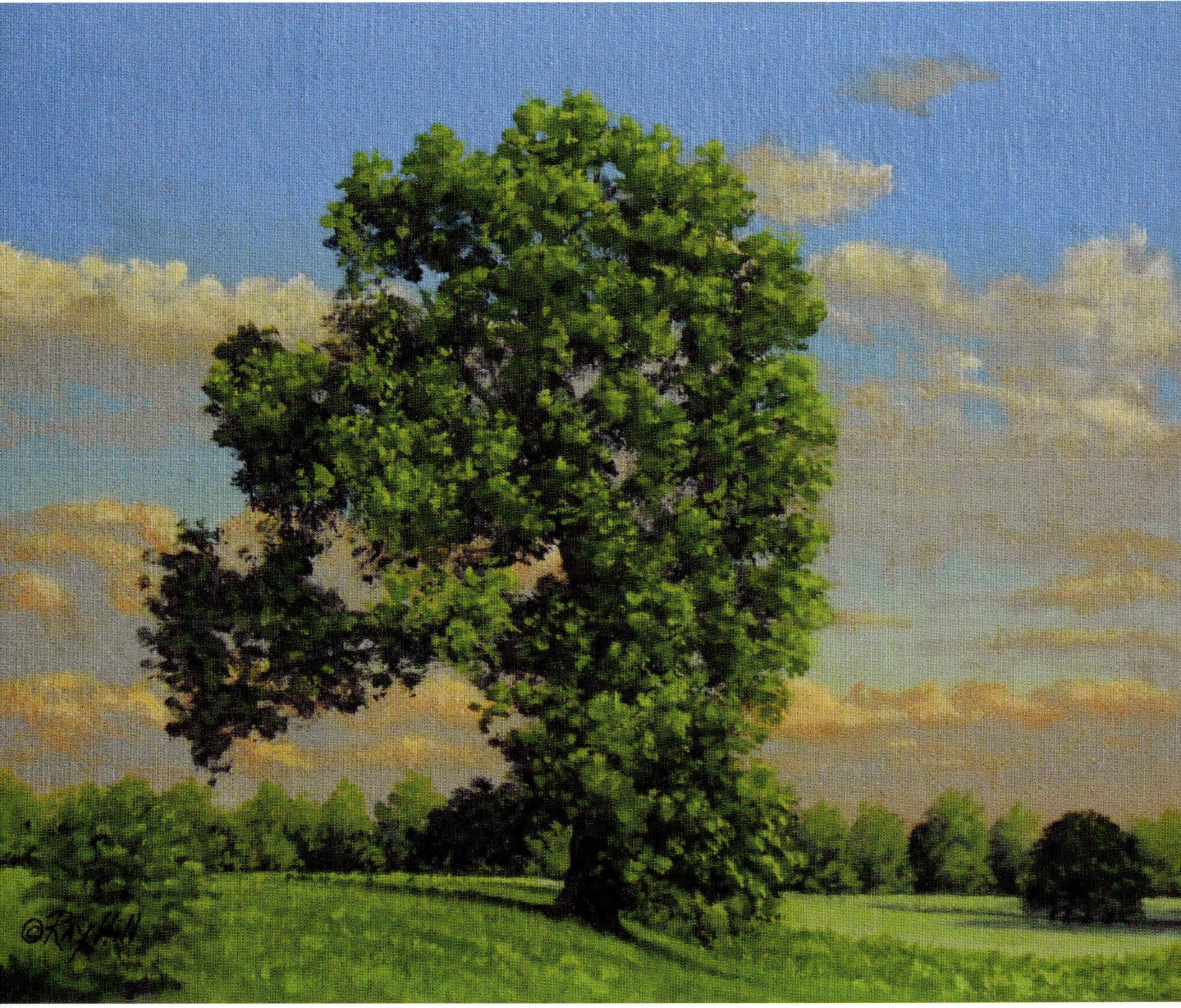

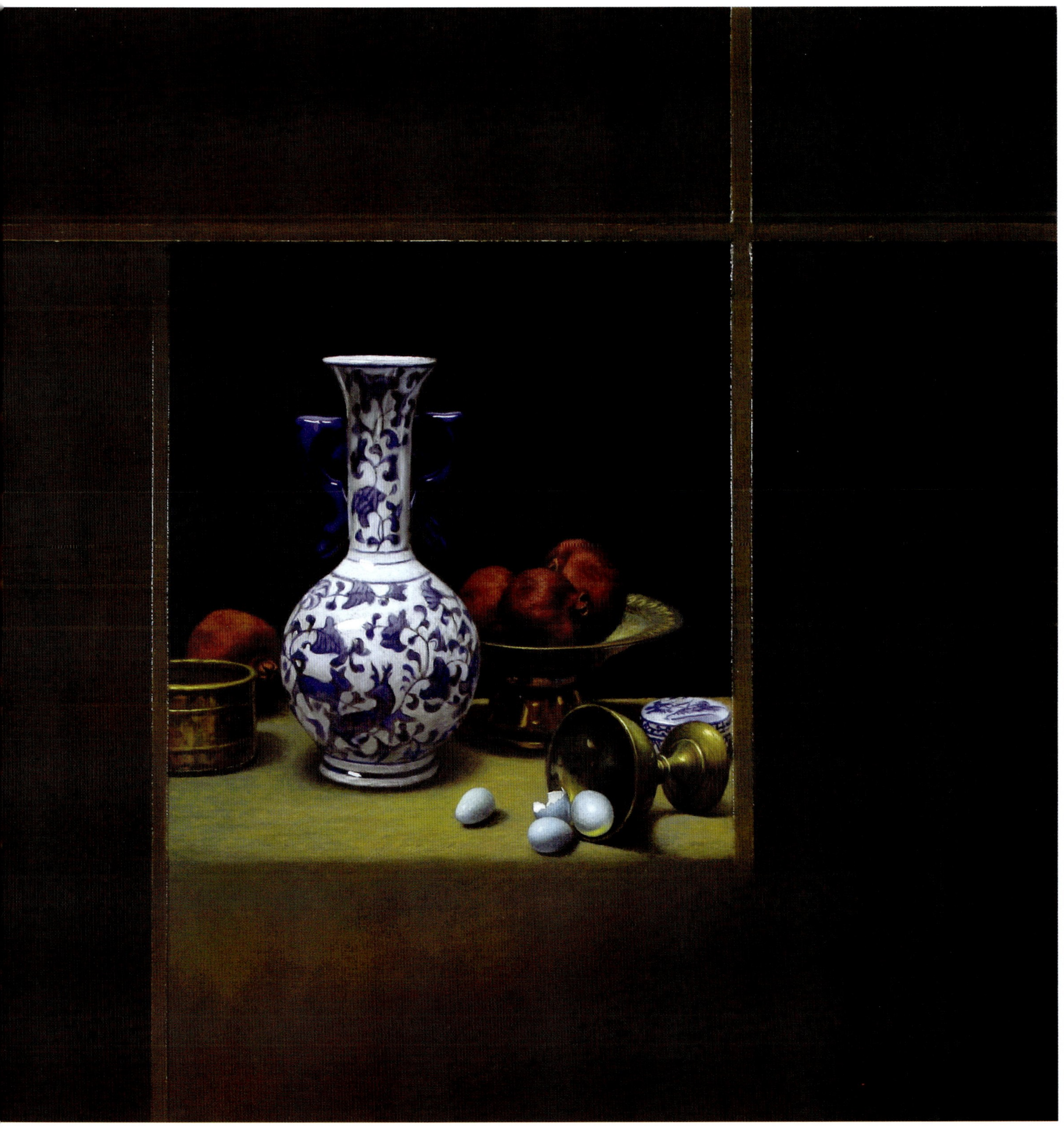

THE DYNASTY VASE | Bruno Capolongo
Acrylic on panel, 16" × 16" (41cm × 41cm)

This painting began as a geometric thumbnail in my sketchbook. Only after composing the larger Mondrianesque design did I work on the still-life arrangement. The raised lines framing the still life are made of extra thick acrylic medium, and the rest of the piece is very thinly painted using regular gel medium to aid in blending colors. All of the props were sourced from my prop collection and set up very close to my easel. By limiting the palette but emphasizing color and light in the right place, a touch of drama or focus is created. The result is a classical/contemporary balance.

"The larger design of a painting is more important than its details and sets the tone for the whole."

—BRUNO CAPOLONGO

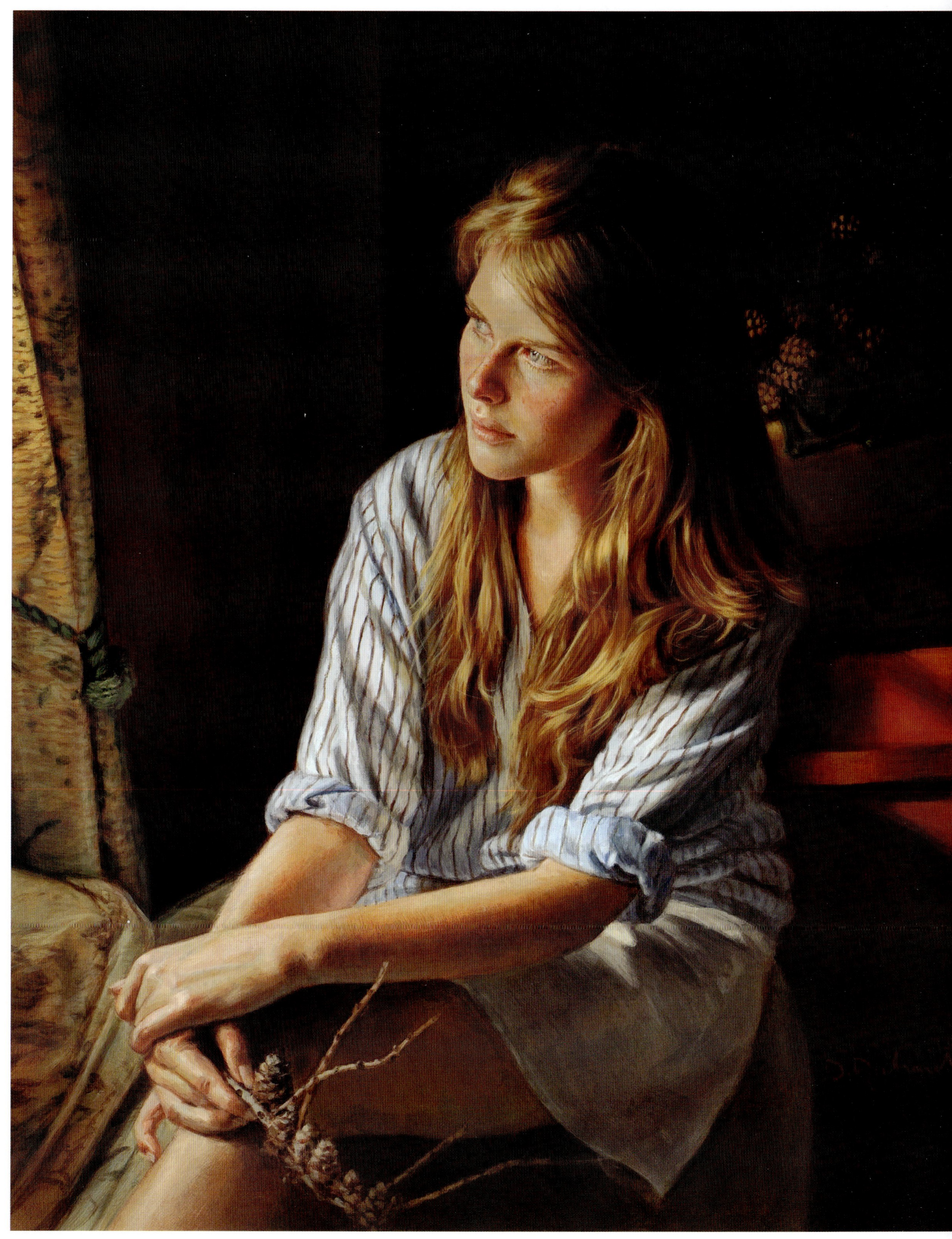

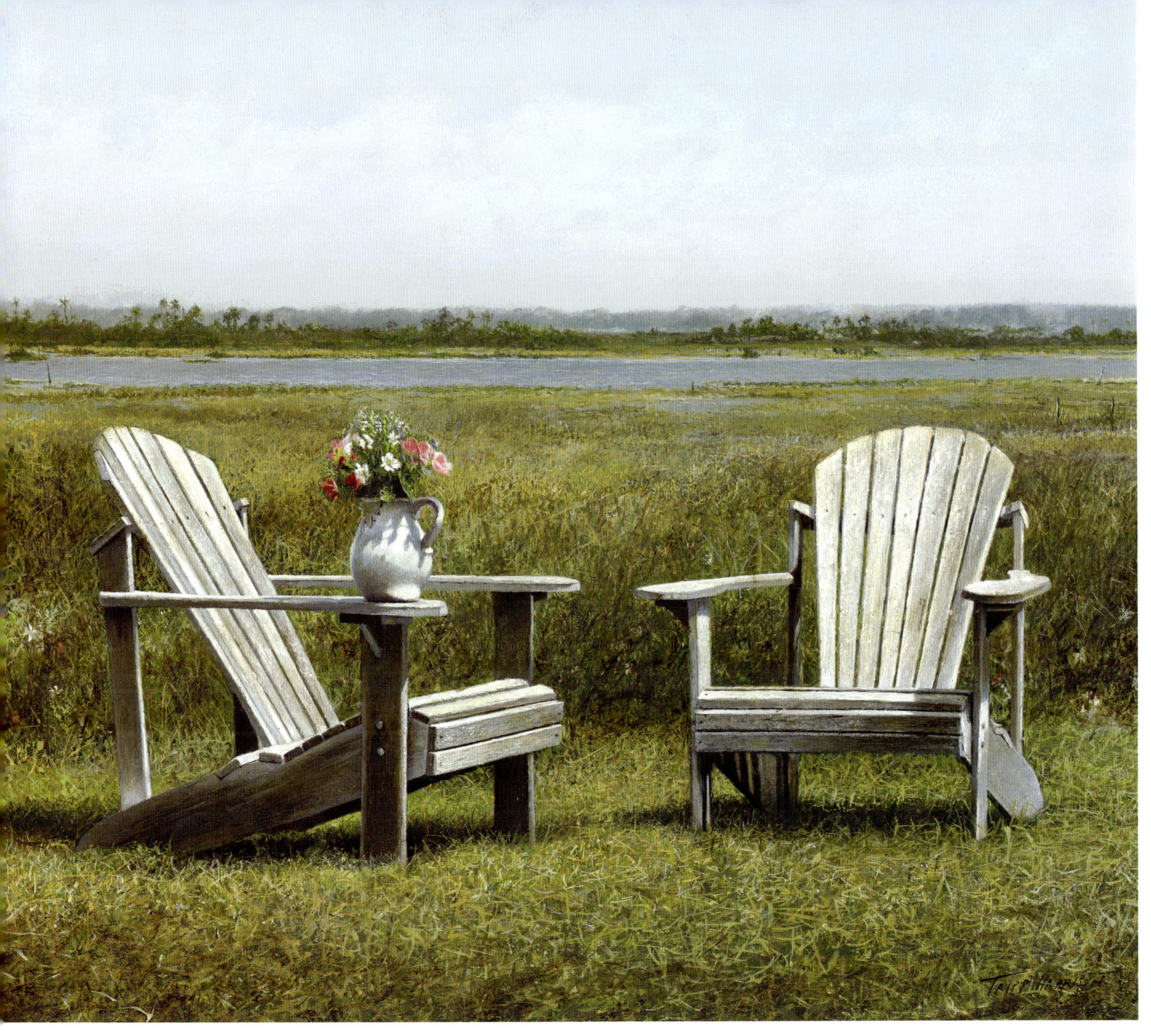

◀ HIS BLUE SHIRT | Danielle Richard
Acrylic on linen, 30" × 24" (76cm × 61cm)

▲ ADIRONDACK CHAIRS | Tripp Harrison
Acrylic on Twinrocker hot-pressed paper, 21" × 24" (53cm × 61cm)

A visit to an old domaine with dark walls reminded me of the light in some paintings by A. Wyeth and even A. Zorn. The perfect place for modeling the figure in a limited light source. I asked my model to wear a blue men's shirt to reinforce the idea of precious memories.

Acrylics allow me to work with glazing without the poses required for oil. I can ceaselessly polish up without being afraid of altering previous layers. I love the luminosity produced by the use of transparent colors. I build my underpainting with a mixture of transparent Burnt Sienna and Van Dyke Red. I establish my values and begin with faces and skin tones, which are going to be the references for harmony of the whole painting. I like quite fluid colors, so I add water and medium (a mix of matte and gloss) and for the soft edges, some fluid retarder. Sometimes when I look at some of my pieces, I ask myself did I paint it with oil or acrylics!

As these two special Adirondack chairs sat outside my studio at the water's edge, the urge to paint them was irresistible. Nature has a way of reclaiming things and these two good friends were in a state of deterioration, so I felt I must pay tribute to them before they were gone. The almost dry chalky nature of these chairs lent itself to the medium of acrylic. That might sound like a contradiction knowing that acrylics can at times have a kind of plastic, unnatural look to them. Acrylics, though, can be manipulated. I prefer mixing dry pigments with my tube colors allowing me to get a more beautiful, organic look while never compromising the integrity of the paint film. Introducing and experimenting with dry pigments and conventional high-quality tube colors can open new doors to limitless possibilities. I paint in very thin layers, building slowly in a very transparent style. This process gives the painting a more luminescent quality as seen in many casein and egg tempera paintings but with all the advantages of acrylics. For me acrylics are limitless in their possibilities, limitless in their inspiration.

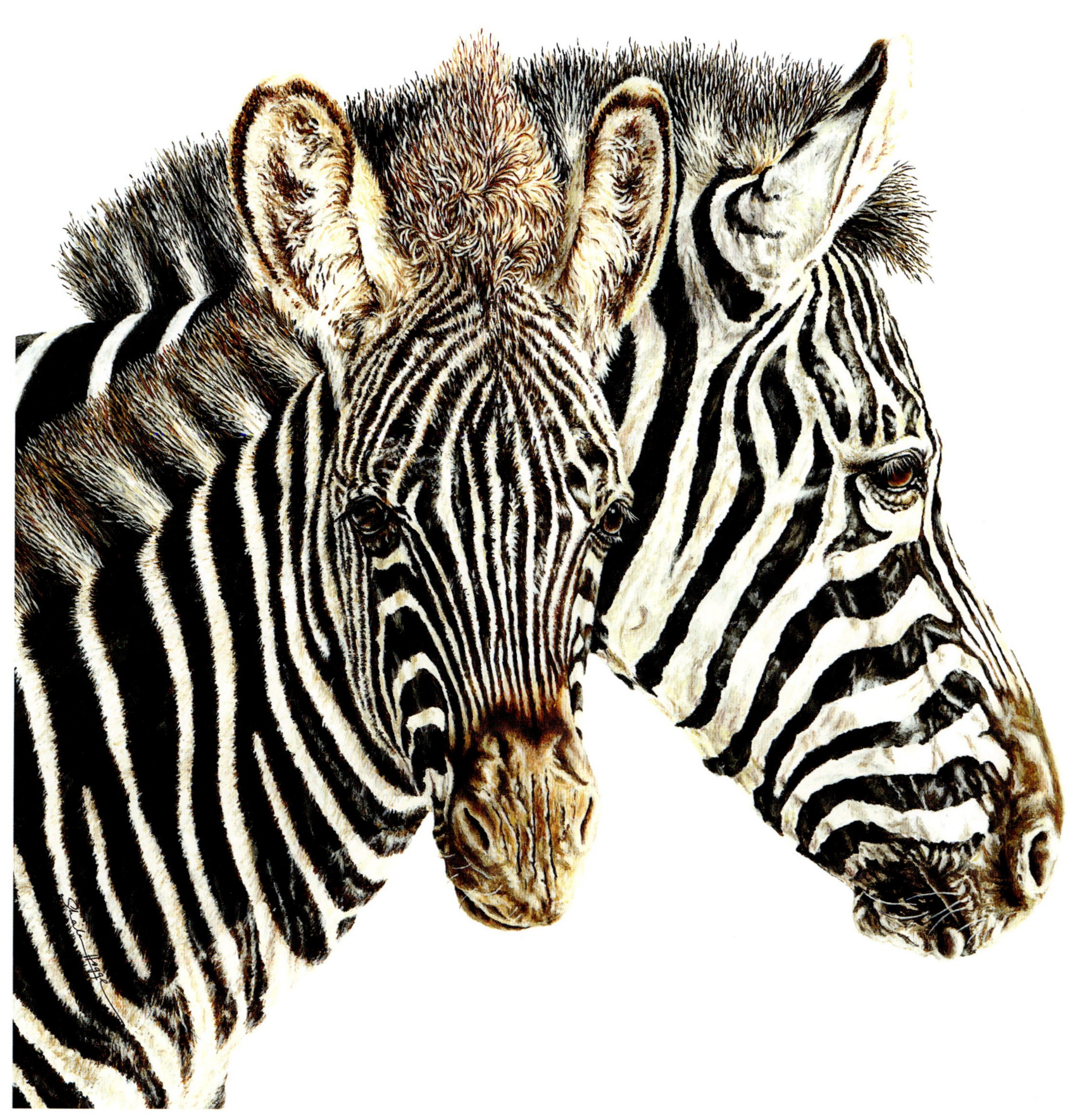

MOTHER AND SON | Sheila Hogge
Transparent acrylic and Titanium White on 3-inch (8cm) deep beech panel
24" × 24" (61cm × 61cm)

Observing the young zebra with its mother was enchanting, a subject I just had to paint. From my various photographs I finalized this compositional idea. I wanted an accurate anatomical but graphic representation. On-site I had sketched in watercolor for color reference as zebra are not just black and white. The beech panel was prepared with five layers of diluted acrylic gesso to achieve a fine crosshatched surface. Using various synthetic watercolor brushes and starting with the eyes, I gradually built up the painting with both mixes and glazes of transparent color (French Ultramarine, Quinacridone Burnt Orange and Quinacridone Gold) and Titanium White (all Winsor & Newton Artists' Acrylic) mixed with glazing medium and/or retarder when necessary. The image was continued around the sides.

EDEN ROAD #1 | Barbara L. Clark
Acrylic on gesso board, 24" × 36" (61cm × 91cm)

Having spent many years as a decorative painter and trompe l'oeil muralist, I have only really painted with acrylics. The ability of acrylics to paint layers and work transparently creating the illusion of depth, yet have the medium dry quickly, has kept acrylic my partner. I paint in the studio with Golden Fluid Acrylics. These paints have the perfect combination of opacity when I need it and transparency when I don't. The classes I have taken studying oils have only made me more comfortable with acrylics although I have learned some great techniques. (However, I do believe oils get more respect.) My imagery is always from my own photographs. Complicated, challenging images interest me, and for me, it is all about the challenge. My artistic goal is painterly realism.

"An unusual artistic characteristic of my paintings is the realism reads the same at 2 feet as it does at 20 feet."

—BARBARA L. CLARK

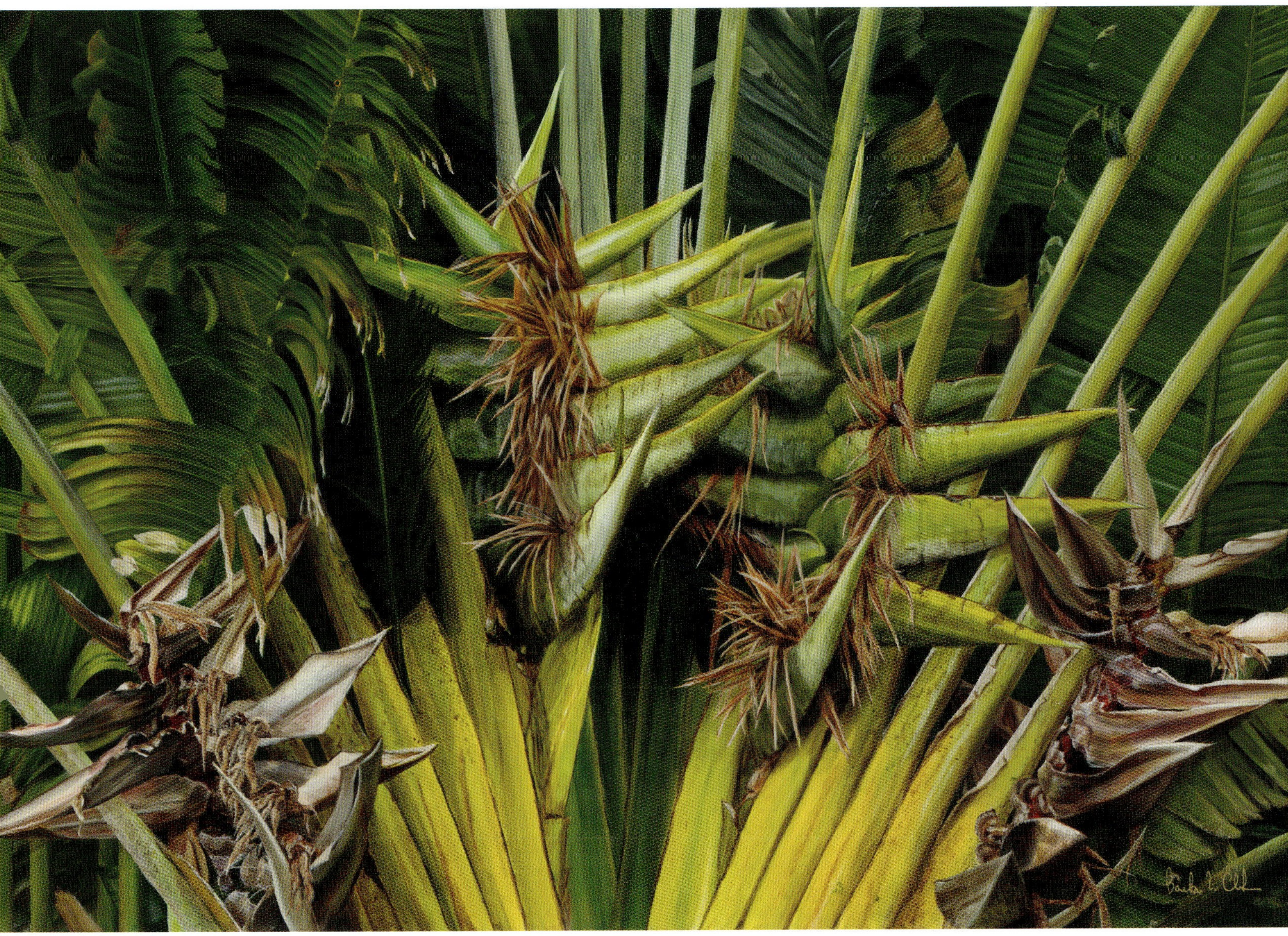

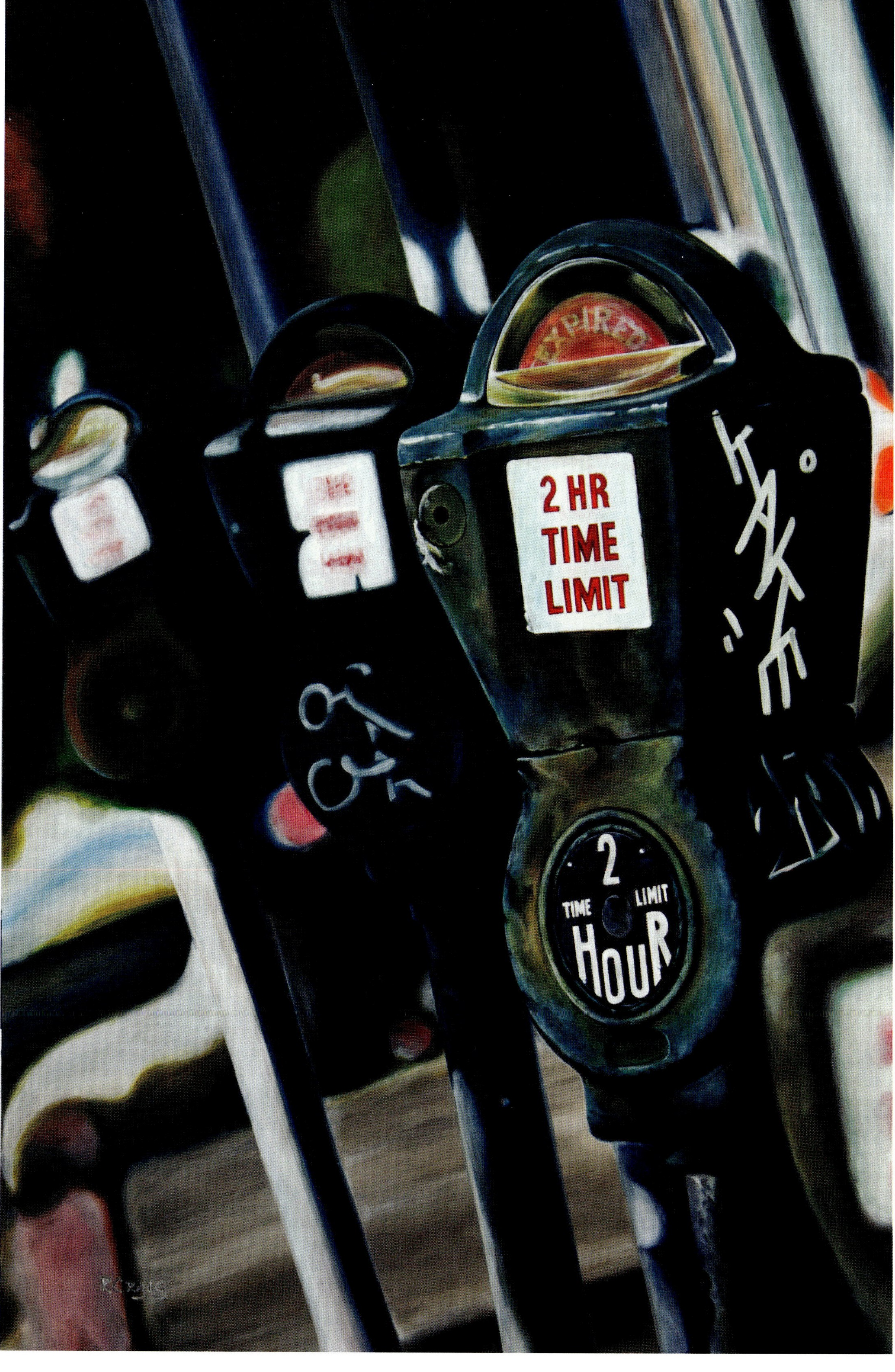
2 HR
TIME
LIMIT
EXPIRED
2
TIME LIMIT
HOUR

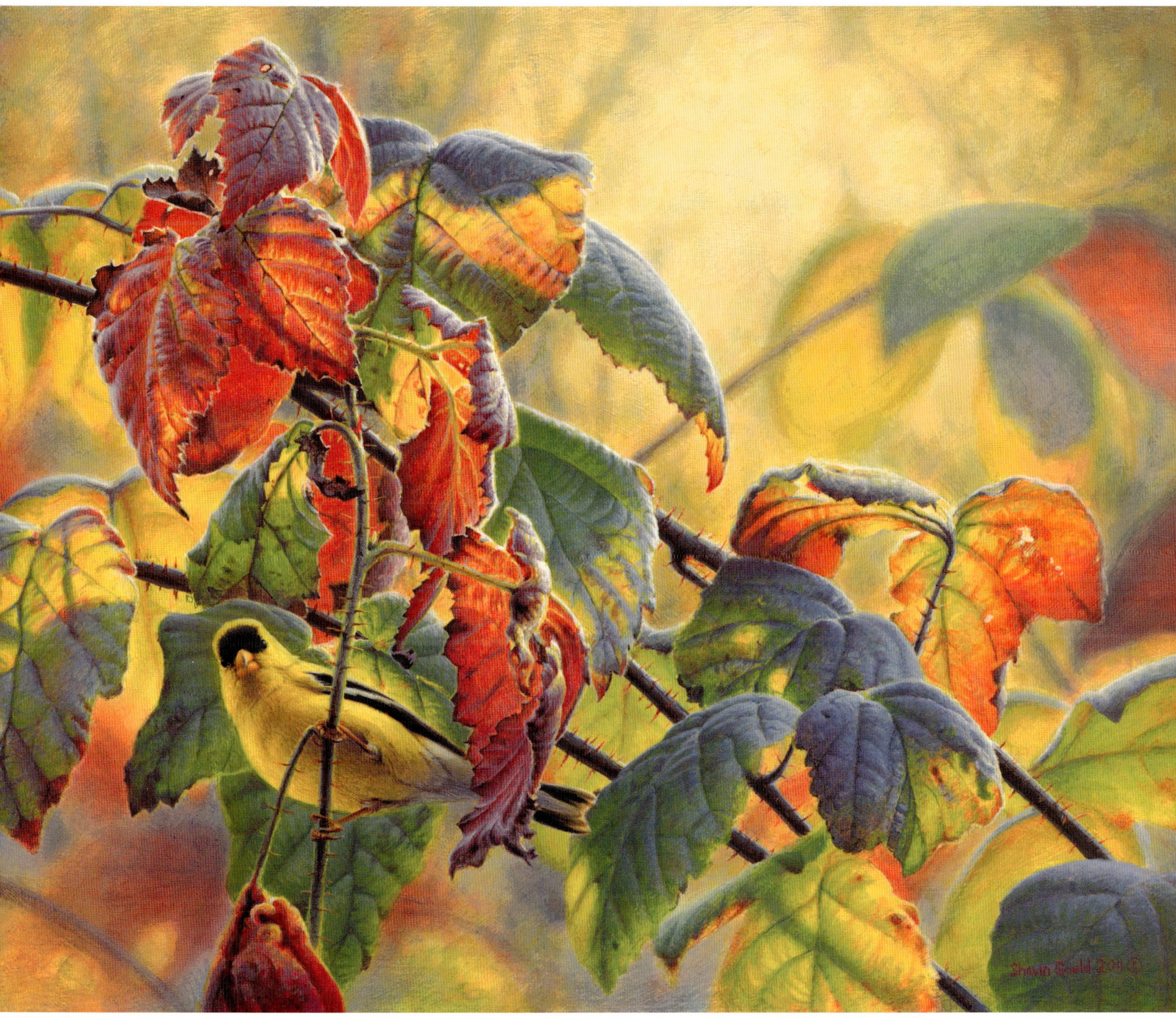

◄ 25 GETS YOU 15 | Ron Craig
Acrylic on gesso board, 36" × 24" (91cm × 61cm)

Interpreting my view of realism has always been a challenge, one that I truly enjoy! With this painting, I wanted to express the dilemma we experience with parking. How it dictates our time while controlling the moment—25 cents gets you 15 minutes; is it ever enough?

Acrylics have always been my medium of choice. The quick drying time benefits my layering process used to achieve the proper tones and detail. Another integral part of my process is the use of retarder and glazing mediums to help with paint flow and blendability. My studies always consist of numerous site visits along with the photographs and sketches I've obtained as reference for when I return to my studio ready to paint.

▲ CHIHULY'S GARDEN | Shawn Gould
Acrylic on hardboard, 16" × 20" (41cm × 51cm)

I really enjoy the versatility of acrylic. Each painting begins by blocking in areas of color and value with thin glazes of paint over a pencil sketch. As it progresses, I use a thicker, more opaque application of the paint with smaller brushes to achieve the sharp details. This range of opacity works well for capturing the warmth of the light as it passes through some of the leaves versus the cool reflected light on the others. The short drying time of acrylic is also important to my technique because it allows me to quickly go back into an area and add more layers of color.

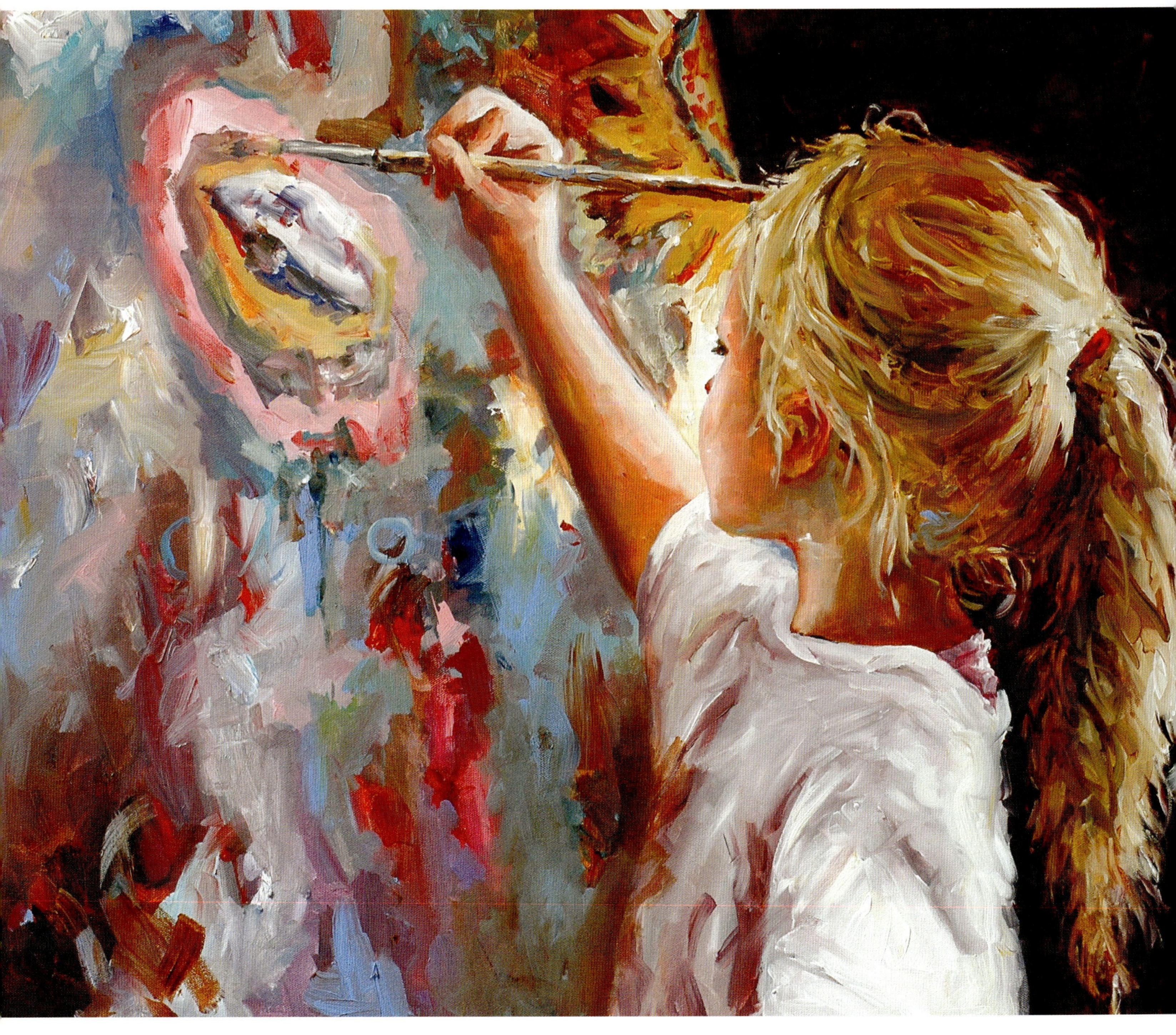

UNIVERSAL CANVAS | Bev Jozwiak
Acrylic on 2-inch (5cm) gallery-wrapped canvas, 24" × 30" (61cm × 76cm)

While participating in an art fair, a vendor set out a canvas for anyone and everyone to paint on. Most passing by added a stroke or two until this little girl got ahold of a brush. Her mother threw a big T-shirt over her clothes and she went to work. Photographs were taken, and once back in the studio I also went to work. This was an interesting piece to work on as I wanted the viewer to see the difference between the little girl and the abstracted canvas she was painting on. To achieve this I painted her skin tones smoother and with more subtle colors. Her hair painted thick and oil-like, and the canvas colorful and abstracted.

HOW DO YOU LIKE THEM | Laura Crabtree-Hollenbeck
Acrylic on canvas, 12" × 16" (30cm × 41cm)

I love painting with just about anything but try to prioritize the safety of water-based mediums. A gallery owner once requested I attempt to create acrylic works that resemble oil paintings, and that was indeed a goal here. I apply multiple layers of paint to build up the highlights and depths, then employ the transparent colors as washes to achieve the final pop of my subject matter. As I frequent farmers' markets, I photograph (and purchase) items from which to compose and sketch in my studio for the painting that will depict whatever I fall in love with there. After much hard work on this I stepped back, sighed and to no one spoke the words of my father: "So how do you like THEM apples?"

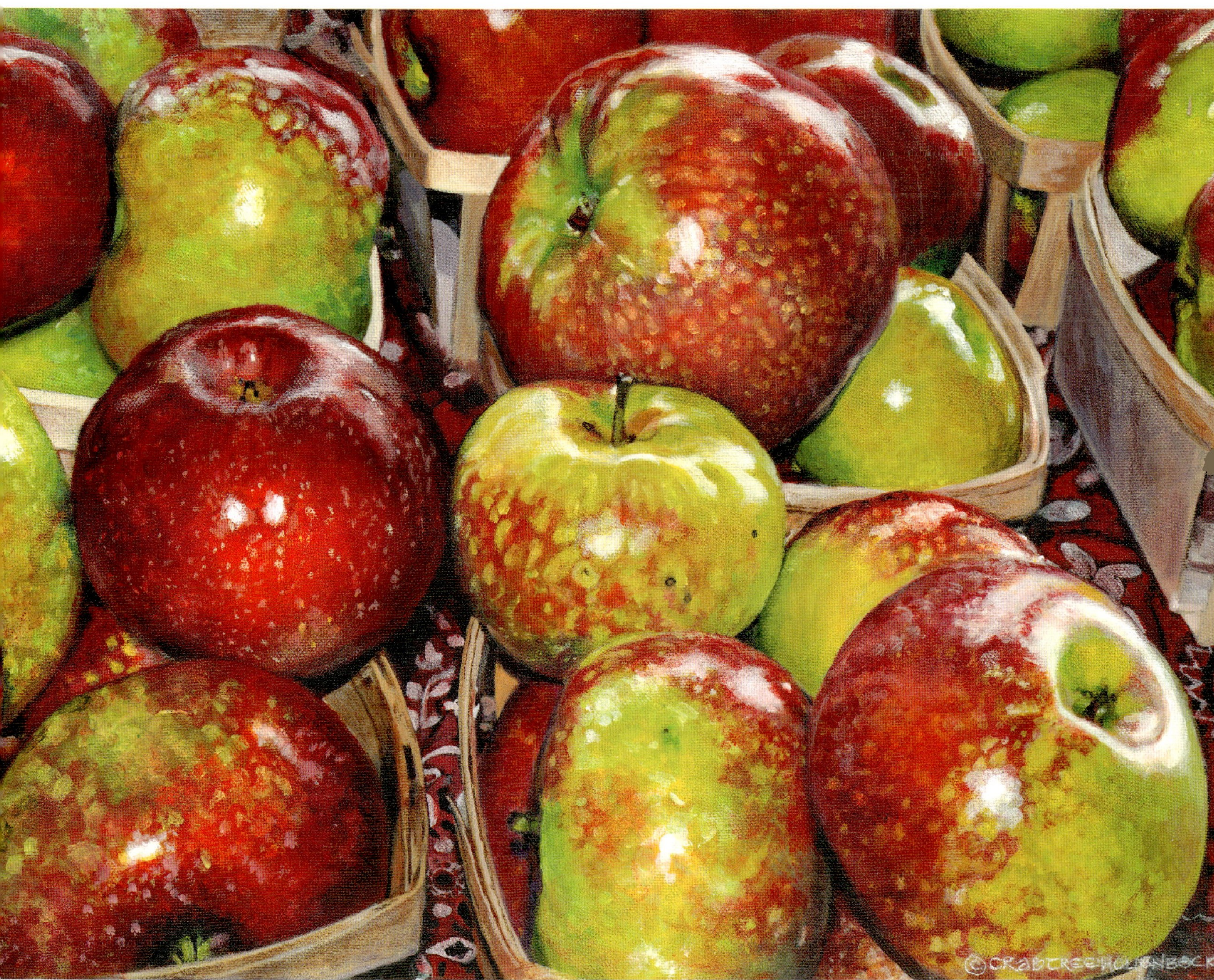

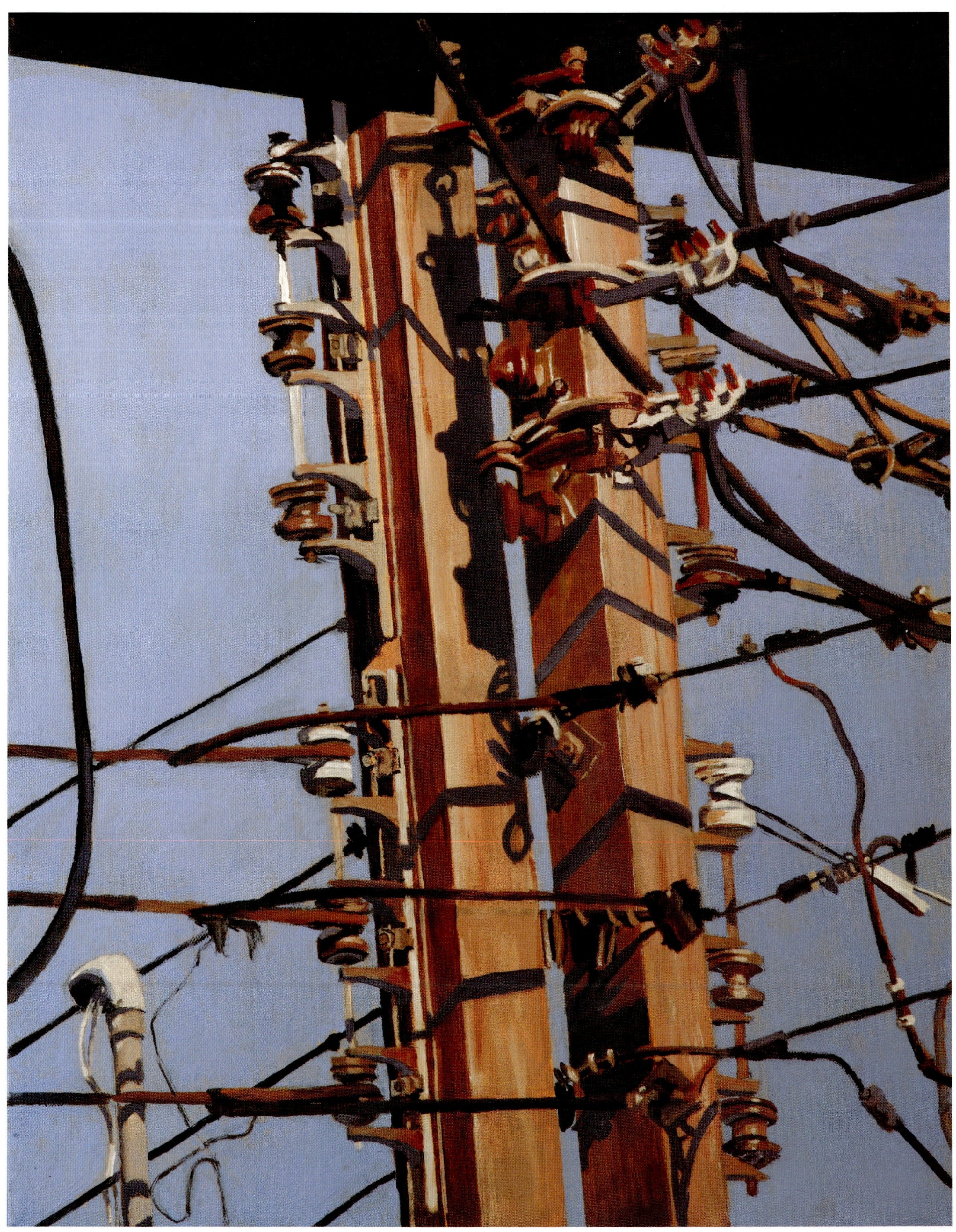

"I set a few rules and then use them as a game plan to create variations on a visual theme, being always mindful of the abstraction that underpins visual expression."

—KRISTIN KRIMMEL

◀ CONNECTIONS 1 | Kristin Krimmel
Acrylic on canvas, 20" × 16" (51cm × 41cm)

I use power poles with their complexity of cables as a metaphor for connectivity and communication. We pass them by, not even thinking of their significance to our lives. The poles and their wires traverse perfect landscapes or clutter our alleyways while bringing us telephone, electronic information and cable. Where would our technically driven society be without these resources? The Power and Communication series is about observation and finding beauty in common objects, elevating them to iconic symbols of our era. I choose to look at power poles for what they are, focusing on them as subject matter.

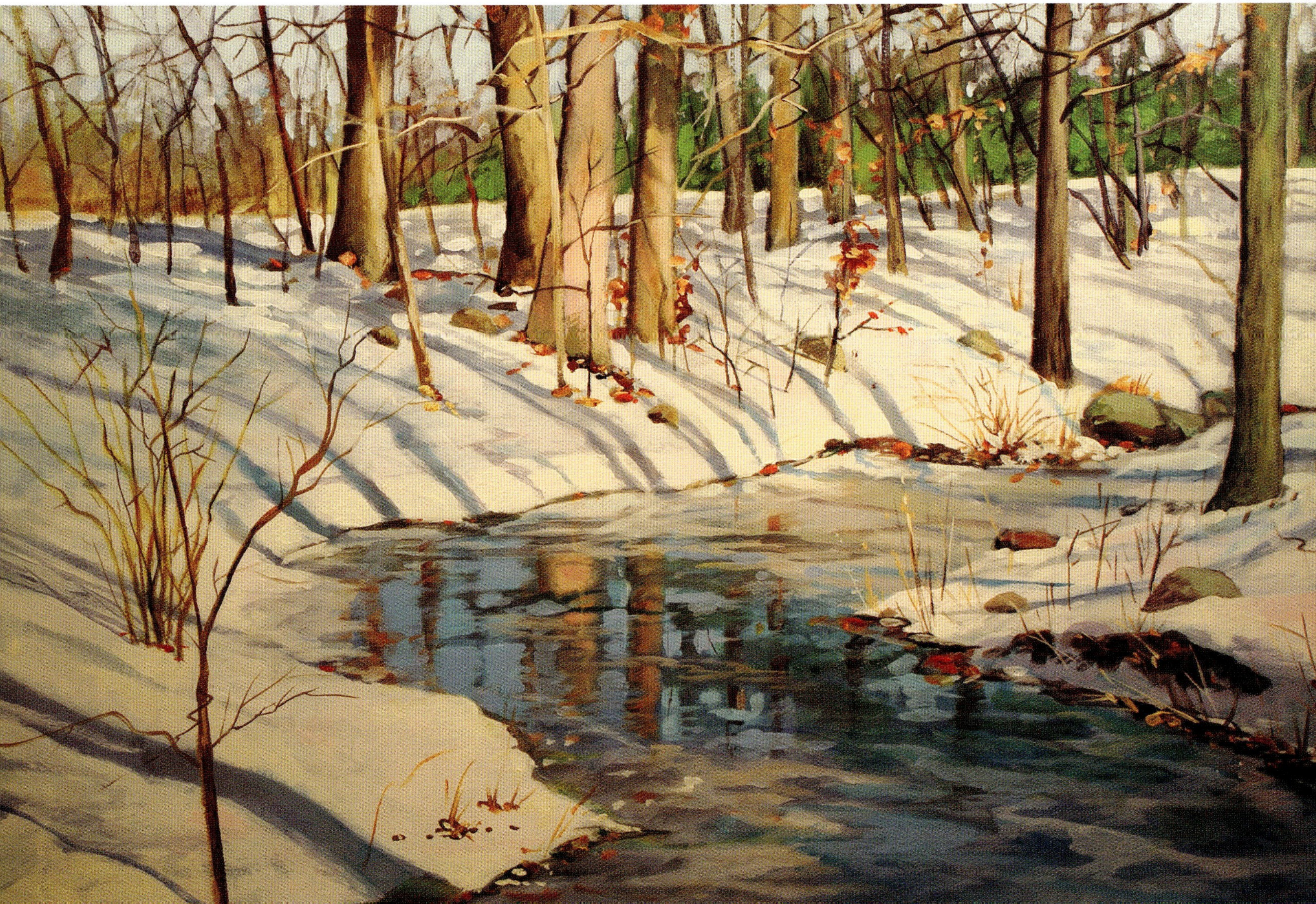

▲ SNOW BUSINESS | Derek Cameron
Acrylic on hot-pressed watercolor paper, 15" × 24" (38cm × 61cm)

I took several photos of this lovely little stream near my home. Working in the studio, I used a variety of acrylic paints and mediums including fluid acrylics, slow drying and heavy body. Glazing medium enriched the colors. Slow-drying medium helped in developing the soft shadows and edges needed in the snow.

I started with a light pencil sketch and then worked in layers building from large washes to a thicker final layer.

I was able to use a watercolor wash technique, a gouache-like technique with medium viscosity and a thicker oil technique at the finish. I have no problem with the drying time of acrylics. The quick decision making helps to make me a better painter in other mediums.

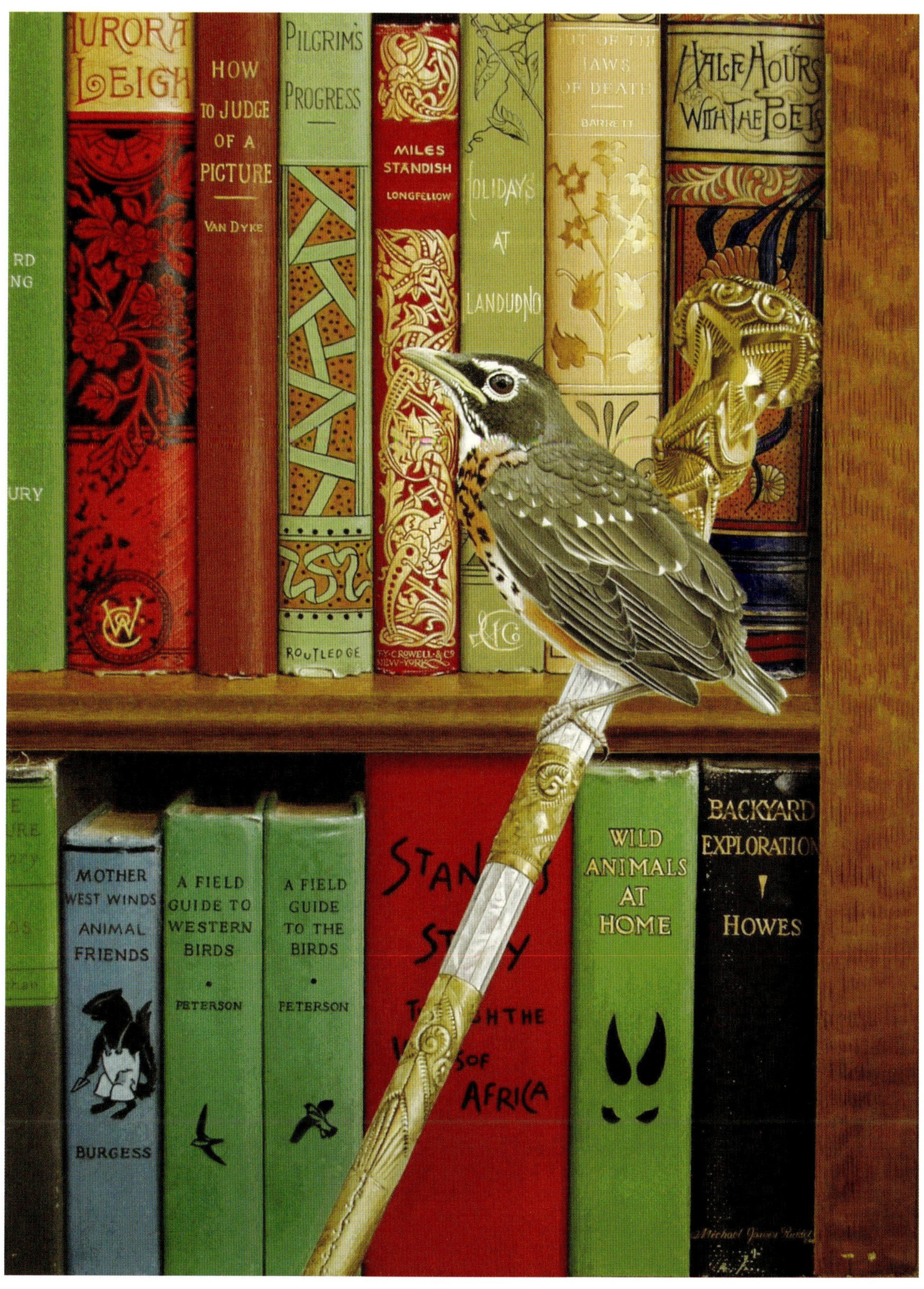

KNOWLEDGE IS POWER | Michael James Riddet
Acrylic on hardboard, 12" × 9" (30cm × 23cm)

After I had used oil and watercolor for many years, my wife told me to try her acrylics. Being a purist, I wanted nothing to do with this new plastic medium. Out of curiosity, however, I decided to do a small painting with this alien medium and to my surprise I was delighted. The year was 1977 and I've used nothing else since. In *Knowledge Is Power* the books are from my library, and most titles were selected to represent the past, present and future of the newly fledged robin. As a side note, the robin was initially sculpted in clay life size and stuck to the old cane as a working model before painting began.

MOUNTAIN REFLECTIONS | Pamela Dittloff
Acrylic on canvas, 48" × 60" (122cm × 152cm)

My usual process is to start with plein air studies to establish color notes, light and values for the final painting. Using the studies and photo references, I paint the larger works in the studio. The inspiration for *Mountain Reflections* was a picnic spot on a beautiful fall day off the Blue Ridge Parkway in North Carolina. In the final painting I combined elements from three different spots along the river to give a stronger composition. The immediacy of acrylic highlights the importance of the planning stages. I start with a somewhat abstract value study to make sure I like the shapes, movement and contrast. Next is an underpainting on the canvas, in this case Burnt Sienna and Ultramarine Blue. Answering these basic questions first allows me to paint quickly and spontaneously (the fun part!). I am a big fan of the versatility of acrylics and often use multiple glazes to get light refracting through several layers, helping to establish depth and mood.

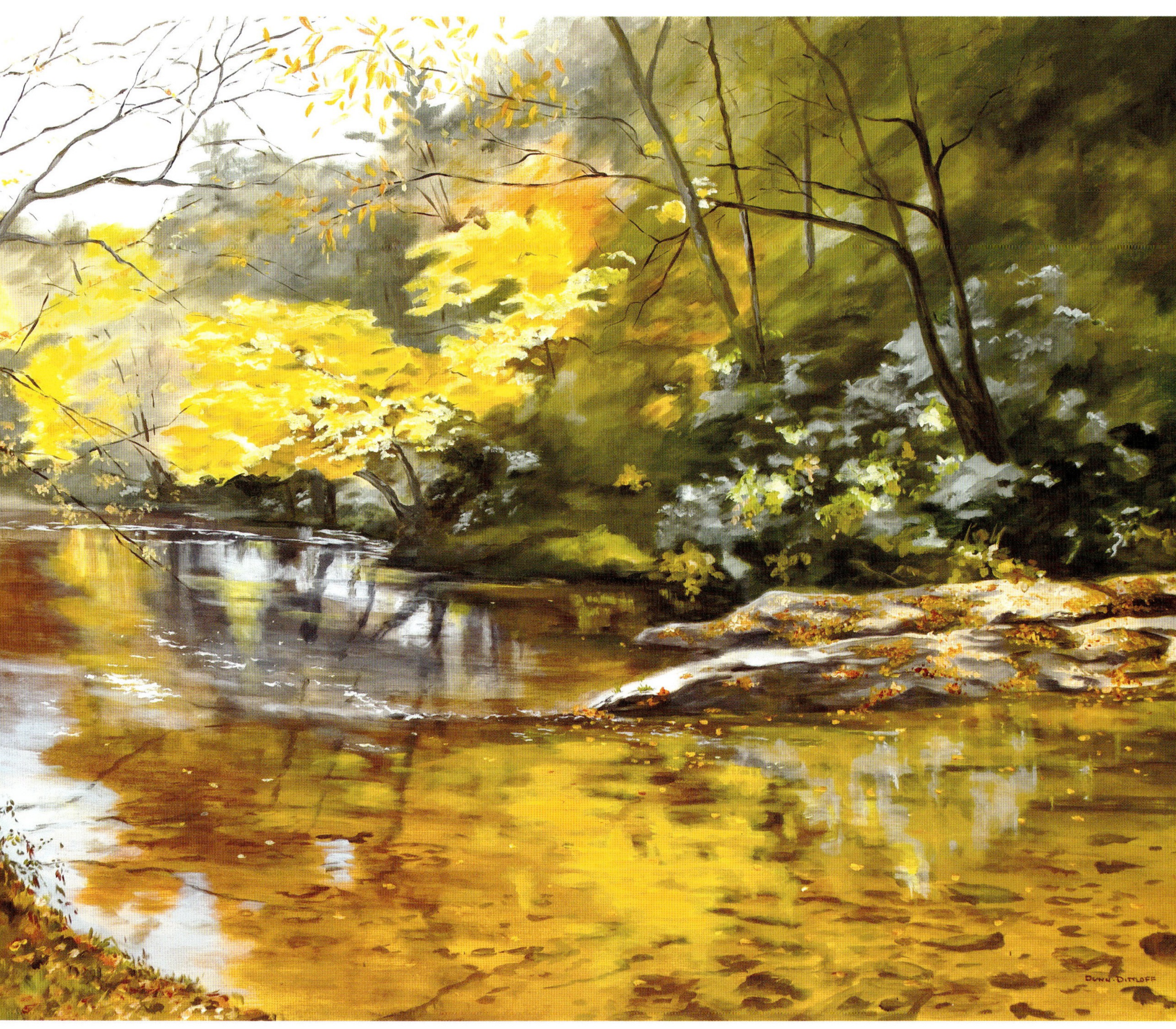

"When working with glazes, work quickly. Overworking may lift previous layers off the ground."

—PAMELA DITTLOFF

SIBERIAN SUMMER | John Mullane
Acrylic on cradled art board, 16" × 20" (41cm × 51cm)

Siberian Summer began like all of my paintings do, from a personal experience. Because most of my work is nature themes, the inspirations and ideas come from being outdoors. That can range from looking out my kitchen window at a bird feeder to traveling to amazing destinations like Yellowstone Park and Botswana in Africa. From these experiences I gather tons of reference material to draw from. I take hundreds of photos of animals, backgrounds, grasses, leaves and landscapes. I also do sketches, take notes on weather conditions and jot down ideas. This particular painting came from an outing at the Bronx Zoo. One morning, this cub and two others playfully chased each other for hours. When one cub took a break to rest on this rock, I was instantly taken with the pose, light and potential for a good composition.

Acrylics are the ideal medium for this. The drying properties allow me to develop areas rather quickly. I usually start with the background and build up layer by layer. This process can be done in minutes with acrylic as opposed to hours or days with oil. It's also ideal for painting fur and feathers or texture on rocks. You can work up these areas by glazing transparently or adding more color for opacity. You can experiment with the various mediums and pastes, but give me a spray bottle with water and a brush and I'm good to go.

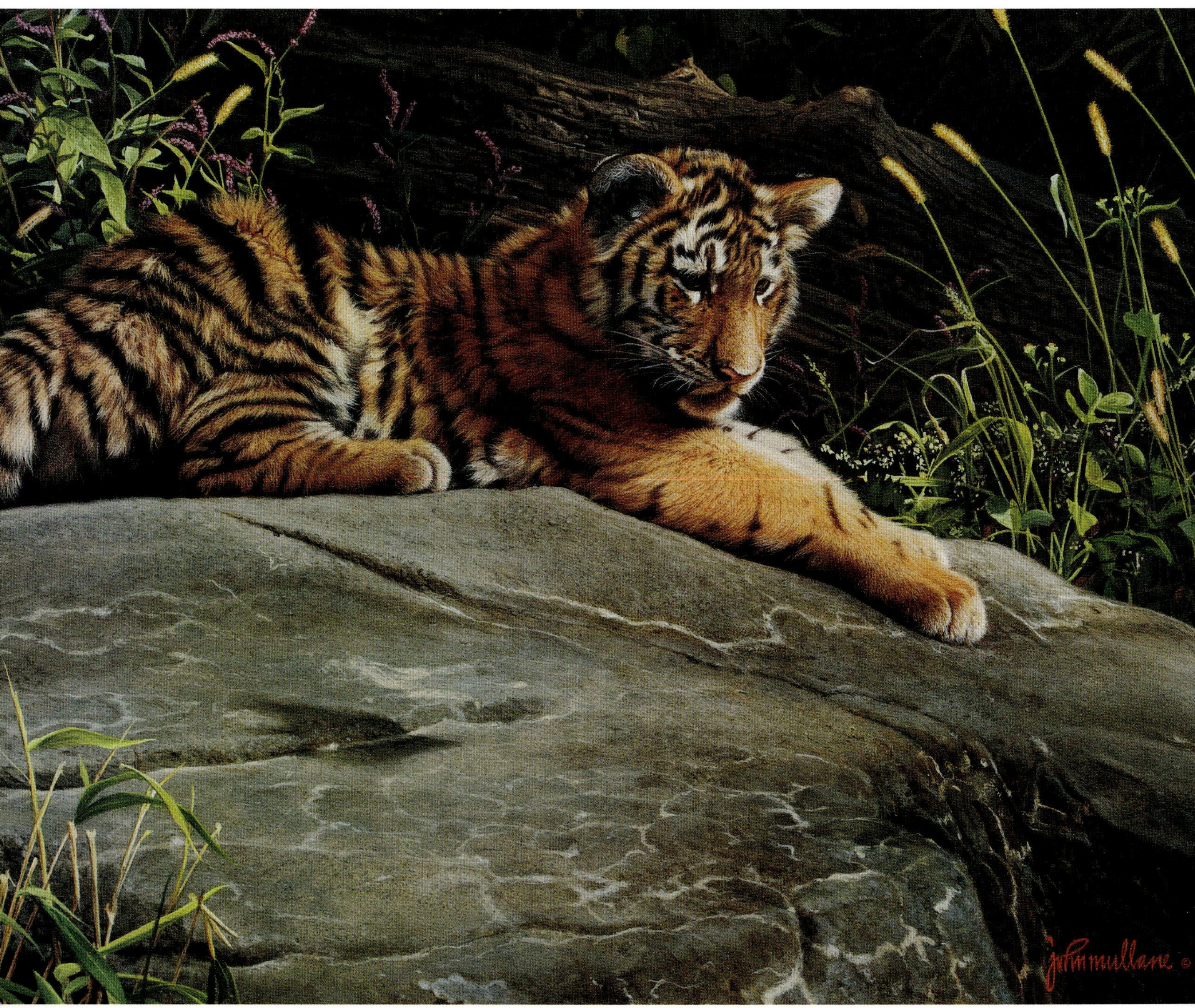

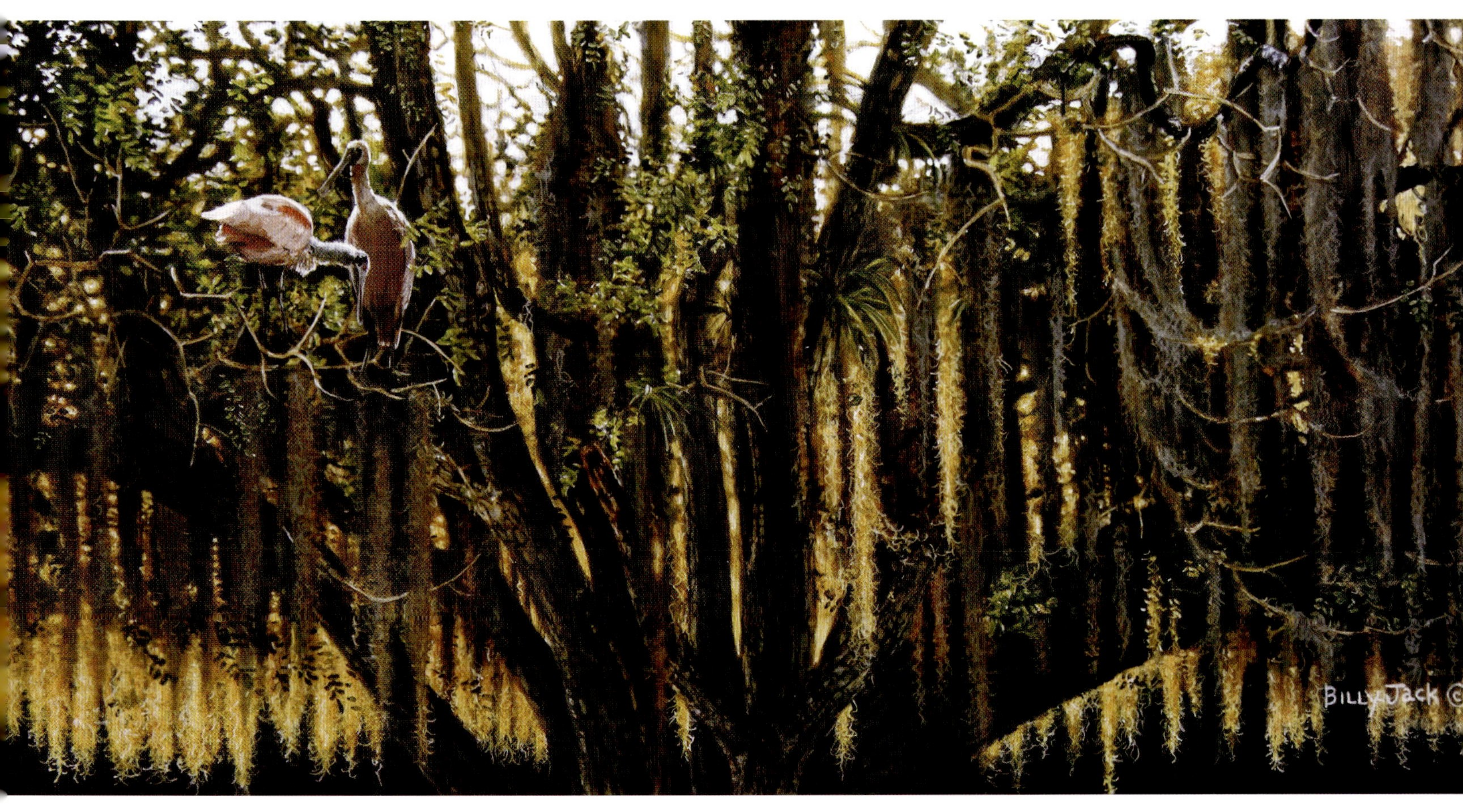

SPANISH SYMPHONY | Billy-Jack Milligan
Acrylic on Masonite board, 8" × 16" (20cm × 41cm)

One of my most memorable bird sightings in the Everglades was that of the Roseate Spoonbills. Their swampy environment is beautiful and unique; every tree seems to be draped with Spanish moss. The late afternoon light was soaking up the moss and peeking through the branches creating a symphony of tones and contrasts. An amazing sight!

HIS ROYAL HIGHNESS | Syndi Michael
Acrylic on stretched canvas, 30" × 40" (76cm × 102cm)

It was one of those times that I was in dire need of inspiration when the most remarkable thing happened! I stepped outside for a breath of fresh air when much to my amazement this beautiful peacock was strutting in the street in front of my house! This was not a typical sight in this neighborhood. I knew I had my inspiration and quickly snapped a picture of him. For about three weeks he made himself at home, perching on our porches, napping in the shade of our trees, and suddenly he was gone as quickly as he appeared. I later learned some peahens had also appeared in another neighborhood near me. Boys will be boys!

As I began this painting, I became so enthralled with the richness of the colors that I carried them over into the background of the painting. I almost always tend to work from dark to light, starting with a black gessoed canvas. Because the peacock itself had so much detail work in it, the background gave me the opportunity to just flow—drybrushing layer after layer of color with no real plan, just feeling.

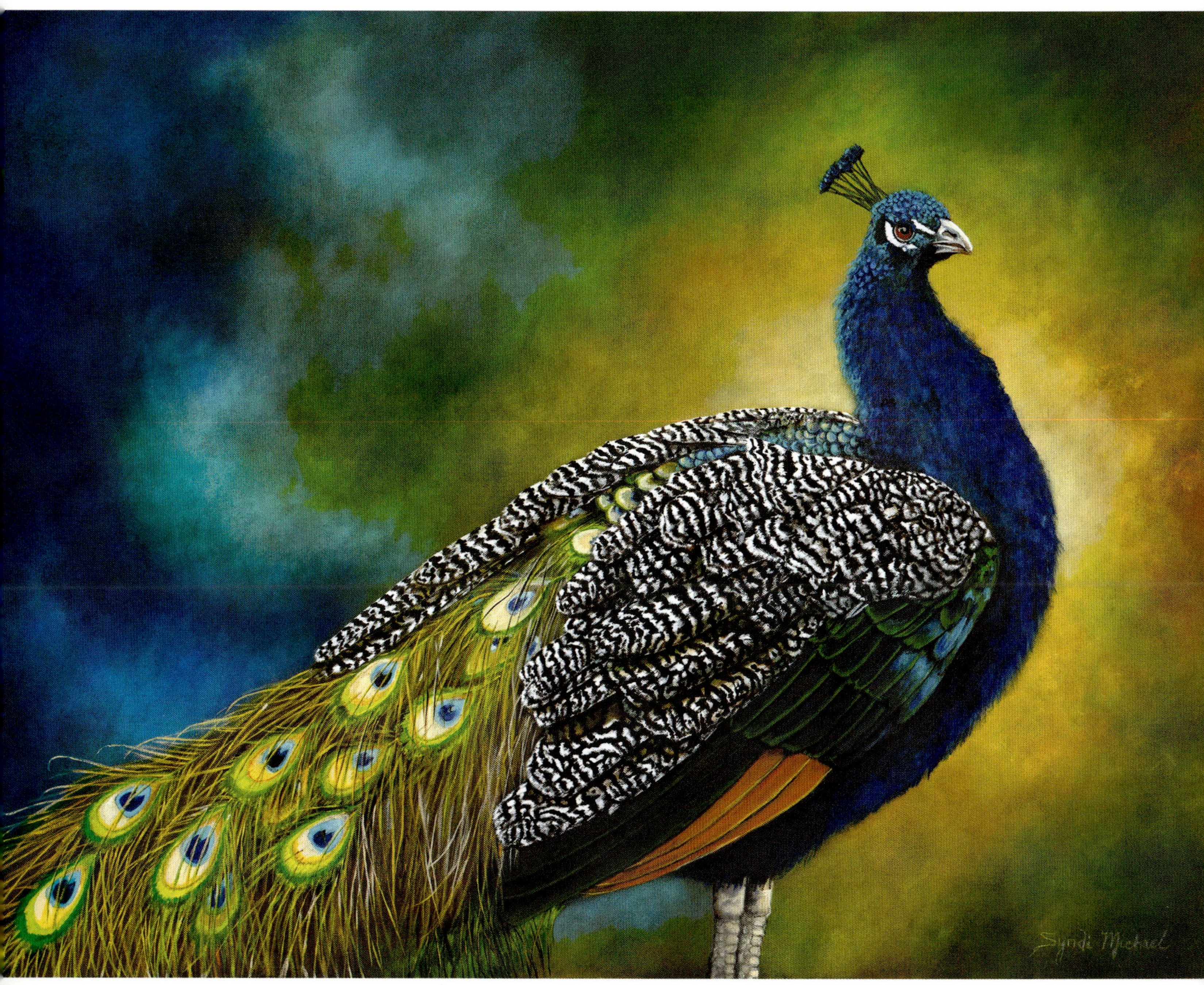

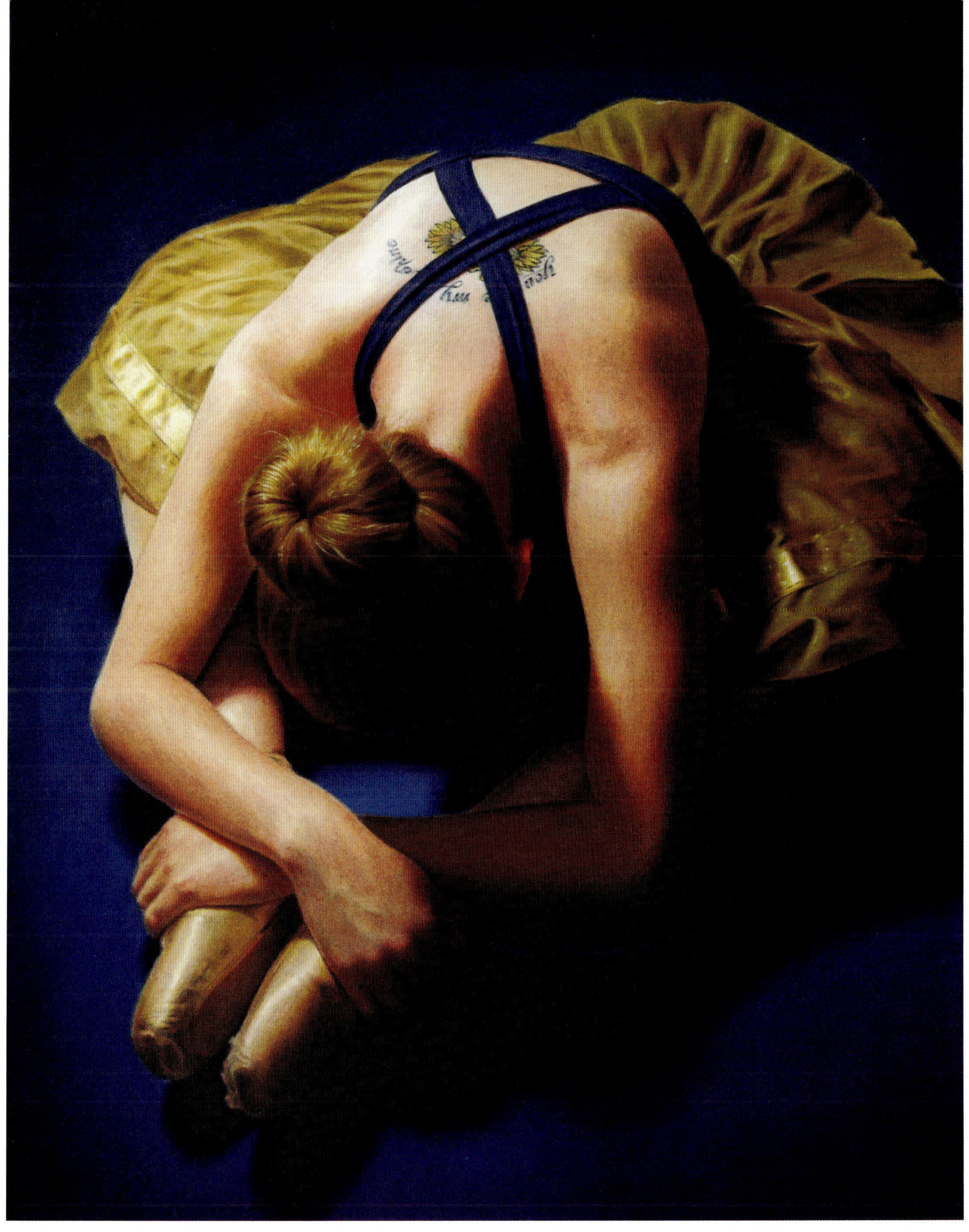

BALLERINA IN BLUE | Marissa Madonna
Acrylic and colored pencil on hot-pressed watercolor board
15¼" × 12" (39cm × 30cm)

I have always been inspired by the beauty and elegance of dance. Transcending the conventional grace of a dancer's performance, *Ballerina in Blue* showcases a quieter moment of preparation and self-reflection. This piece was made using FW Acrylic Inks and Prismacolor Colored Pencils. Using the acrylic much like watercolor, I build up my paintings in many thin layers. Then for finer details I use the colored pencils. This mixed-media approach combines the freedom of laying broad washes with the tight control of drawing. It can take quite some time to build up a rich surface working this way, but it is a process that I have grown to truly embrace.

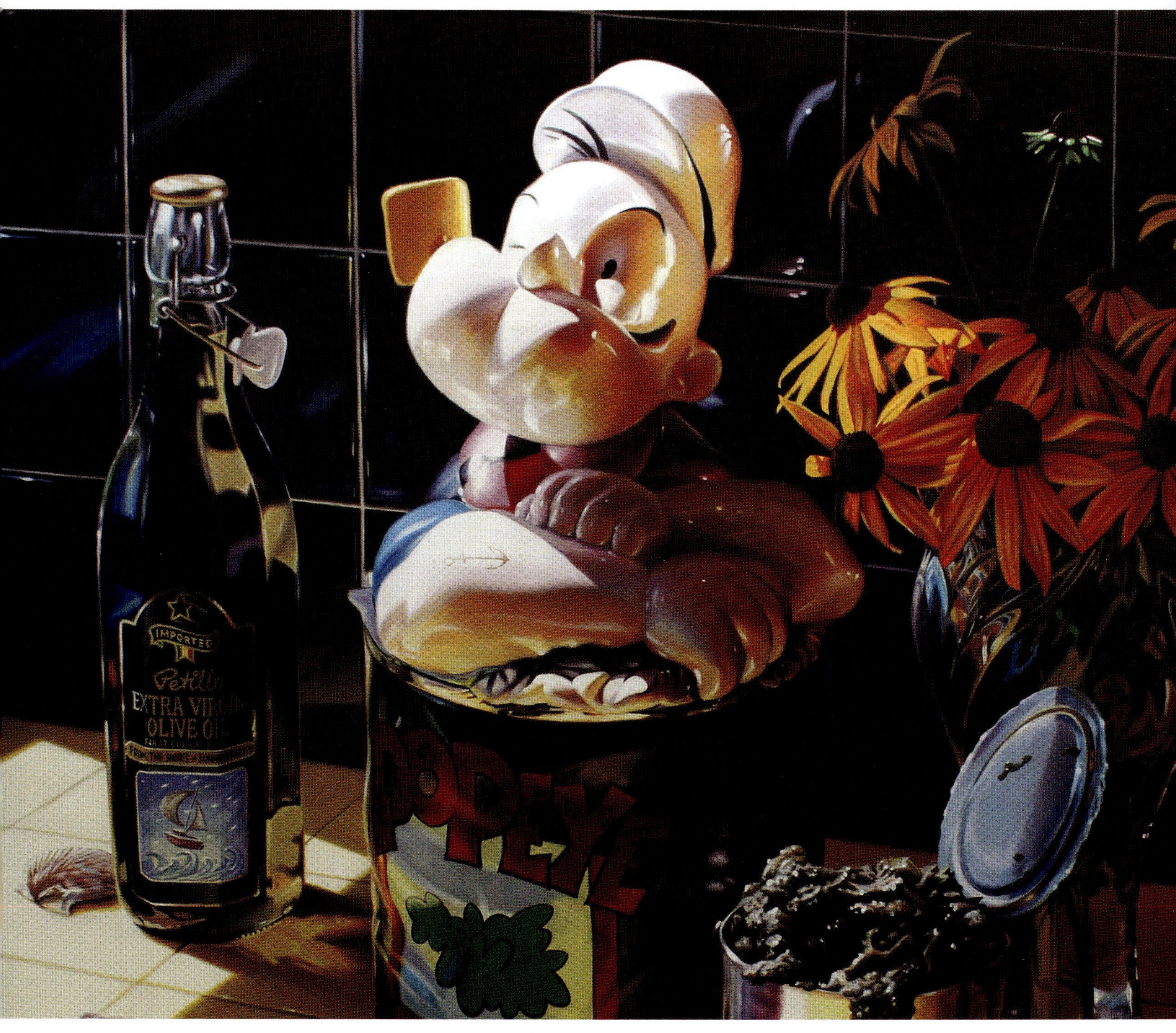

NAUTICAL STILL LIFE | Bob Petillo
Acrylic on canvas, 35" × 31" (89cm × 79cm)

In the late 1990s, I decided to do a series of cookie jar paintings as part of a nostalgic Americana theme. This painting was inspired by a number of items owned by myself and friends. After setting up the still life with dramatic lighting effects and taking about forty photographs, it was a matter of using the best of each element to create the final composition. I achieved these final results by painting directly on the canvas using solid color mixes and washes.

TENEMENT | Bob Petillo
Acrylic on canvas, 32" × 48" (81cm × 122cm)

A friend and I decided to spend a day visiting some Soho galleries in New York City. After we parked a few blocks away, the walk there revealed this amazing reflection. Camera in hand, I just couldn't help myself. I took a bunch of photos and thus began the start of a new nostalgic Americana series of paintings called *Reflections of America*. I painted this piece in photorealism on a large textured canvas for a more painterly effect. Colors were mixed and applied directly with brushes blending intermediate tones on the canvas itself. With forty photographs, it was a matter of using the best of each element to create the final composition.

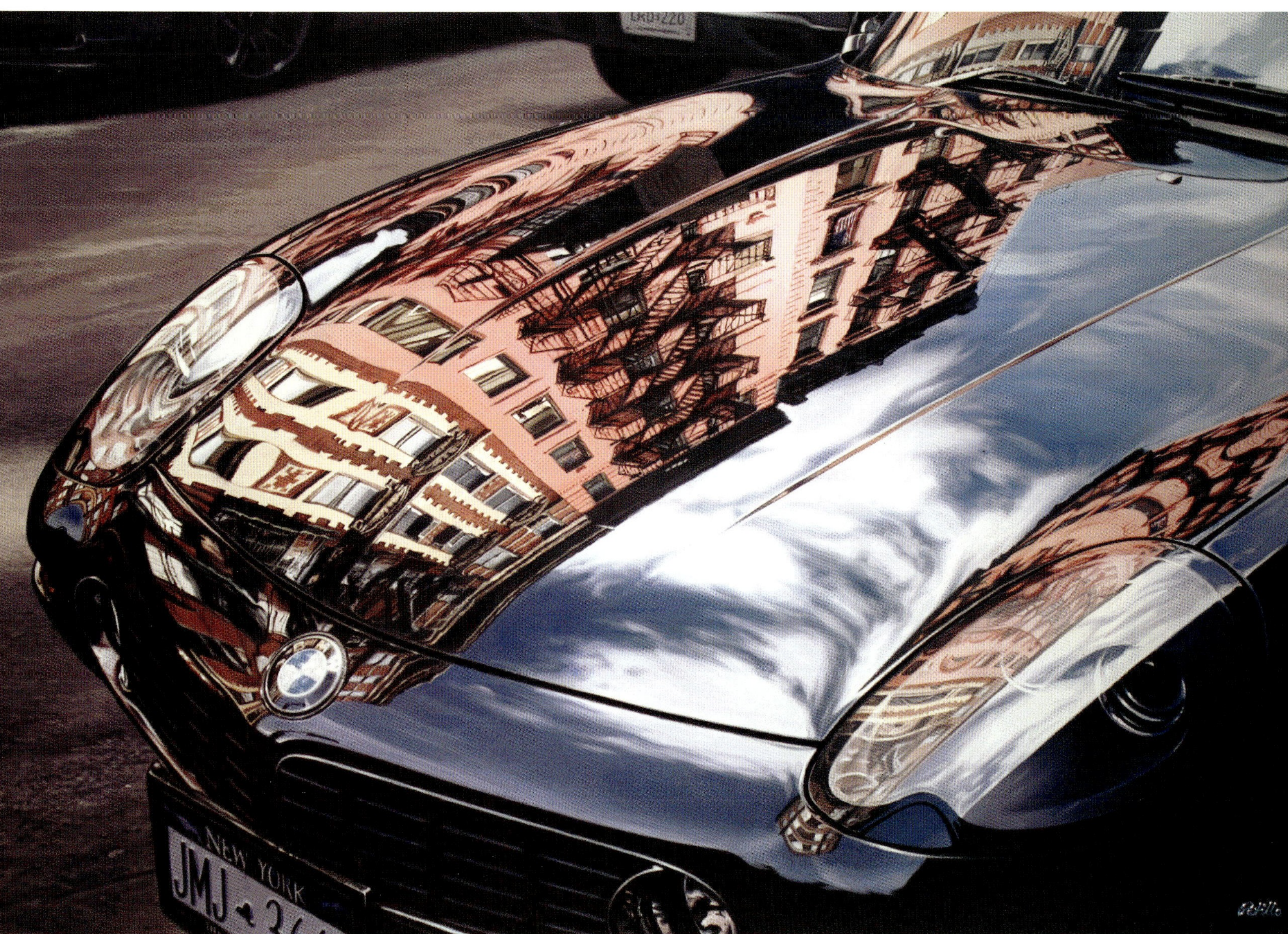

SURFSIDE | Keith Wilkie
Heavy body acrylics on cotton duck archival canvas, 36" × 48" (91cm × 122cm)

Most of my recent work has been driven by my love of water—usually the salty variety—marshes, the beach and related coastal scenes. Countless hours spent observing a subject and absorbing the environment from my boat or sitting on a beach are essential. I paint in my studio using sketches, studies, photos and memories. I started painting with oils but eventually discovered the advantages of working with acrylics. Their flexibility is an advantage in my work as they can be applied thin or thick, opaque or translucent, in fast-drying situations or extended with slow-drying blending medium for wet-into-wet applications.

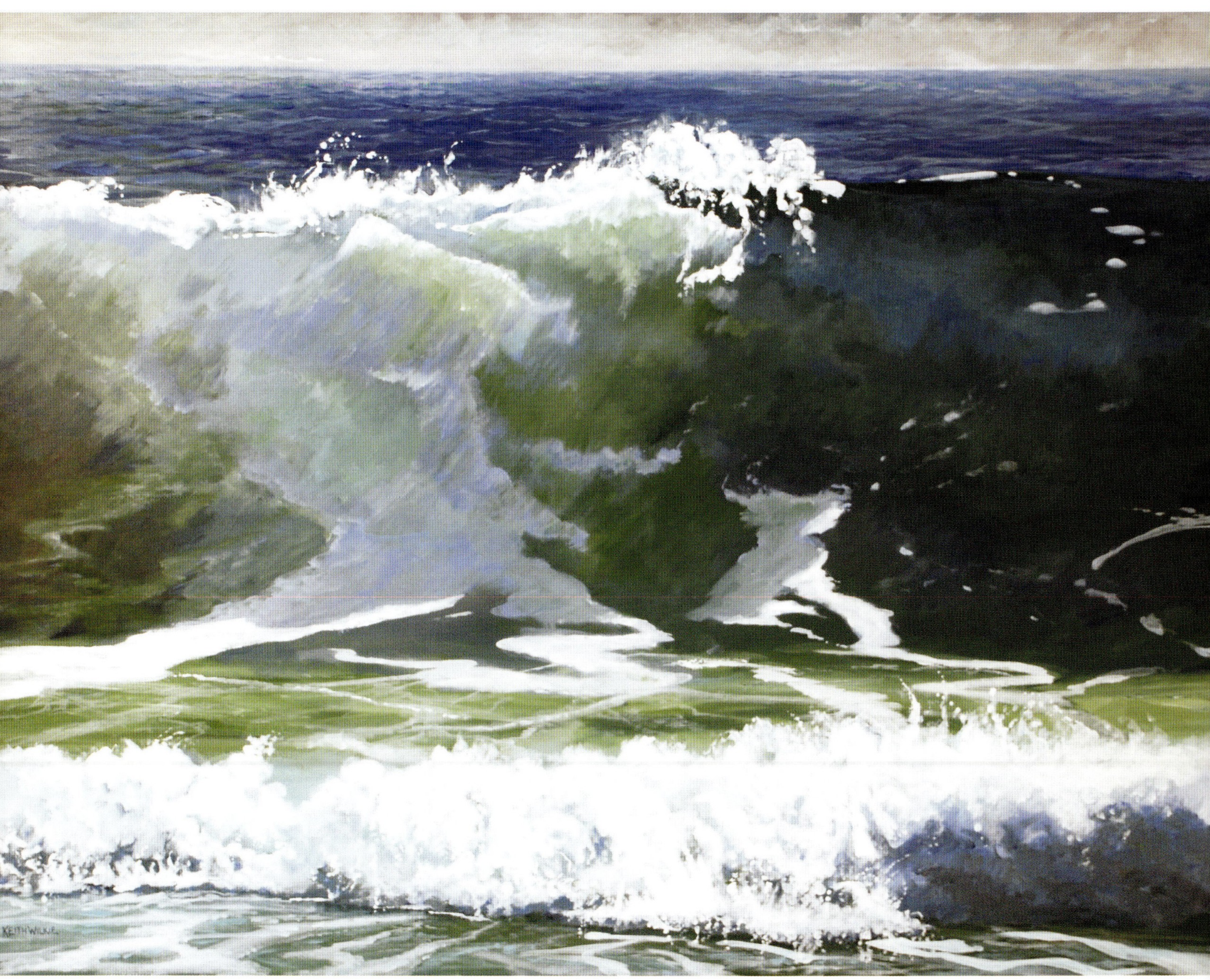

"Relax, enjoy the process of painting and delight in the joy your work provides others."

—KEITH WILKIE

"Don't be afraid to use lots of paint—it will make a far better painting."

—ANDA J. STYLER

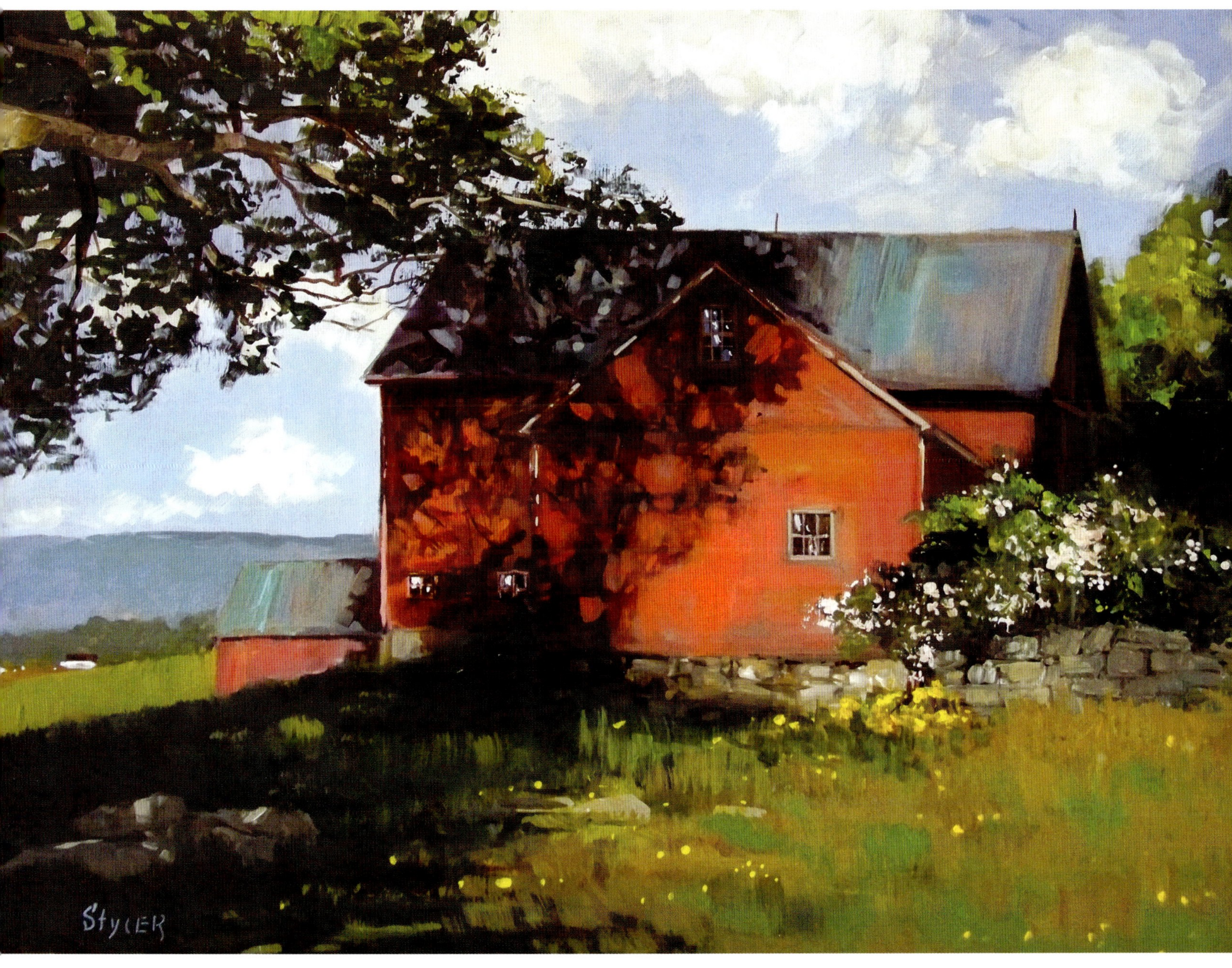

AUGUST | Anda J. Styler
Acrylic on linen, 22" × 28" (56cm × 71cm)

August was inspired from a smaller on-site painting. My technique is to stretch a linen canvas, gesso it with a Burnt Sienna background color, then use a thin mix of Van Dyke Brown and Crimson for underpainting a value study. Finish work begins with heavier paint, brushes, knives or rags to create effects. My process is building many layers of paint to create a rich texture and color. Using a palette knife adds interest, texture and accidents that add life to the painting. Light and shadow create drama and movement—for me it's about that fleeting moment—I see it everywhere in the landscape. This painting was challenging because of the perspective of the tree branch and capturing the shadows on the barn.

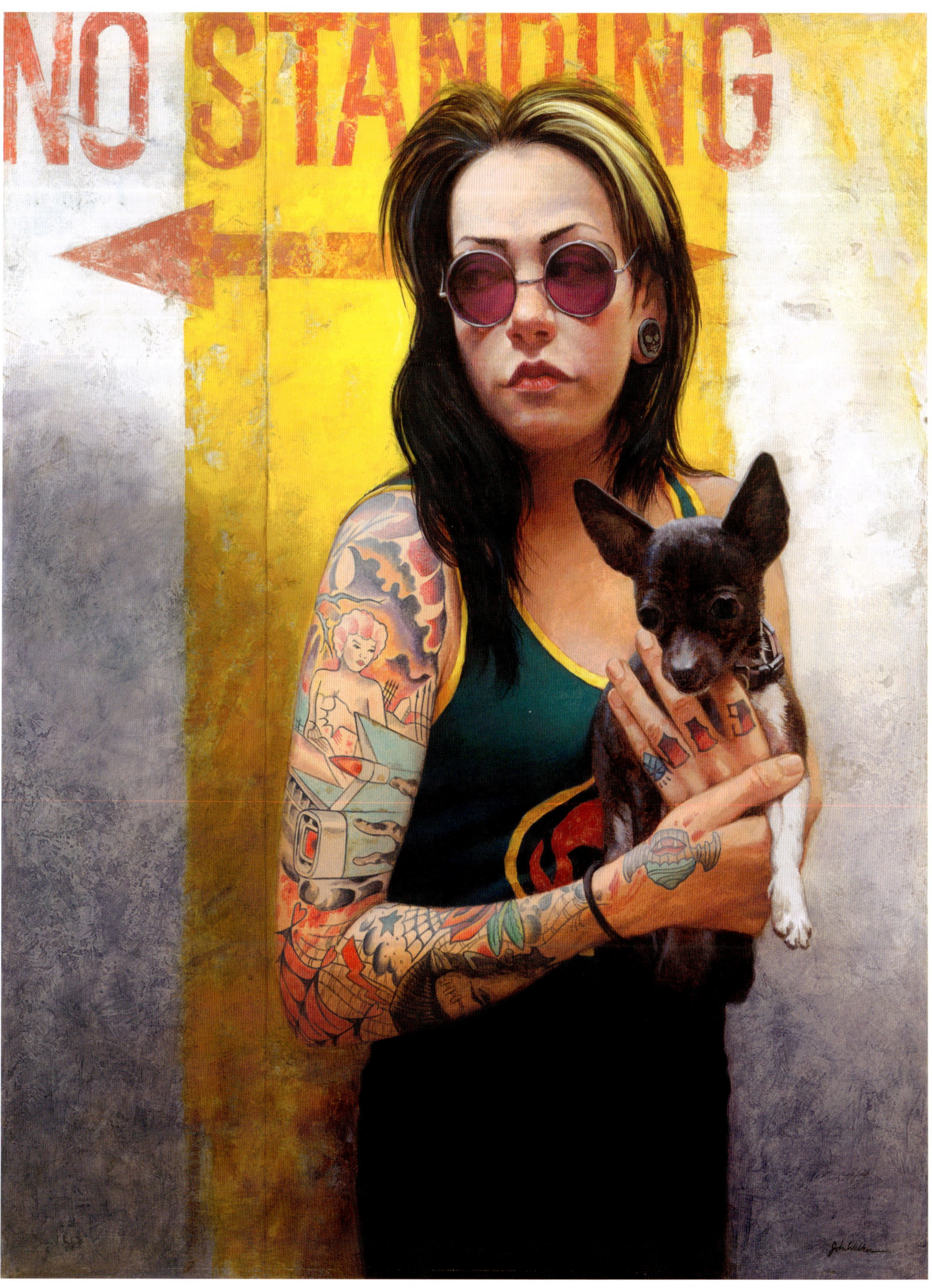
NO STANDING

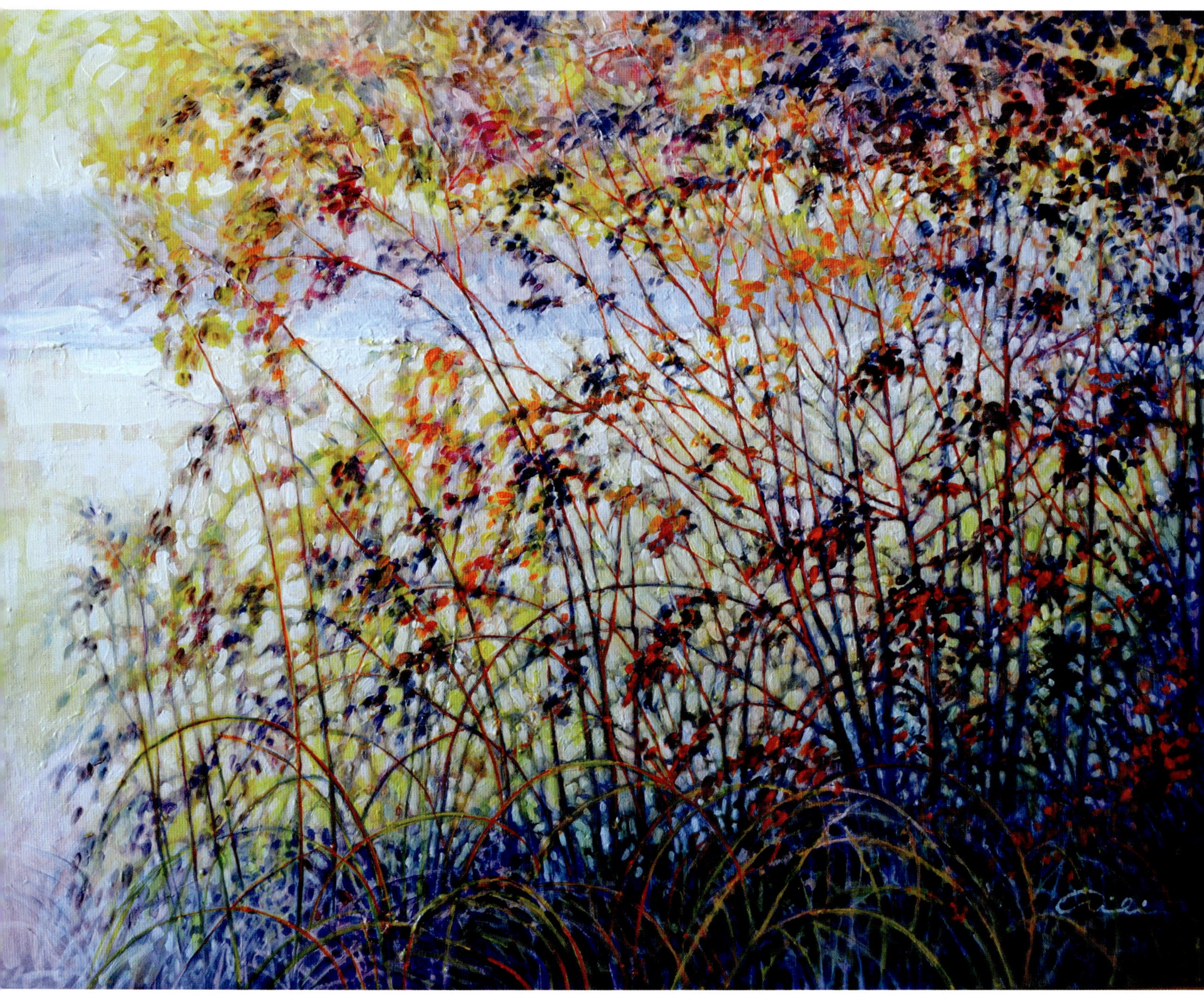

◀ VOODOO STEPS OUT | John Walker
Acrylic on hardboard with textured background
32" × 24" (81cm × 61cm)

While the model was taking a break, I made the offhand suggestion that she try posing with her little dog, VooDoo. The resulting scene was more interesting than the one we had originally been working on. Technically, the challenge was to combine a dimensionally textured background wall (gesso applied with a palette knife in a knock-down style) with the smooth surface underlying the figure in a way that didn't look contrived or foreign. A strong light source, sweeping across both foreground and background, helped the two relate to each other and became a powerful compositional element that strengthens the mood.

▲ WHITE LAKE | Aili Kurtis
Acrylic on stretched canvas, 30" × 40" (76cm × 102cm)

I painted *White Lake* on my balcony, which overlooks a beautiful freshwater lake. While I was painting I continued to glance at the trees and bushes in front of me to help me remember the way branches and leaves interconnect, but mostly I was interested in designing the painting to portray the rhythms and patterns in nature. It was important to me that the painting have an abstract feel to it, while still retaining the charm of a theme. Acrylic is a very important medium for this technique because of its quick drying power. I was constantly layering one color on top of the other. For instance, to simplify the pattern of the branches and create interesting negative spaces, I painted opaque layers of Titanium White to block out the bright colors of the foliage and then used acrylic glazing liquid tinted with Phthalo Blue to soften the white to make it look like the lake.

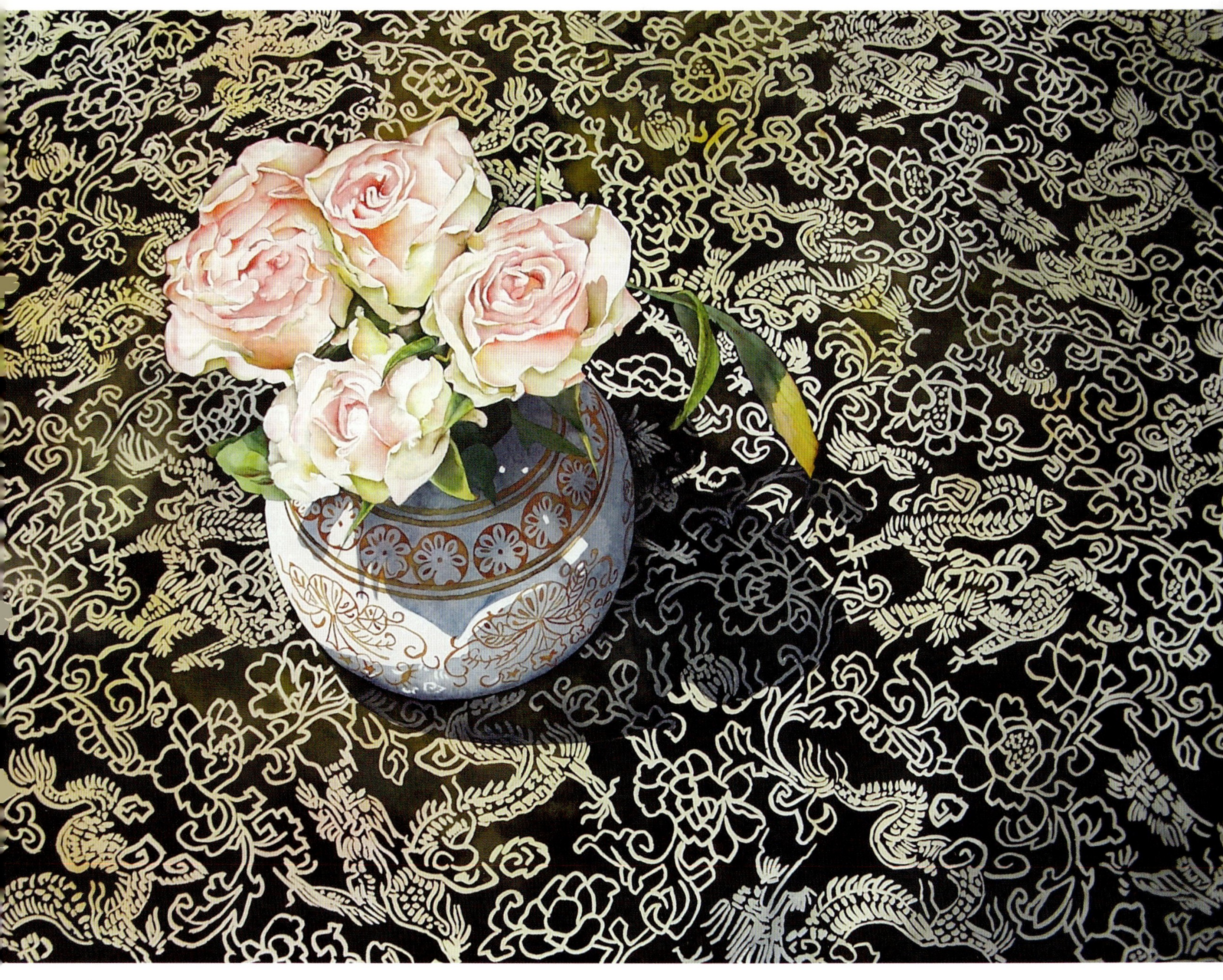

ORIENTAL ROSES | Deb Ward
Fluid acrylic on 300-lb. (640gsm) cold-pressed Arches
22" × 30" (56cm × 76cm)

This is one painting in a series based on my collection of oriental fabrics. Painting in series alleviates the stress of what to paint next and lets me master either a technique or a subject. Background colors were laid in; then quantities of Pebeo drawing gum were used on the dragons. Similar in usage, look and handling of watercolors, fluid acrylics allow me to glaze and the paint to flow. I challenged myself to create a shadow on black and to create interesting black fabric with other colors. Painted slow and steady, with attention to detail, created during my annual painting retreat with friends, this is one of those rare paintings that came out on paper just the way I visualized it!

▶ KARYN AND KAYO | Lindsay Watson
Acrylic on gesso-primed stretched canvas, 16" × 12" (41cm × 33cm)

Although acrylics offer a complete range, my favorites are the sheer vivid fluids and buttery soft body paints. After photographing Karyn and her grandson, I could picture the work—Kayo, cuddled gently against her. The eye would follow an oval shape, down one arm and up the other ending in his tiny fingers, creating a feeling of harmony and trust. The background was brushed loosely with seven colors, one layer at a time: Naples Yellow, Pale Portrait Pink, Teal, Parchment, Nickel Azo Gold, Light Blue and Burnt Sienna. These hints of color added texture and interest against the figures' neutral palette.

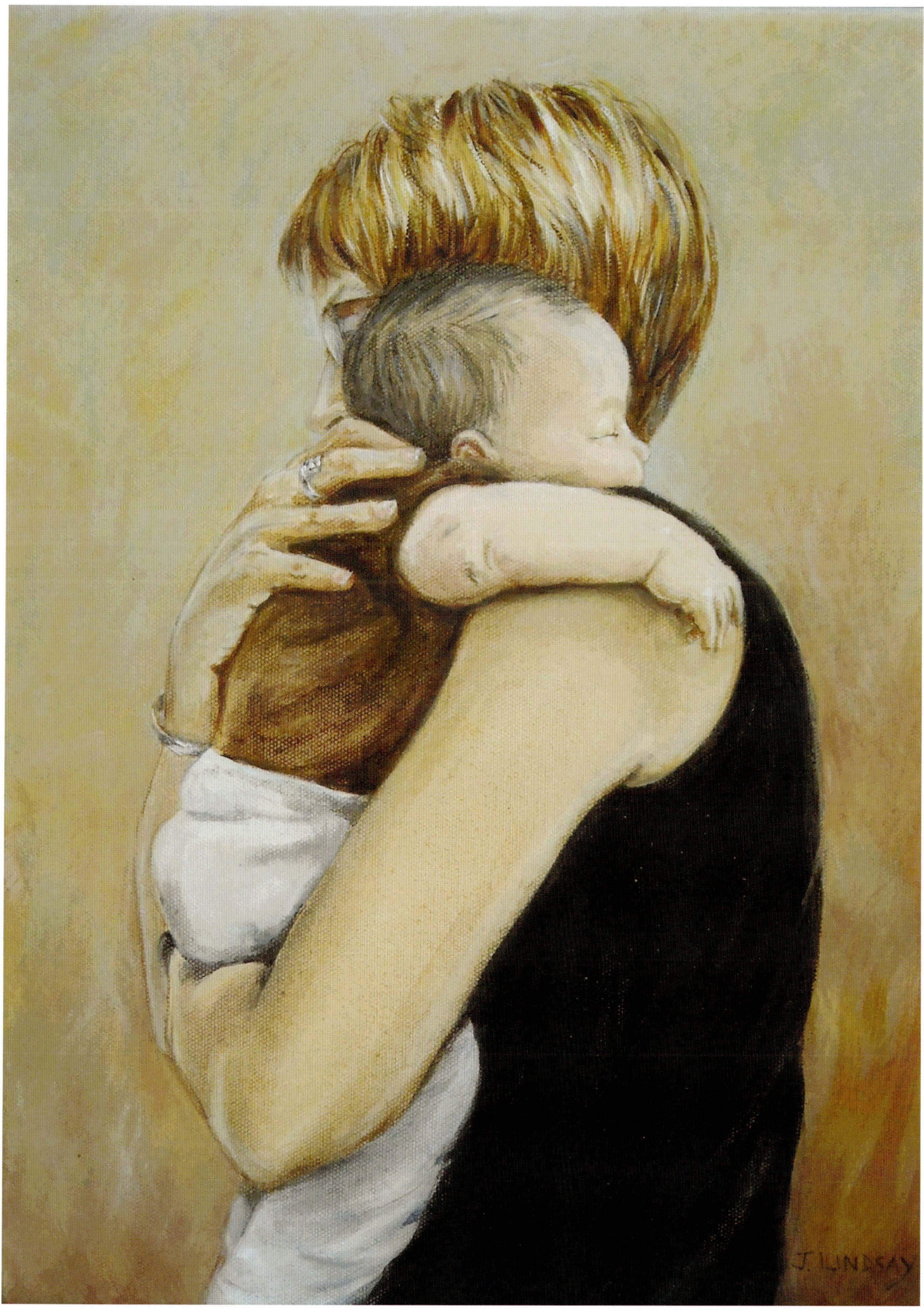
J. LINDSAY

"Creative composition, cropping and color can often transform a representational, illustrative depiction of a subject into art."

—DAVID WICKS

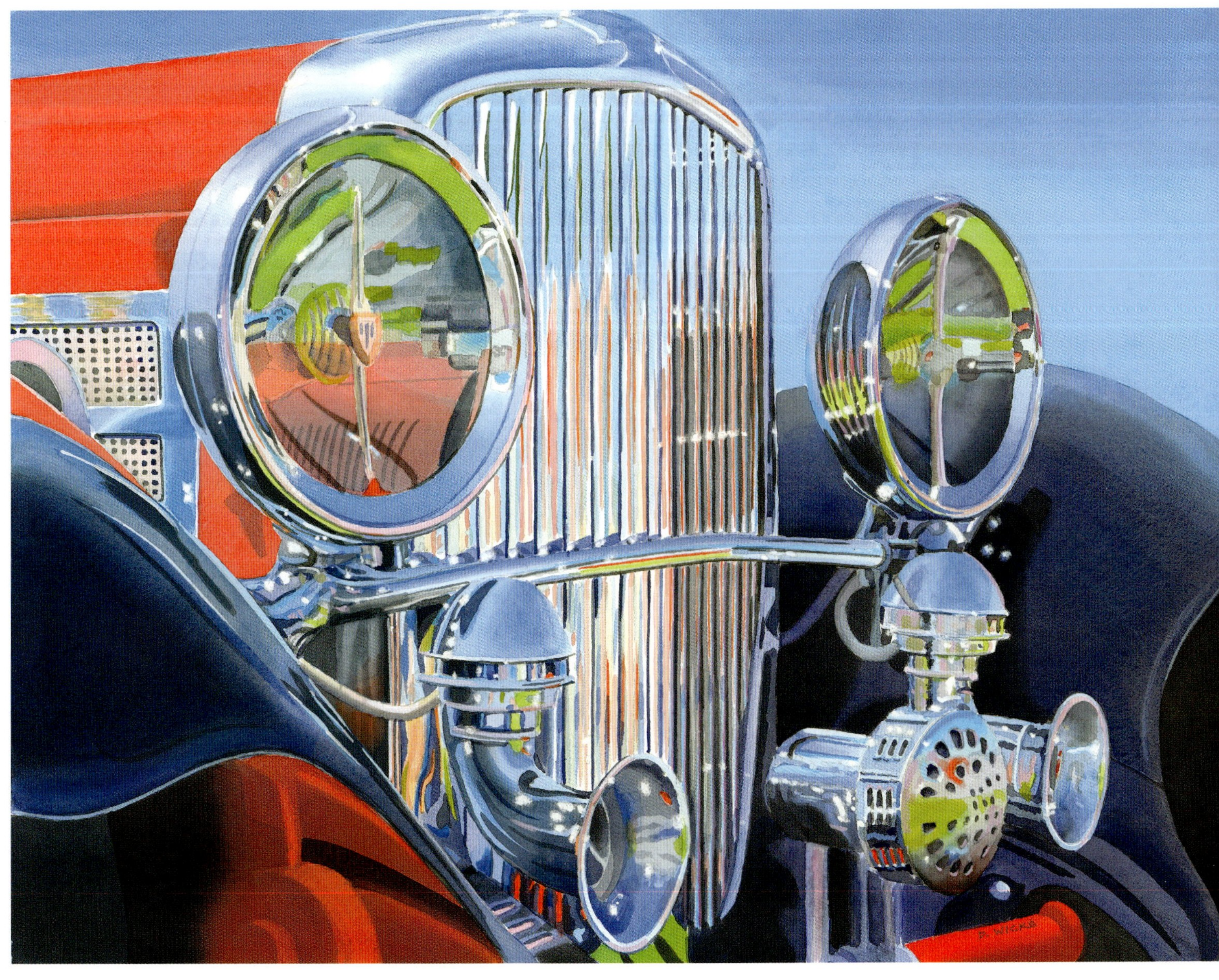

▲ DUESY | David Wicks
Acrylic on 300-lb. (640gsm) cold-pressed Arches
17½" × 23½" (44cm × 60cm)

I chose to use acrylics for this painting because acrylics would allow me to paint multiple glazing layers without loosening and muddying the underlying layers, and because acrylics would best facilitate the highly saturated colors that I desired. The painting is based on photographs of a Duesenberg (Duesy) taken at a car show, but the colors and reflections have been altered and amplified for a more dramatic effect. Extensive use of wet-into-wet techniques allowed me to soften edges and to blend colors, both of which can be a challenge with fast-drying acrylics.

▶ EMPIRE STATE BUILDING | Joe Bergholm
Acrylic on 1½-inch (4cm) deep panel, 24" × 18" (61cm × 46cm)

I captured this motif from the top deck of a cruise ship on the Hudson River while heading for Bermuda on a beautiful late summer evening. The composition highlights the size of the Empire State Building compared to the surrounding structures and conveys the diversity of New York City where the top of every building has a different shape sprinkled with various signage and water tanks! The controlled drying times of my Golden OPEN Acrylics and my color pool painting method facilitated the execution of this complex painting. The controlled drying time of Golden OPEN Acrylics has revolutionized my painting techniques. Color pools of the same paint were workable on my palette to reuse and modify to achieve the many subtle colors required to execute this work over several months.

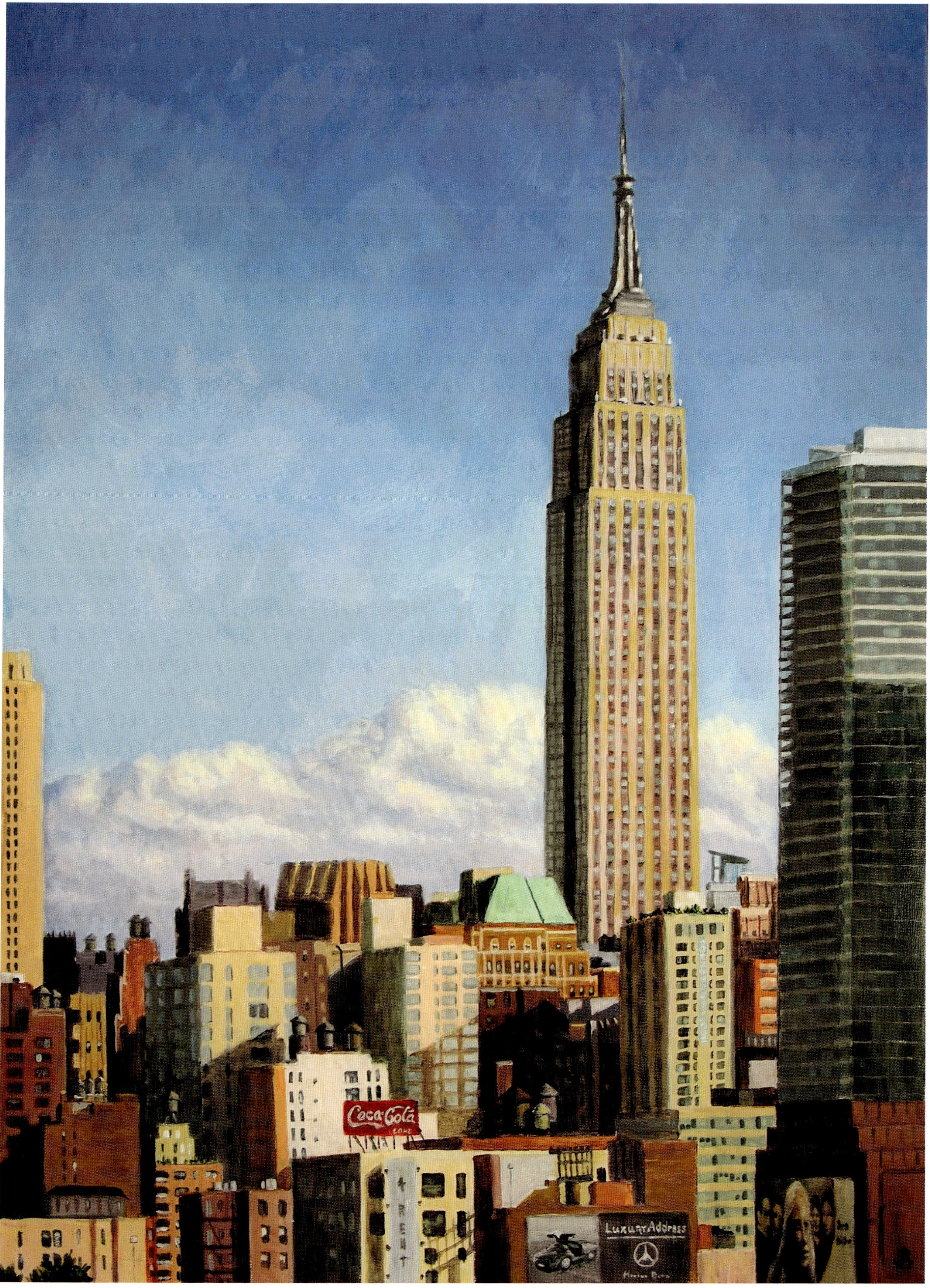
Coca-Cola
LuxuryAddress

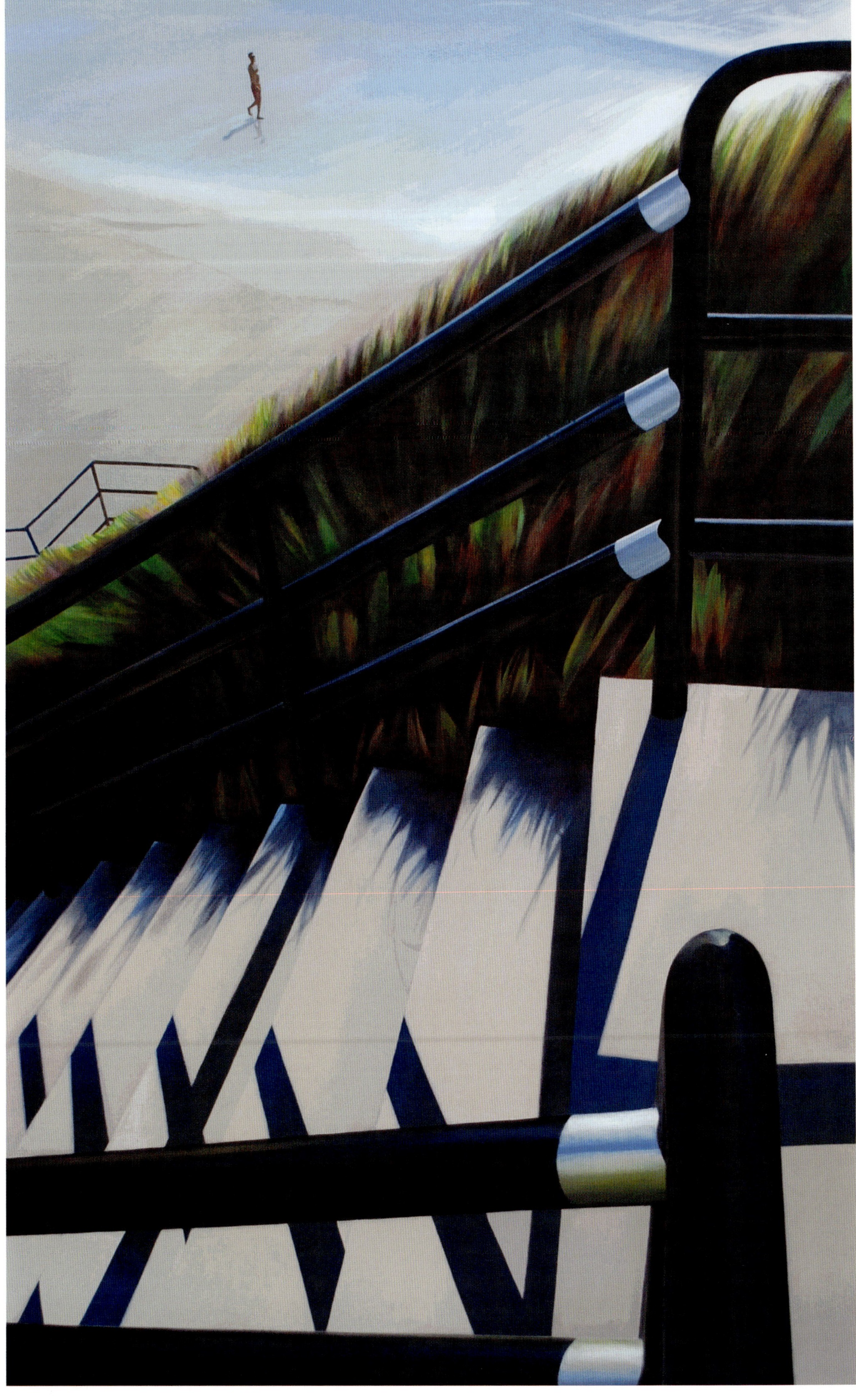

MOSS COVE | Nancy Yaki
Acrylic on canvas, 48" × 30" (122cm × 76cm)

This piece is one of a series of paintings in which I depict stairs descending to the ocean. These hard, angular human constructs juxtapose brilliantly with the elemental complexion of the water, illustrating how humanity perpetually seeks to construct its own pathways back to simplicity and origin. I enjoy acrylic because of its drying qualities—it allows me to work on a large scale at a swift pace, with sweeping marks and large blocks of shape and value. From this foundation I look for patterns to emerge that I can use to create movement and visual rhythm.

MEDITATION, ASHLEY | Hal Yaskulka
Acrylic and oil on canvas, 50" × 60" (127cm × 152cm)

This painting was created using both acrylic and oil paint. I sometimes like using acrylic in my underpaintings using a limited palette of Ochre, Raw Sienna, Napthol Red, Alizarin Crimson, Burnt Sienna, Ultramarine Blue, black, white and yellow. The painting was first sketched with willow charcoal, and then I start to block in my shadow pattern and background. From there I like to proceed from dark to light, working from big shapes to small shapes. This painting was painted mostly in acrylic with a bit of overpainting in oil. The drips were integrated into the overpainting process.

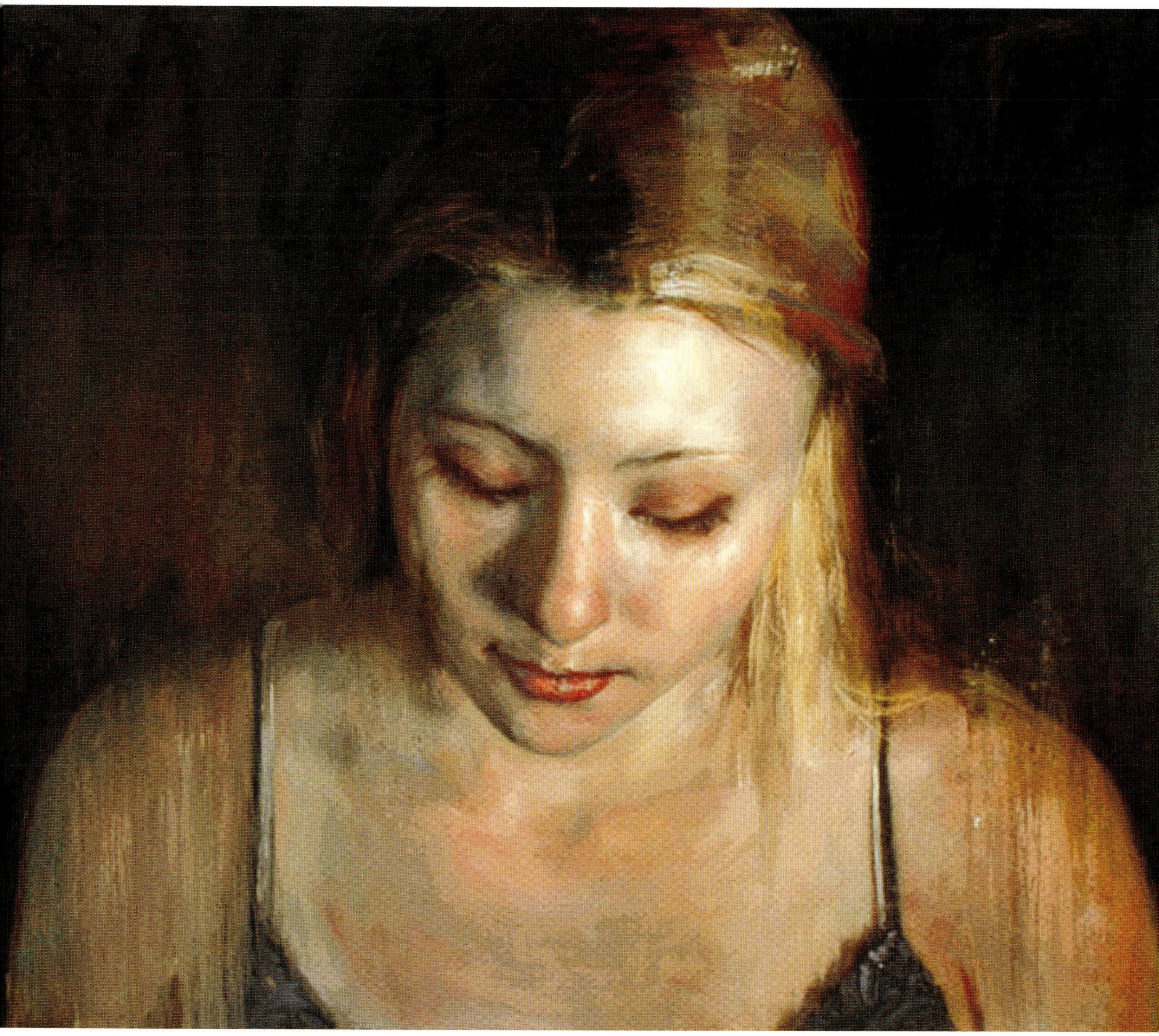

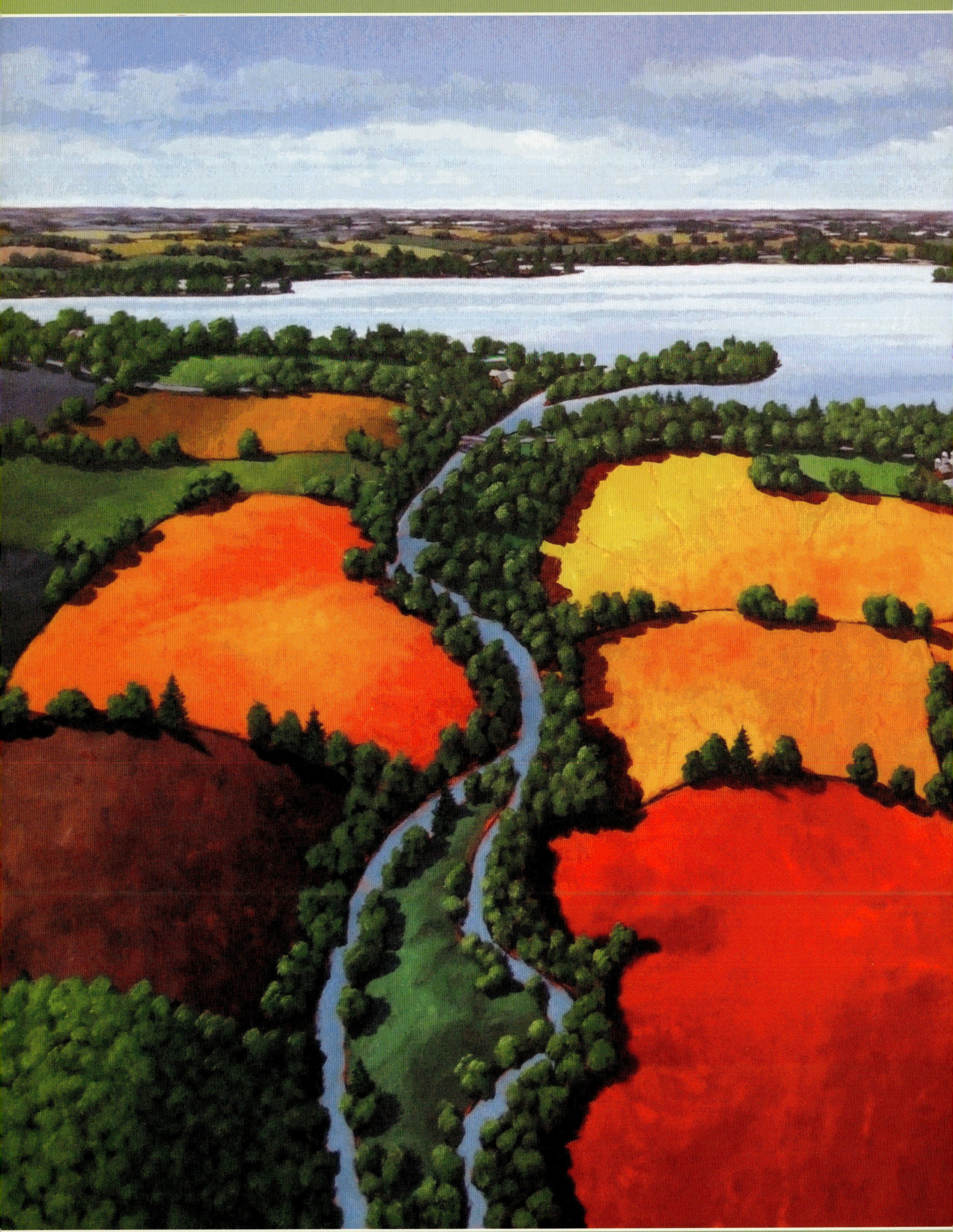

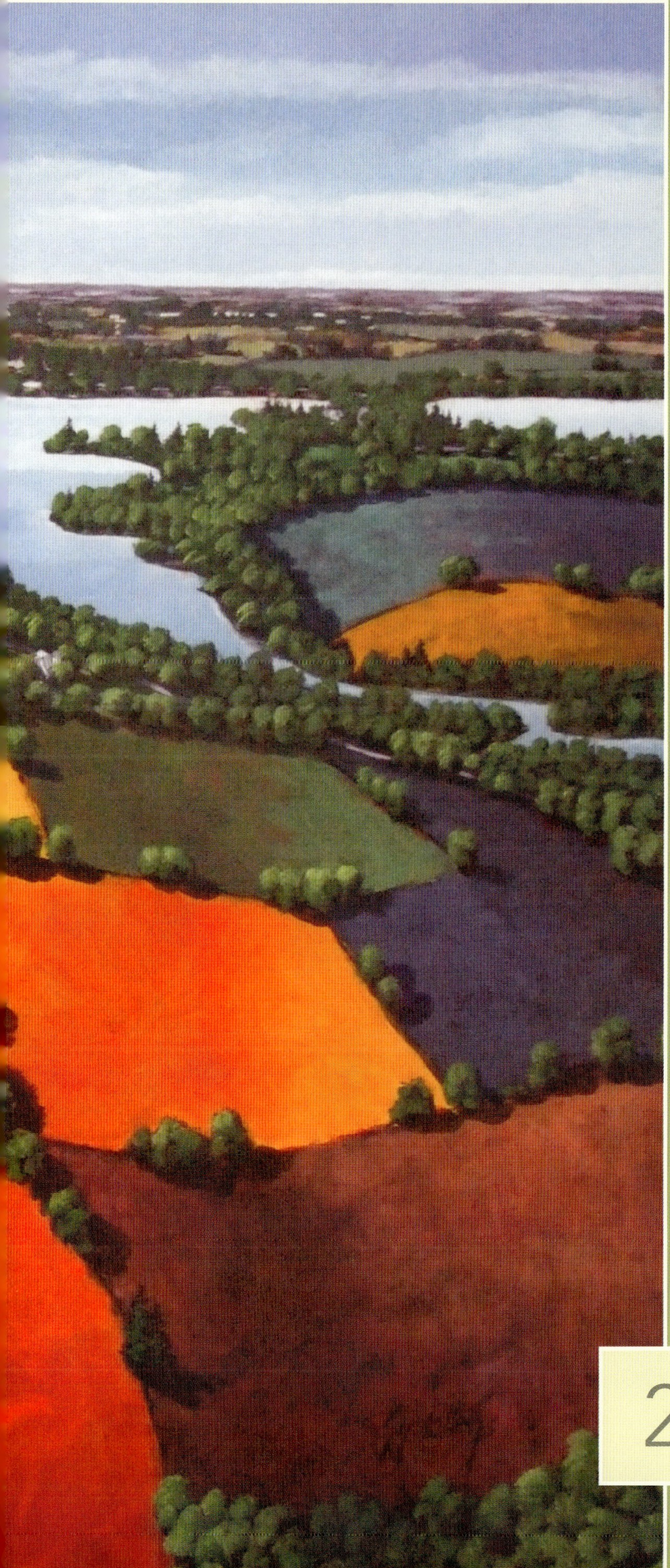

"From my point of view, the sky's the limit."

—SY ELLENS

SUMMER SHIMMERS | Sy Ellens
Acrylic on canvas, 48" × 60" (122cm × 152cm)

Having grown up on a farm in northern Michigan and later having traveled frequently by air during which I observed the variation of field patterns, I developed an interest in painting landscapes in a colorful, creative style. *Summer Shimmers* was created in my studio with no reference materials. I began by painting the canvas with thinned-down Cadmium Red. When that had dried, I painted in the sky and waters. I painted the fields by dividing the canvas into interesting shapes and filling them with my usual bright colors to create balance and harmony. Acrylic is fast drying, which allows me to paint the desired layers.

2 | STYLISTIC

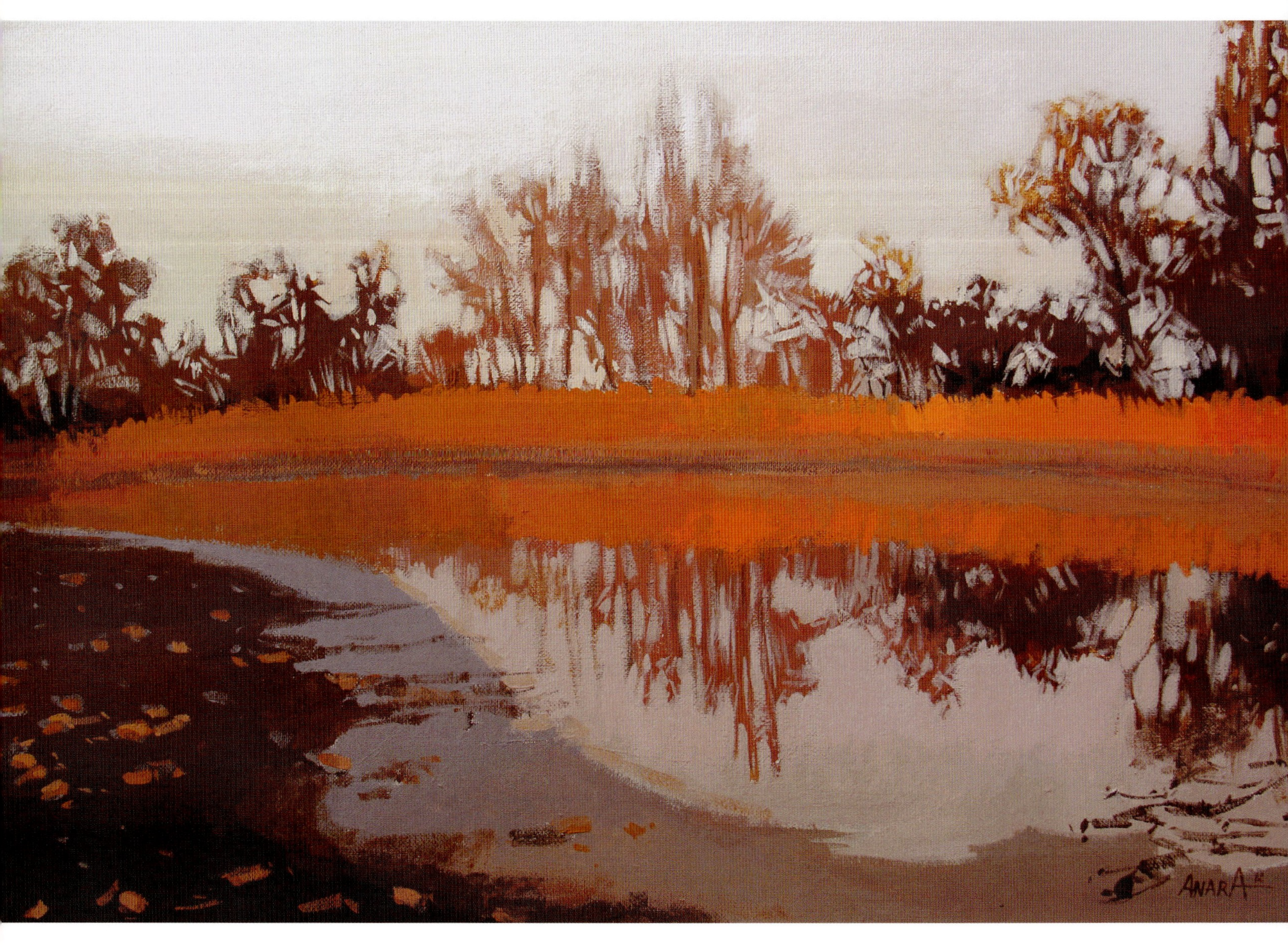

AUTUMN REFLECTION IN WATER | Abzhanova Anara
Acrylic on canvas, 16" × 24" (41cm × 61cm)

A murky day of late autumn. A beautiful view appears in front of us, a beautiful landscape. Here I conducted a workshop for children, teaching them how to draw an autumn landscape. In my creation I admiringly depict the river, I show a sincere love. There are some murky clouds together with autumn gold, and the weather gives us the warmth of the leaving days of summer. Reflection in the river can be divided into two parts: the gray-blue and the milky white. The light side seems to be hidden behind numerous stems of ghostly trees. It can be seen that part of my soul froze in my creation, filling it with warmth and soft inner light. While looking at this picture we would want to forget about the work and problems for a second, to dissolve in a gentle beauty and harmony, to think about the fluent and leisurely stream of life, which is so far from today's cities full of energy.

MOUNTAIN FLOWERS | Abzhanova Anara
Acrylic on canvas, 20" × 27½" (51cm × 70cm)

The main thing that attracts us in this painting is nature expecting spring. Mountain steppe, as the major artistic image of the Kazakh landscape painting, shows vitality. The steppe is the symbol of Kazakh culture, a place where the present meets with the past and the future. The landscape of mountain steppe is worth thousands of words. Fascinating charm and the grandeur of mountain steppe, its miraculous beauty tempts the power of space, style of life and principles of philosophy. I try to re-create its soul and breath, deliver true feelings of a human being. The mountain steppe full of contemplative depth and grandeur might be a comfortable home and a soul-stirring harmony of the universe, the poetry of the soul. Steppe does not just emotionalize me, but it stays as a source of my spiritual inspiration and gives me the possibility of dialoguing with my cultural heritage.

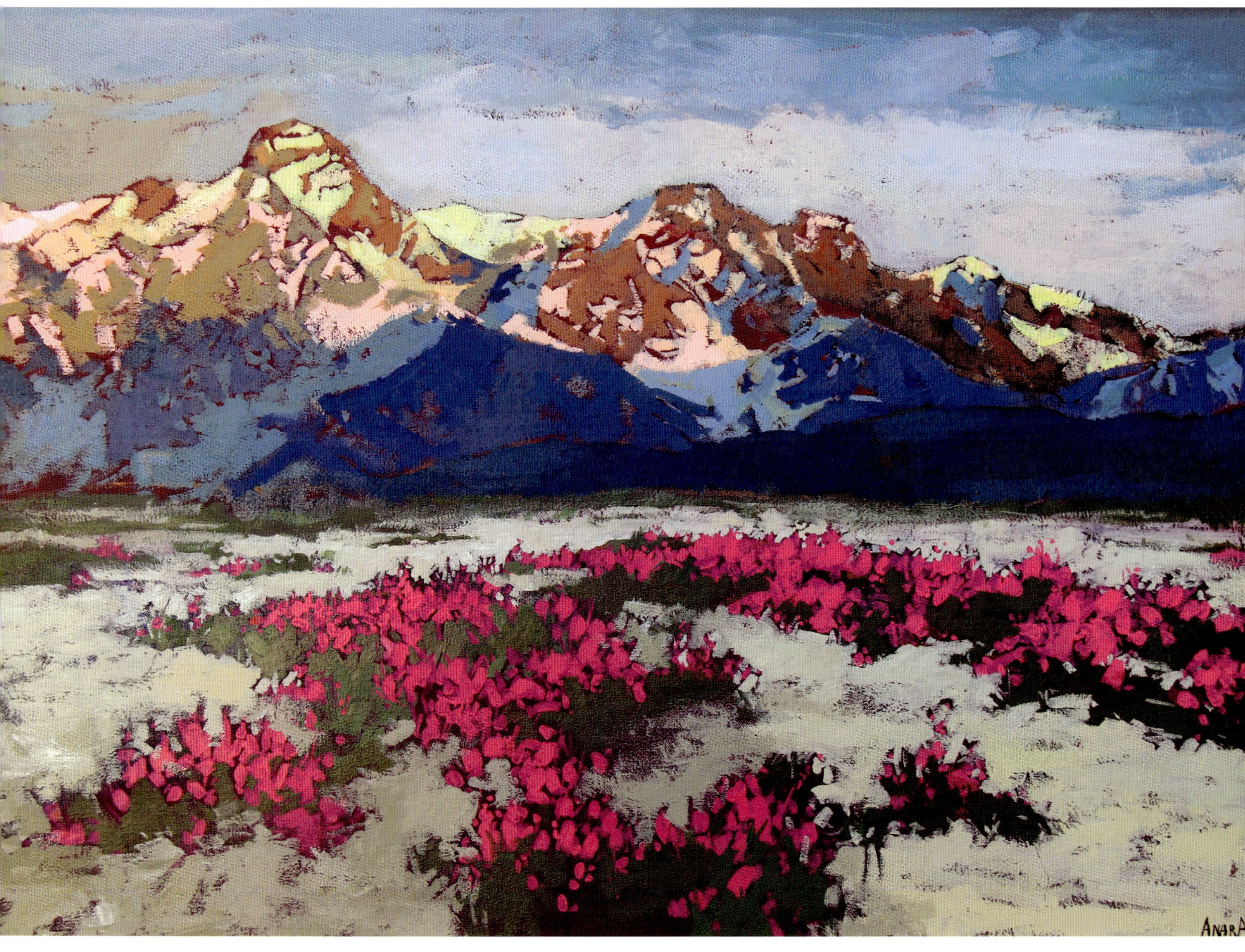

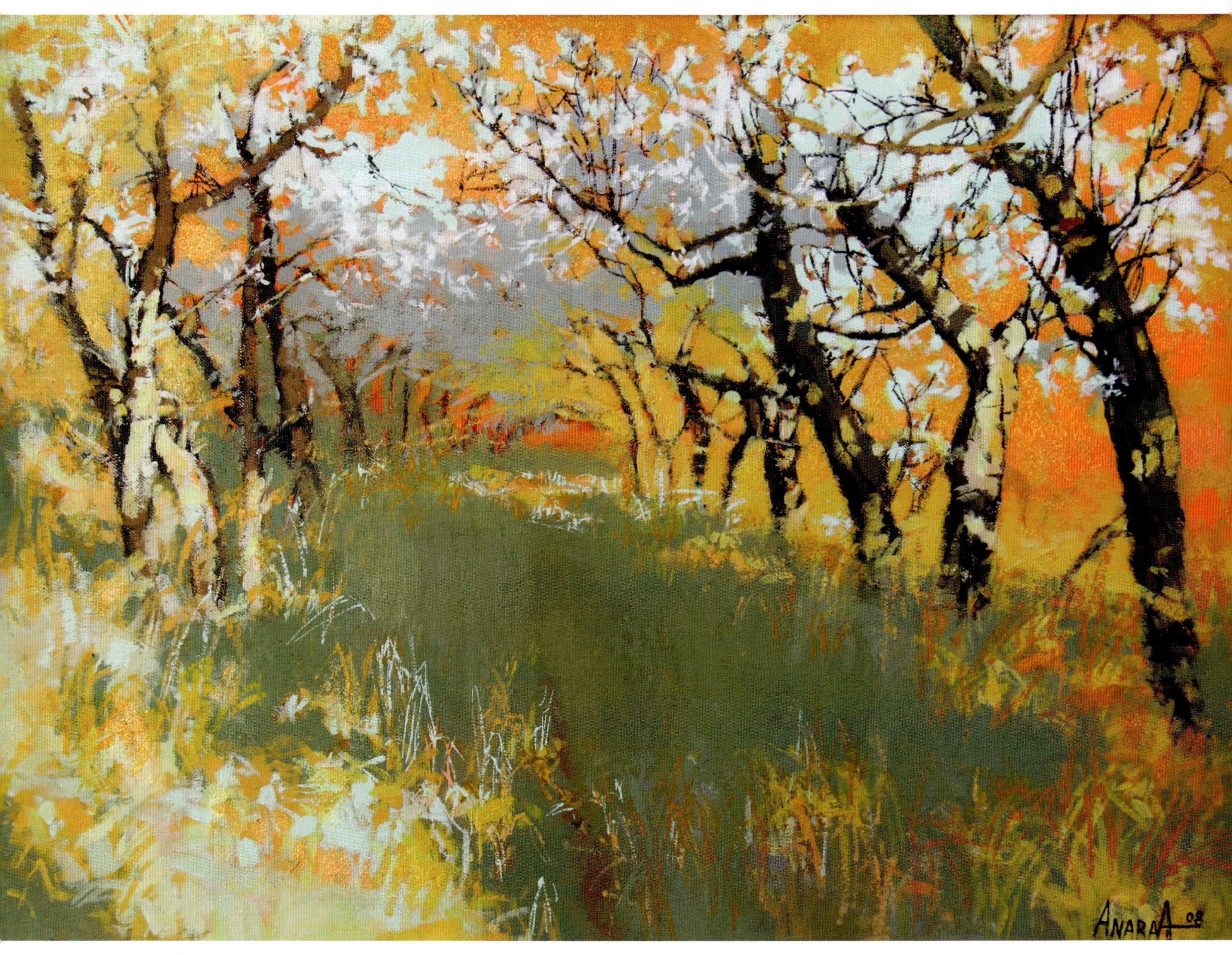

▲ FALL | Abzhanova Anara
Acrylic on canvas, 20" × 27½" (51cm × 70cm)

The beauty of autumn is the romance of my mood with light sorrow. This is a wonderful picture of nature, Almaty alleys dressed in scarlet and gold. Emotional impressions pouring some kind of special warm light are expressed here. I like to paint autumn; however, it is not easy to capture the harmony of autumn cold. This subject gives the richest choice of colors. The leaves on the trees change from green to different shades of gold and aureate. Yellow sienna, greenish brass, brown bronze, pale yellow and orange-yellowish gold all remind me of my favorite autumn. And the mood is a little sad because this beauty disappears so fast.

▶ READING RAILROAD | Shirley Jeane
Acrylic on 300-lb. (640gsm) cold-pressed Arches
30" × 22" (76cm × 56cm)

I wanted to produce paintings with simplified shapes, a limited palette and a matte finish similar to old posters. After trying to do this in watercolor with little success, I tried acrylics. At first my acrylic paintings looked more like glossy plastic rather than the subdued images I sought. I experimented with acrylic mediums and paint of varying viscosity until I found a combination that provided the look I wanted. Neutral grays mixed with fluid acrylics and matte medium are essential to my technique. I discovered painting clear gesso over my drawings sealed in graphite, stopping smudges; and using clear gesso between layers eliminated the pooling effect of painting plastic on plastic, giving a more even look. *Reading Railroad* is one of a series of paintings I have done from photos using these techniques.

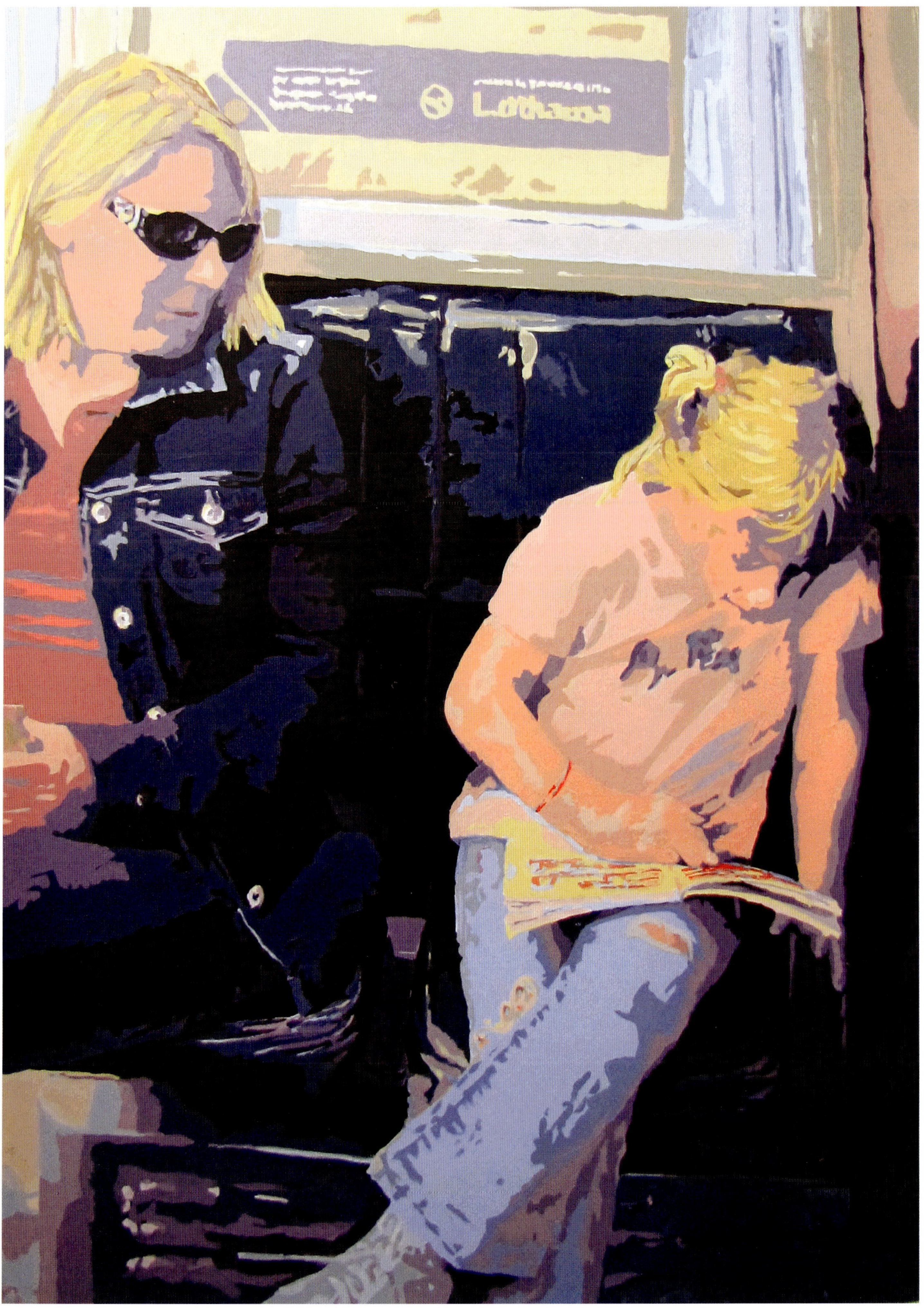

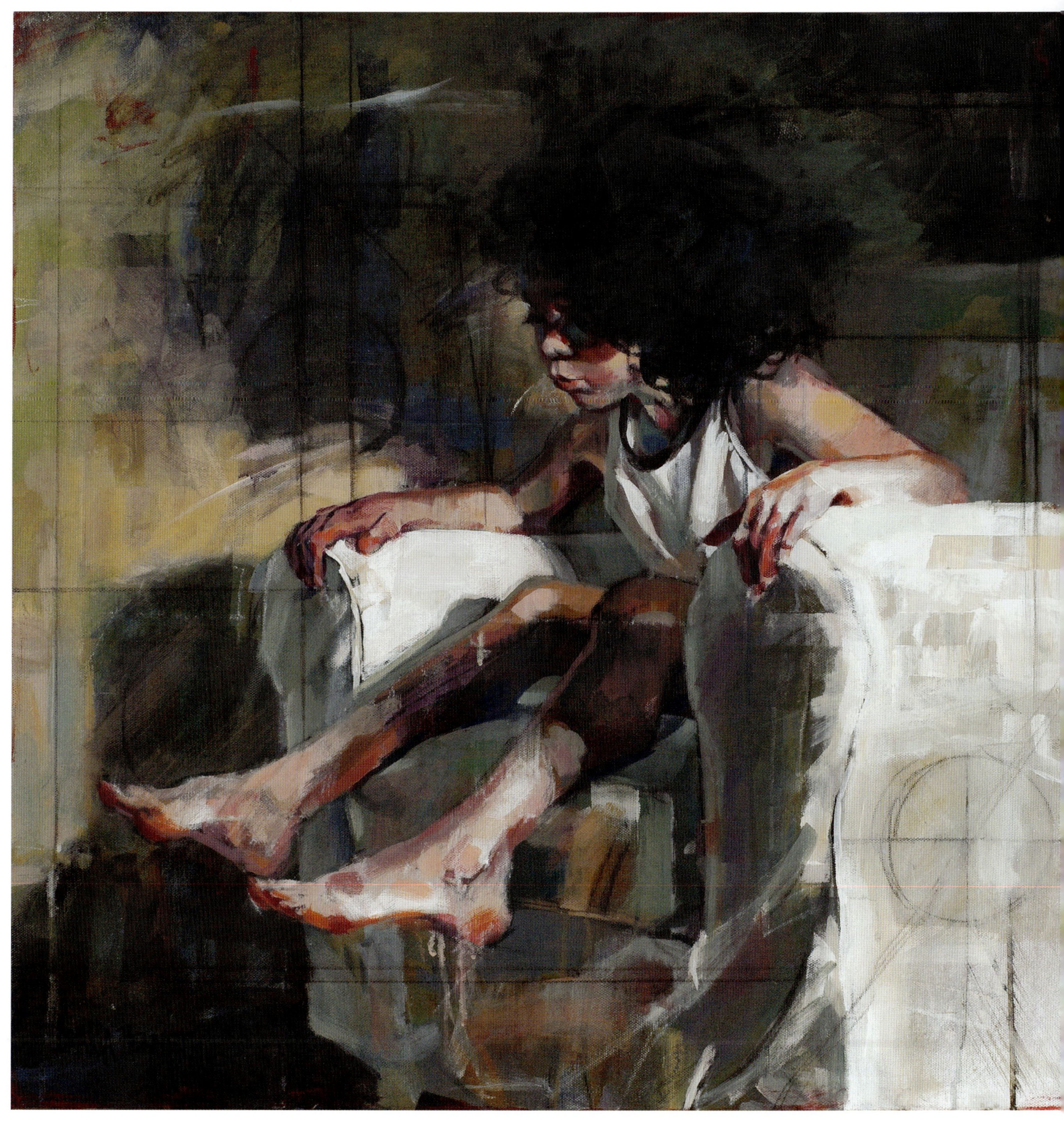

SHADOWS | Liana Bennett
Acrylic and china marker on canvas, 24" × 24" (61cm × 61cm)

I started using acrylics in 1967, primarily Liquitex. My palette now includes Golden, Utrecht and Daniel Smith. Subject matter runs from highly rendered figures to pure abstract. Mixed media plays a large part in my work. I'll try anything, some with wonderful surprises, others with disastrous results! I always use an acrylic block-in under my oil paintings. I need to feel a connection to the people I paint. I know the stories of those closest to me. The little girl in *Shadows* is my niece's daughter. I did a photo shoot and painted directly from my computer screen. Leonardo da Vinci inspired the black lines, and I was experimenting with applying masking tape, pulling them and adding layers.

ASCENDING | Diane Cannon

Acrylic over tissue on 300-lb. (640gsm) Arches, 20" × 22" (51cm × 56cm)

The momentum of flight against the blue of the gulf became imprinted in my memory. To capture that fleeting moment of elation, I began experimenting with configurations, textures and diverse mixtures of Golden's blue liquid acrylics to express the mood and atmosphere that I experienced at that time of day.

Repetition and variation in form and value allow the singular color scheme to do its job. The pattern for the birds was created after the background was painted on tissue and adhered to 300-lb. (640gsm) watercolor paper with matte medium. The variety in the blues helps express my feelings of initial excitement, followed by the aura of tranquility that provoked my vision for this piece.

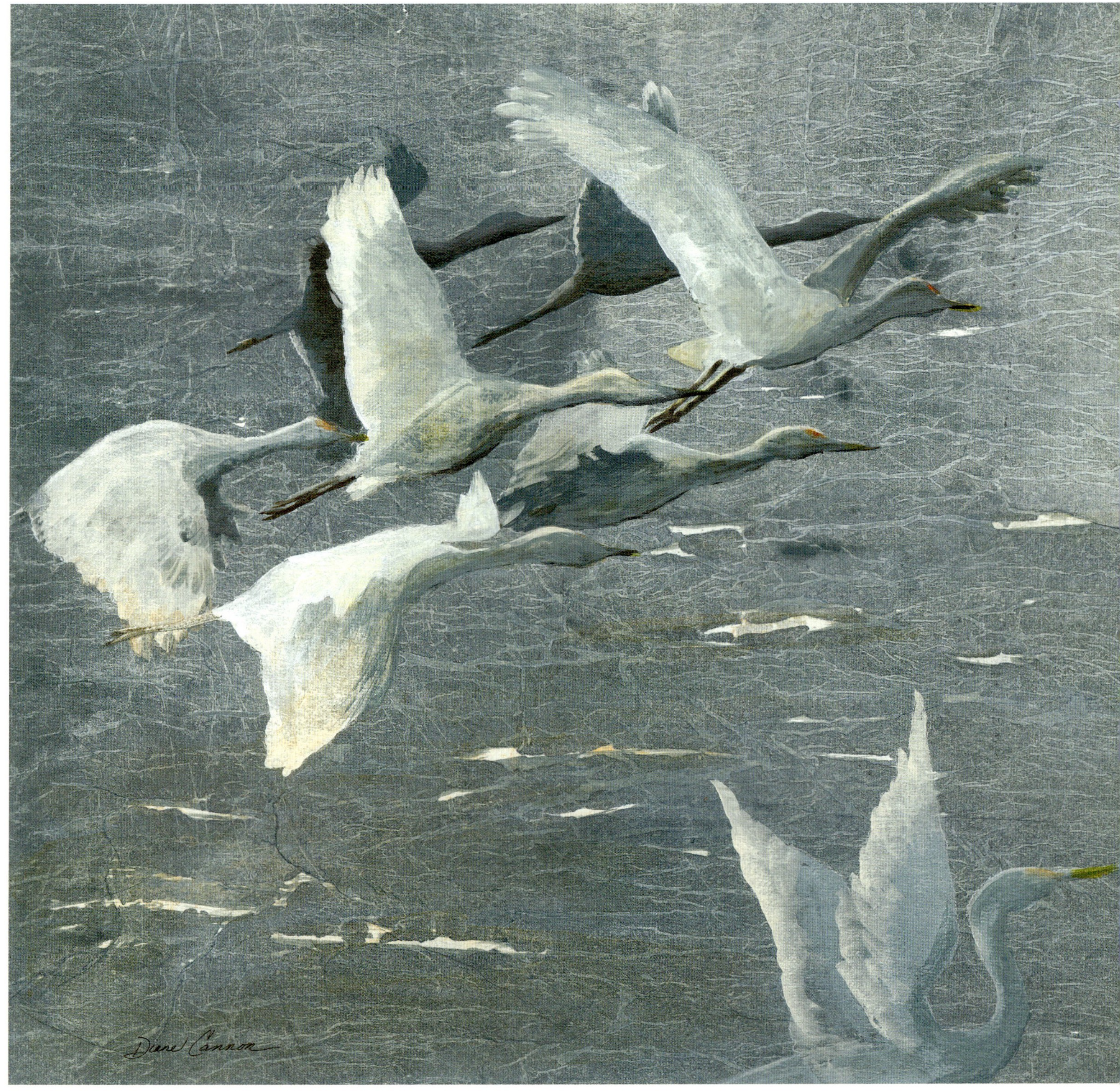

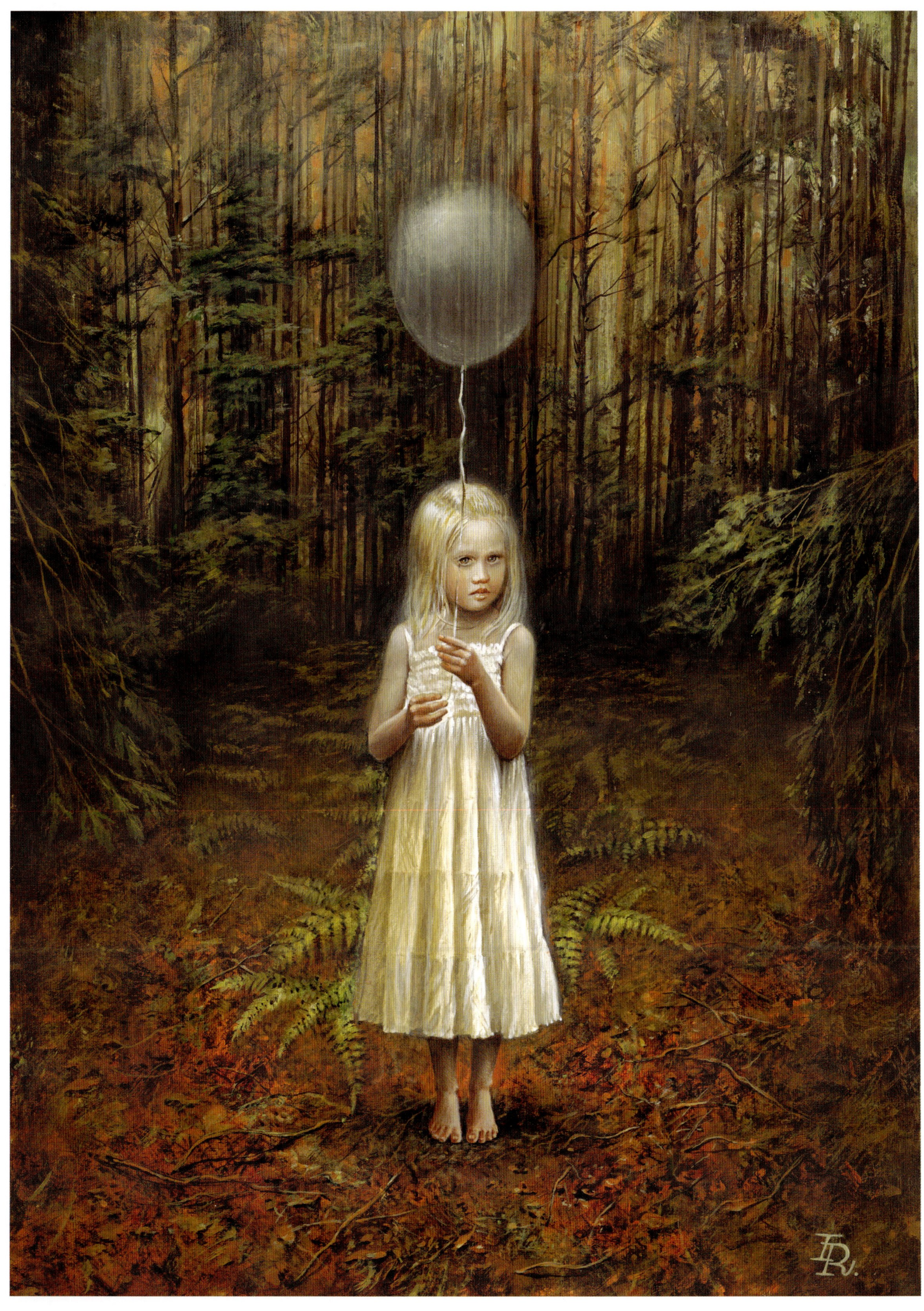

▼ OPEN HOUSE | Nancy Curry
Acrylic with permanent ink on canvas, 6" × 12" (15cm × 30cm)

Open House is part of my street series, inspired by a lifelong fascination with neighborhoods and my unrestrained imagination. I want these paintings to intrigue and delight the viewer at the same time. To that end, I chose water-loving acrylics and canvas because both lend themselves to the subtractive techniques I like to use to variegate my pieces. I used a combination of fanciful facades with varied textural accents and lush, natural settings to create movement and interest throughout the painting. The houses' unique personalities emerge when they are detailed with permanent ink in varied thicknesses. It is my hope that this series creates a place where our imaginations can mingle.

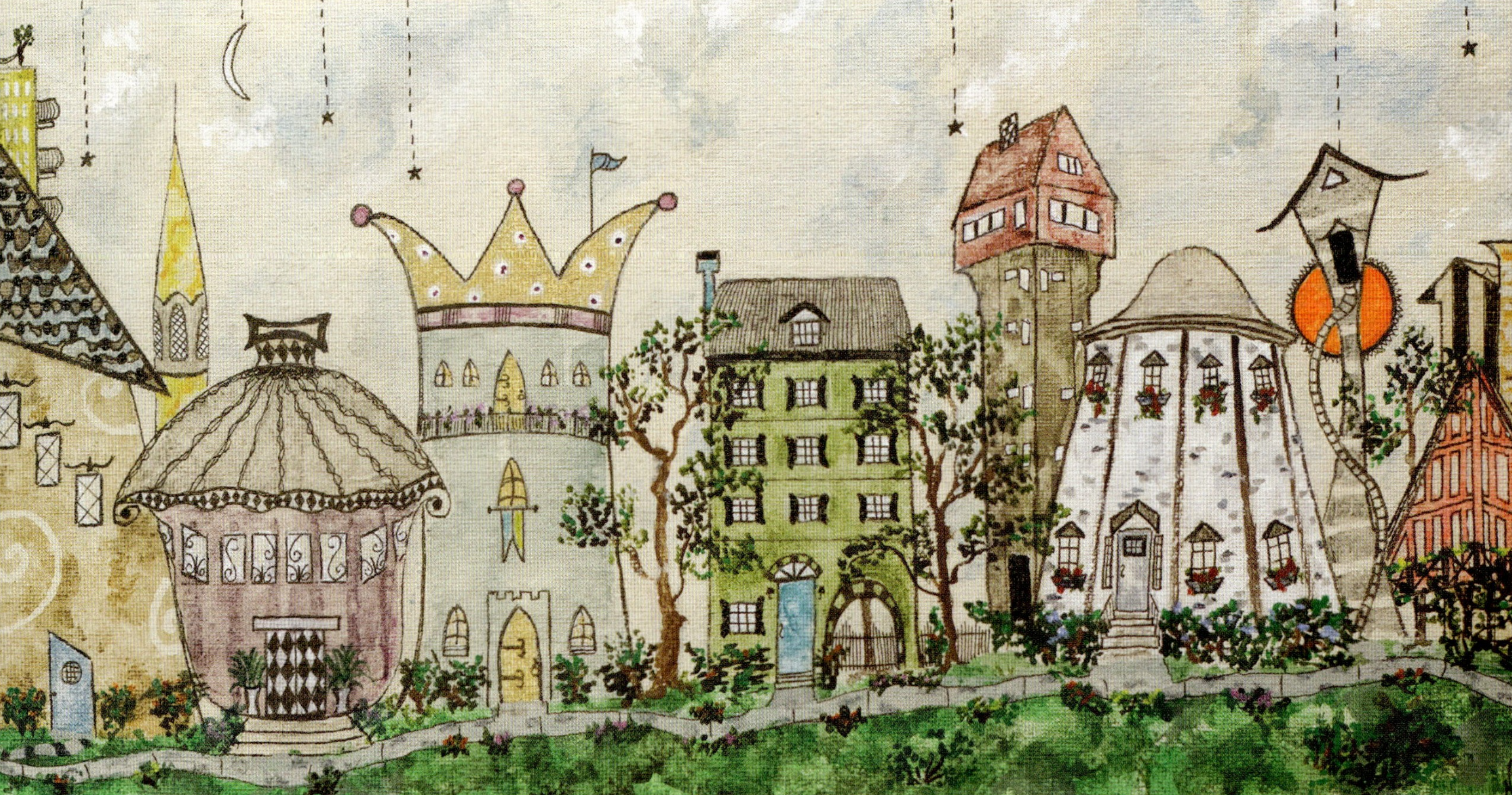

◀ BIRTHDAY GIRL WITH YESTERDAY'S BALLOON | Igor Raikhline
Acrylic on board, 30" × 22" (76cm × 56cm)

This painting was done from my dream life, my second life that exists only when my head touches the pillow. This separate life is quite fulfilling and has plenty of turns and twists. It endlessly surprises me with vivid and sometimes otherwise unimaginable ideas. Dreams always come in handy for me to catch, develop and perfect ideas to a point where they become applicable to the surface of a canvas. I am strongly tied to the theme of childhood, which I have slowly evolved into my *Child Versus the Unknown Universe* series.

I have found that acrylic paint is indescribably versatile and matches my personality. It has a lot of substance and gives me room to maneuver from a heavy brushstroke emphasizing the roughness of the fabric of nature to a gentle and soft touch for transparent layers, bringing fresh air and breathing room to the surface of a painting.

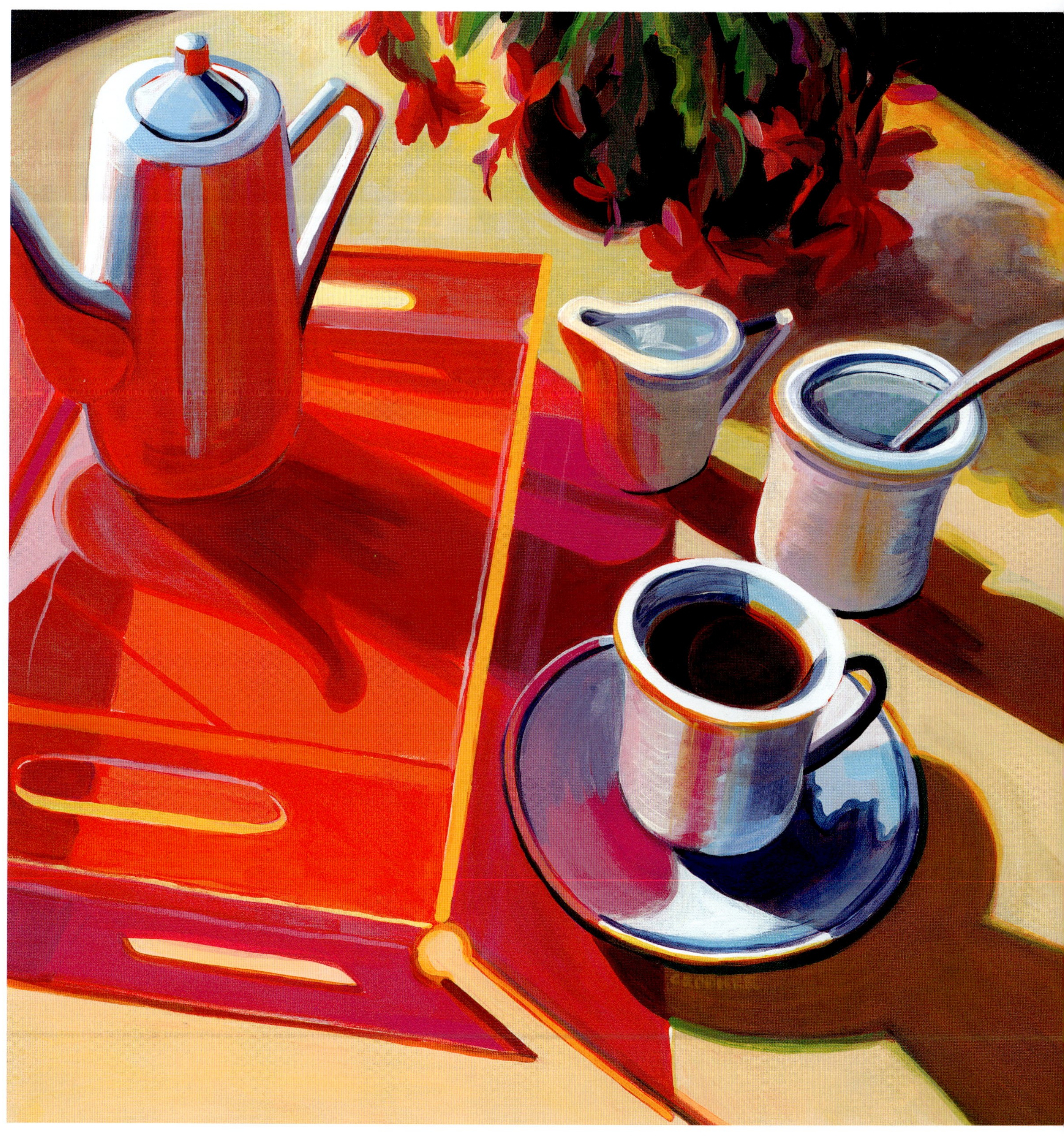

MORNING COFFEE | Jan Crooker
Acrylic on canvas, 24" × 24" (61cm × 61cm)

Morning Coffee illustrates the way acrylic paint can accomplish both opaque and transparent effects. I am interested in the effects of light and simultaneous contrast, so I start with a deep canvas primed with Cadmium Red. I sketch the layout from life with chalk as it shows up well on the midtone value and begin with opaque acrylic and lay in both the lightest and darkest areas. I am thinking of the light from the onset. I work from opaque paint to more transparent colors, ending with multiple layers of glazing and details.

"A shadow further reveals an object's form."
—JAN CROOKER

NAPA RED | Preston Craig
Acrylic on canvas, 24" × 30" (61cm × 76cm)

"Artists see with their eyes, heart and soul, and create based on their own personal story."
—PRESTON CRAIG

This is one in a series of landscapes I created to explore the possibilities of utilizing a split complementary color scheme. The subject matter I choose to paint varies between landscapes, portraits, fantasy and social commentary.

Photoshop was used to rearrange some of the elements in a photo for a better composition, and then I created an 11" × 14" (28cm × 36cm) value and color study. My value study was used for the finished sketch on the canvas, and a split complementary color scheme was chosen for my palette. I use a Masterson covered palette and keep the palette in the refrigerator between uses. When mixing my colors, Liquitex Slow Dri and Golden OPEN Acrylic mediums are added, which helps keep the pigments fresh over an extended period of time. These give me the most control over my medium.

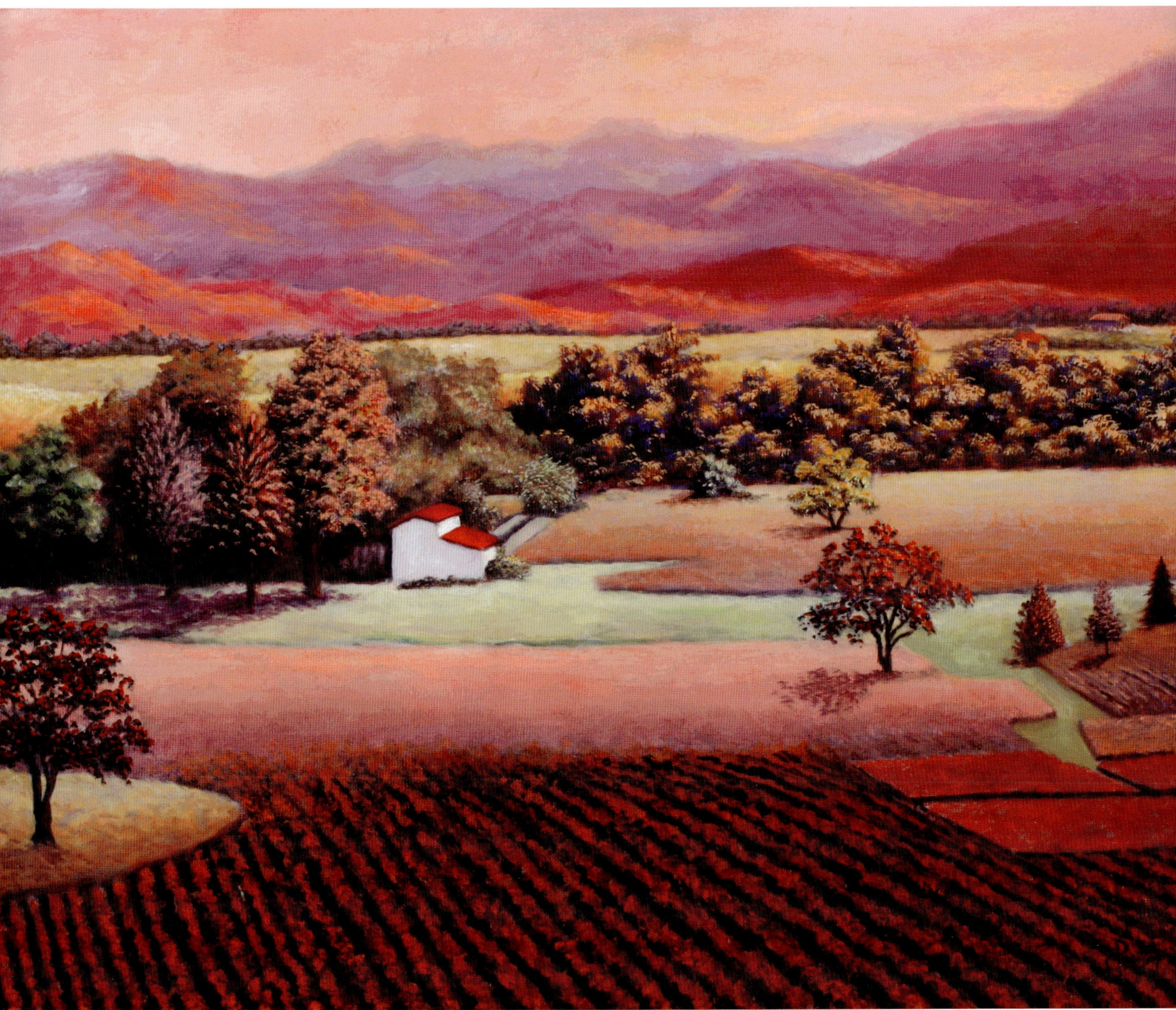

WITCH ISLAND | Philippe Fernandez
Acrylic on oak wood panel, 48" × 36¾" (122cm × 93cm)

Witch Island is a combination of translucent acrylics in various shades of black, yellow and turquoise. I layered them throughout the entire painting to create a mirrored effect balancing the sky, water and land. *Witch Island* was a personal challenge. I had never painted a seascape with such lightning and various tropical plants on a canvas of this size. Originally, I was scared and excited to take on this challenge, but after a month of ten to twelve hour days, I finally called it finished. *Witch Island* helped me to grow as an artist in that I now see challenges as opportunities.

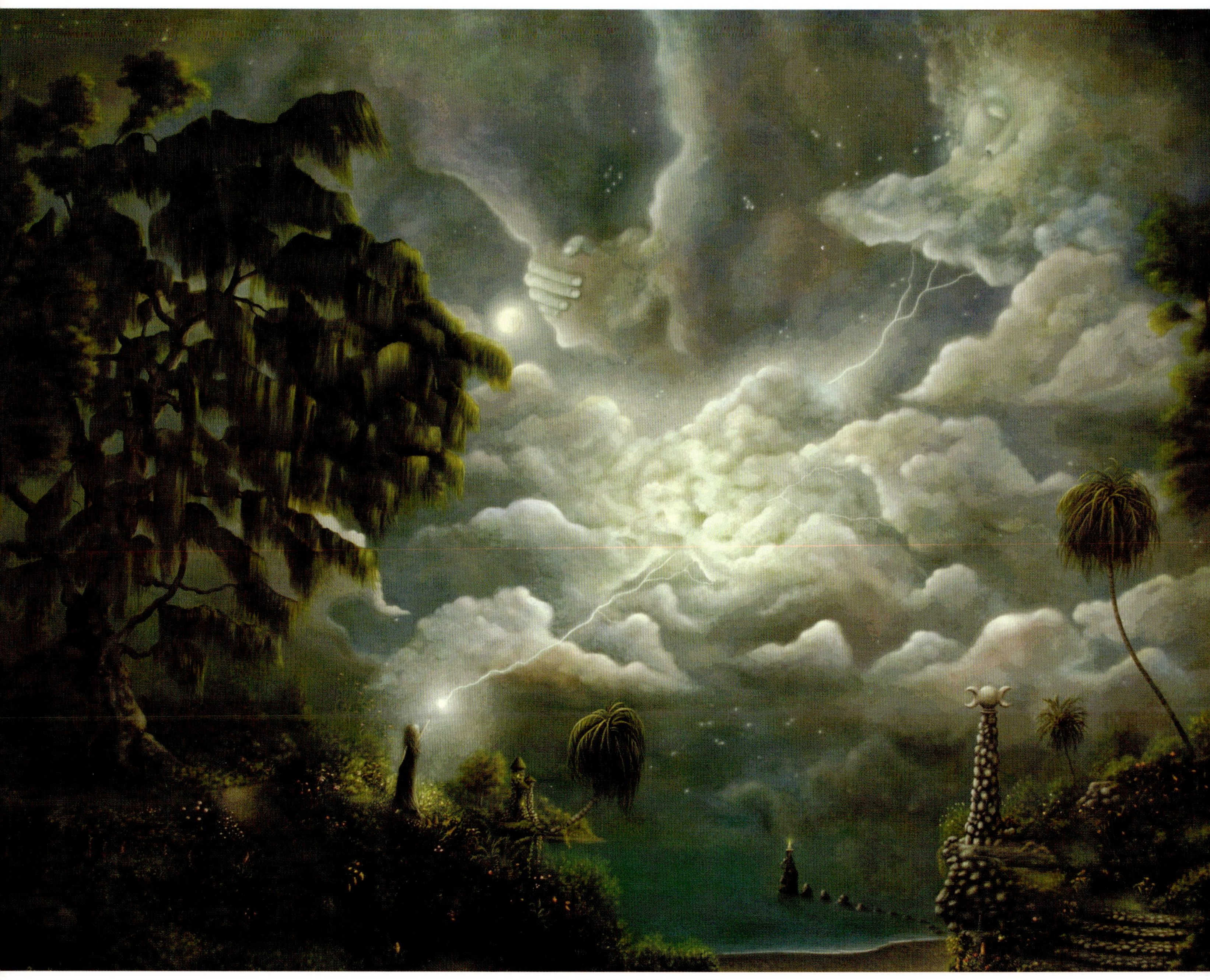

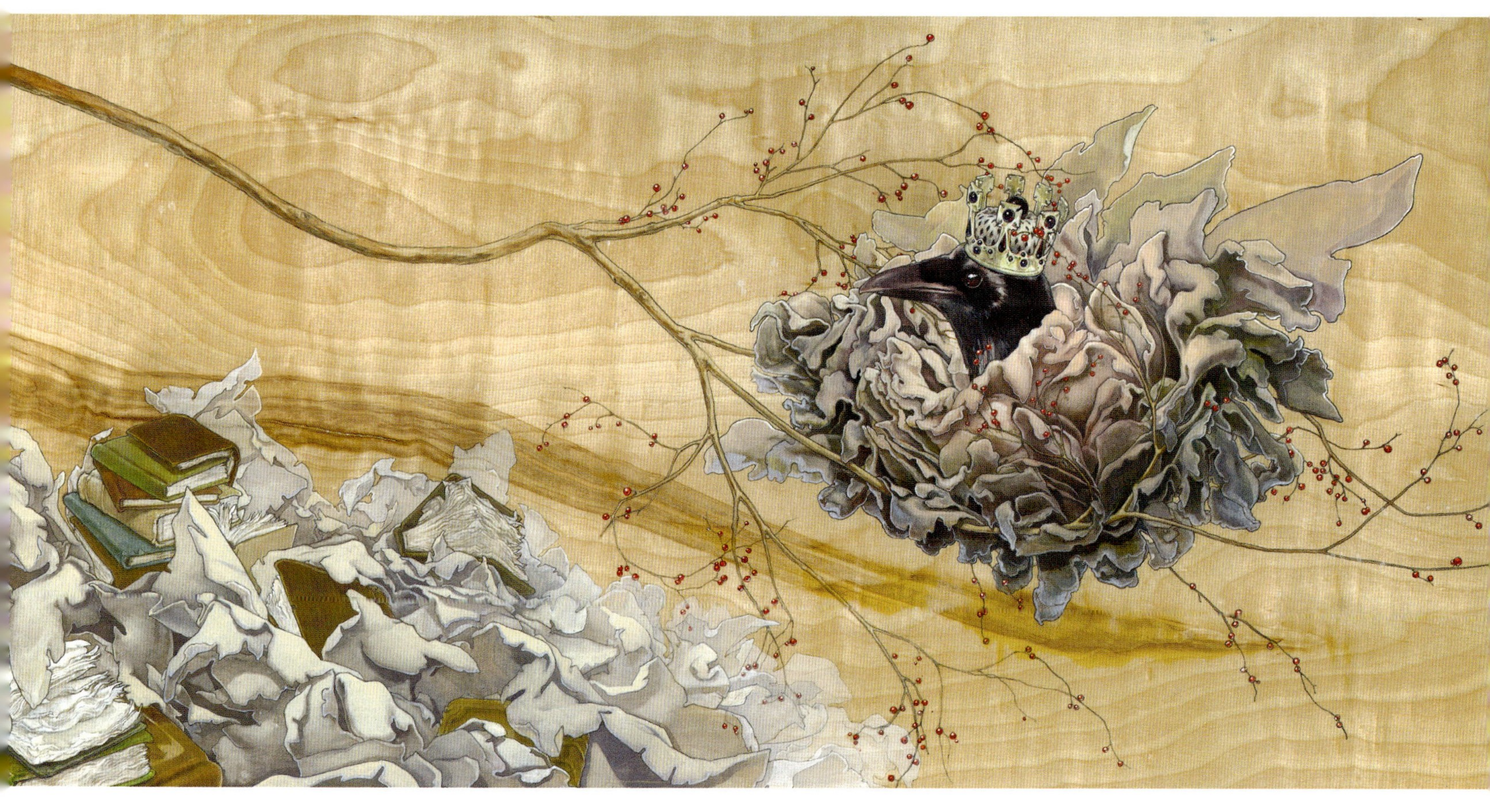

WHAT TO DO WITH IT? | Kyle Fisher
Acrylic and graphite on birch panel, 32" × 65" (81cm × 165cm)

We process our experience of the visual world and the iconography we gather—of wildlife, of the mundane, of markings of physical space—in countless and unimaginable ways. A spattered wash of color may resonate. For another, a line mimicking brittle, tattered fabric conjures familiarity. I believe that through reinterpreting the representational use of one's unique understanding of how things feel, fold, move, tear, bloom and decay, we're able to introduce imagery in a way that challenges predispositions. We're then able to better communicate the nuances of perception that connect us.

My process involves layering many transparent washes of acrylic along with light sanding—examples of the versatility that acrylic affords not present in other mediums.

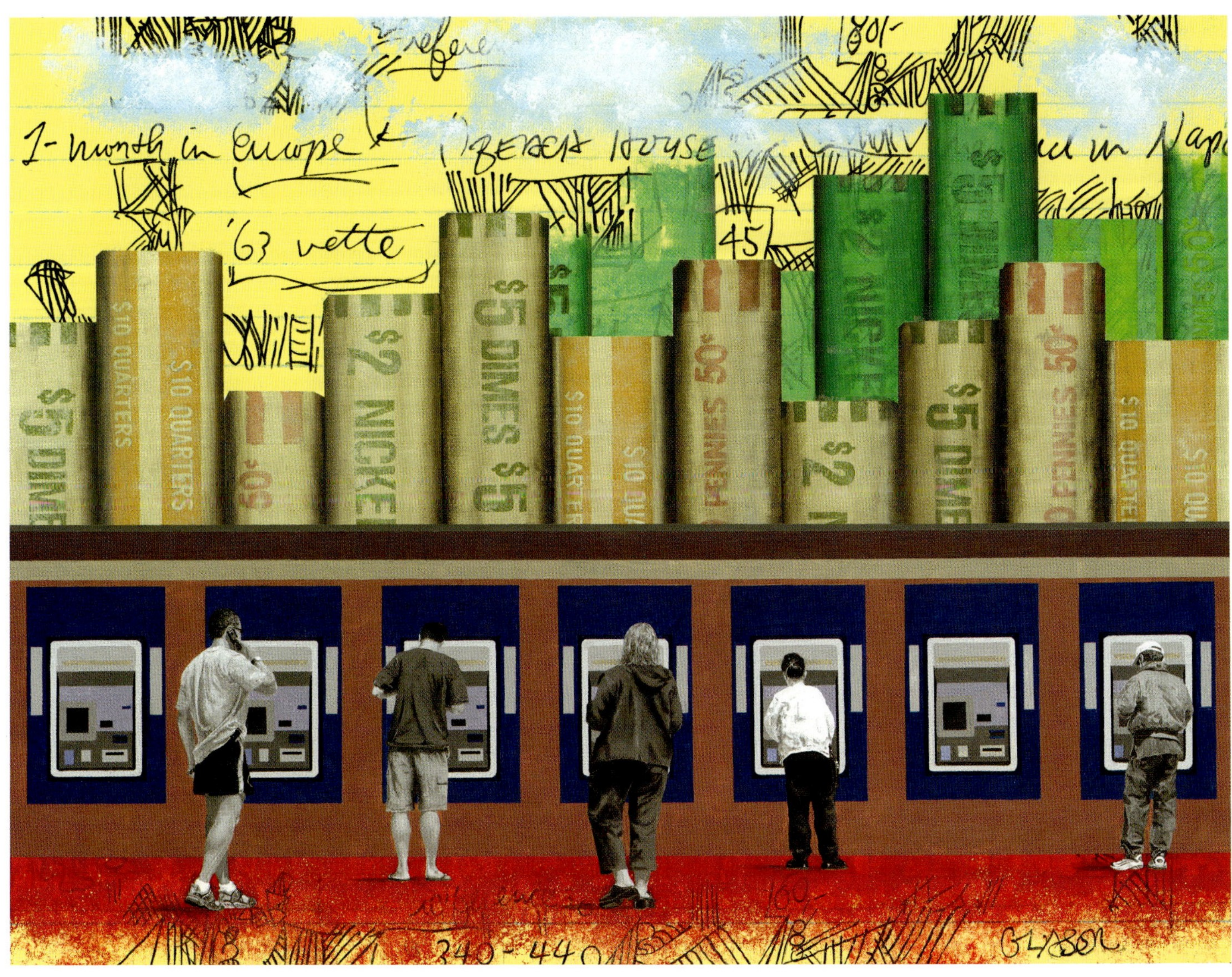

▲ WITHDRAWAL SYMPTOMS | Scott Glaser
Acrylic on canvas, 30" × 40" (76cm × 102cm)

The concept for this piece was quite accidental. I had gone to the San Jose Public Library in search of reference material for another project. Sirens started to blare and people evacuated the building—there was a bomb scare. While sitting on the library steps waiting for the all-clear sign, I started taking photos of people as they approached a bank of newspaper dispenser boxes. I had quite a few shots of various buyers by the time the library reopened. Weeks later, going through my photo library, I decided to build a painting around these "newspaper people."

The process of creating my final sketch was done by taking a photo of an ATM machine, repeating that unit seven times, taking a photo of coin wrappers to create the "skyline," selecting five of the dozens of photos of people from my bomb-scare day at the library, scribbling some wish list items on a yellow legal pad and assembling them all in the computer. I enjoy combining realism, pop and messaging in my work. The message aspect comes from twenty-five years as a creative guy in advertising. This piece took me just under 300 hours to complete using the grid system.

▶ PRAIRIE DOG | Scott Glaser
Acrylic on canvas, 24" × 18" (61cm × 46cm)

I love portraiture. I don't call them portraits, I call them personalities. It's not about anatomy, bone structure, epidermis or skin tone—it's about the inner being. And that's how I approach every piece I create. Whether it's a person, pet, piano or piece of popcorn, it's about personality. The concept of *Prairie Dog* was simply to present the personality of our precious twelve year old French bulldog, Zsa Zsa.

To me acrylics are the more playful brother of oils. Why be so serious? It's a painting, not rocket science. Have fun. Acrylics are fun. So what if you blow it? One of my friends, the master digital scanner and fine art printer Don Sigovich, told me that an artist said to him that he wants to sell prints of his work, not the paintings. Don's response was, "What are you painting for?! You can always make another painting." I agree. If you're a painter, paint. If it's your profession, sell. If it's a hobby, hang them on your walls, give them as gifts or hide them in your attic.

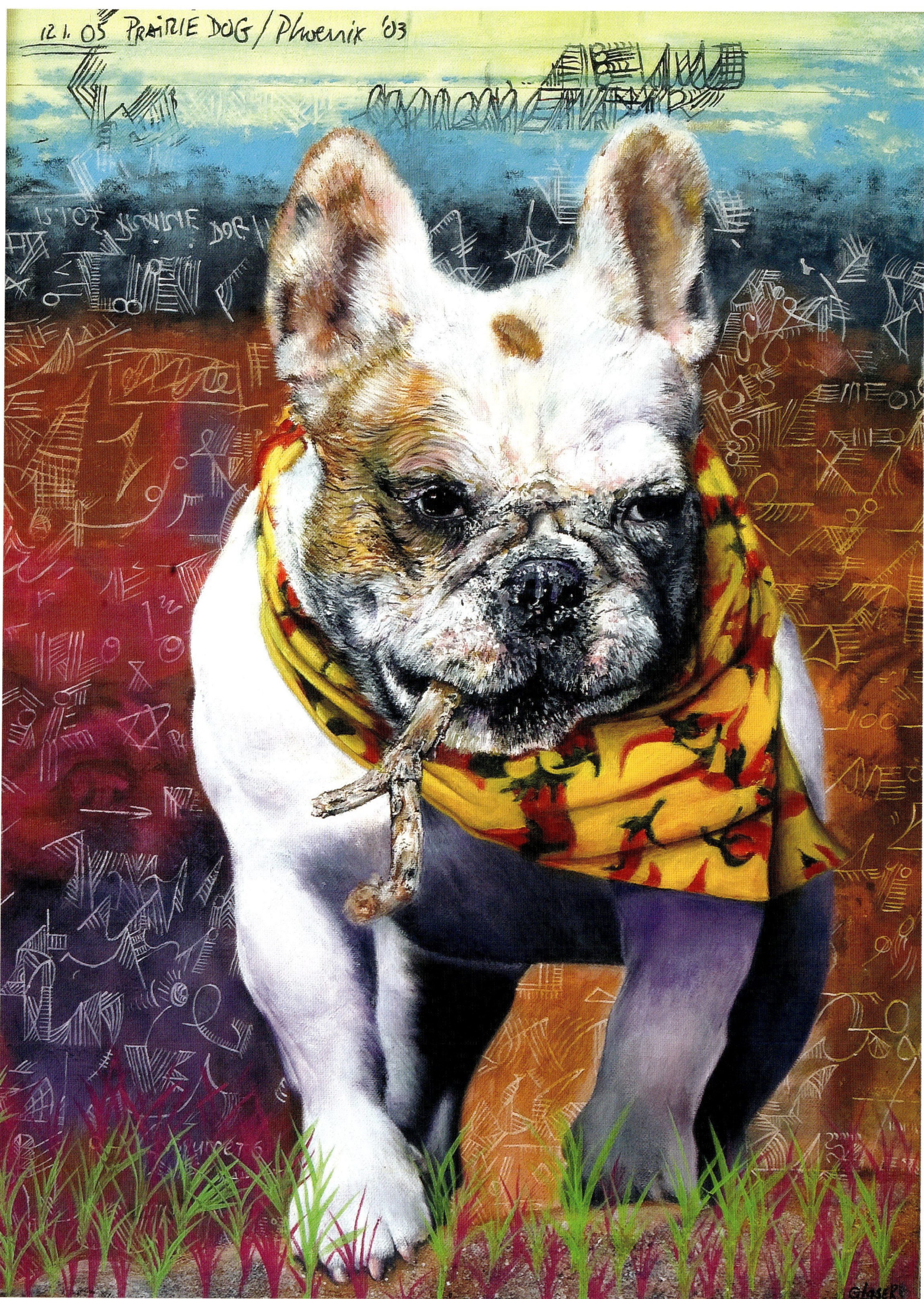
12.1.05 PRAIRIE DOG / Phoenix '03

NJ BEACH UMBRELLA | Bernie Hubert
Acrylic on stretched canvas, 40" × 72" (102cm × 183cm)

My painting style is photorealism interspersed with improvisation and stylizing. I saw this image of a beach umbrella in a photo. Of course, it had distractions in it, people and other nonessentials. With the help of vivid and bold acrylic tones, I transformed it into this simple, bright kaleidoscopic painting. I never know what I'm going to paint next, except to say, "When I see it, I know it."

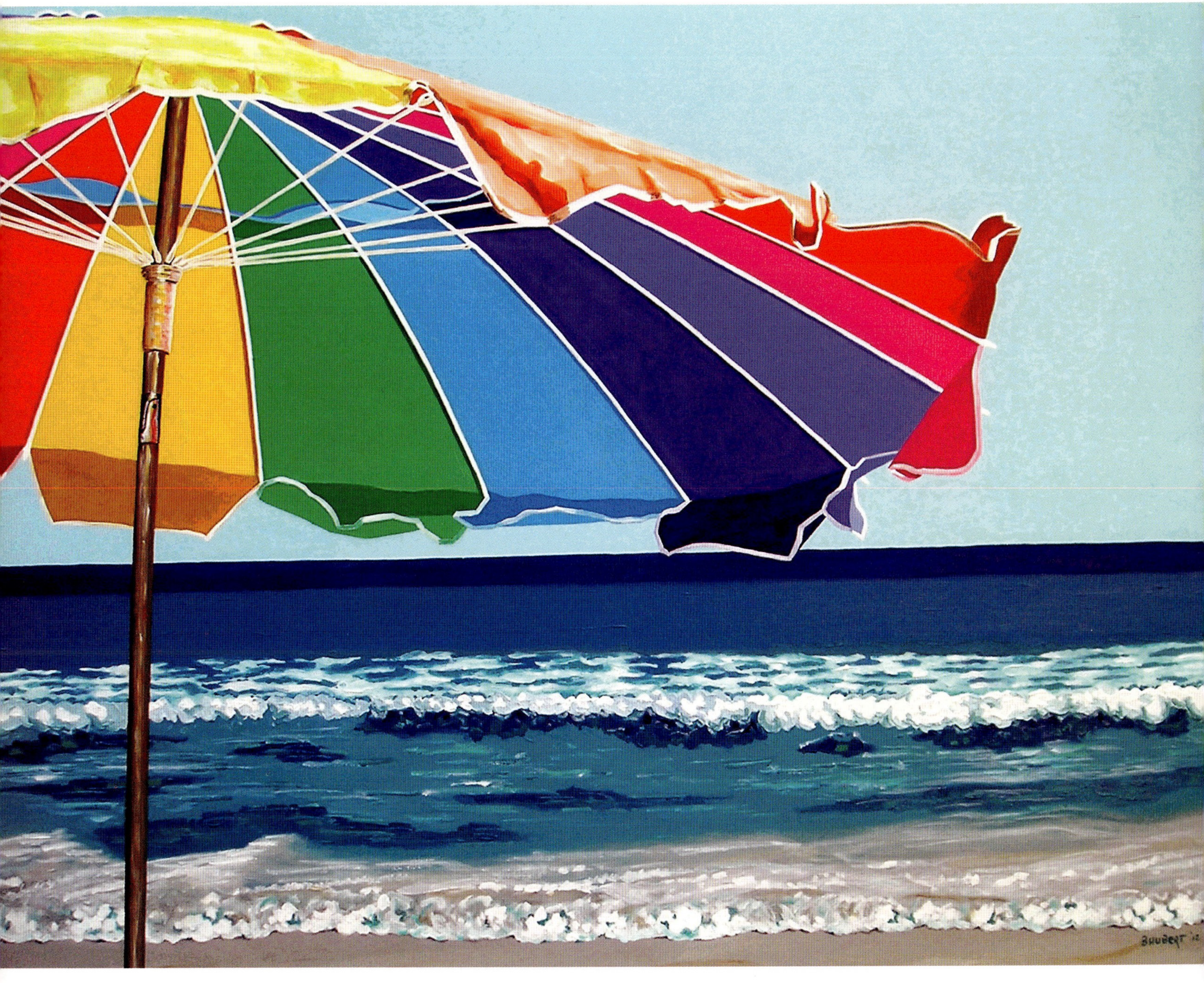

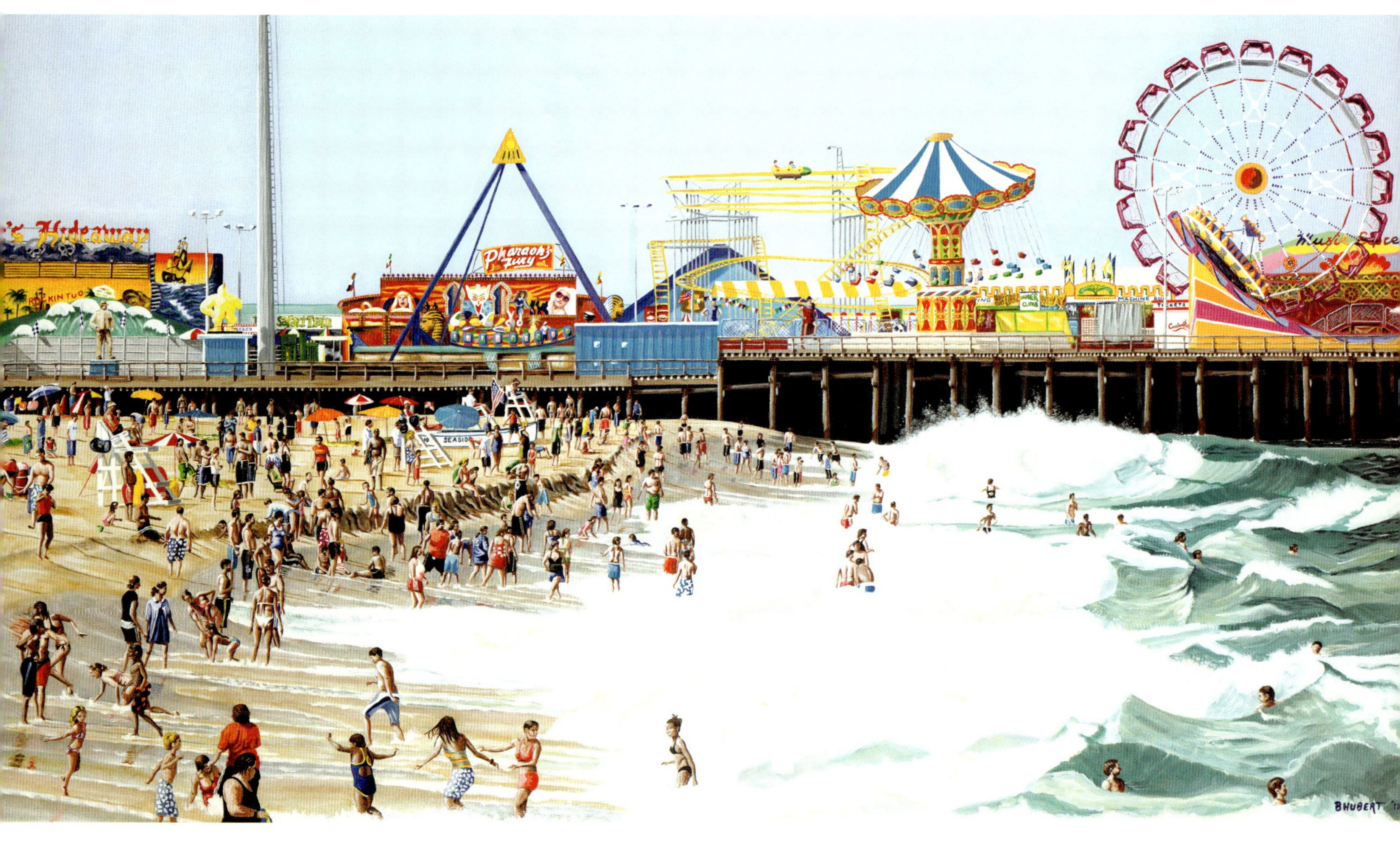

SEASIDE HEIGHTS, NJ BEACH AND CASINO PIER | Bernie Hubert
Acrylic on stretched canvas, 40" × 72" (102cm × 183cm)

I saw this image in a Jersey Shore calendar, and because the Seaside Heights Casino Pier is a rite of passage for so many New Jerseyans, I knew I had to paint it. Completed in June of 2012, I never dreamed that a short four months later with the onslaught of Hurricane Sandy, the twisted ocean wreckage of the Casino Pier roller coaster would become the universal symbol of this killer storm's devastation. Generally, on a painting of this size I would work with larger brushes, but for this piece, because of all the detail in the rides and the people, I used very small brushes on 90 percent of the project. Each person became a mini-portrait. To personalize it, I inserted my two grandchildren (the two towheads) in the bottom left corner.

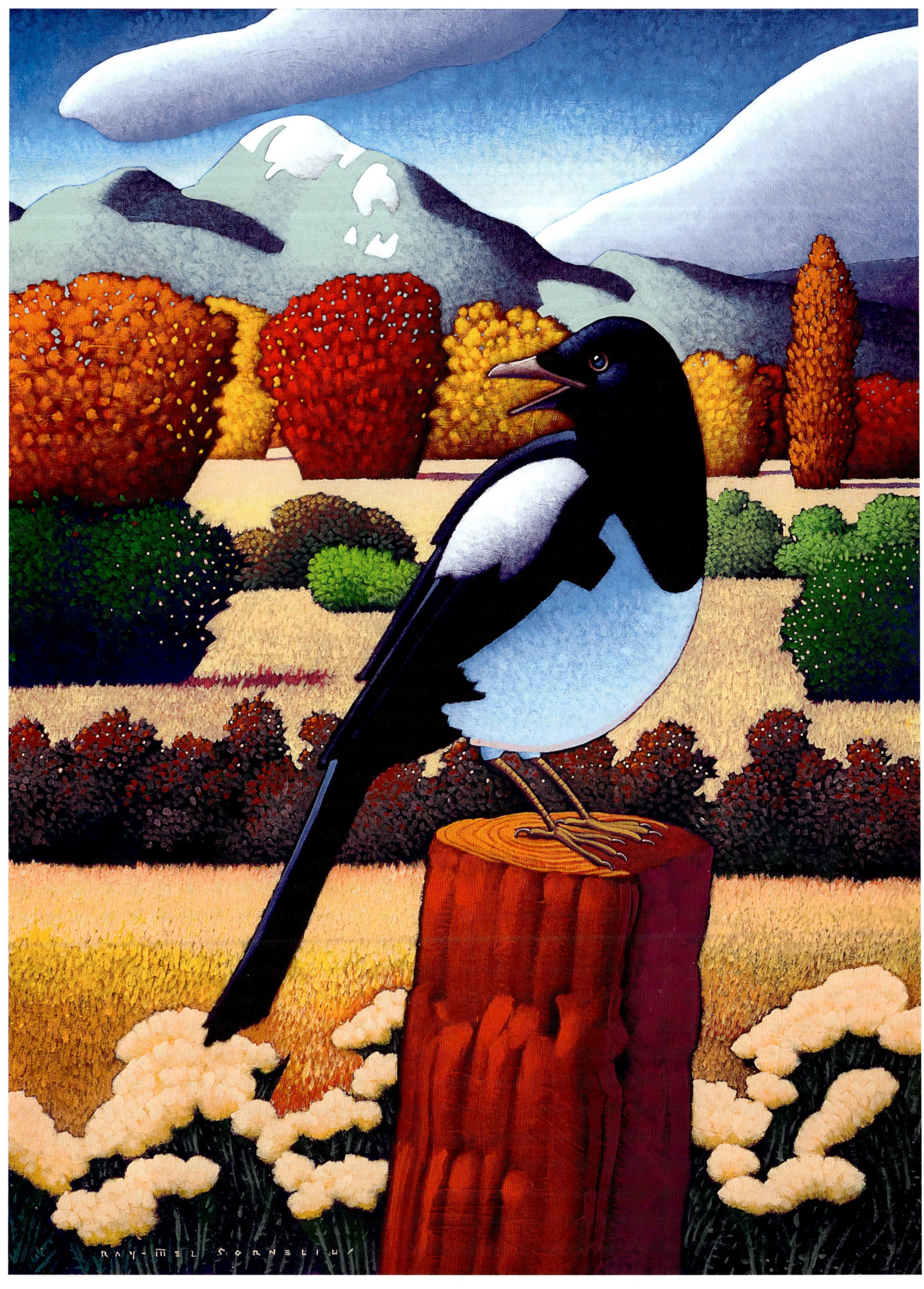
RAY-MEL CORNELIUS

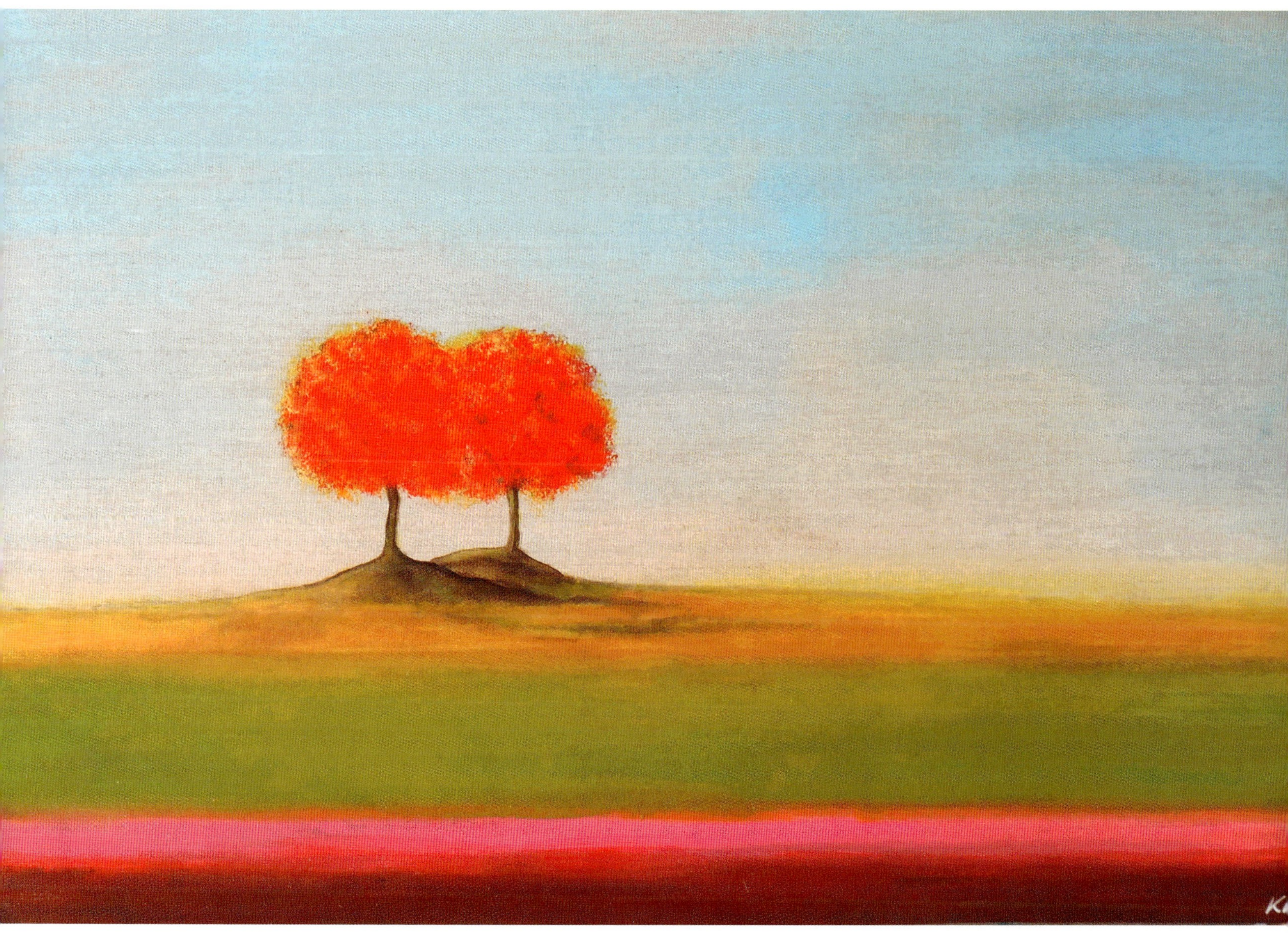

◄ A MAGPIE THIS FALL | Ray-Mel Cornelius
Acrylic on canvas, 40" × 30" (102cm × 76cm)

I have always worked in acrylics. The medium provides my color palette, and its fast-drying property aids my color blending technique. I paint by layering colors, one over another, to achieve a representation of light defining form. I see light as an additive element—an element is totally in shadow and basically formless until light delineates its form. I begin with a dark underpainting and define the form by applying layers using lighter tonal values until I reach the desired chiaroscuro effect. This painting was inspired by observing magpies as they quarreled and went about the business of their day.

▲ IS IT CLOUDY OR BRIGHT? | Vanessa Katz
Acrylic on linen gallery-wrapped canvas, 24" × 36" (61cm × 91cm)

This canvas combines two of my favorite subjects, trees and abstracts created through my imagination. My work thrives through intuition and spontaneity, and sometimes I actually see what I am going to create in my dreams and may dream about the canvas over a period of time. I love working with acrylics as I prefer the fast drying time so I can create lots of layers and build up depth and texture. I also prefer the choice of heavy bodied, soft bodied and liquid acrylics to create many different effects from impasto to washes. With this canvas I wanted to create very bright, bold colors with a contrasting delicate wash for the sky creating a luminous effect. I also wanted to make it very clean and visually demanding. I feel the bold pink band near the bottom enlivens the whole canvas and takes it from being ordinary to dramatic, more abstracted and visually impactful.

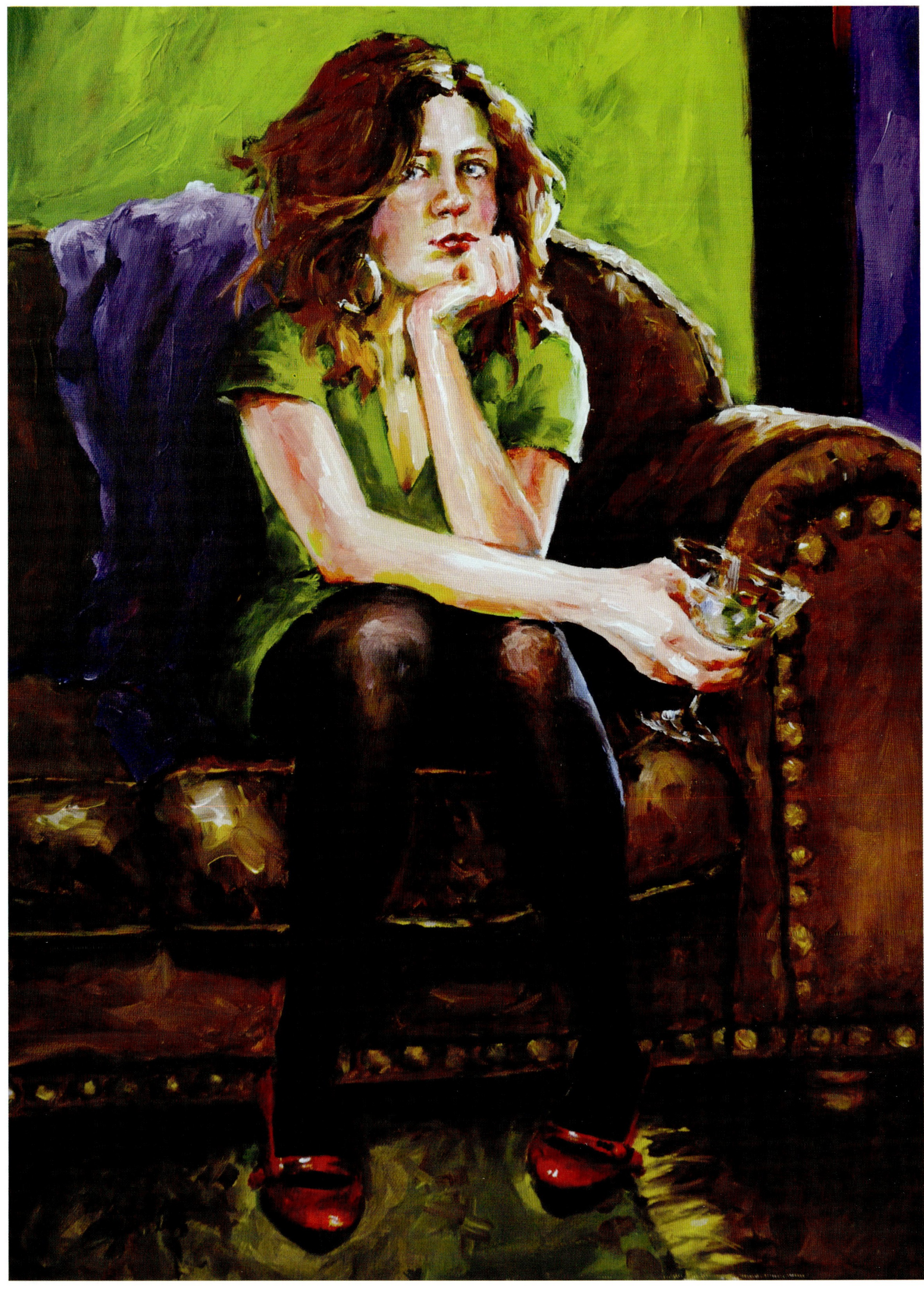

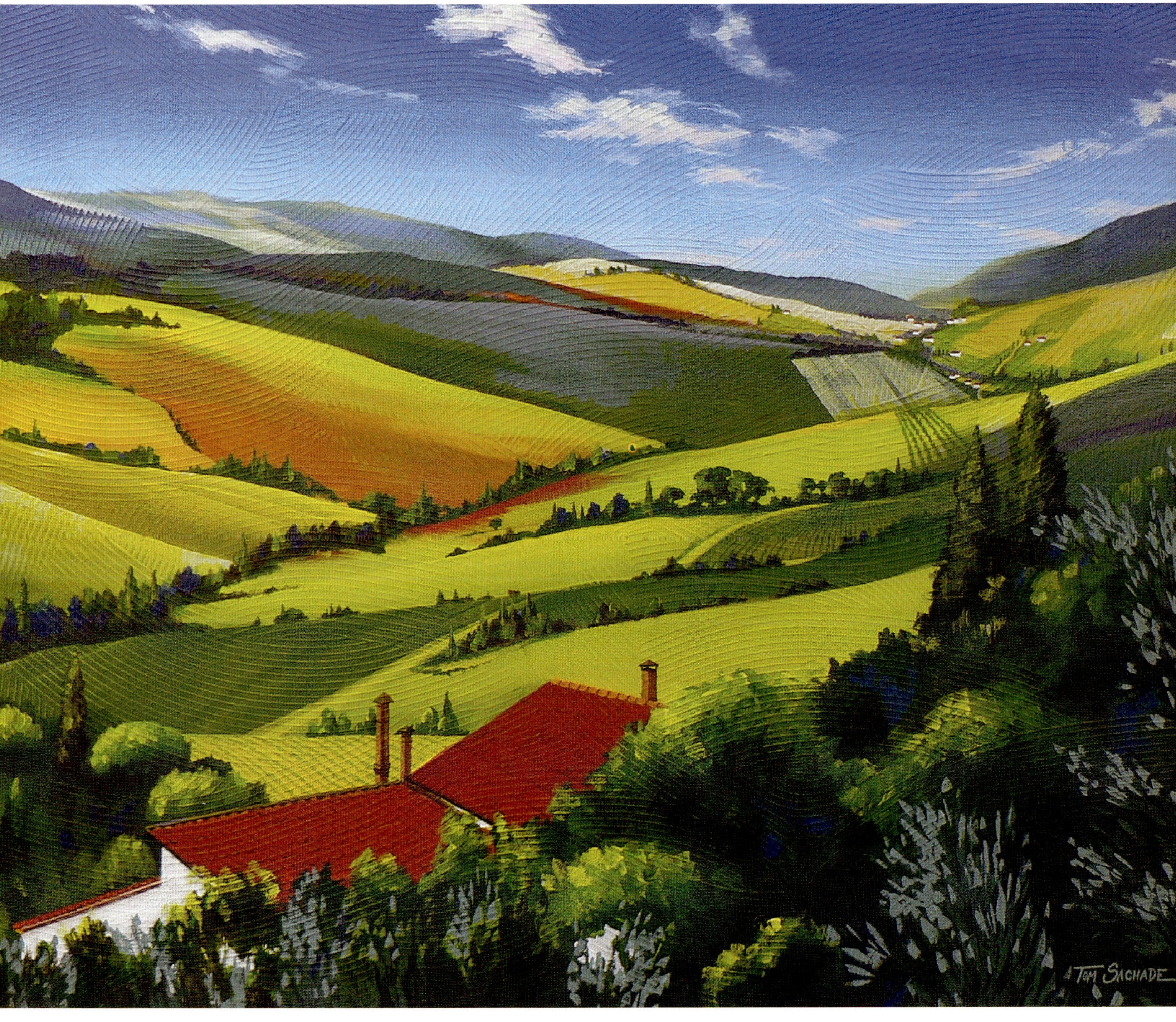

◀ BROWN LEATHER, GREEN OLIVES | Bev Jozwiak
Acrylic on stretch canvas, 24" × 18" (61cm × 46m)

I have come full circle. Early on, my painting career started with acrylics on canvas. The results were becoming so watered down that they almost looked like watercolor, so I made the switch. It was an instant love affair, but after many, many years and much studying of some of my favorite oil painters, my watercolors became thick and heavy-handed. I didn't want to work with the solvents and smelly oils, so I again decided to give acrylics a try. I don't use mediums, so to get that oil look I paint each area fairly fast so I can blend before it dries. Now I happily paint watercolors that look like watercolors, and my acrylic paintings fill the void I was feeling about oils.

▲ A TUSCAN VIEW | Tom Sachade
Acrylic on Canvas, 20" × 30" (51cm × 76cm)

My favorite medium has always been watercolor, but in my pursuit to find another, I quickly learned to work with acrylics and found that the versatility of the medium worked well for my applications. I often succeed in achieving a watercolor appearance in my large acrylic murals by using loose washes. In my smaller paintings such as *A Tuscan View*, I sometimes achieve a more opaque oil look. I recall the thick warm air over the expanse of softly rolling hills when I visited Tuscany and tried to depict that wonderful atmosphere. The landscape was a tapestry of color patterns and texture. To emphasize texture I pulled a comb through a layer of wet gesso and once dry, worked from my photograph to complete the painting.

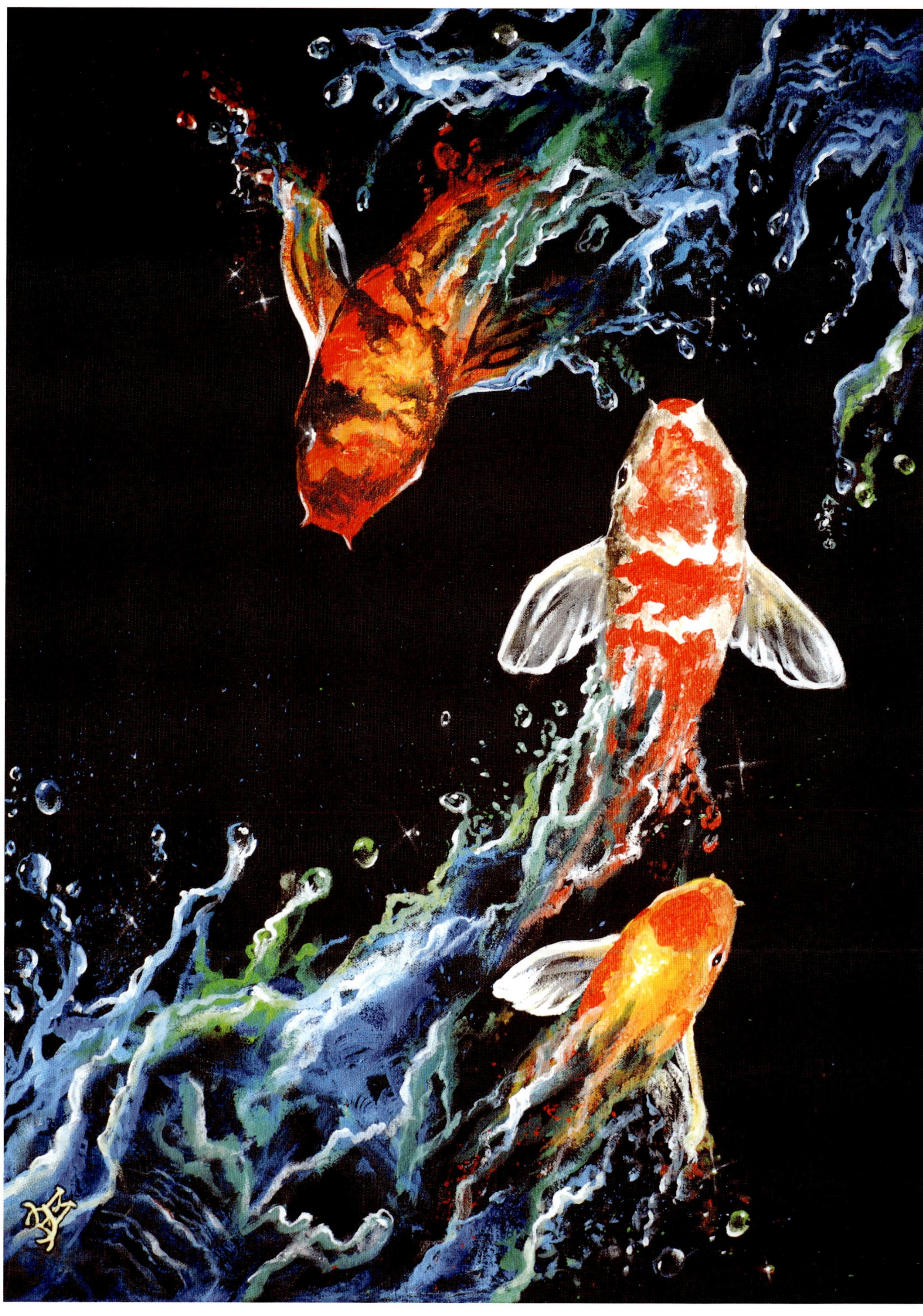

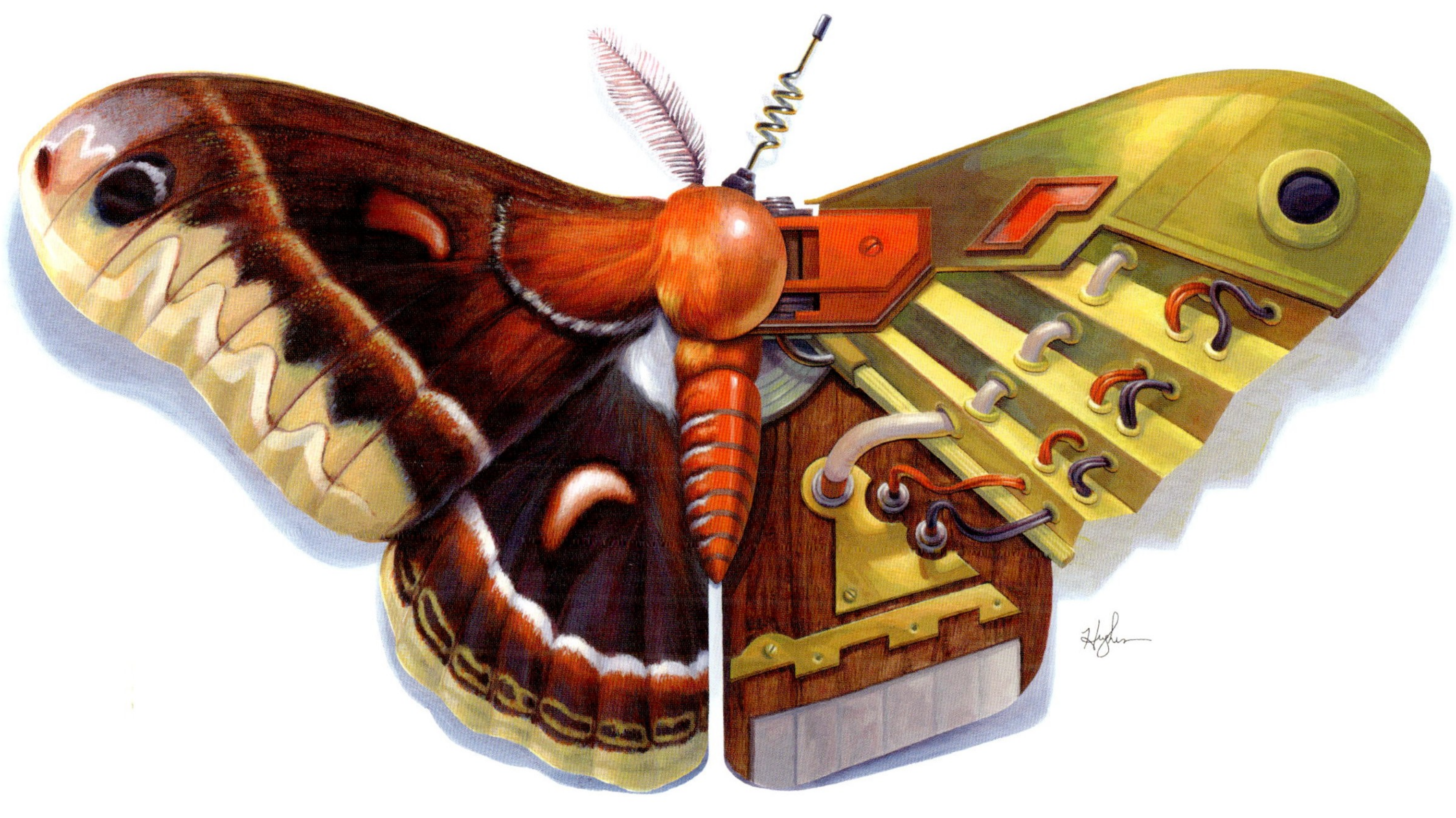

◀ ENDLESS JOURNEY | Marco Antonio Aguilar
Acrylic on canvas, 24" × 18" (61cm × 46cm)

This is from my series called *Splash of Color*. The idea started out as water splashing into the shape of different animals. It has now evolved into the water patterns morphing into solid animals. The resulting image is part splashing water and part aquatic life. The choice to paint them against a black background gives that extra punch and drama that I usually strive for. This project has forced me to look at water in a whole new way, and I find that I am constantly searching for interesting splash patterns. I also find myself spending hours sketching different splash patterns for future projects with my strokes being formless, shapeless—like water. I keep my mind open and fluid, and eventually the shapes reveal themselves.

▲ CECROPIA BOT | Steven E. Hughes
Acrylic and collage on illustration board, 9½" × 17½" (24cm × 44cm)

Research into the movements of bugs and insects has led to great advances and experiments in the world of robotics. It is this unlikely combination that I have chosen to depict. Beginning with similarities in patterns of the Cecropia moth and by making comparisons to steampunk and wiring designs, I constructed the robotic side of the image with plain bristol paper in collage, glued with acrylic medium. The resulting substrate creates a subtle relief that adds depth to the imaginative realism when the final acrylic painting is applied on top.

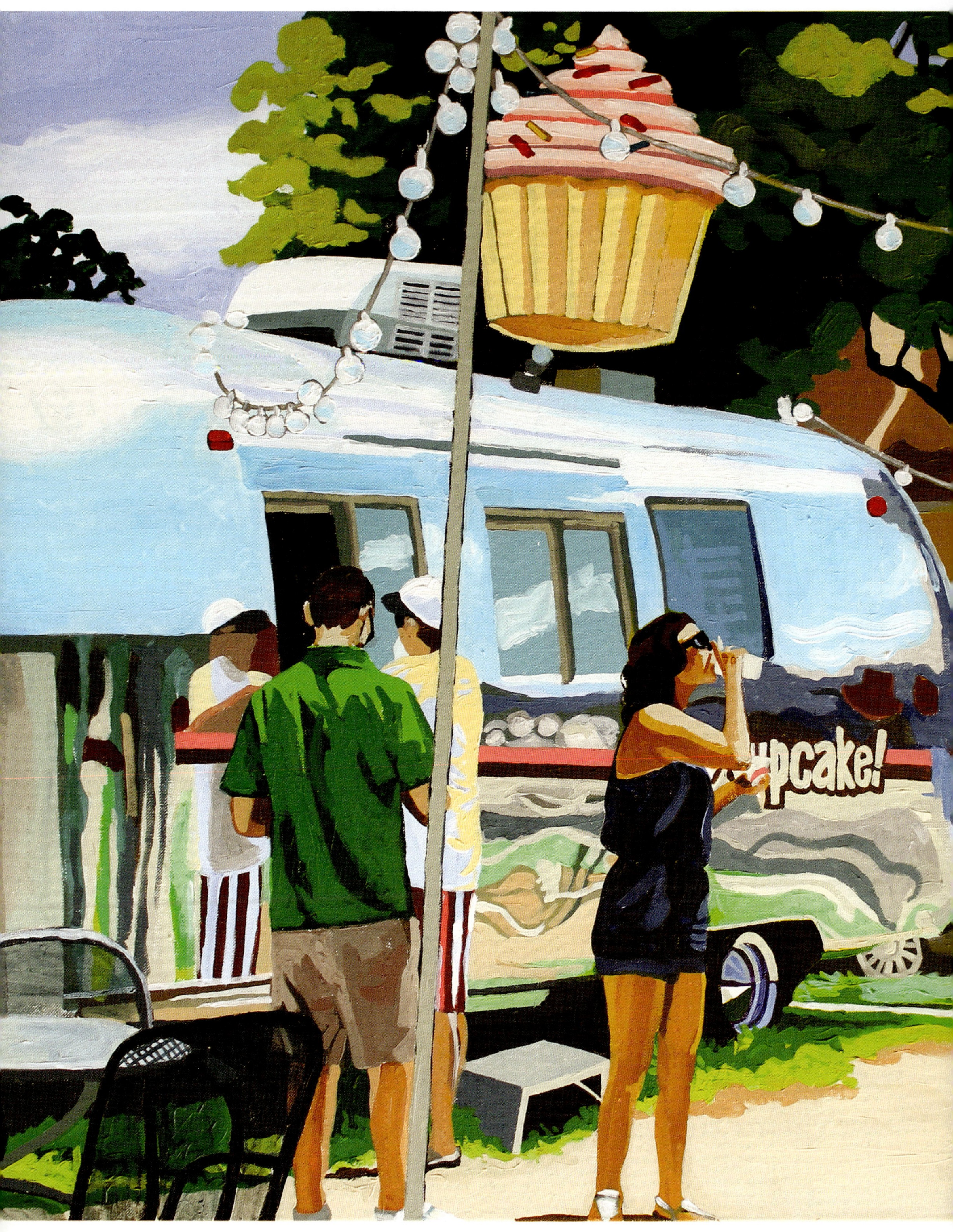
pcake!

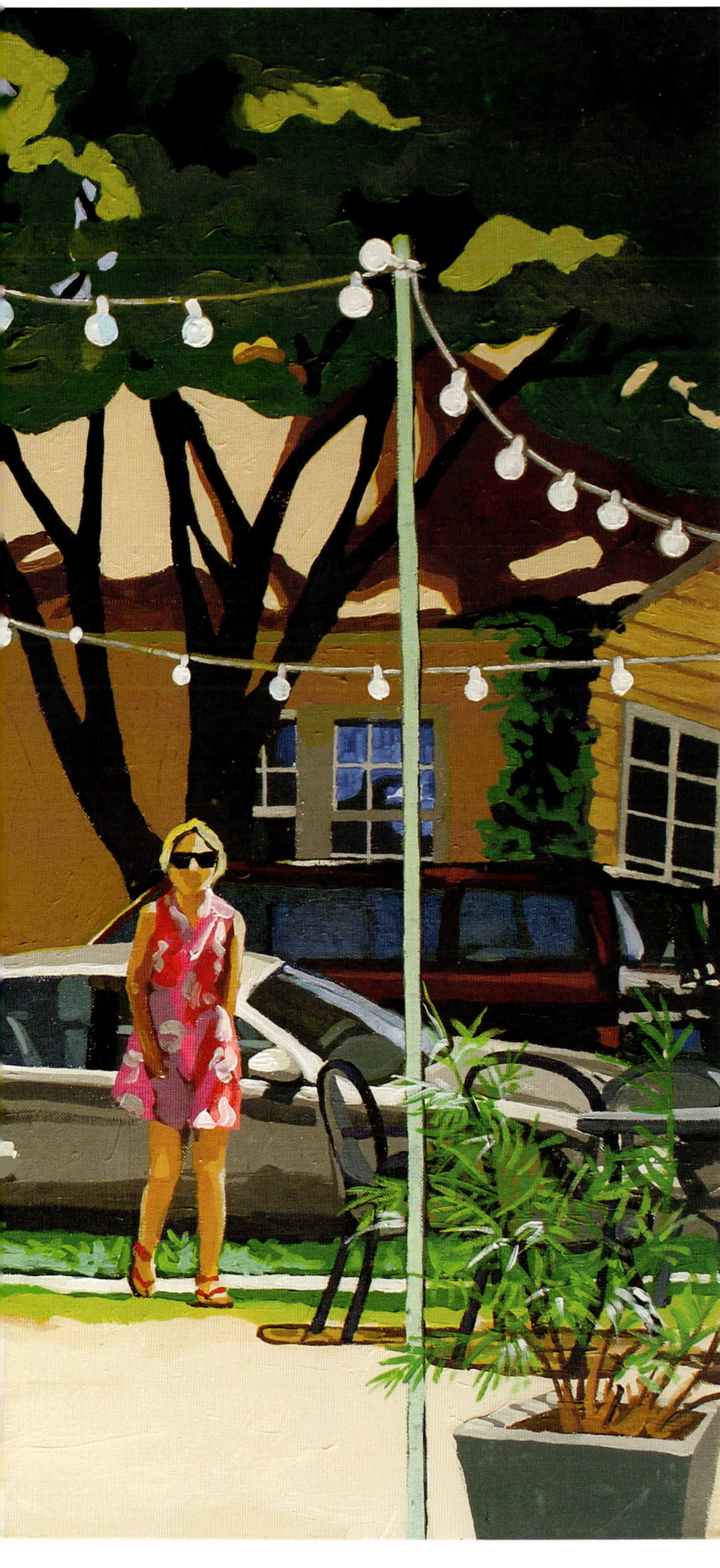

HEY CUPCAKE! | Melinda Patrick
Acrylic on canvas, 30" × 40" (76cm × 12cm)

After growing up painting in oil, I decided to give acrylic a try just to see if either of us had changed over the years. I love the fast-drying element of acrylic. I paint in layers, so the faster the paint dries, the faster I work. I am able to create crisp, bright layers of paint that build into a somewhat realistic image. I am a rabid photographer and shoot from the aspect of what will look good on canvas. My favorite subject matter is urban landscape. I include a lot of detail in each painting, but my goal is always to simplify.

"A good painting is poetry made visible—music for the eye."

—PAUL KINSLOW

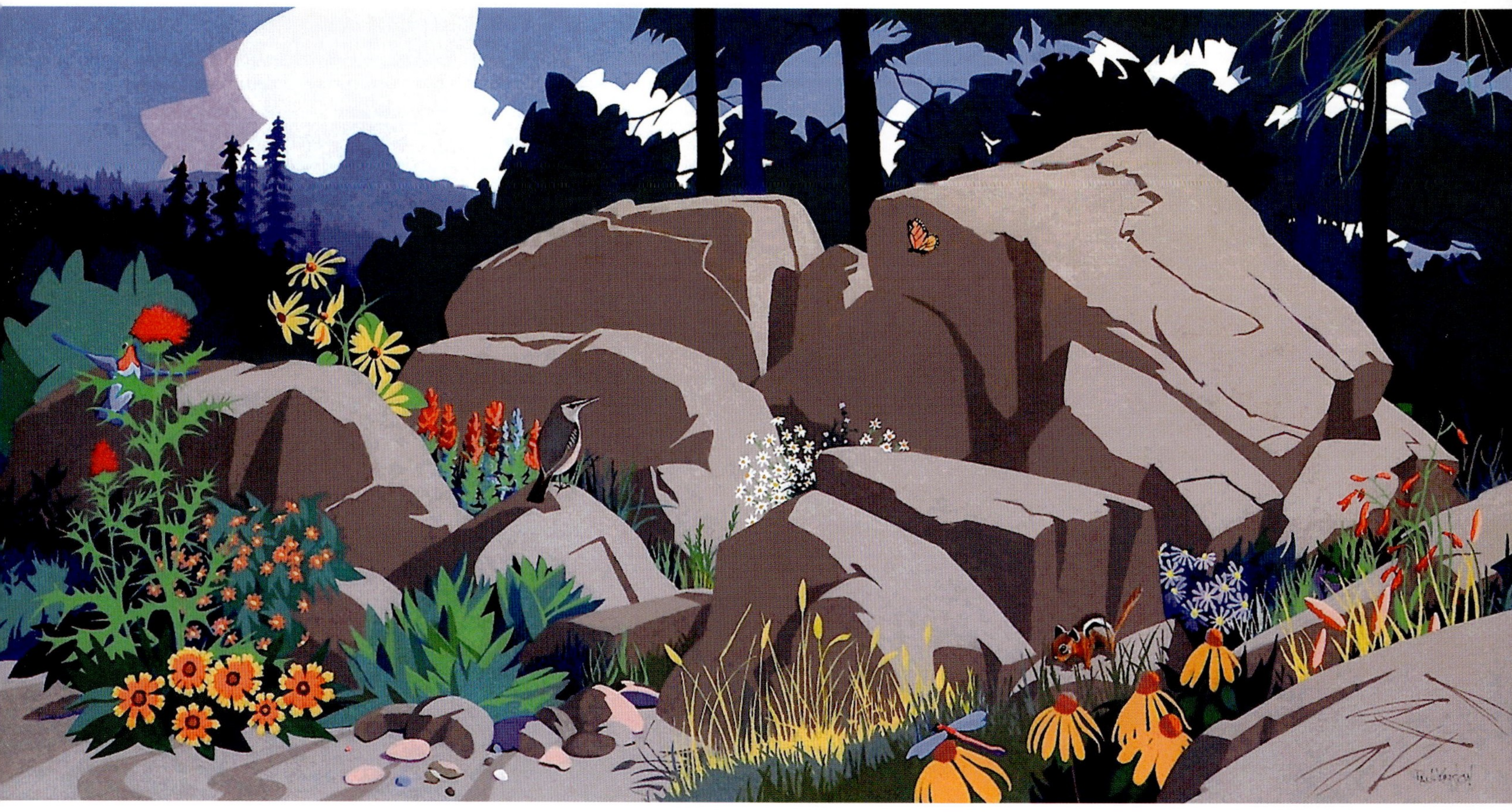

UNDER THE RIM | Paul Kinslow
Acrylic on canvas, 18" × 36" (46cm × 91cm)

I am happy in two places—walking through the wilderness and standing before my easel. The former is my well of inspiration—The Real World—where I spend what time I can. Sometimes in the wilderness I make small paintings with oils. However, in my studio the quick-drying, self-leveling qualities of acrylics allow me to compose simple forms, sharp edges and areas of flat, unvarying color that model impasto.

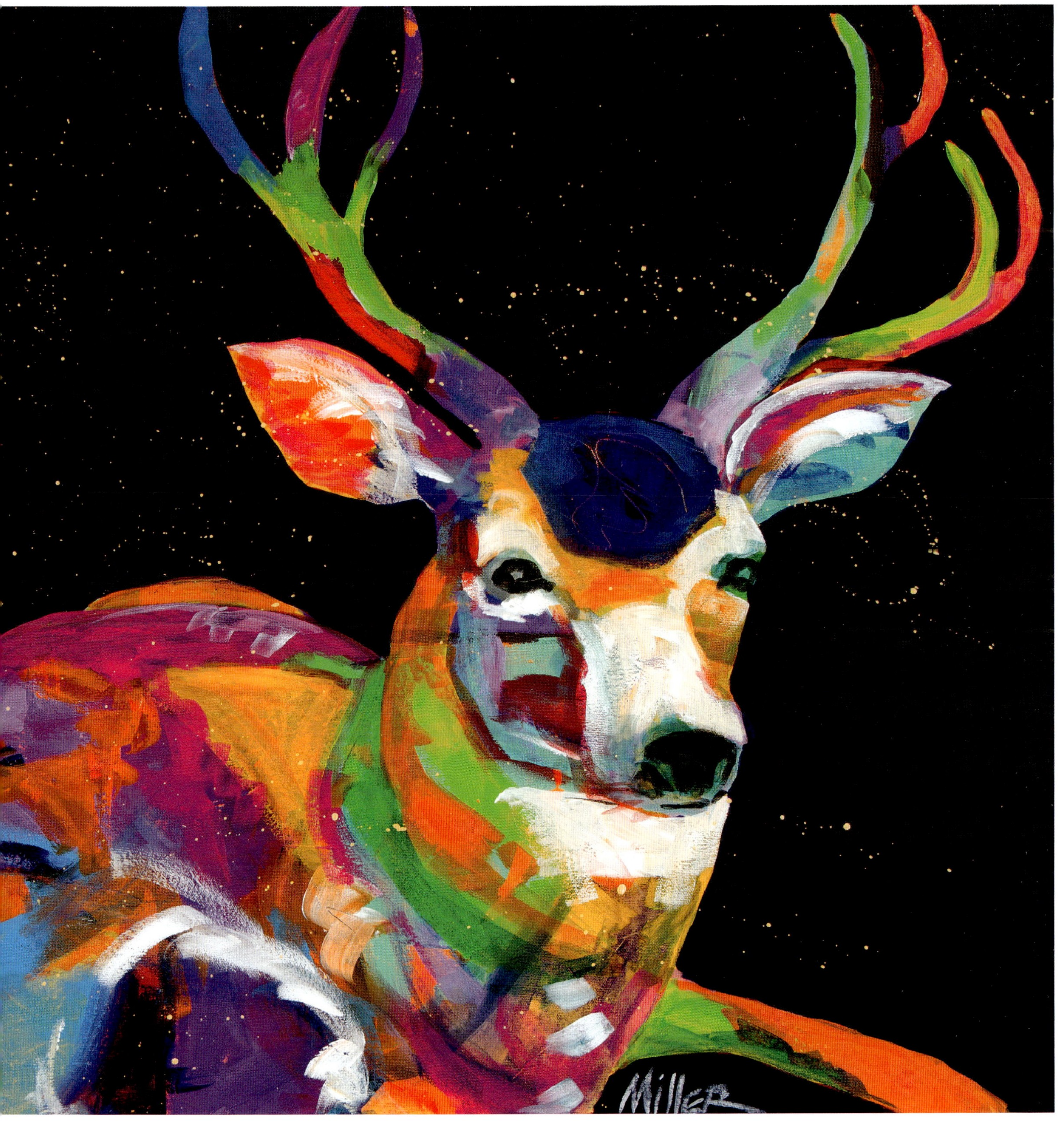

PASSIVE AGREEMENT | Tracy Miller
Acrylic on canvas, 24" × 24" (61cm × 61cm)

My painting of a mule deer was based on a photograph I took of a robust, healthy male who was taking a break in our front yard in the shade. My title comes from the fact that I was standing a mere few feet from him while he passively stared at me and let me take photos from several different angles. I got to work in the studio using a layering process that I do with all my paintings. I start with a wash of solid color followed by a visual haiku of black lines. The work starts out as a total abstraction, and then I decide where to place the animal within that framework. From there it's a process of negative space painting followed by many brushstrokes to build up form, musculature and features unique to the animal. I believe my work captures the spirit and inner essence of the animal subjects I paint through my bold use of color.

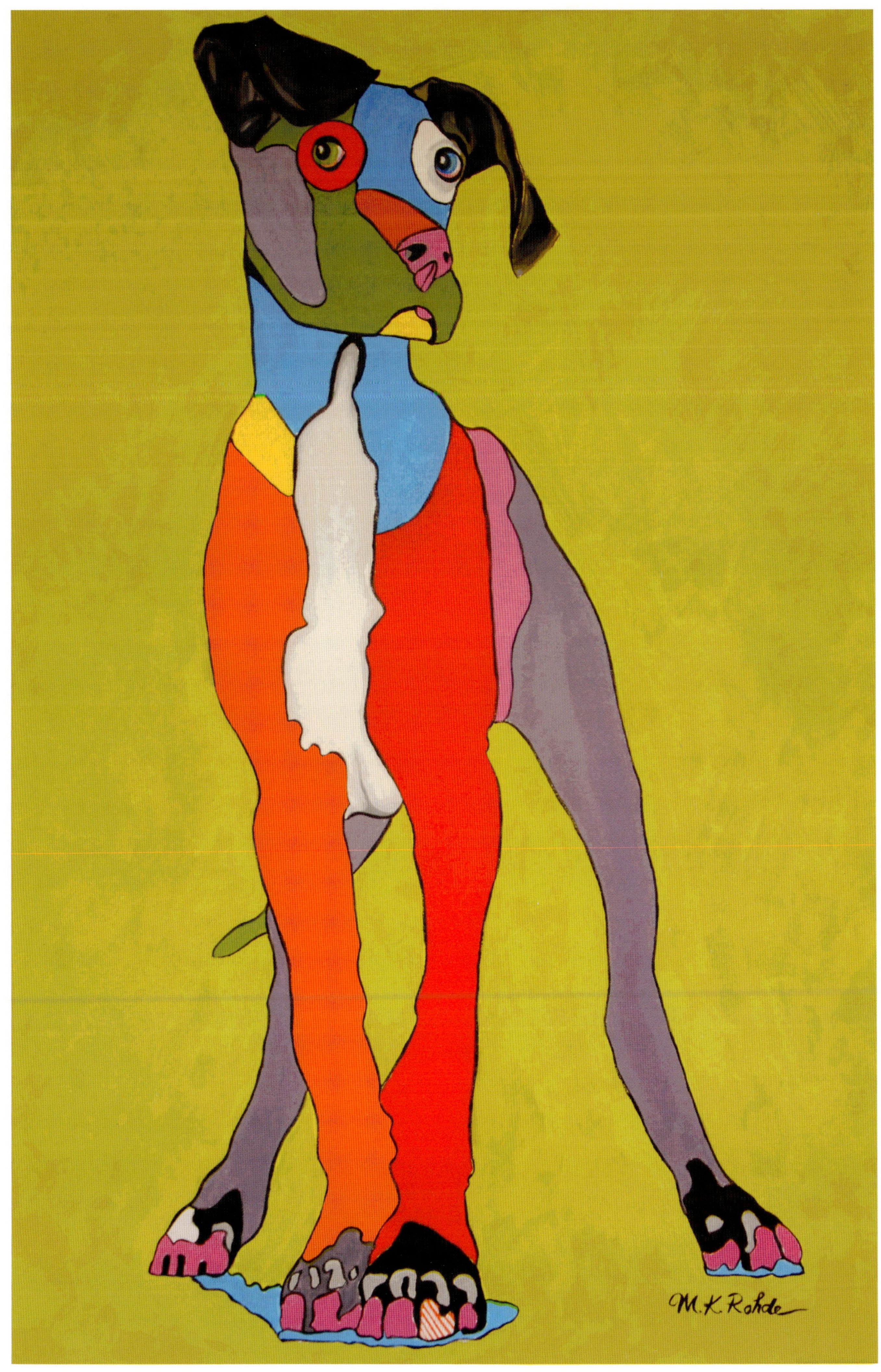
M.K. Rohde

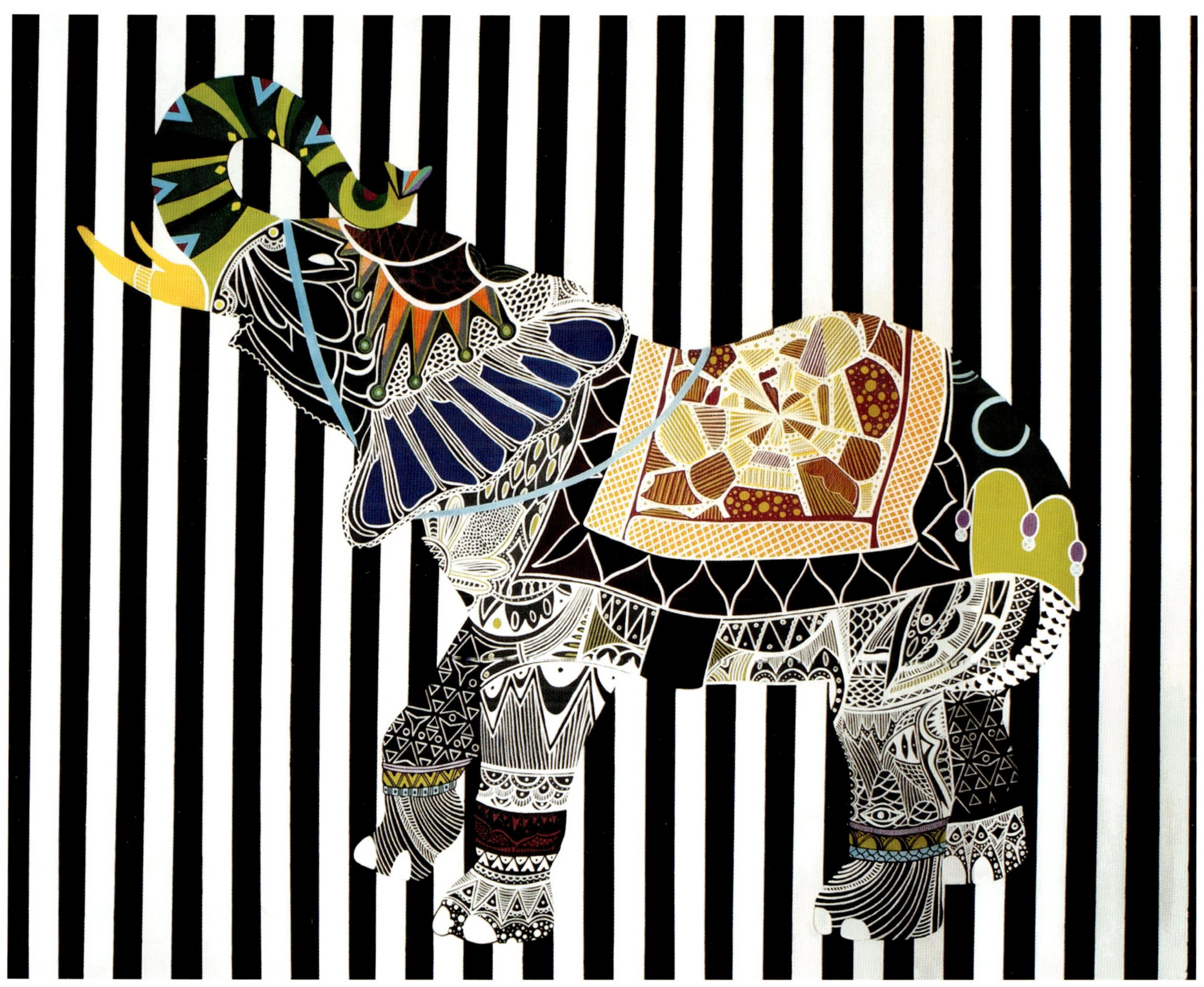

GAYLA | Mary K. Rohde
Acrylic on cotton canvas, 36" × 24" (91cm × 61cm)

Gayla was painted from a photograph. I love animals and often shoot photos of them. I am always looking for some type of conveyance of emotion from my animal friends. *Gayla* represents that awkward feeling one may have felt when growing up—an adolescent dog who is not yet sure of her elegance, only of her legs and big paws. Her self-conscious pose enamors me, and I watch her eyeing me suspiciously. You see, she just had her toenails painted!

After painting watercolor for more than thirteen years, I decided I wanted a fresh, new approach and tried acrylic painting. For *Gayla*, I used Matisse Derivan Victorian Gray for the background. I then used a mixture of yellow and green I like to call chartreuse on top of the gray, allowing some of the background to peek through to create some texture against the very flat, two-dimensional figure. I began my color placement with one hue, then determined what looked good balanced against it. I also added some shading and contour to the important features of Gayla—mainly her eyes.

▲ LUCK | Yelena York Tonoyan
Acrylic on canvas , 48" × 60" (122cm × 152cm)

All works of art are the fruit of the human imagination. We can conjure up infinite ideas, and within this infinity we are sometimes given a gift when one out of the thousands of fantasies comes to the forefront. The difficulty, however, consists in turning visions of the imagination into reality on a canvas. I am not certain why or how the elephant became the central idea for *Luck*. Whereas in India elephants are sought in the quest for good fortune, here I did not seek out the elephant. Instead the elephant found me. Once I embraced this vision I knew for certain this piece was going to be special! However, when I began painting I found that the various mediums of painting I tried did not give me a desired result. To resolve this dilemma I tried acrylics and realized it was the ideal medium for my vision. Acrylic paints have a rich, deep color pattern that allows the artist to combine the drawing with the painting, making the painting more true to life. I found that when the mind, the hand and the brush became the continuation of one another, my "lucky" elephant appeared on the canvas. I painted this canvas with the love in my heart, and when a part of the soul is invested, there can never be any falsehood.

JAZZ HORNS | Rosa Vera
Acrylic on 140-lb. (300gsm) hot-pressed Fabriano Artistico paper, 29¼" × 29½" (74cm × 75cm)

The idea for the piece came from watching musicians at a jazz festival at the San Antonio Botanical Garden. I took a series of photographs and put them together to get the horn players lined up the way I wanted them. Over time I have attempted to visually depict the sound of music. In *Jazz Horns* I used stamps in the shape of spirals and waves to represent the image of jazz sounds surrounding the musicians.

Coming from a watercolor background, I find that acrylic offers many opportunities for layering and building up a painting. In *Jazz Horns* I used acrylic molding paste mixed with paint for stamping and for making an impasto relief to make the piece three-dimensional in parts. Acrylic paint was also dripped to give a sense of movement.

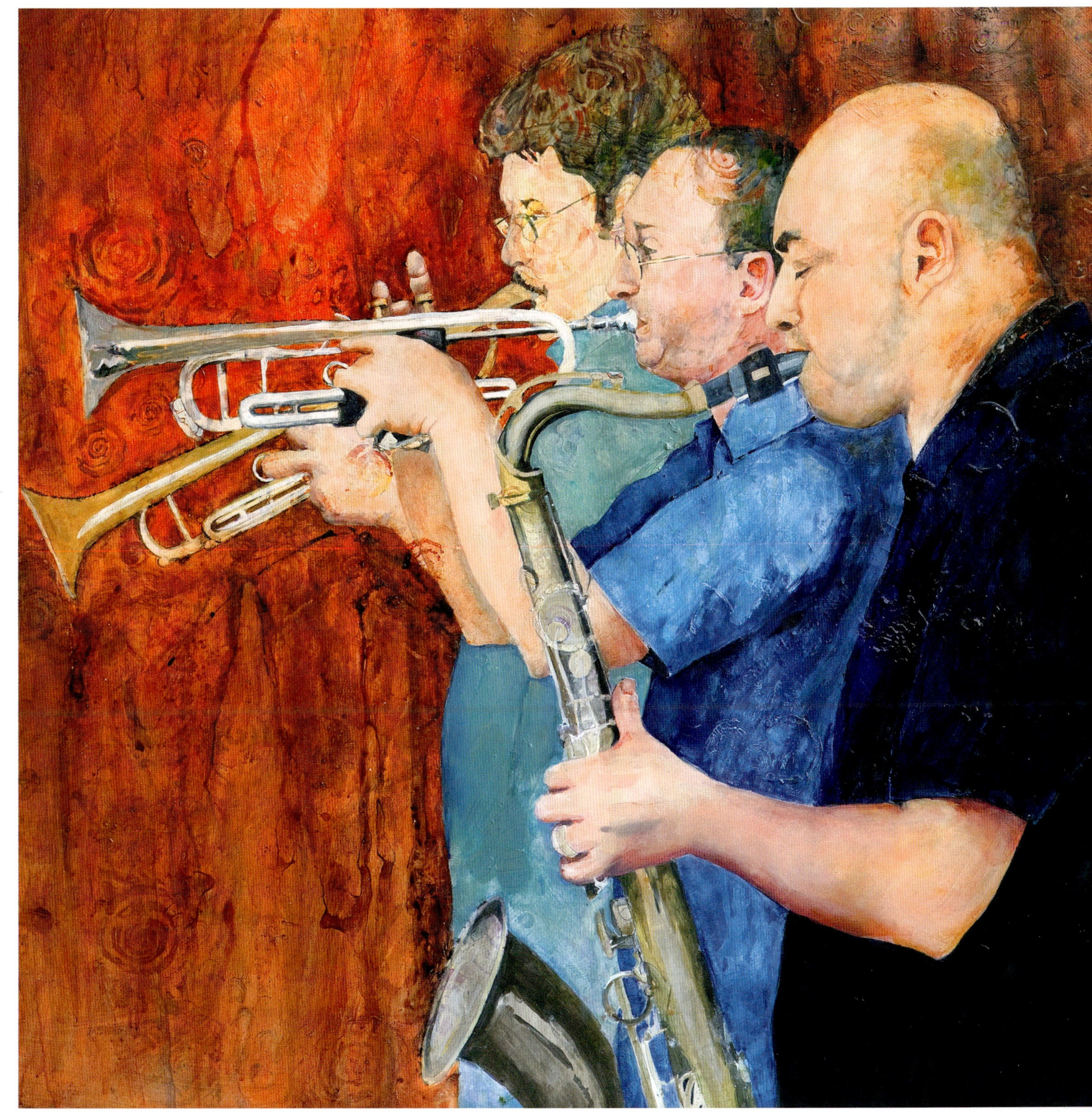

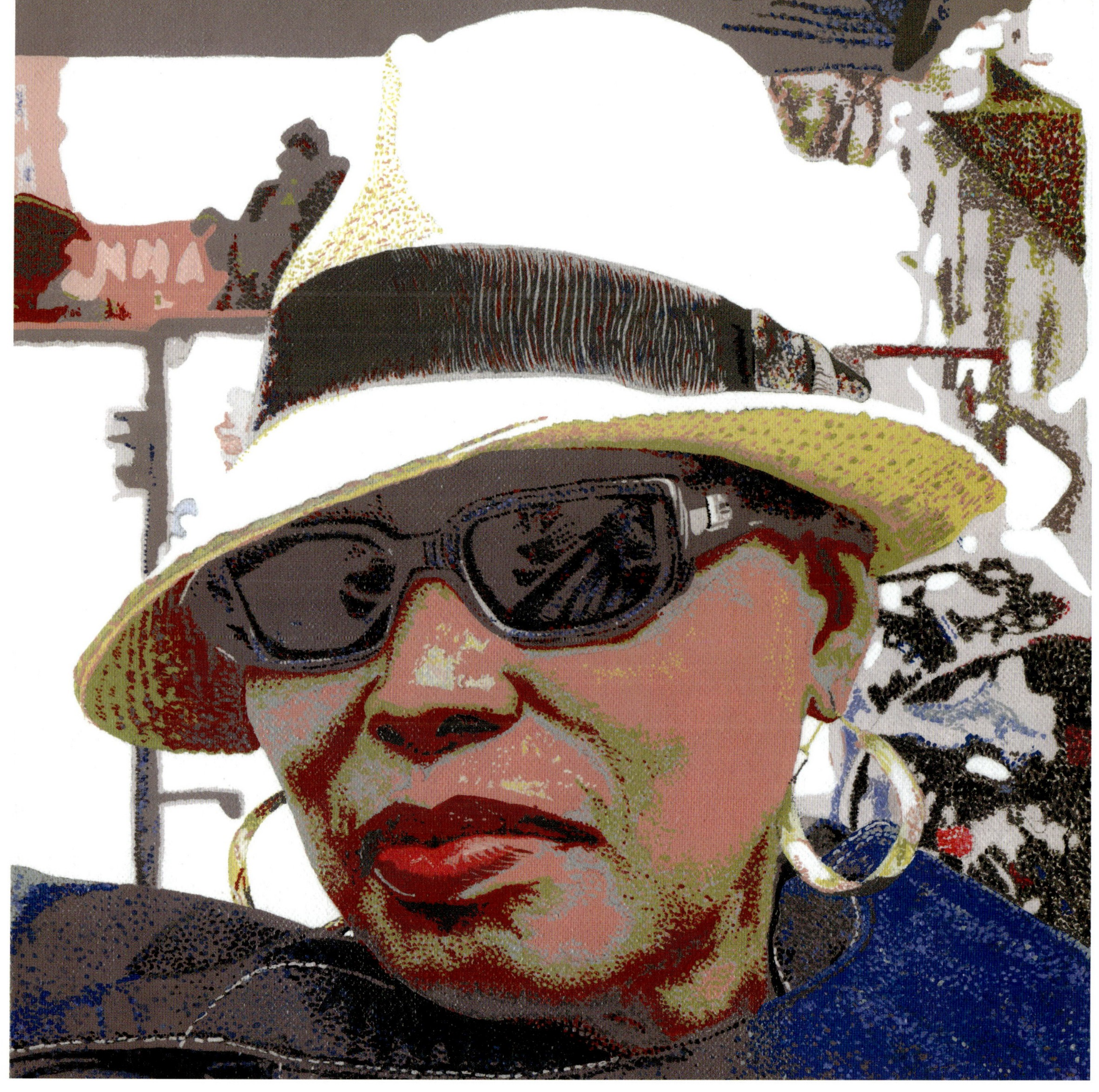

OPW | Hank Washington
Acrylic and gloss varnish on 8-oz. (225g) natural cotton duck, 12" × 12" (30cm × 30cm)

Consistently over the last forty years, acrylic has been the medium of choice for me and the high school students I teach in California. As an artist and teacher I love the versatility and flexibility that acrylics provide, their ease of use, affordability, clean up and storage, color variations and drying time.

OPW is a manipulated photograph of my beautiful wife taken at a local California beach. As a teacher and artist I am constantly exploring new mediums, techniques and technologies that can be applied to learning. One area I am exploring is the editing of images using different software programs like Photoshop and CorelDRAW. When the multitude of effects and filters is combined with the explosion of point-and-shoot cameras and mobile digital software, the technology becomes a powerful artistic tool. In *OPW*, I used the process of layering color in conjunction with the application of stippling techniques.

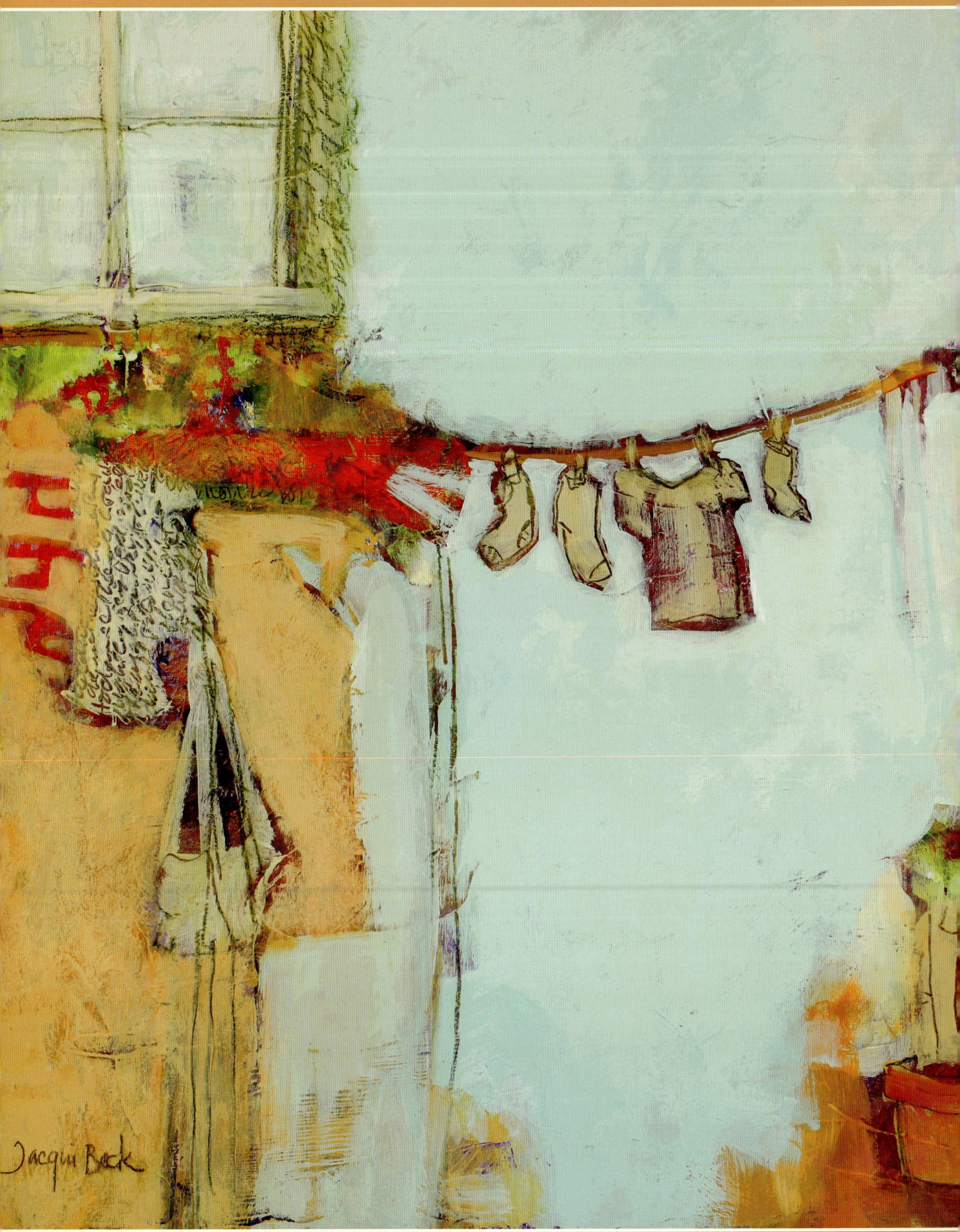
Jacqui Beck

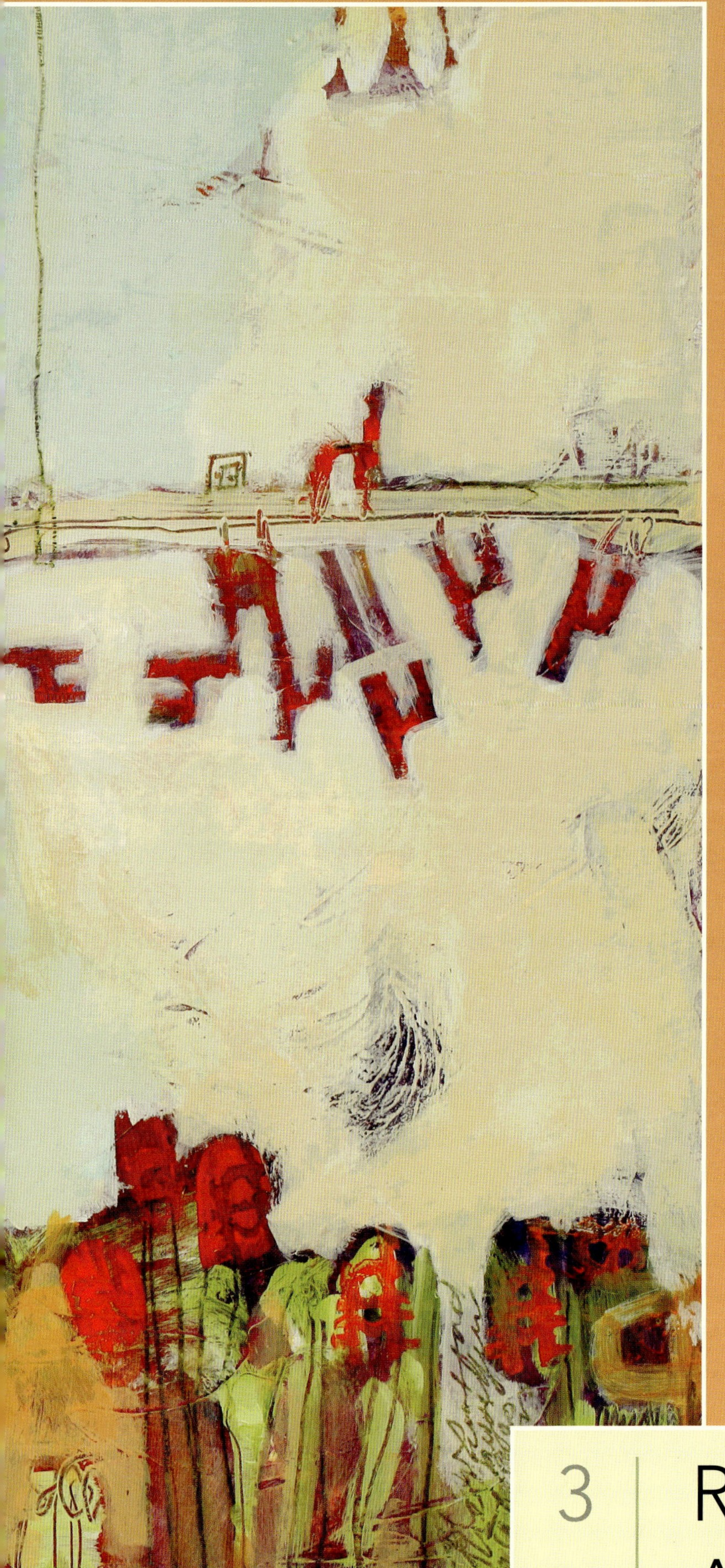

DECORATING THE ORDINARY | Jacqui Beck
Acrylic and colored pencil on board
16" × 20" (41cm × 51cm)

I don't plan much before starting a painting though I may have an idea in mind. I start loosely, applying texture (mediums, collaged materials) and color directly or in other ways such as using handmade stamps. I may write or draw into the paint at this stage, too. As I work, I bring out aspects of the design that I like and am fascinated by. I use a combination of loose expressive application and more controlled work.

I paint in acrylics for many reasons. Because I use multiple layers, I appreciate that it dries quickly. I use the paint in many ways, from thin transparent coats to thick, textured impasto. In *Decorating the Ordinary* I used a variety of techniques including stamping and colored pencil for writing words, creating line and texturing. I use the pencil on wet, semiwet and dry paint for different effects. It is a good way to scratch through a top layer to reveal a contrasting value or color below.

My subject matter is deeply personal to me. *Decorating the Ordinary* is about the beauty of simple and functional parts of life. I love clotheslines, the color and pattern of clean laundry blowing in the breeze.

3 | REALISTIC ABSTRACTIONS

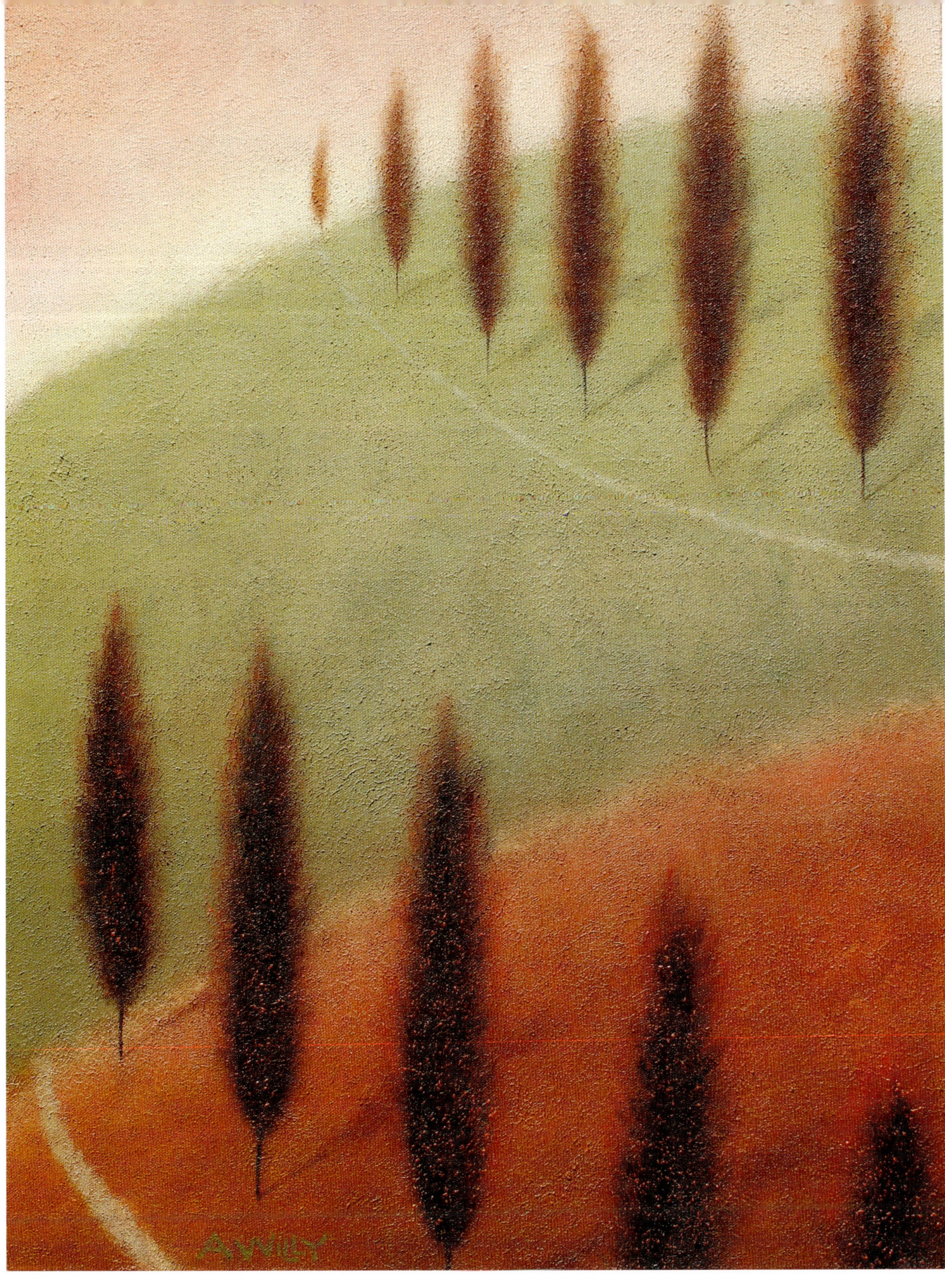

RELATIVE DISTANCE | April Willy
Acrylic on sanded stretched canvas, 20" × 16" (51cm × 41cm)

My imagery is generated mostly from my fascination with color, form and movement within the landscape. As both an illustrator and an artist, I challenge myself to tell a story revolving around the theme of a cyclical world, the changing seasons, weather and a pivotal moment in time.

When working in acrylic, I first texturize the painting surface with sand mixed into gesso. When dry I paint a blended background starting with the farthest point back (the sky), working my way toward the foreground. This often creates multiple layers depending on the complexity of the composition.

One great aspect of working in acrylic is that mistakes are easily painted over. This gives me the confidence to work quickly and spontaneously. Acrylic is the perfect medium to use for rendering tight details. The colors reproduce well and the quick drying time is essential when a large body of work needs to be produced in a timely manner.

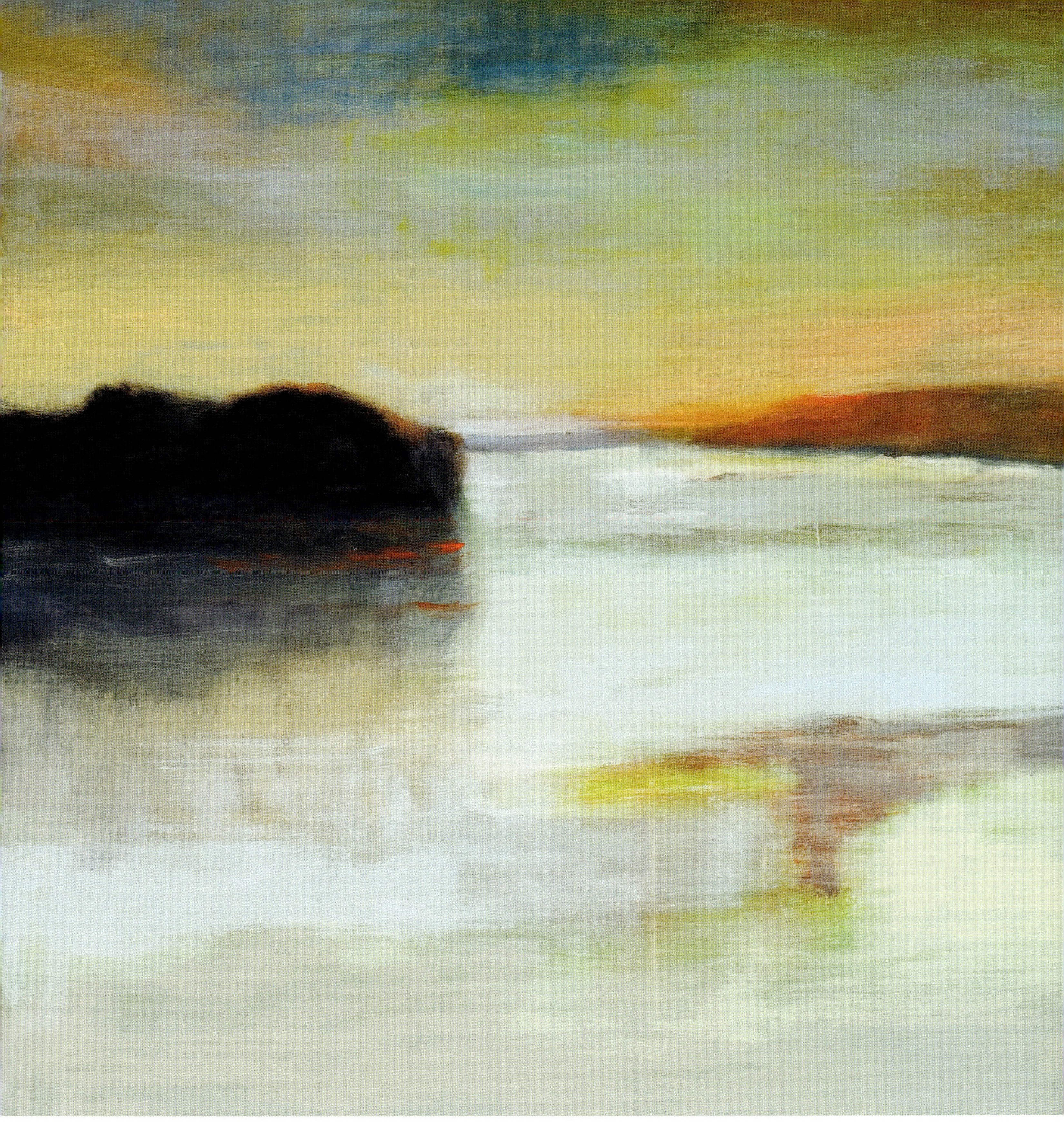

DISTANT SHORES | Donne Bitner
Acrylic on canvas, 36" × 36" (91cm × 91cm)

When I returned to art after raising my family, I worked in watercolor on paper. After a few years, looking for more spontaneity and layering ability, I switched to acrylic. The paint was applied in thin layers, a leftover from the watercolor years. This new approach also gave me the chance to work on different textures such as wood, canvas, paper and even glass. I like to add mixed media to my surfaces, and oil pastel, charcoal, spackling and joint compound opened new doors of exploration. My abstracted landscapes are a recent series. Since I work from memory and not a reference, there is a discovery process as I don't start with an end result in mind but rather let the painting evolve over time. It's painting by discovery! Words to remember: A painting doesn't have to be something; it's a painting and could be about the paint, line, shape and texture!

RED TAXI | Mac Mak
Acrylic on canvas, 36" × 48" (91cm × 122cm)

I often found the red taxicab at corners of my city, Hong Kong, an energetic cosmopolis at all hours. At night she was stunning next to the highly condensed buildings with layers of colors ranging all around. The luminescence, reflections, abstractions and motion were an endless supply of inspiration. I chose in-motion red taxicabs as a motif to illustrate my inner feelings related to the fast-paced city.

For *Red Taxi*, I started with a drawing in Carbon Black, then added cool and transparent darks, building up the layers. I worked into the midtones and painted the scarlet body of the taxi to establish a key that would influence the rest of the painting. Finally, I tackled the light tones and highlights using the thick-on-thin technique. I often use thick layers of paint I applied to reflections and push and mix them on the canvas to produce interesting and spontaneous palettes. My goal in *Red Taxi* was to indicate the complexity of the scene with as few brushstrokes as possible. In order to demonstrate my reaction to the dynamics and stress of the city, I depict my subjects loose and expressive.

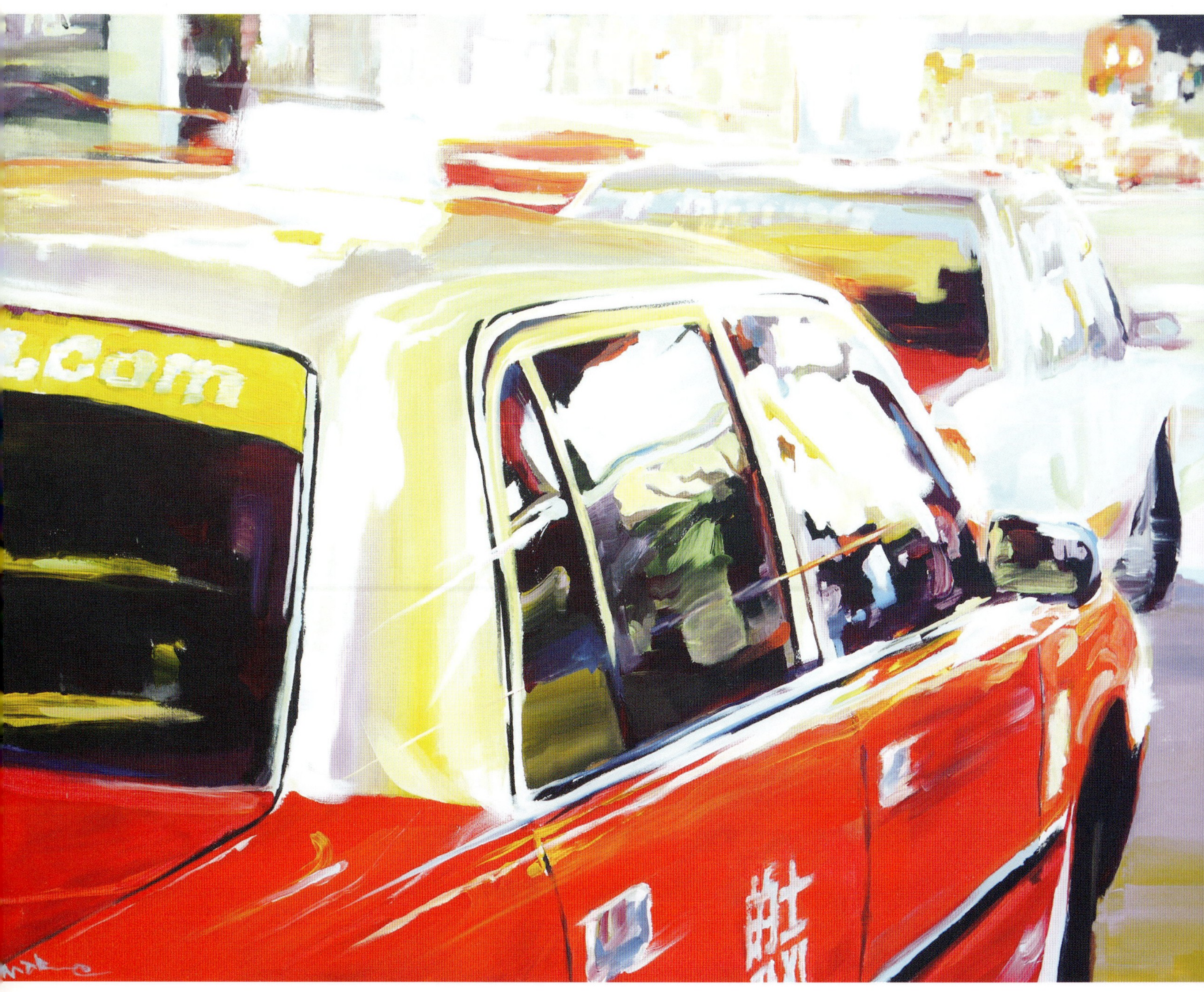

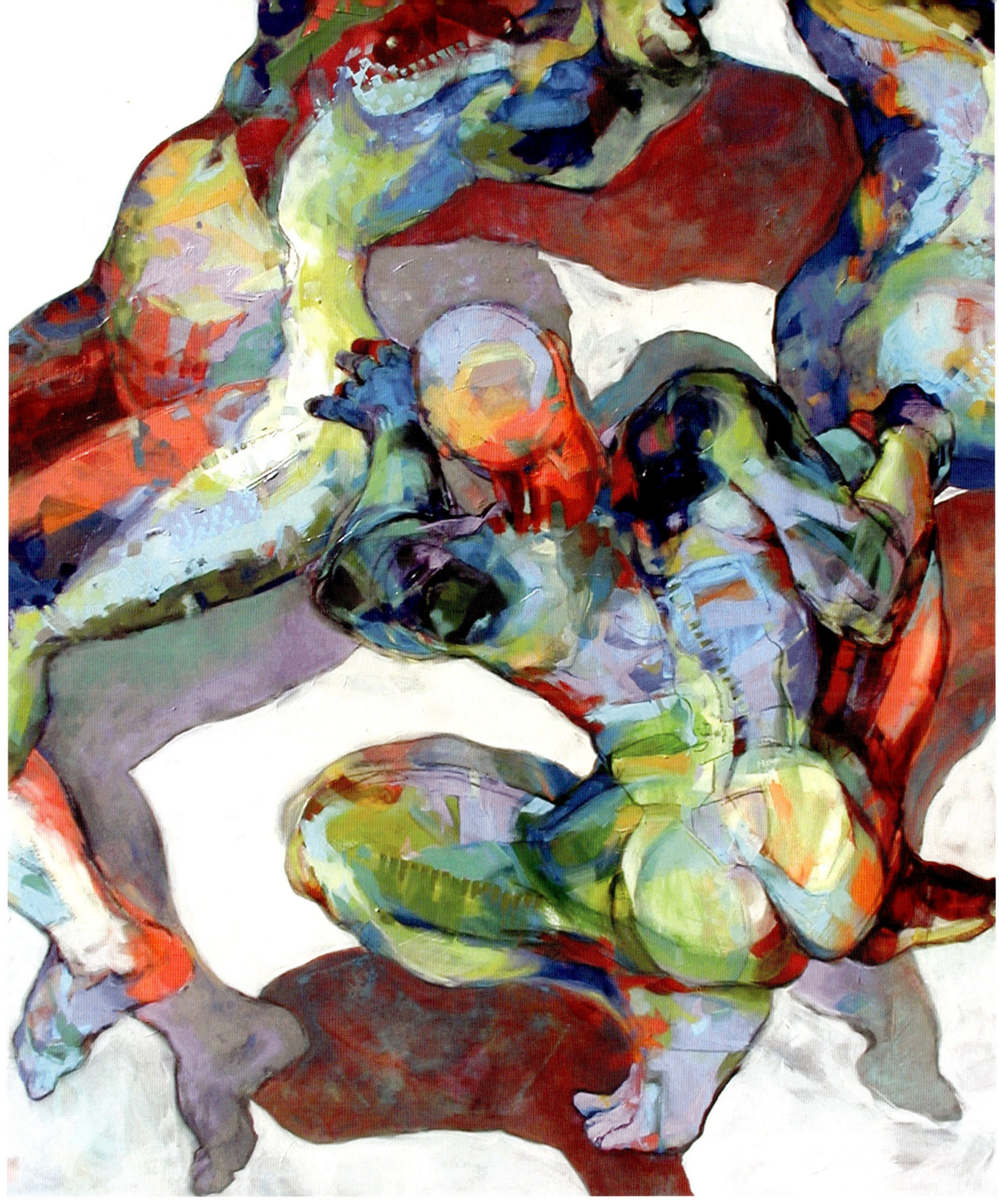

IN MATTERS OF THE HEART | Joanne Beaule Ruggles
Acrylic with charcoal on stretched canvas, 60" × 48" (152cm × 122cm)

My paintings usually start from fields of abstraction—visual chaos. The canvas field is playfully filled with drips and splashes, organized patterns and wildly expressive marks until I begin to have an interest in the abstract expressionist stew that I have started cooking. At that point, I consider what figures might already live on the canvas, and I take my cues from it. After years of studying the human figure, I have found that body language becomes a solid tool to create narratives. Inevitably what my charcoal stick unearths within the abstract acrylic painting pertains to the topic already on my mind.

"Build child's play into your process—periods of time when you do not know where you are headed."

—JOANNE BEAULE RUGGLES

BREEZES THROUGH THE COTTONWOODS | A.S. Helwig
Acrylic on cradled board, 30" × 40" (76cm × 102cm)

I was fourteen when I started to paint outside in the coulees by my Lethbridge, Alberta, home. That romantic vision—that all painters went outside to paint—was what I thought all painters did. The imagery of this piece reflects those first encounters with acrylics. These cottonwoods grow beside the Oldman River that runs through Lethbridge. They are resilient, tough trees

There is still often a bias toward acrylic painters as people assume more serious painters use oil. Often I'm told my paintings look like oil, but they are unabashedly acrylic. I love working with thin and thick passages of paint. The gels and mediums give me more options for surface manipulation. The colors, especially the newer formulated organic pigments, are juicy and rich. My advice to painters new to acrylic: put more paint on your palette and use it all!

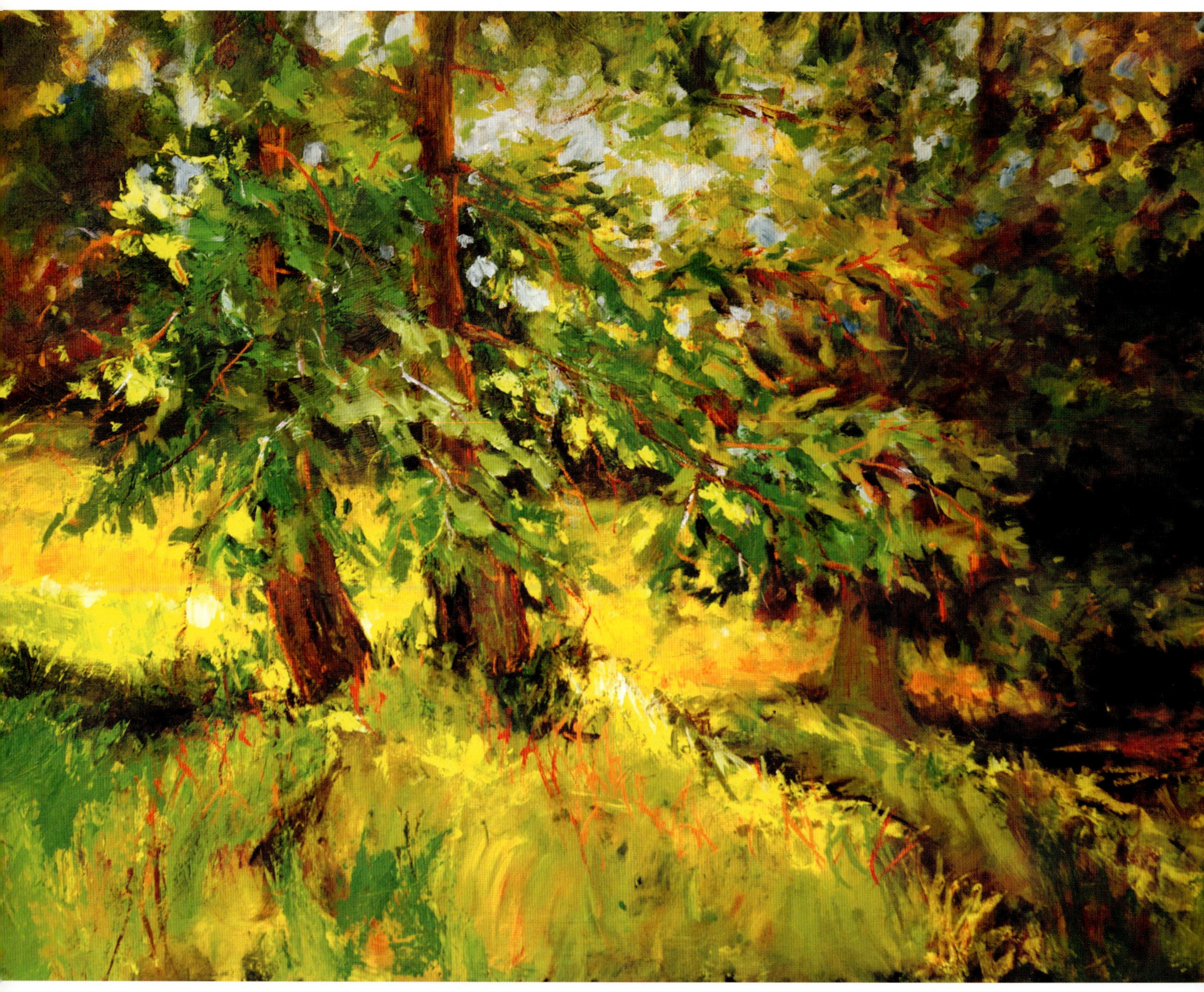

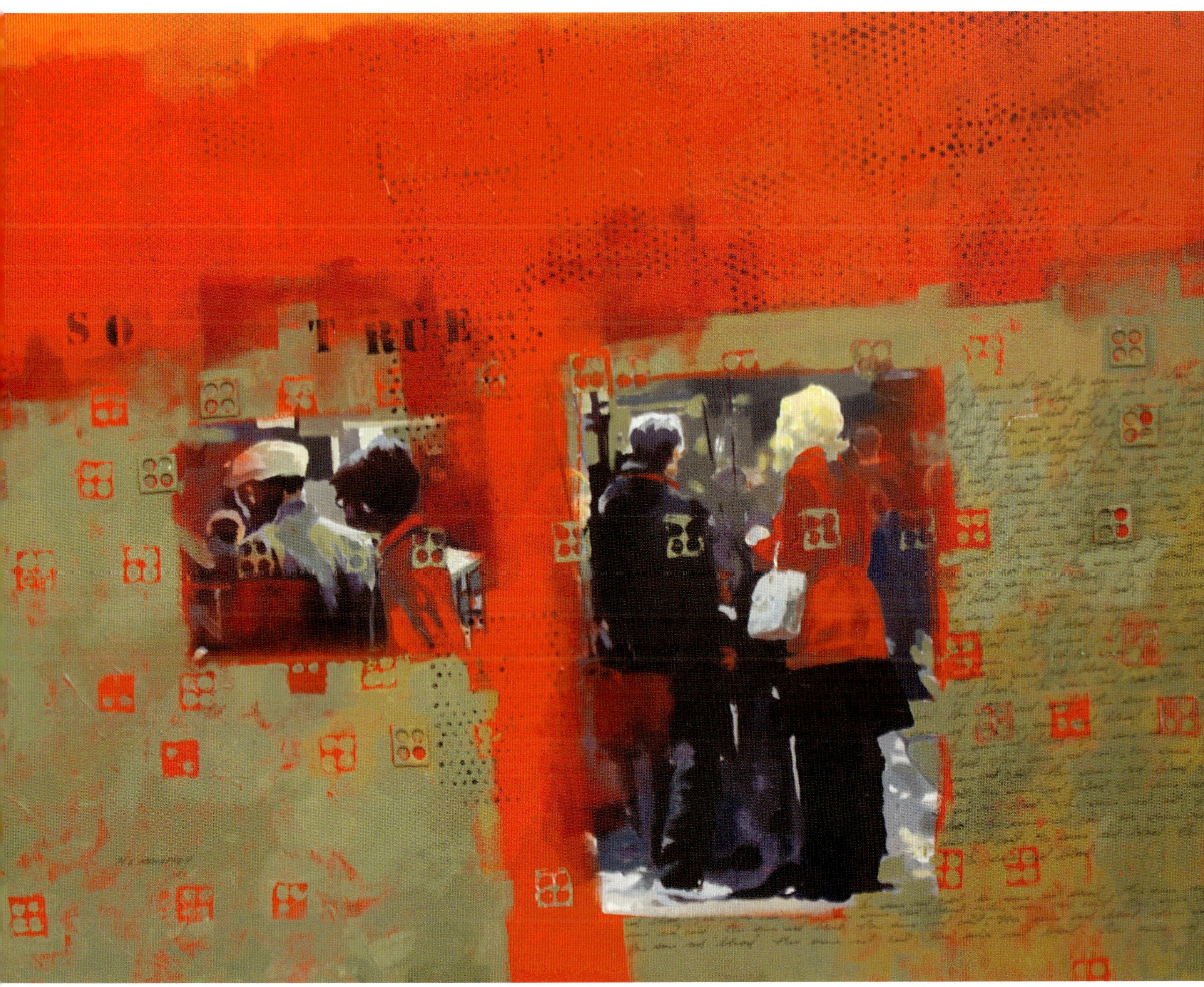

SO TRUE | Mark E. Mehaffey
Acrylic with some ink and collage on canvas, 30" × 40" (76cm × 102cm)

So True started life as a painting of an indoor flea market complete with a crowd and vendors. The original painting was competent both in terms of drawing and paint handling but lacked . . . something. As I studied the completed painting (already signed and framed), I noticed that both the white couple and the black couple were looking at the same items *and* both women had on the *same* red coat. Skin color is literally skin deep . . . so to drive this point home I wrote over and over in black ink "same red coat, same red blood . . . it is, so true." I used a sponge roller and covered any and all of the original painting that did not have meaning, keeping focus on the two women who share so much. The cursive writing that contains the message also acts as an area of texture, especially from a distance. I hope it also acts to draw the viewer in to both enjoy the texture and to actually read what was written. The little square shapes are both painted and collaged in to add a repeating pattern (with variety) and to remind the viewer that this is a two-dimensional surface, a painting. I much preferred the new painting to the old. It now has meaning, content and emotion. It makes viewers think, and I hope it gets them involved.

"To create a work of significance, make sure your work has meaning to you. Just reporting or repeating something often done will not get you to where you want to be."

—MARK E. MEHAFFEY

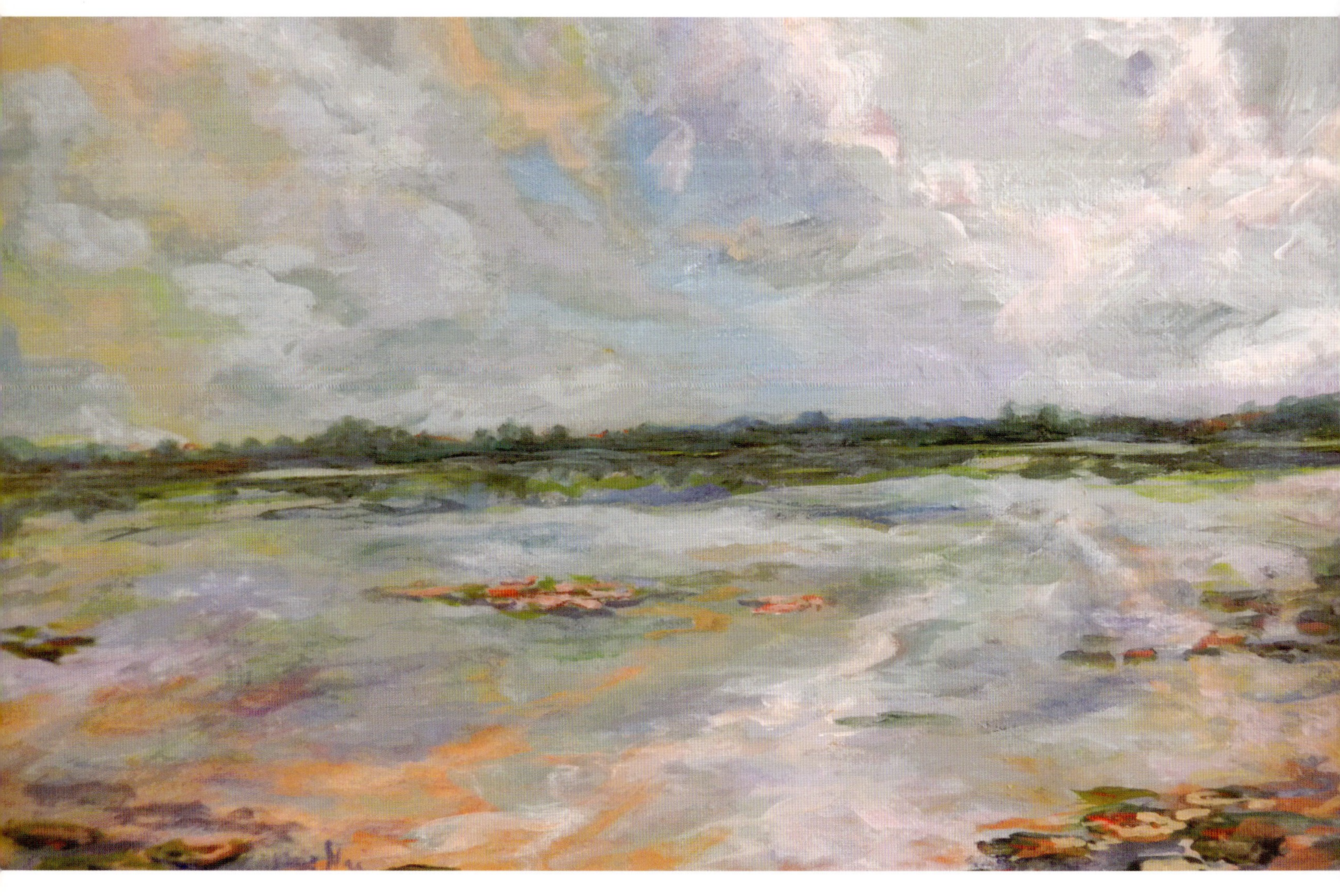

MORNING CLOUDS | Patricia Maguire
Acrylic paint on canvas, 30" × 40" (76cm × 102cm)

Morning Clouds is a larger studio version of a plein air painting I did on location in Delray Beach in Florida. It was early morning and the light and the reflections in the water were changing rapidly. Acrylic paint was the perfect medium for a fast sketch. Once in the studio, my challenge was to give the larger painting the feeling of movement, light and heat that I had experienced outside. I started by covering the whole canvas with shades of pink and peach to mimic the early morning light. I then selected a limited palette of colors and used only zinc as my white. Working with layers of transparencies, my goal was to re-create a feeling rather than a place.

EARLY MORNING LIGHT | Patricia Maguire
Acrylic paint on canvas, 20" × 24" (51cm × 61cm)

This is a plein air painting. Before the heat sets in, Florida skies are full of color. I thinned acrylic paint with water to create transparent layers, and I used big brushes to quickly achieve my composition. Before starting, I toned the entire surface of my canvas with a turquoise blue.

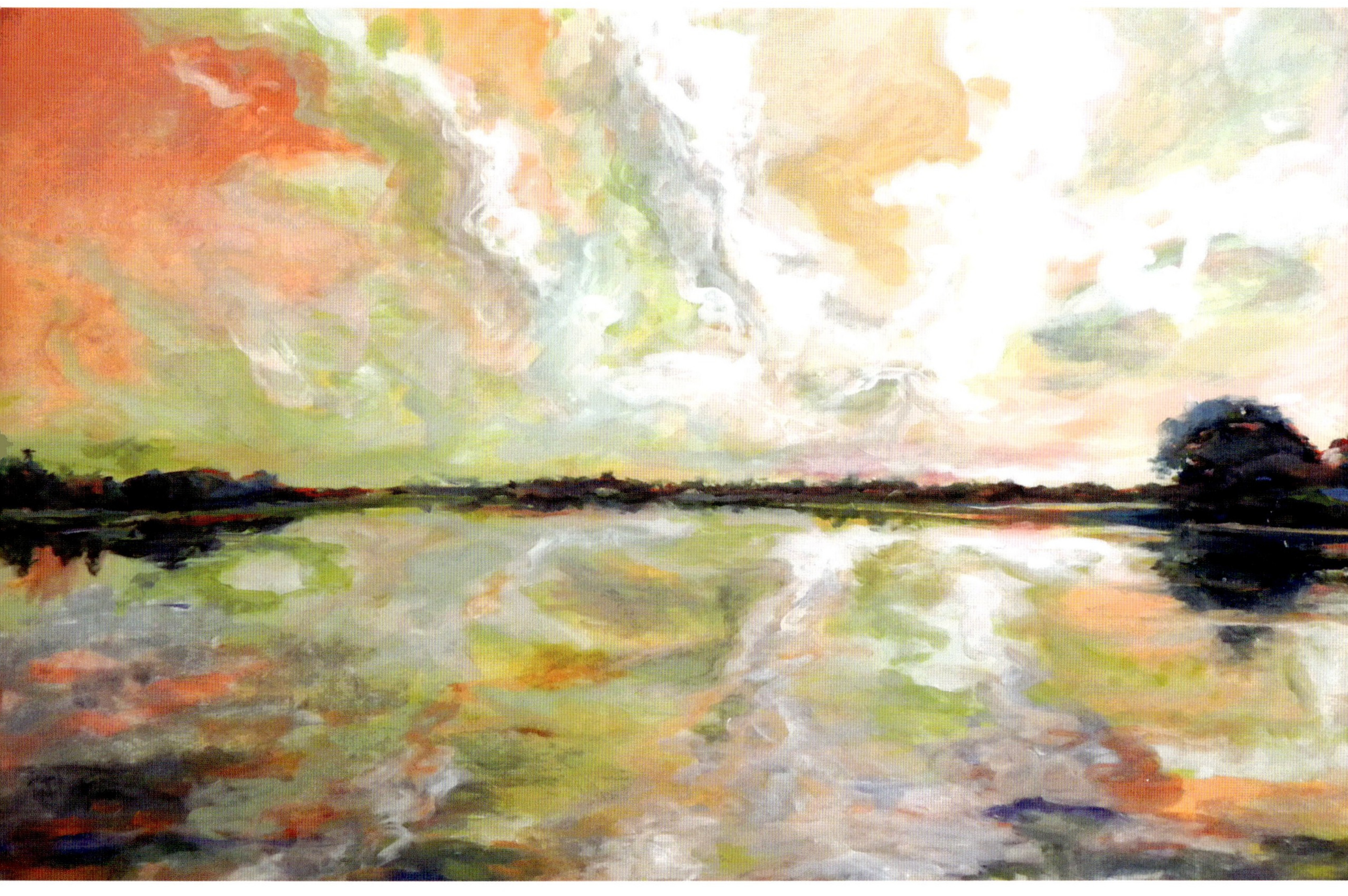

▼ SITTING ON THE CATBIRD SEAT | Linda Olmstead
Acrylic with sheet music and rice paper collage on stretched canvas
15" × 30" (38cm × 76cm)

After many years working in oil and watercolor, I finally returned to acrylics and what fun I've had with such a versatile paint! My work has totally changed—I'm especially excited about how acrylic works in collage, the most freely creative of all painting genres. I love the physical characteristics of acrylics, especially the short drying time. My impatient side can layer colors or entirely redo the painting. Usually I have a plan for every painting, but with acrylics that plan can change within minutes, which allows me to approach each painting as an adventure.

"Crows are the most joyous, brave, fascinating, annoyingly loud birds on the planet!"

—LINDA OLMSTEAD

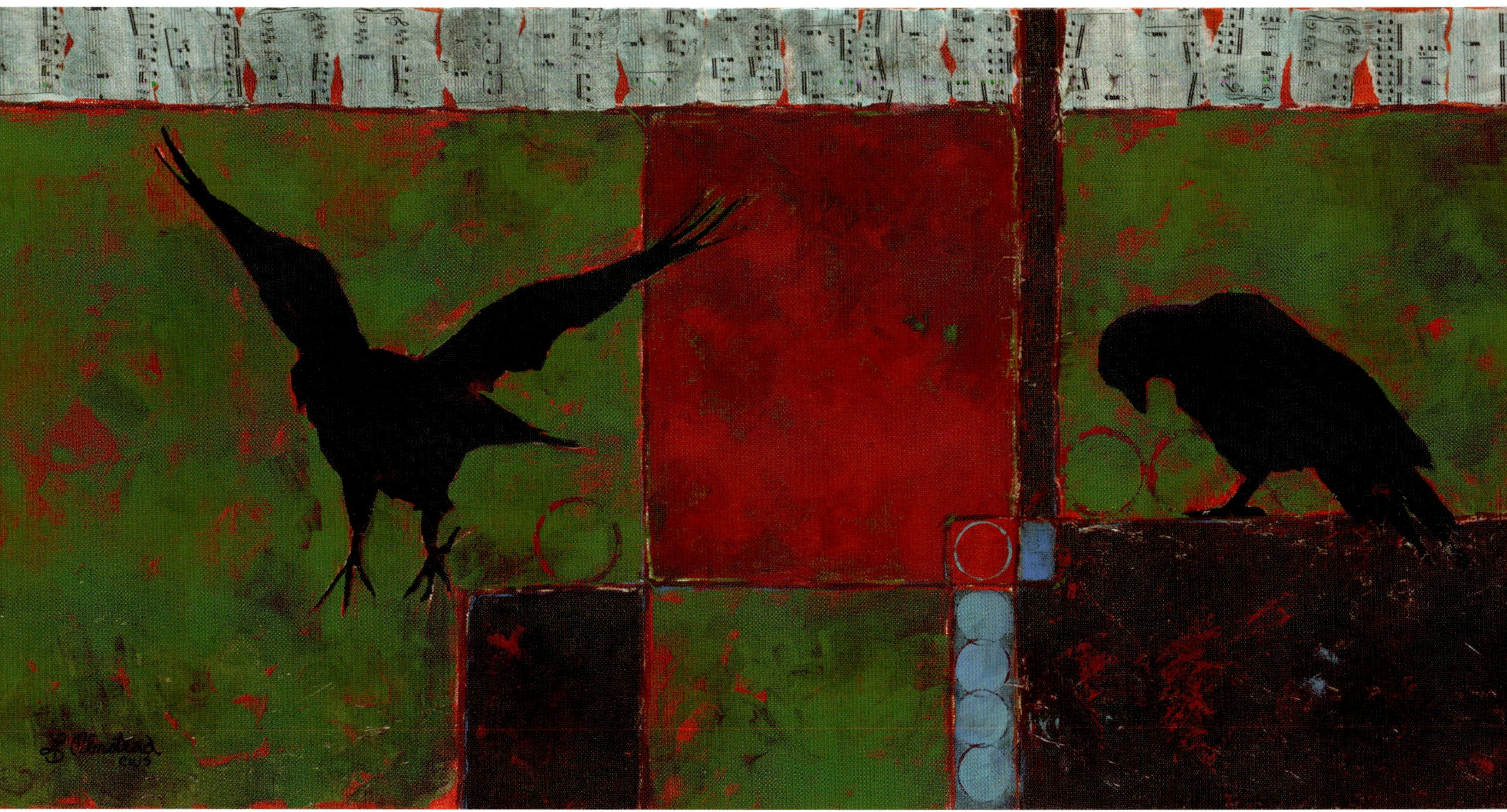

▶ GUITAR MAN: BLUES GUITAR | Suzanne McCourt
Acrylic and mixed media on canvas, 48" × 36" (122cm × 91cm)

When I was four and a half years old, my preschool teacher informed my mom I would become an artist. At six years old, I won a bike in an all-state drawing contest. After I became a nurse, insurance agent, coffee shop owner and mother of three, her prediction came true.

A brush with a benign brain tumor led me to expand my palette and make the change from watercolor to acrylic. In my vulnerability I found my own voice. I can't help but think that whatever I was going through in spirit transferred into this artwork and connected with people of all ages. It is my biggest seller to date.

To begin *Guitar Man: Blues Guitar* I experimented with mixed media and thus emerged a turning point in my career. I call my unique style of "painterly storytelling." I play by embedding handmade papers, imagery, photos, quotes and layers of acrylic. I hope to engage viewers with surprise by drawing them into the heart of the artwork.

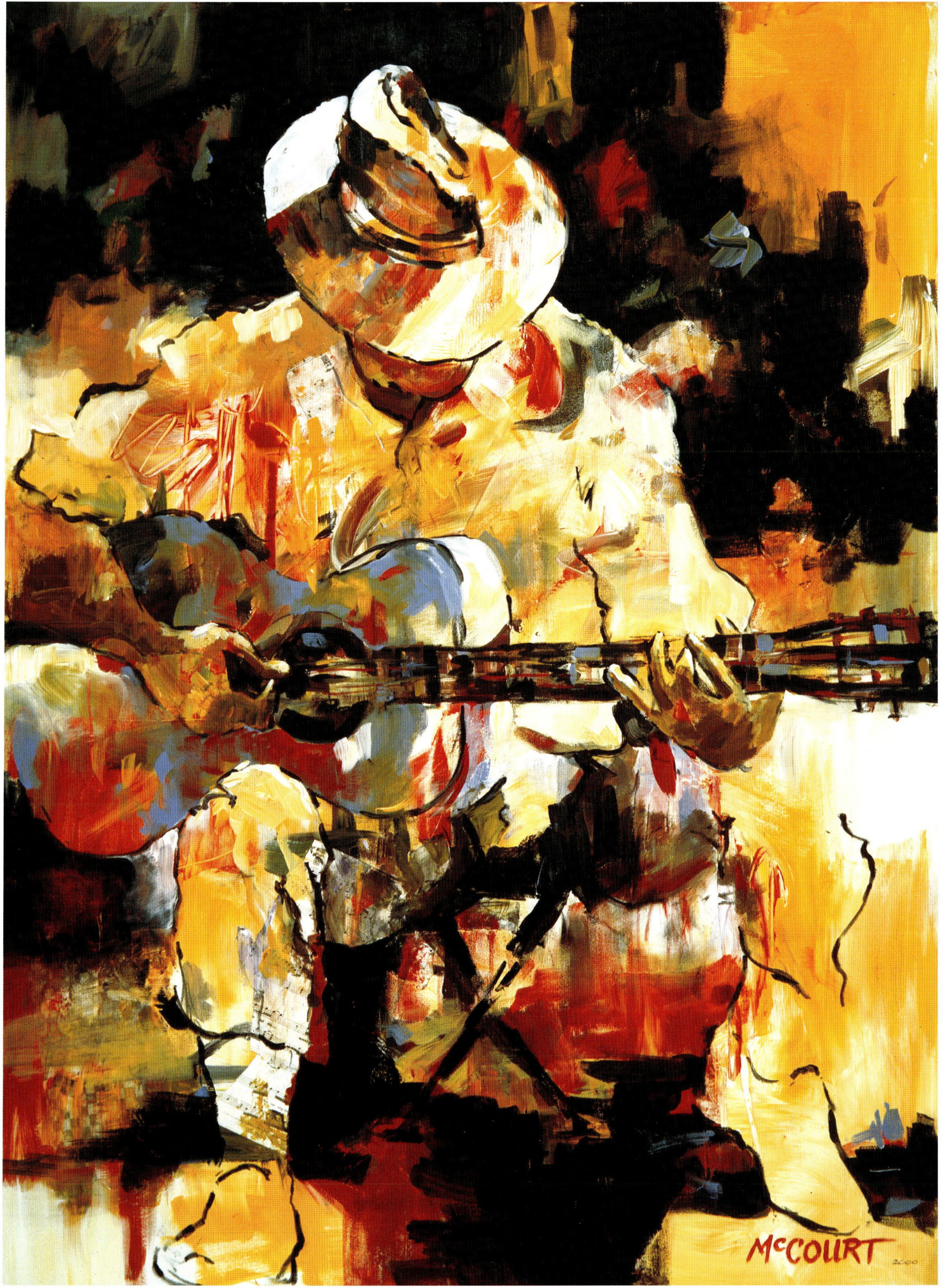
McCOURT

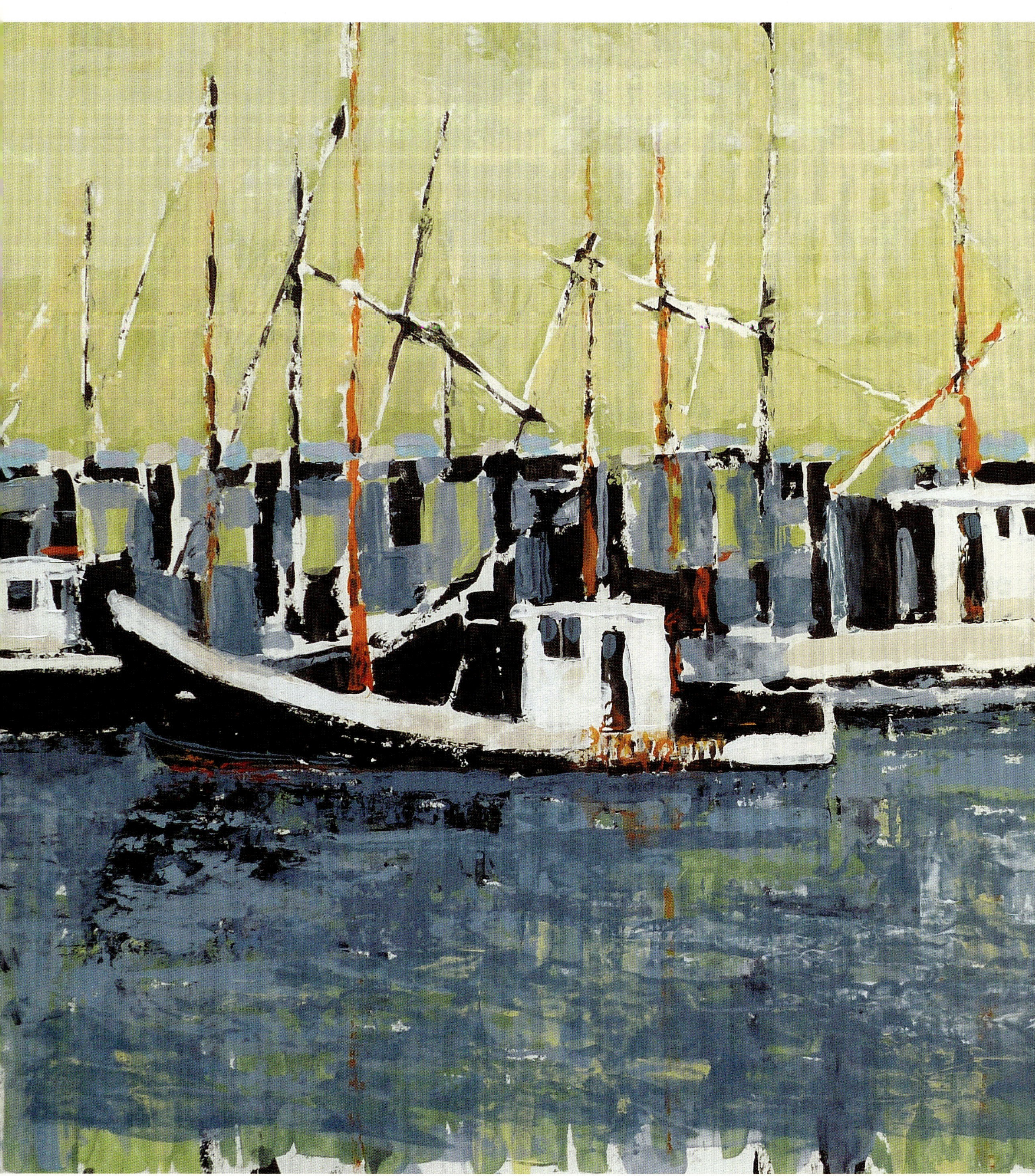

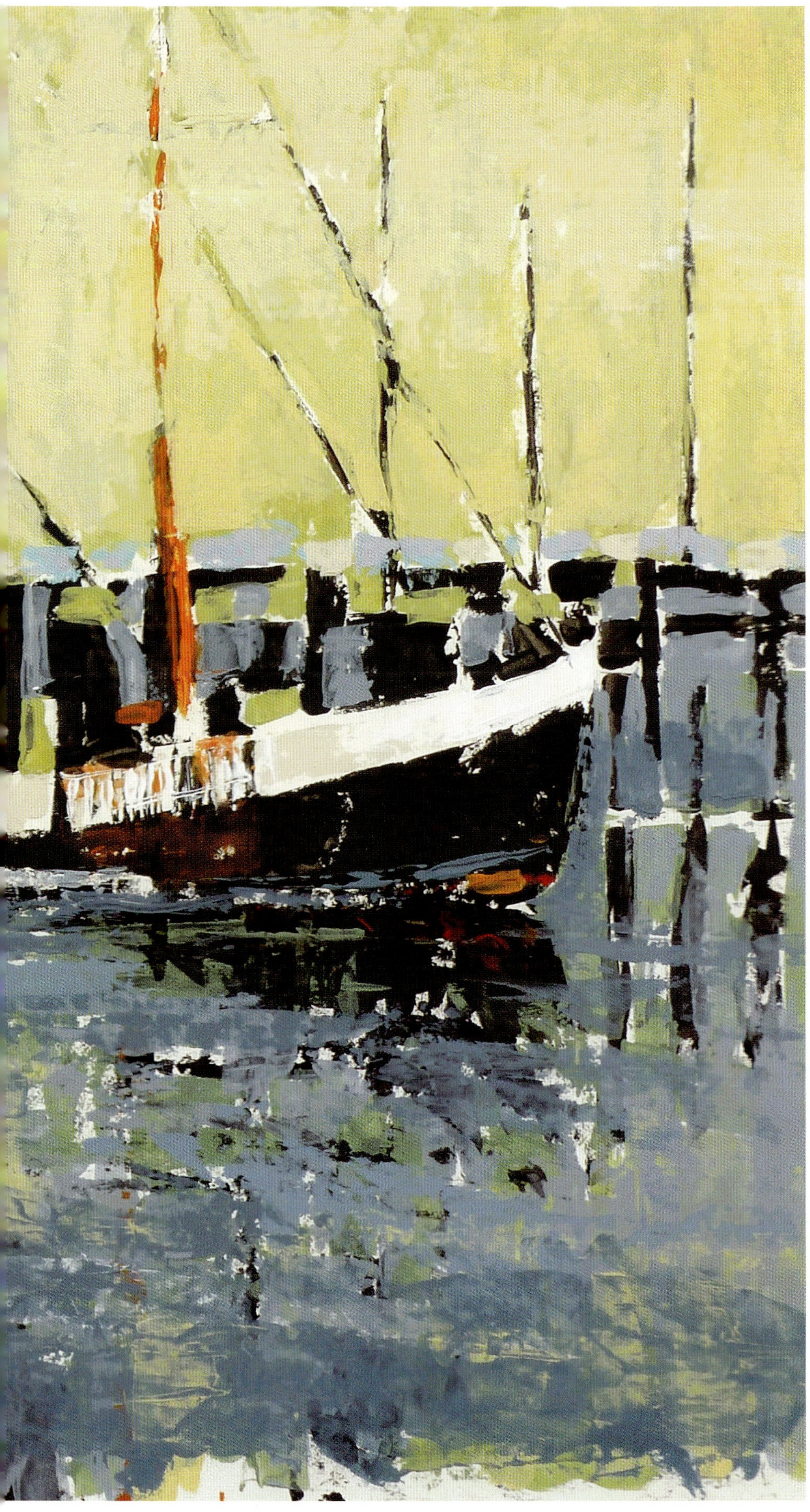

WORKING DOCKS LINEUP (AKA LINED UP IN BLUES) | Ann Trainor Domingue
Acrylic on watercolor paper mounted to Ampersand deep-cradled Gessobord
24" × 36" (61cm × 91cm)

I captured a series of reference snapshots rich in color and location specifics of hard-working fishermen who use this main wharf in Provincetown, Massachusetts. Back in my studio I worked on several ink and watercolor sketches to develop a semiabstract design structure. I began the final piece on 140-lb. (300gsm) hot-pressed watercolor paper by drawing bold black compositional lines with fluid acrylic paint, then adding and scraping away many transparent and opaque color layers building texture as I worked, primarily using a palette knife. The layering and scraping echoes the rough textures found on the wharf—boat paint, barnacles, weathered surfaces. I am interested in the imperfections, the rough beauty of the place. Acrylic paints and various other mediums allow me to change at my pace working alla prima, a benefit that suits my painting approach.

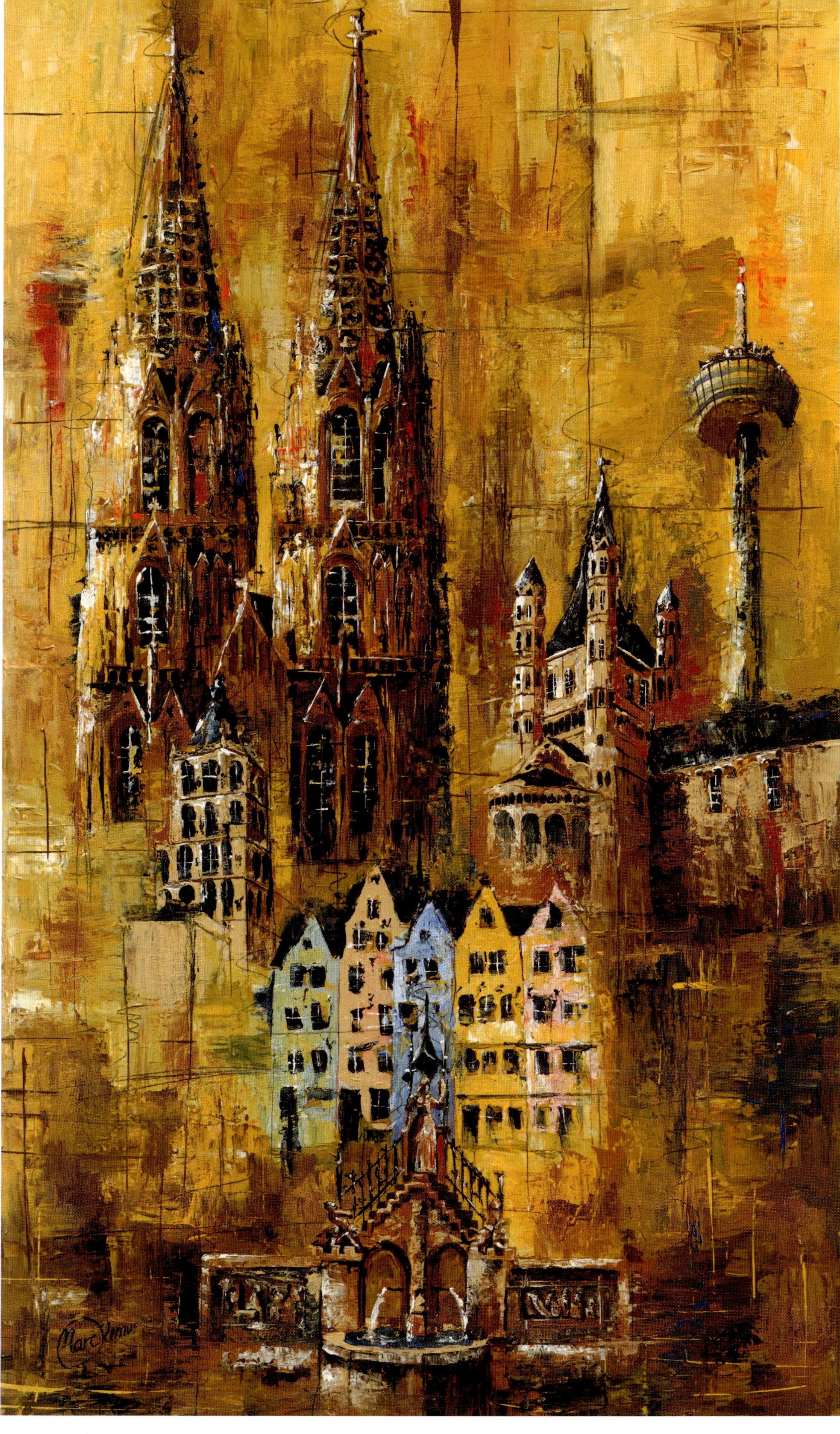

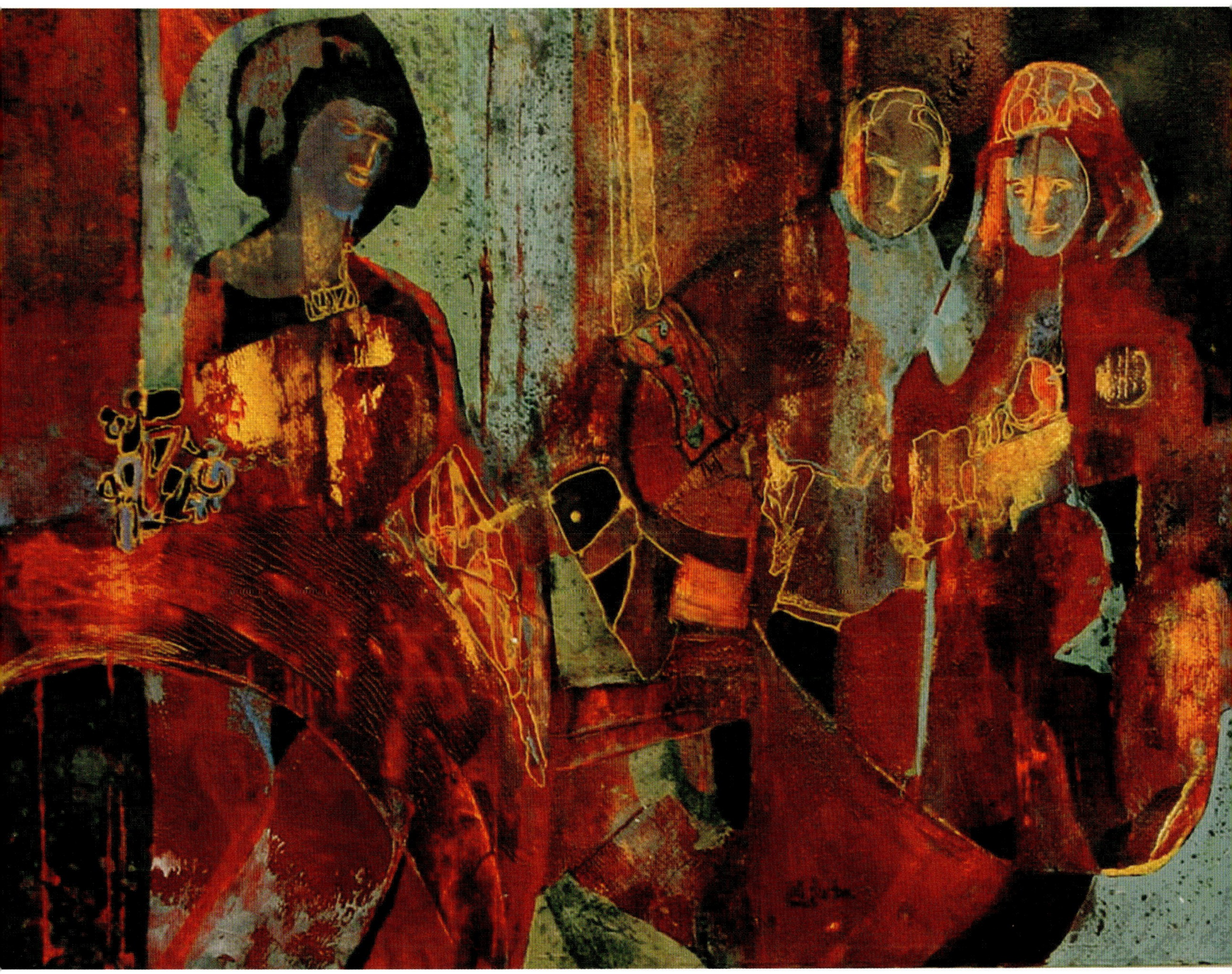

◀ EXPRESSIONS OF COLOGNE | Mark Remus
Acrylic on canvas with a matte medium finish, 55" × 31" (140cm × 79cm)

Since my studies at Art Center College of Design in Pasadena, California, I have worked with many different mediums and styles but have always come back to acrylic due to its versatile nature. Over the past ten years as a cityscape painter, I have rendered children's illustrations, created abstract compositions and painted over 200 cities in various styles, including pop art. A gallery in Cologne gave me my first solo show, thus making this city very special for me.

Traveling is a perfect tool to develop creative ideas. The more images you see in the world, the more you want to put them on canvas, helping your art to grow. This piece was solely created with palette knives. It was finished with a glossy varnish to give it the feel of an oil painting.

▲ THREESOME | Dotti Burton
Acrylic on 140-lb. (300gsm) soft-pressed Fabriano watercolor paper prepared with gold gesso, 14½" × 19¼" (37cm × 49cm)

Threesome emerged with figures that were not planned. However, once discovered, they became my painting inspiration. Creating a good composition was a problem as the painting seemed to be split in the middle. I solved this problem by putting a panel of blue on the top portion, dividing the left and right sections into unequal shapes. Carla O'Connor's teaching inspired me to add small symbols on the figure's clothing, which was my first-time use of this design technique. While the paint was still damp, I lightly sprayed small areas, then placed tissue over the area and rolled a brayer over the tissue to expose either the gold gesso underpainting or the painted layer underneath, creating multiple layers of paint and texture.

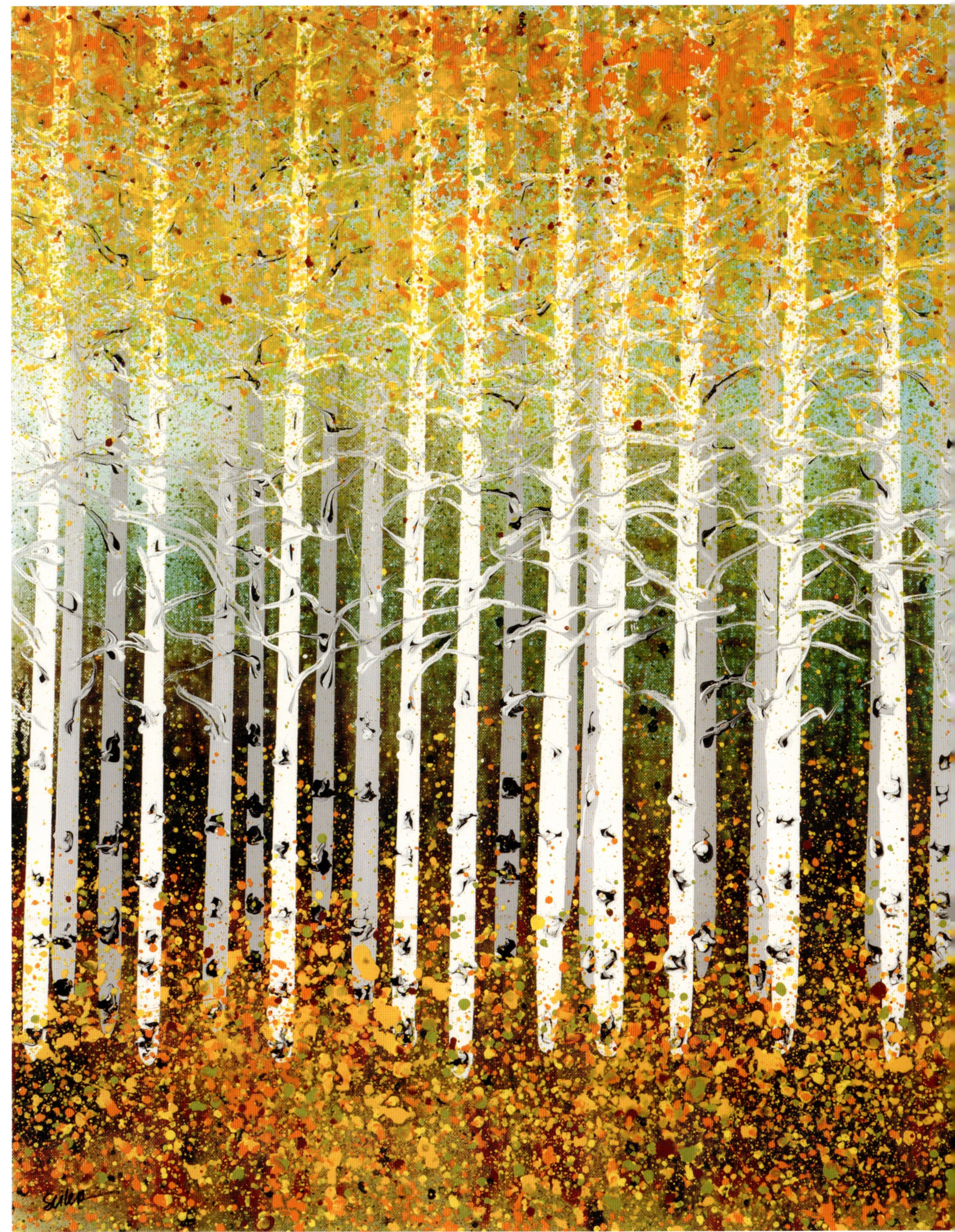

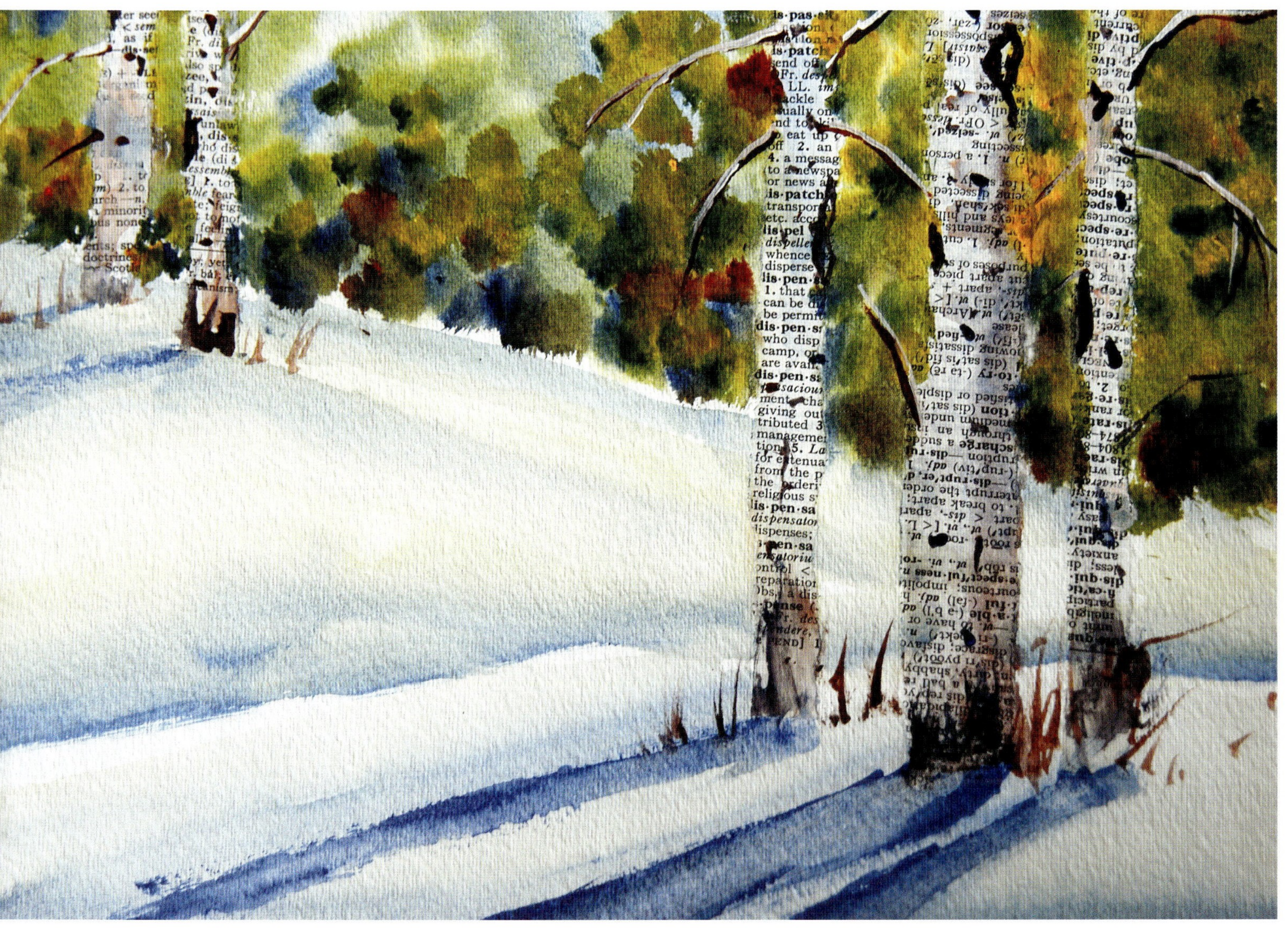

◀ ASPENS XX | Nancy Seiler
Fluid acrylic on canvas, 30" × 24" (76cm × 61cm)

Aspens XX, painted in my studio in 2013, is the twentieth rendition of my work *Aspens Up Basin Creek* created during a month-long artist residency exploring fluid acrylics in Basin, Montana, in 2010. I am inspired by colors and textures in nature and usually have just a smattering of an idea when I start to paint. I lay the canvas flat and start painting big and fast, letting the paint and water move and blend. I may tilt the canvas to create even more movement. Then I continue to build up layers until I'm satisfied. I usually have many paintings that I work on simultaneously.

▲ WINTER SENTINELS | Patricia Coulter
Acrylic with mixed media on 140-lb. (300gsm) cold-pressed paper
9" × 12" (23cm × 30cm)

After deciding on an idea, I began by adhering pieces and bits of paper from my everyday life—receipts, a narrow strip from a fortune cookie, a piece torn from a newspaper—to a blank canvas. Once dry, I began adding paint in loose washes and drips, turning the canvas upside down and experimenting with various ideas. Then more paint, more drips, possibly more paper collage. At the end I added a few details, possibly with ink and paint.

I have found this method to be tremendously liberating! No more am I paralyzed by the fear of a white canvas. I look at it as though it is already marked up and just join in! I love how the pieces of glued paper and the basic shapes of preliminary color washes take me from thinking it has to be a representational painting to one of an abstract quality.

I use the influence of the prairie landscape for the basics of my paintings. I have some tentative plans in mind when I start but I wait until I've glued some papers, etc. and see what shapes they suggest. I do envision what I want to say, but at the same time I'm working out the elements of the painting—line, shapes, color, value—while being aware of establishing a strong composition.

WHEN IN DOUBT | Myrna Wacknov
Acrylic over liquid watercolor on Yupo, 20" × 26" (51cm × 66cm)

My imagery is almost always a face, but my goal is to experiment with the various elements of art and a combination of materials to create a unique, unexpected and exciting visual experience. In *When in Doubt*, I started with liquid watercolor on Yupo synthetic paper to create texture. I then mixed acrylic medium into the liquid watercolor for a transparent nonliftable layer and continued to build the painting with progressively more opaque layers of acrylic. The extreme cropping and vibrant, unusual color choices contributed to my objective for an expressive and entertaining painting of a most expressive and vibrant individual.

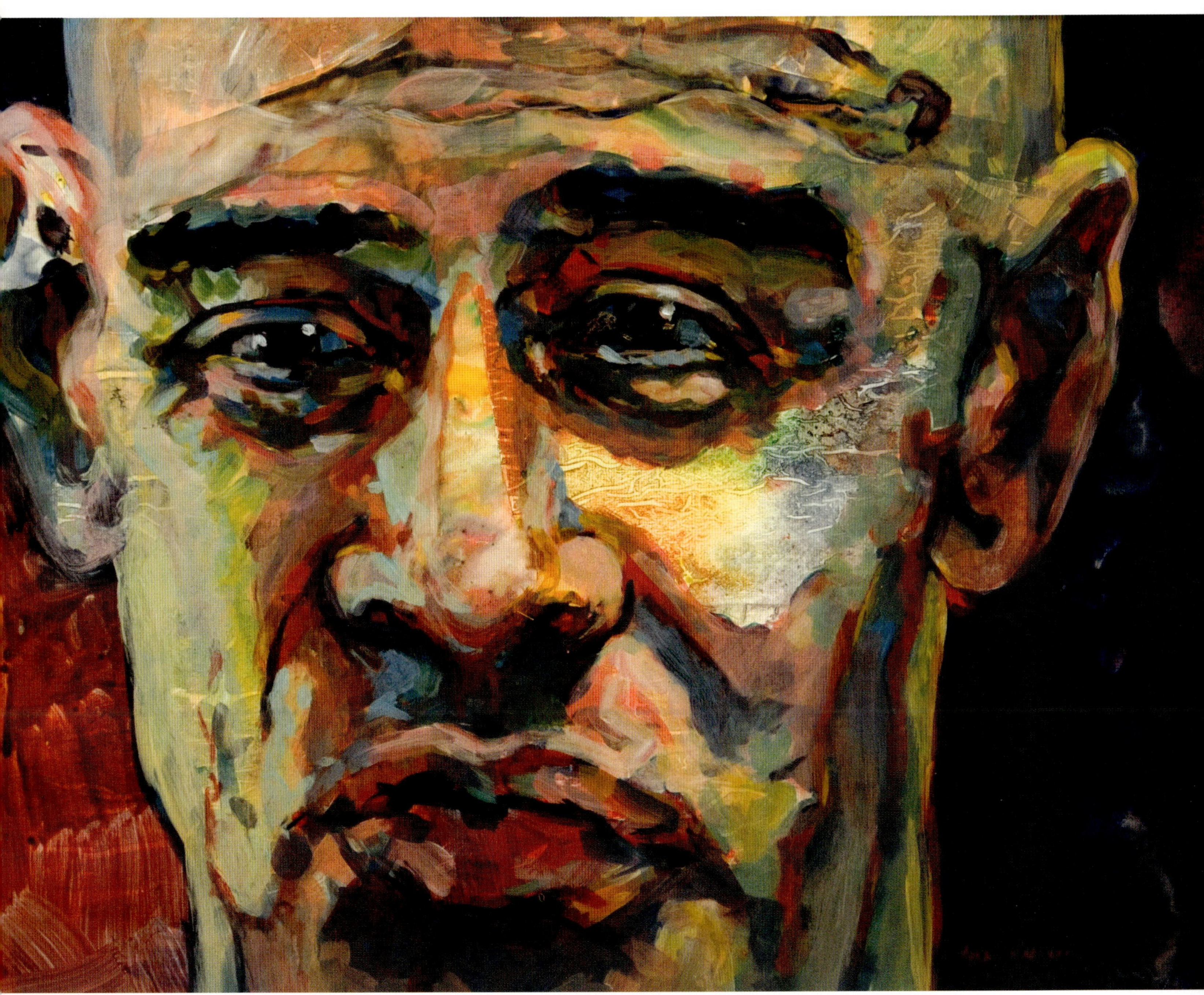

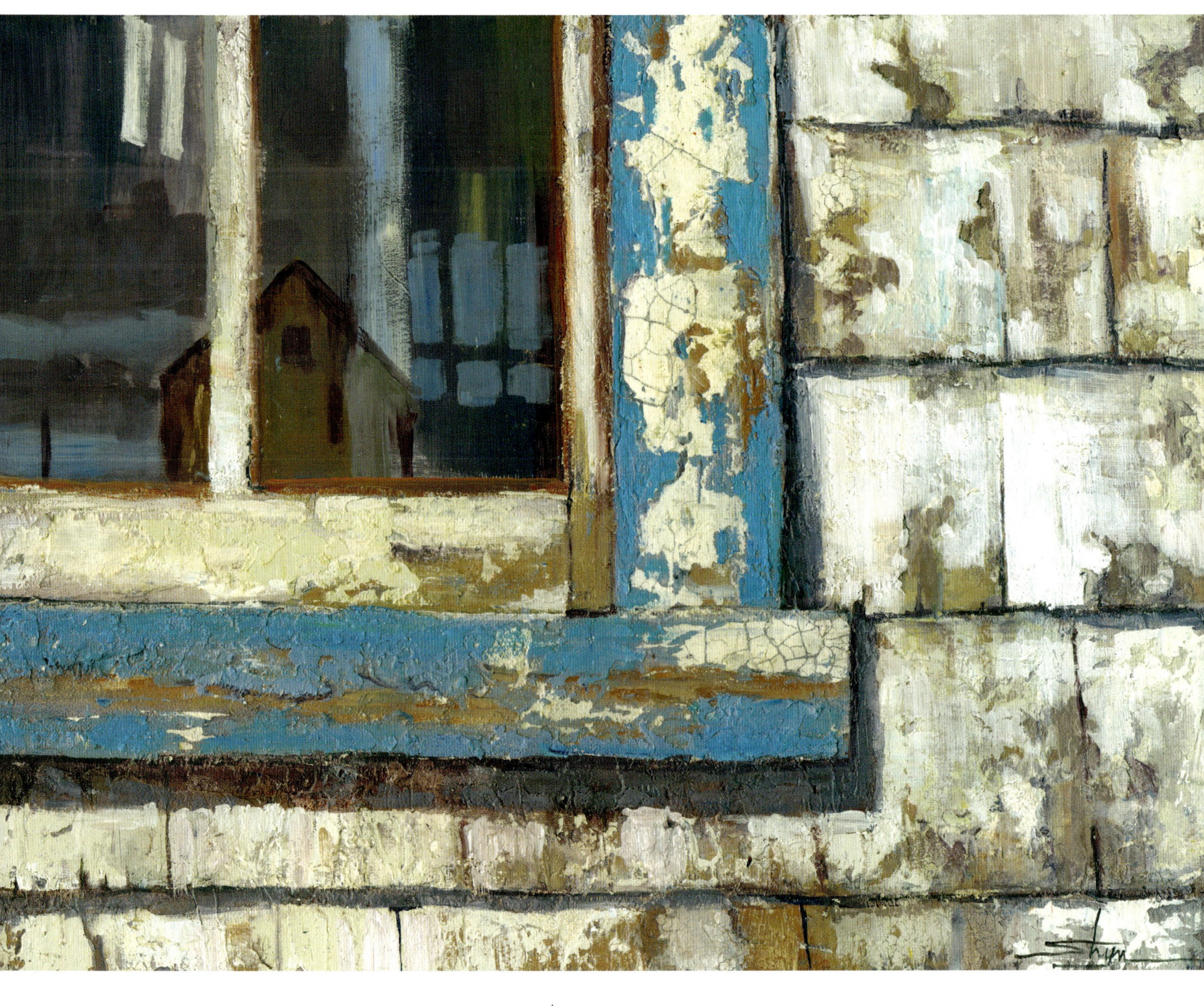

AMERICANA | Dianna Shyne
Acrylic and acrylic mediums on Ampersand Masonite, 18" × 24" (46cm × 61cm)

Recently I used many of the buildings from North Russia's Prince Edward Island as reference for a series of paintings based on abstract compositions with realistic detail. This image was chosen because I could see into and through the building as well as the reflected village in the window. I began by trimming my photograph into an abstract design. After mapping out the values with washes of thinned acrylic, I used a palette knife to lay on heavy molding and crackle pastes. When all that was dry, thin washes of fluid acrylics were applied. A sander was used to recover whites and establish textures. I finished with heavy body acrylics. I used cracked paint and rippled windows to express a slower, simpler era. By saying less about the whole building, I said more about the poetic quality of the aging process and the movement of time.

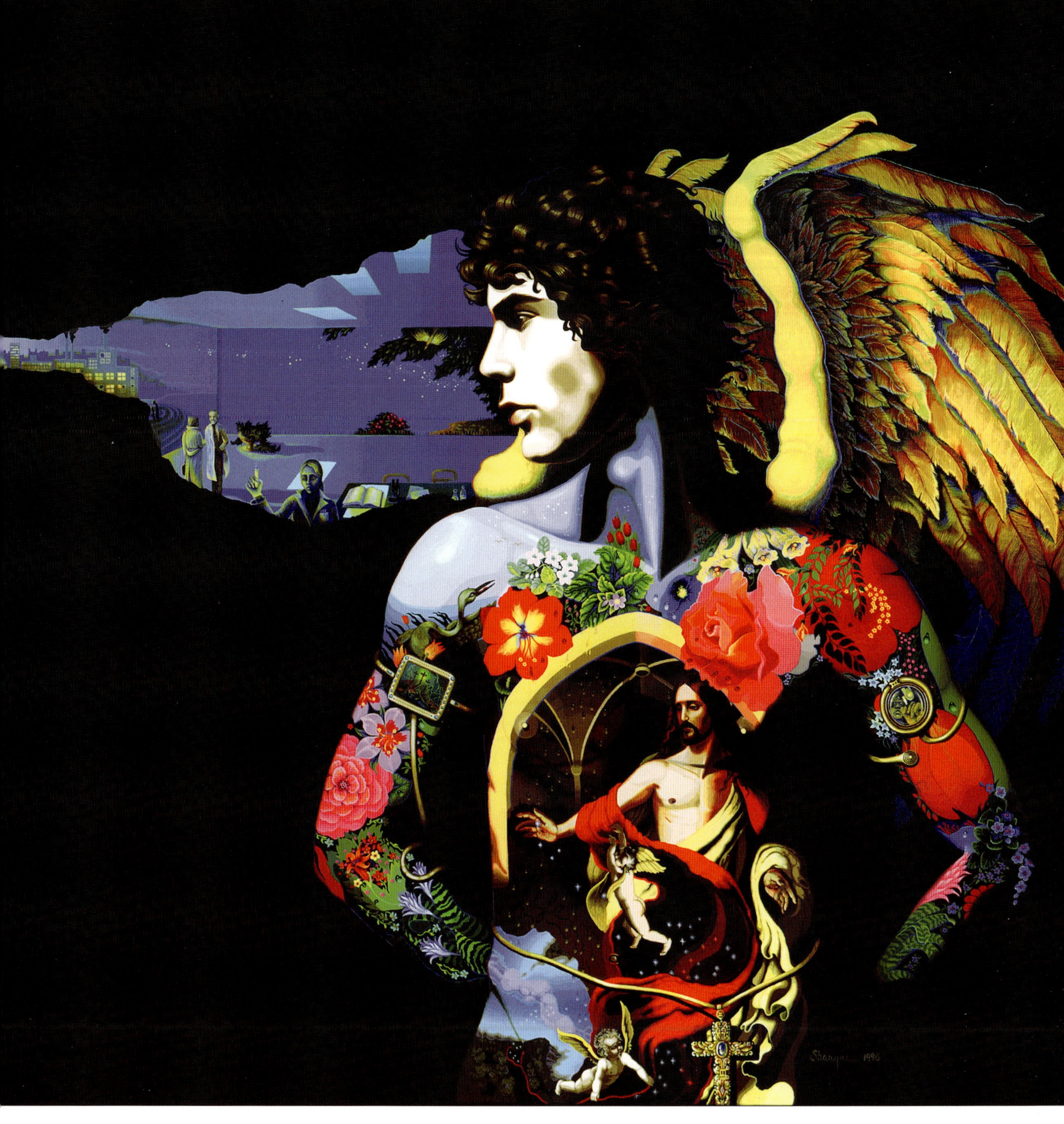

THE TATTOOED ANGEL | Sharyne E. Walker
Acrylic on linen mounted on hardboard, 36" × 36" (91cm × 91cm)

I use a basic photo reference and study faces of interesting and beautiful people. My ritual for painting begins in the bath where I cleanse and clear my thoughts. My visualization always happens while I am in water. My easel is set up next to a large wall mirror so I can check the image reflection as I progress. My imagination is used more than reference photos, but if I need close-up details, I study my features in the mirror. I have a multitude of ceiling lights with natural spectrum. The dimensions of the painting include the angel and what he is witness to, including a reflection of me painted in the gemstone on his left arm.

"Transcend the obvious."

—KATHLEEN YOKOUCHI

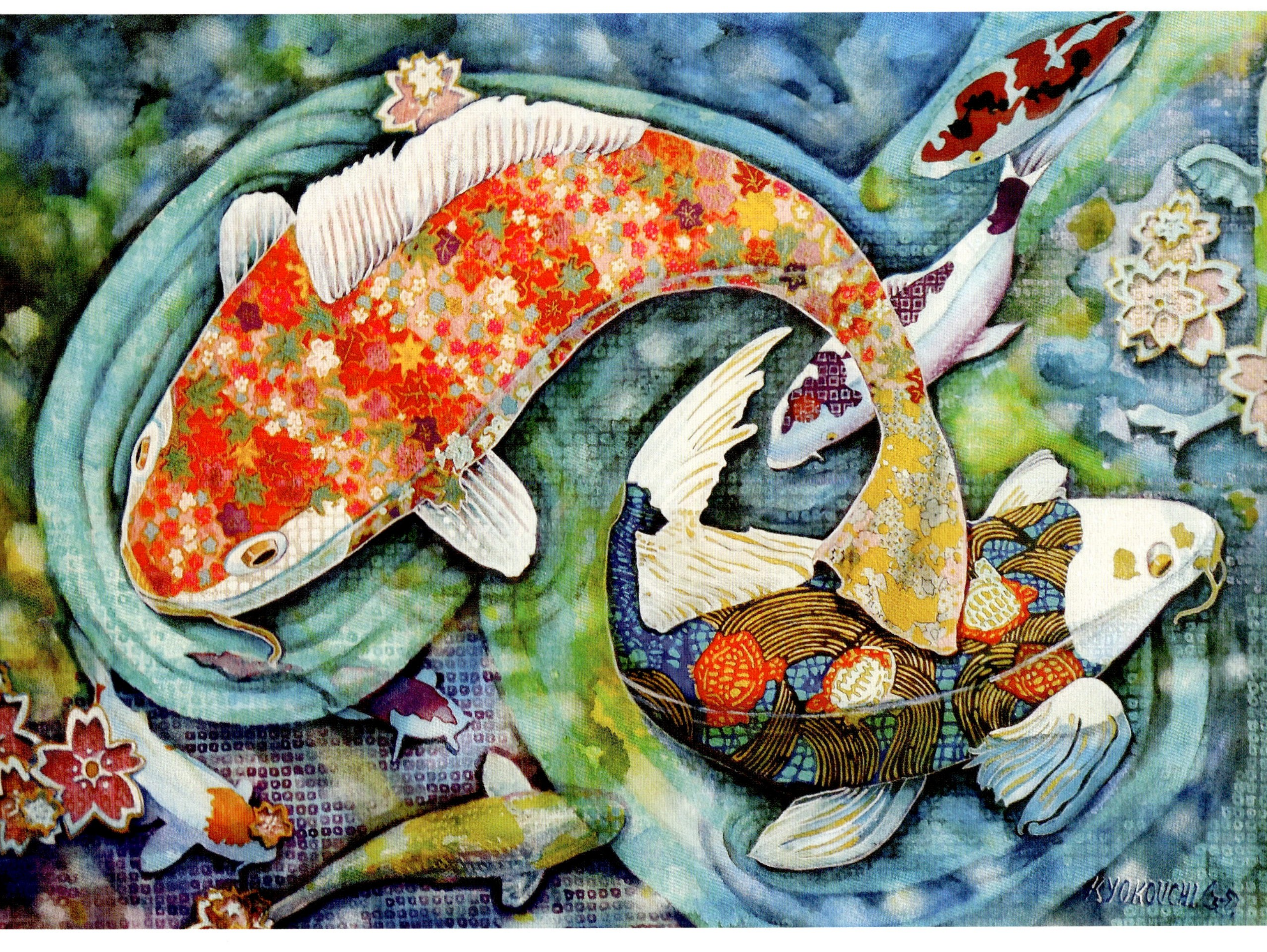

GOOD LUCK AND PROSPERITY! | Kathleen Yokouchi
Acrylic on 400-lb. (850gsm) cold-pressed textured paper, 12" × 18" (30cm × 46cm)

Rather than traditional Asian koi swimming upstream with calligraphy to convey good luck and prosperity, I wanted the koi to embody the blessings. I sketched live koi and used acrylic washes to depict the movement of their bodies and the water to convey the energy and joy of these blessings. For prosperity, I used rich colors and textures that only acrylic paints allow. Fish scales became bright flowers and symbols found in kimono and obi (sash) brocade. The overall painting has the texture of *shibori* (Japanese tie-dyeing). I used applicator squeeze bottles filled with heavy body acrylic colors to outline each flower to obtain a cloisonné effect.

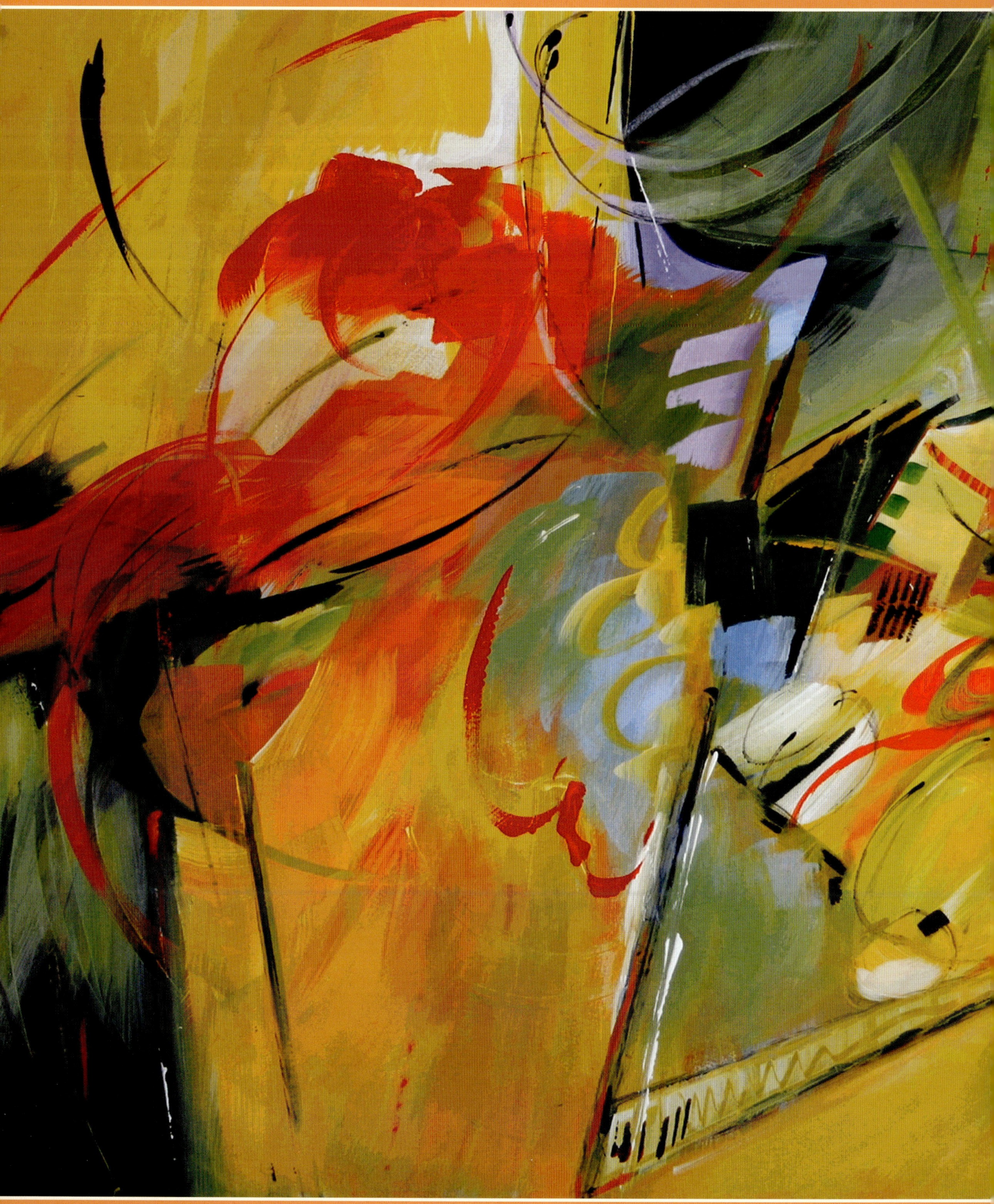

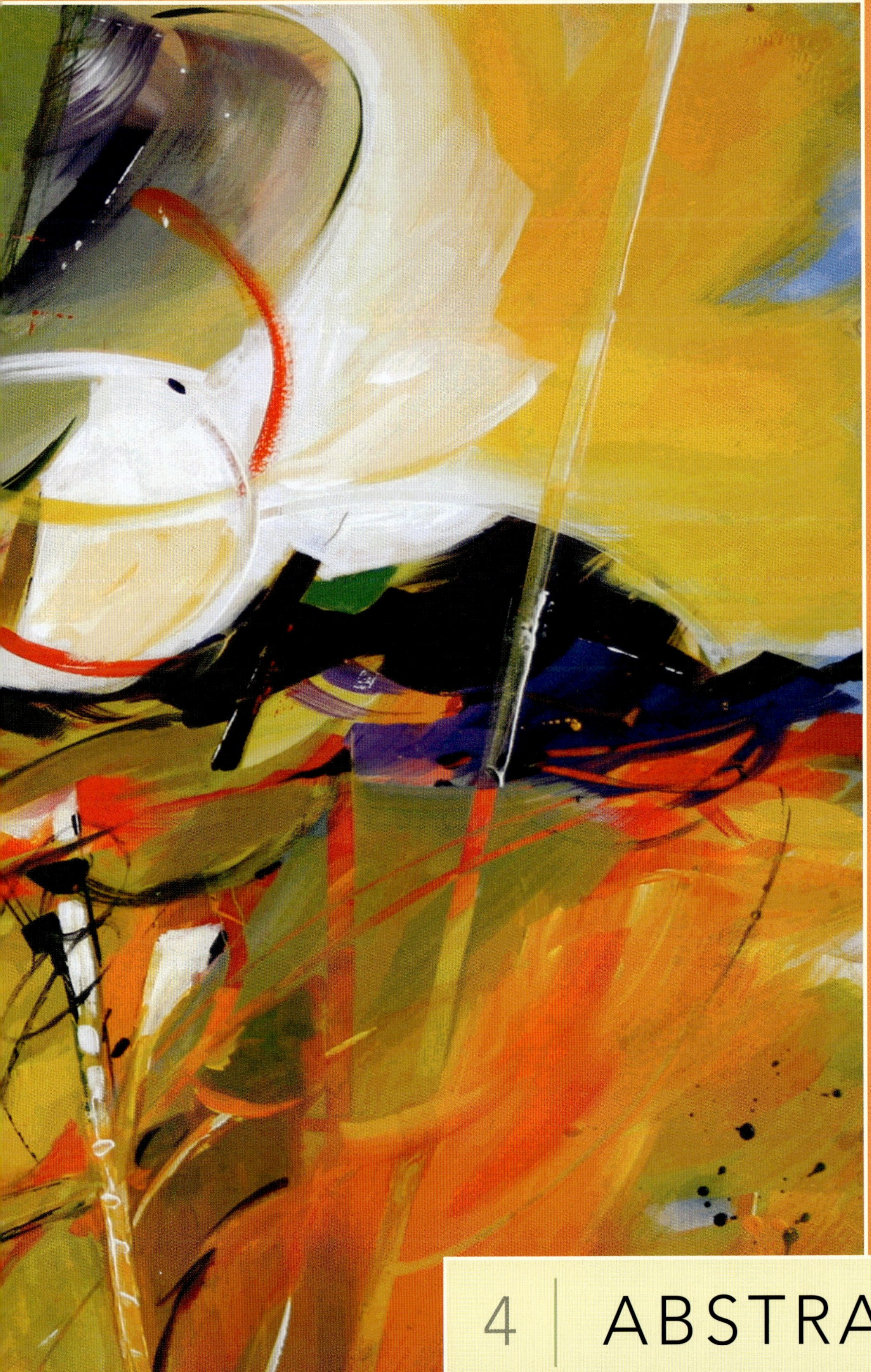

BURST OF COLOR
Denise Athanas
Acrylic on 300-lb. (640gsm)
hot-pressed paper
22" × 30" (56cm × 76cm)

Each of my paintings begins with the seed of an idea or mood and evolves slowly. I paint what I feel and want others to see. I began *Burst of Color* by brushing shapes of color onto hot-pressed paper in order to create design interest. I kept adding rich pigments to different areas. I selected shapes that worked to spontaneously create a more solid design. I like to work quickly using wide brushes. I spend days viewing my painting turned in different directions to see the various shapes, looking at their size and how they relate to one another. By using this approach I am able to paint with a free spirit and take advantage of any accidents that might happen. I experience the joy of painting when I am emotionally involved. I always make my decisions intuitively. The joy lies in the finished painting when I analyze it for good design and find that everything works together. Then I know the painting is born of my spirit.

4 | ABSTRACTIONS

BLOCKING COLOR | Carol A. Gatchel
Acrylic on gallery-wrapped canvas, 30" × 30" (76cm × 76cm)

Four years ago I switched from using watercolors to acrylics. Using the different gels, mediums and molding paste with acrylics provided more texture and expressive possibilities than painting with watercolor. For *Blocking Color* I had no preconceived idea. I began with the colors I use most: Australian Sienna, Phthalo Turquoise, Quinacridone Purple and gold. Next I focused on shapes, contrasting sizes and value. Smooth texture and three-dimensional forms added depth. As an essential element, linework created movement and flow. The tools I used for the linework were palette knives, colored pencils and water-soluble wax pastels.

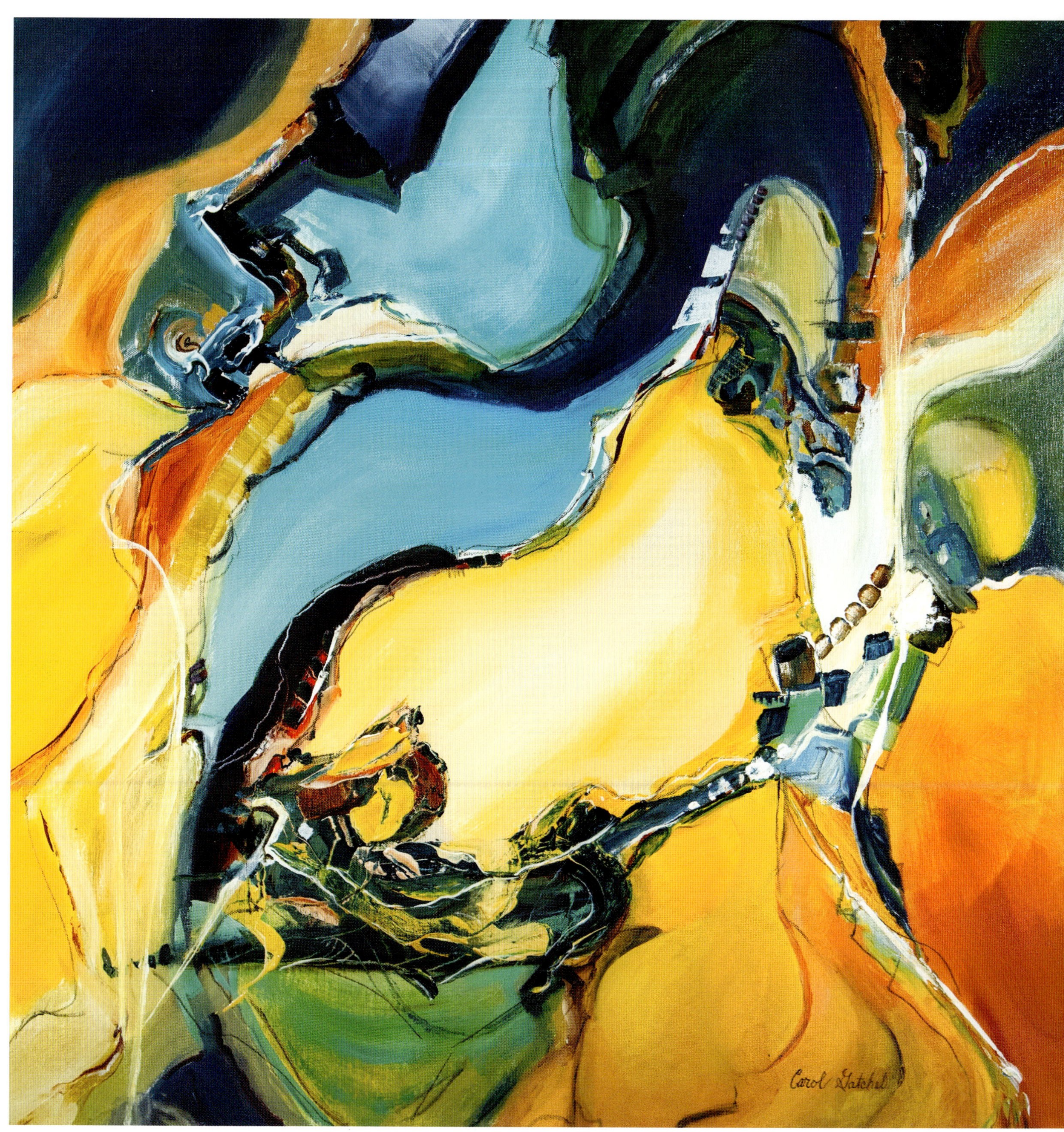

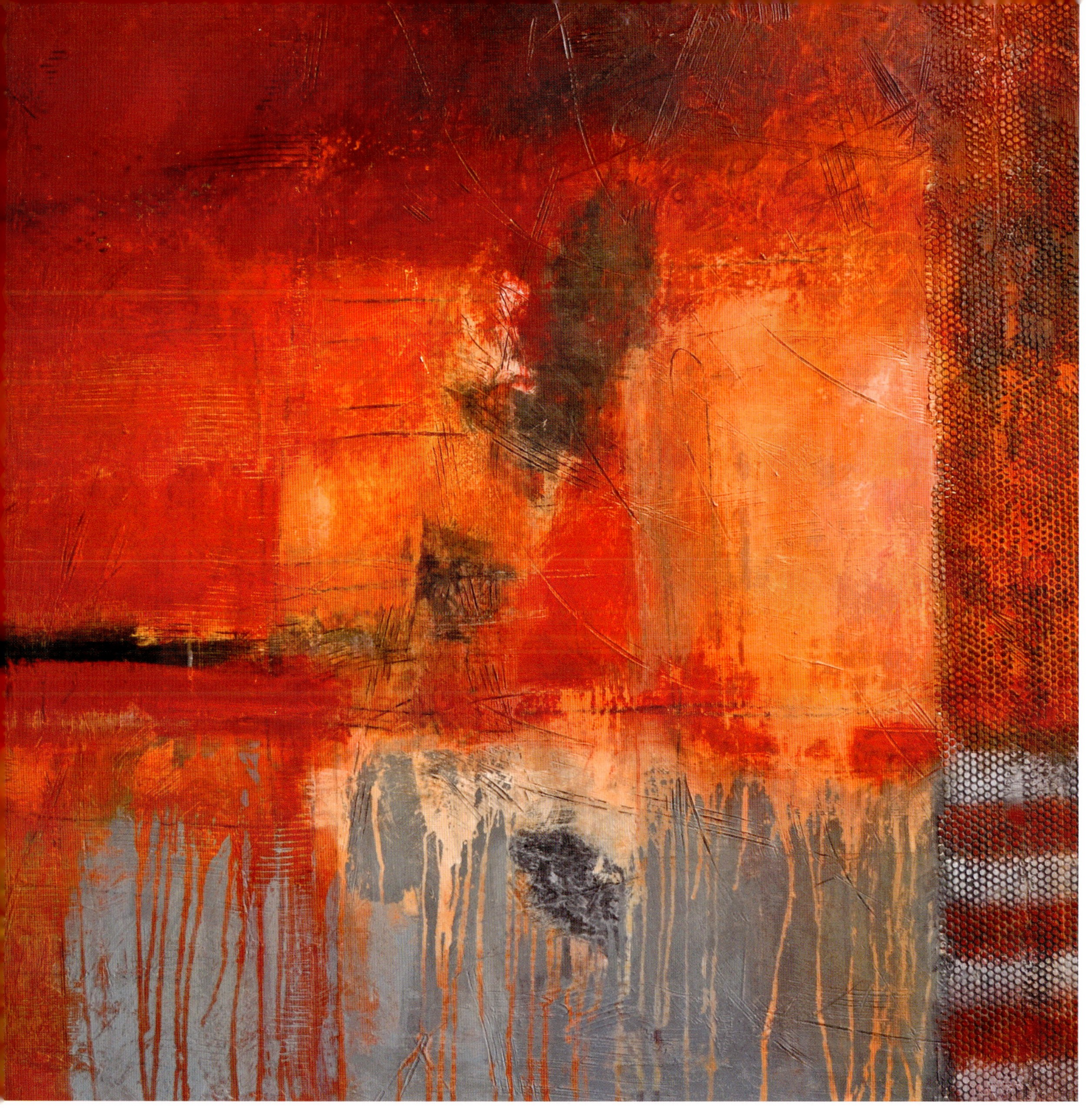

A MATTER TO CONSIDER | Filomena de Andrade Booth
Acrylic on canvas, 40" × 40" (102cm × 102cm)

I rarely begin a painting with a preconceived idea in mind but instead prefer to let it take on a life of its own as I guide it into completion. Frequently I'll get to the point that I call the "ugly stage." This is where the real challenge begins as I shape the painting into existence. This may involve adding more texture, scraping, gouging, adding and subtracting color until I begin to see the form that it will eventually take. If I reach an impasse, I just begin all over by gessoing the entire surface of the canvas. As drastic as this may sound, I actually like working over a bad painting because the underlying colors and textures frequently pop up through the new painting. In fact, this painting was painted over another painting that had not worked out for me.

"Don't ever get so attached to a painting that it frustrates you. Just reach for the gesso and start again."

—FILOMENA DE ANDRADE BOOTH

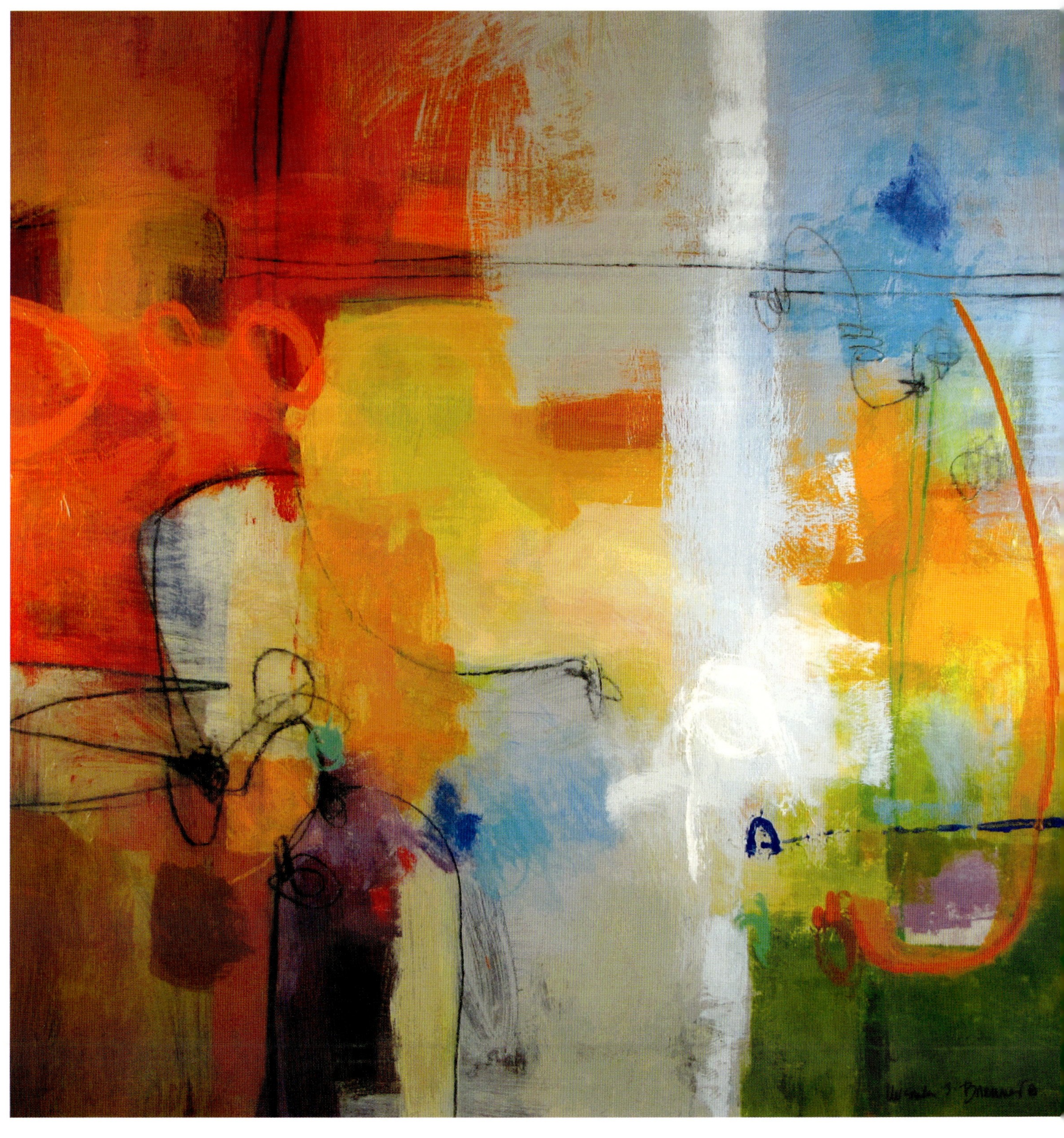

DANCING | Ursula J. Brenner
Acrylic on canvas, 40" × 40" (102cm × 102cm)

The canvas upon which I paint gets stapled to a 50-foot (15m) wall in my studio. I mask off the canvas and then put on a layer of Golden Extra Heavy Gel before I start my painting process. Sometimes I have a general idea of what I want to paint, but I am always open to happy accidents. The painting always tells me what it wants as it progresses. I step aside and simply listen. Painting is about making decisions. I love acrylics because I paint fast and I love the freedom it gives me in my process. The beautiful thing about acrylics is that there are no mistakes in painting; if you don't like it, just paint over it!

MOMENT IN TIME | Ursula J. Brenner
Acrylic on canvas, 40" × 40" (102cm × 102cm)

My work generally tends to be abstract, but composition, values, rhythm and interplay of colors are important to help make the work interesting. I use Lukas Cryl acrylics and Golden paint in my work exclusively. I like to thin my paint with Liquitex Gloss Medium Varnish to help obtain beautiful glazes of color. I am also partial to using Caran d'Ache Neocolor II crayons for my linework, scribbles and scrumbles.

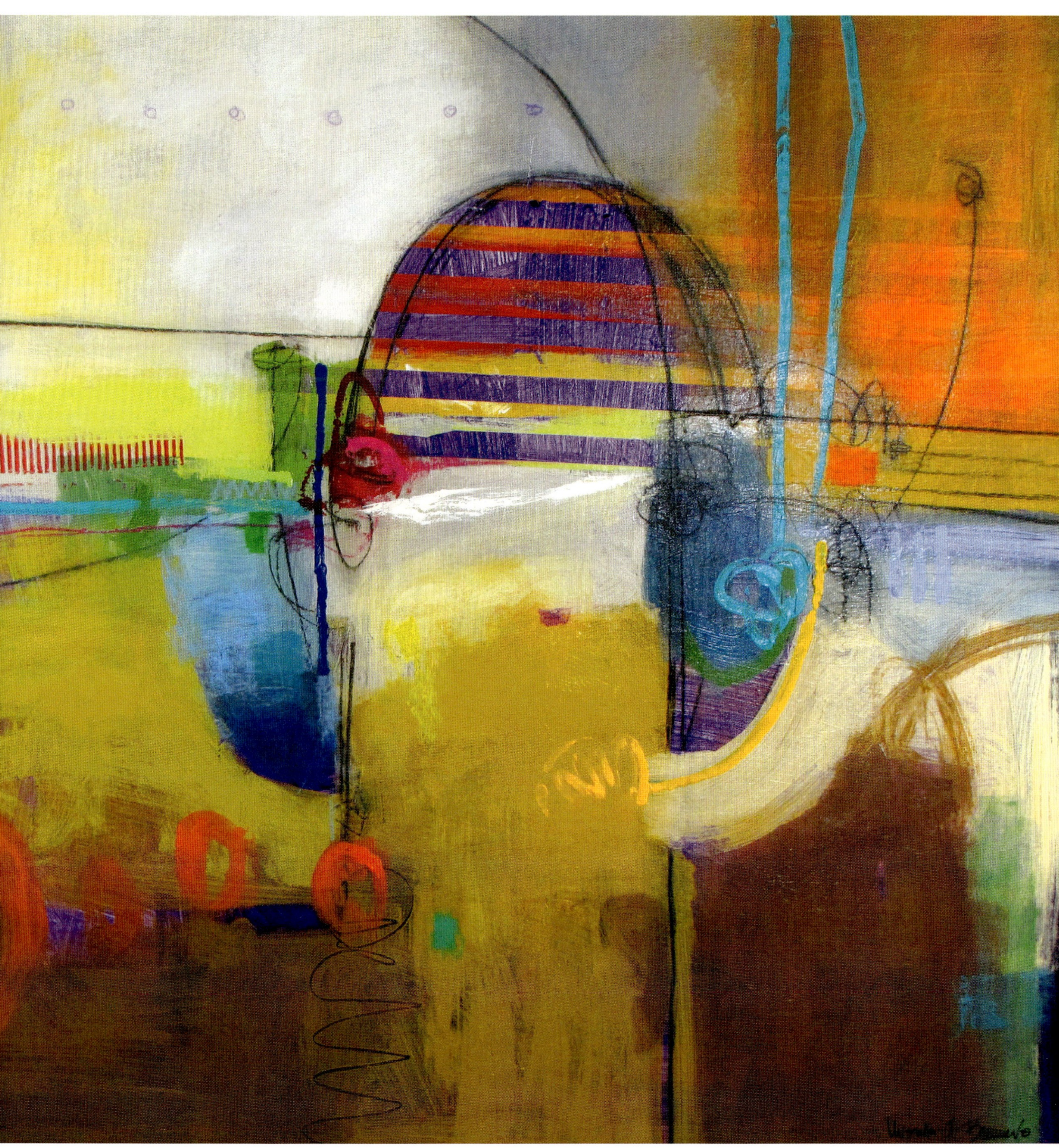

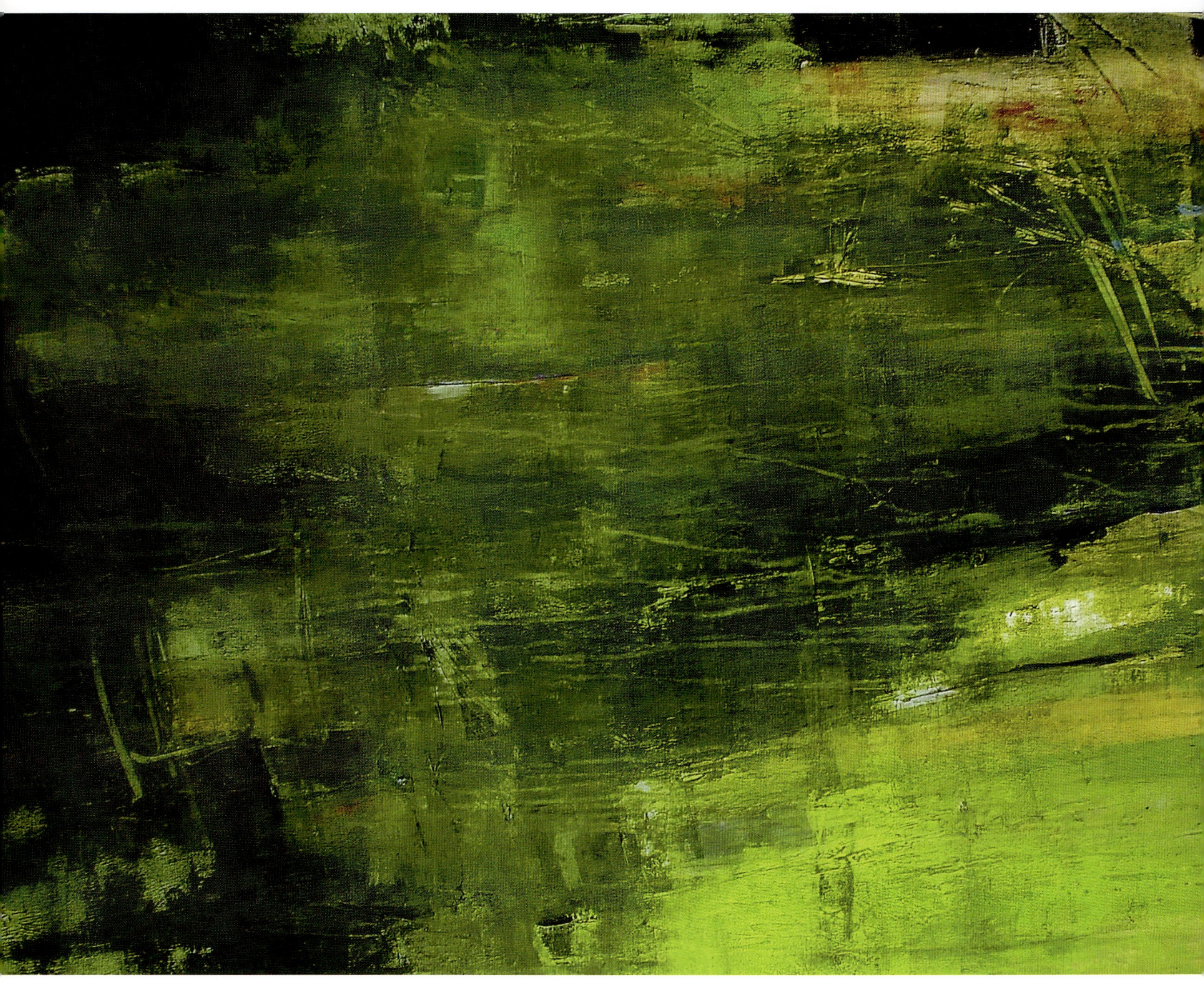

PIERIAN SPRINGS | Jan Brown
Acrylic on canvas, 36" × 48" (91cm × 122cm)

I began *Pierian Springs* in my studio, layering and spreading the acrylic paints with brayers and scrapers on a vertical format. I enjoy acrylic paint because of the speed in which it dries; it matches my own speed quite nicely. I grew a little frustrated with the painting and decided to take a break and look at it upstairs. I started to turn the painting as I often do and when I saw it in this horizontal position, it was like BINGO! I knew I was done! The title came from a search through mythology. Pierian Springs is said to be where the Muses went to get their inspiration. Alexander Pope popularized it in a couplet in the poem *An Essay on Criticism* (1709): "A little learning is a dang'rous thing: Drink deep, or taste not the Pierian spring."

GREEN FRENZY | Loren Kovich
Acrylic on canvas, 40" × 30" (102cm × 76cm)

The inspiration for this painting and most of my acrylic paintings comes from the many trout-filled streams and rivers in Montana. A few years ago I decided to loosen up and experiment with acrylics instead of my usual medium, watercolor. I usually paint the fish first and then let the thinned-down acrylic flow and do its thing. Once one wash dries, I glaze over it with another wash of a different color, sometimes using up to ten washes to achieve the effect I want. For *Green Frenzy* I used blues, greens, oranges, yellows and gold as a final touch to give some sparkle to the water.

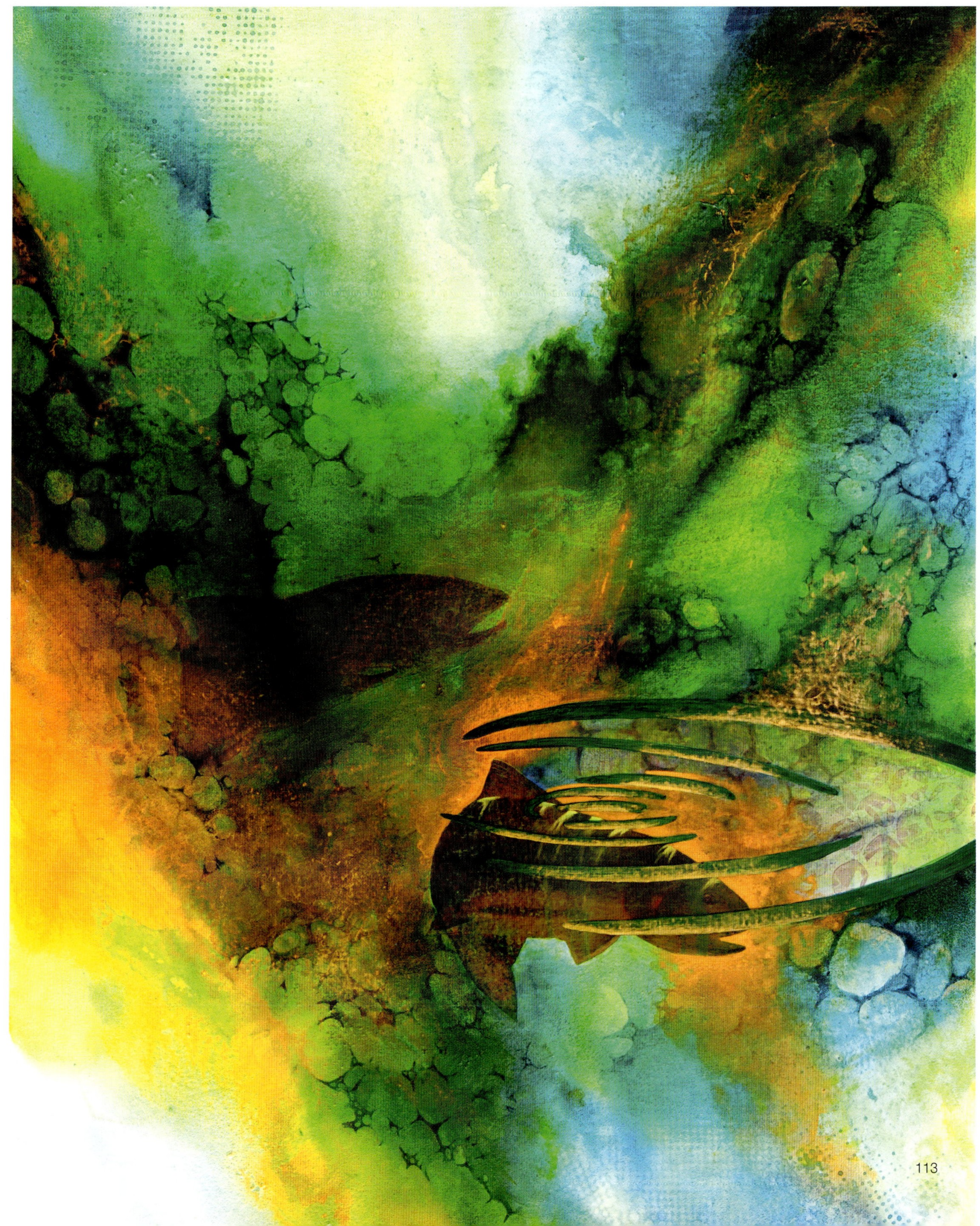

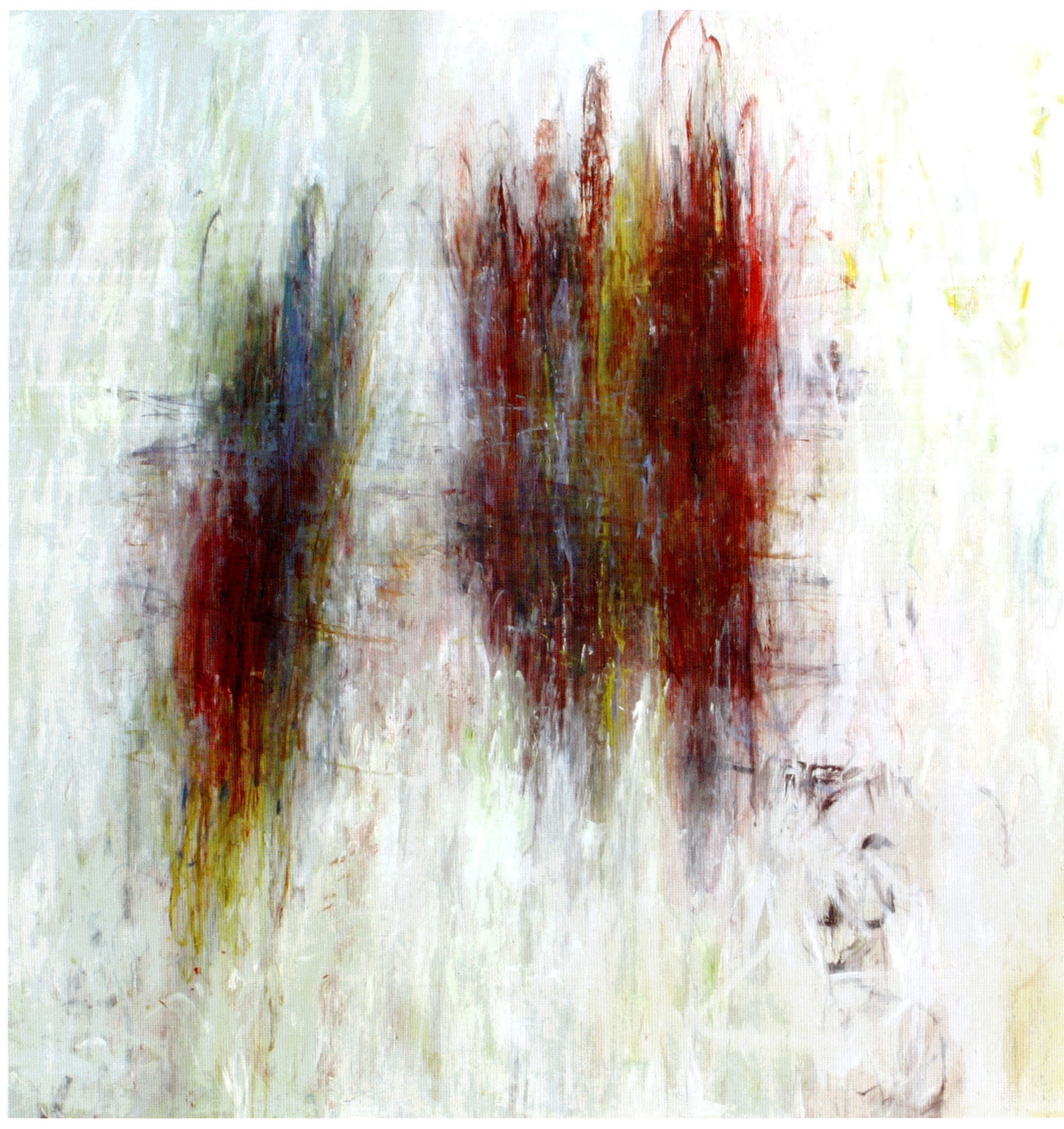

▲ CELEBRATING YIN | Brenda Hope Zappitell
Acrylic with cold wax on panel, 60" × 60" (152cm × 152cm)

I have painted consistently in acrylics for more than twenty years. As an abstract expressionist painter, acrylics suit my creative process well, giving me the ability to move from layer to layer quickly and intuitively. My most treasured tool is a spray bottle with water, which blurs the gestures and enables me to find the unexpected. The flexibility of the faster drying time and using water with acrylics are both reasons that I consistently use only this medium. I have tried other mediums and always ended up back with acrylics.

▶ MIRAGE | Priscilla Greenbaum
Acrylic with watercolor and gouache accents on 140-lb. (300gsm) cold-pressed Arches, 20" × 16" (51cm × 41cm)

I yearned to paint the story of the stark beauty of the Nevadan high desert and capture the feeling of shimmering heat rising high into the atmosphere, creating mirages. Initially I sketched to get to know the land, but once in the studio, I relied on memory to transform mountainous desert imagery into an abstract design, paying particular attention to the placement of lights and darks. Using a cool tonal color palette of brown and blues accented with crimson and gold, much of the painting was done in thin acrylic washes. To pull the foreground forward and provide textural variety, the desert flora was stamped. White gouache was washed over areas to unify and tie elements together and provide a sense of shimmer and mystery. Is there really a stream in sight?

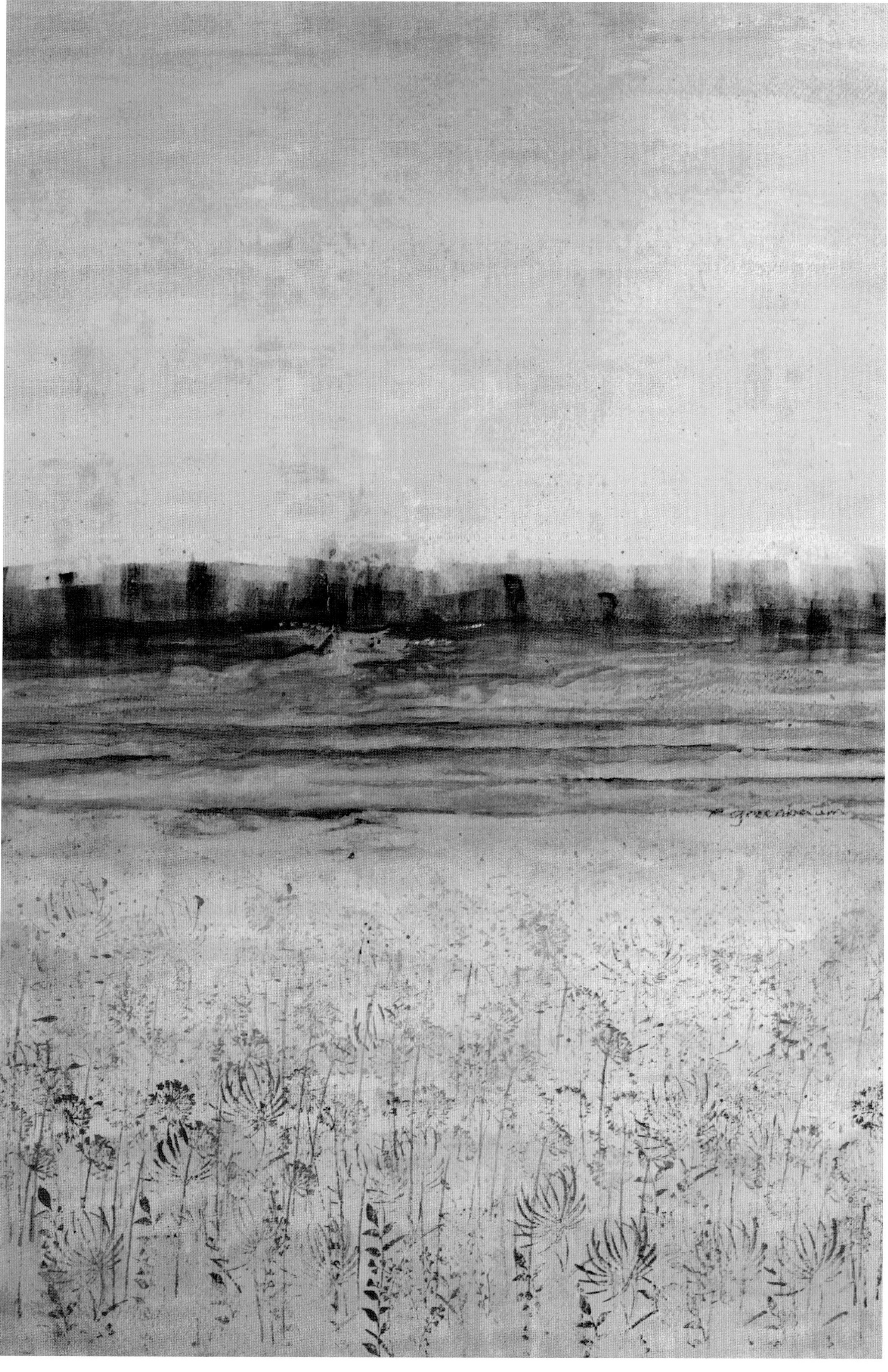

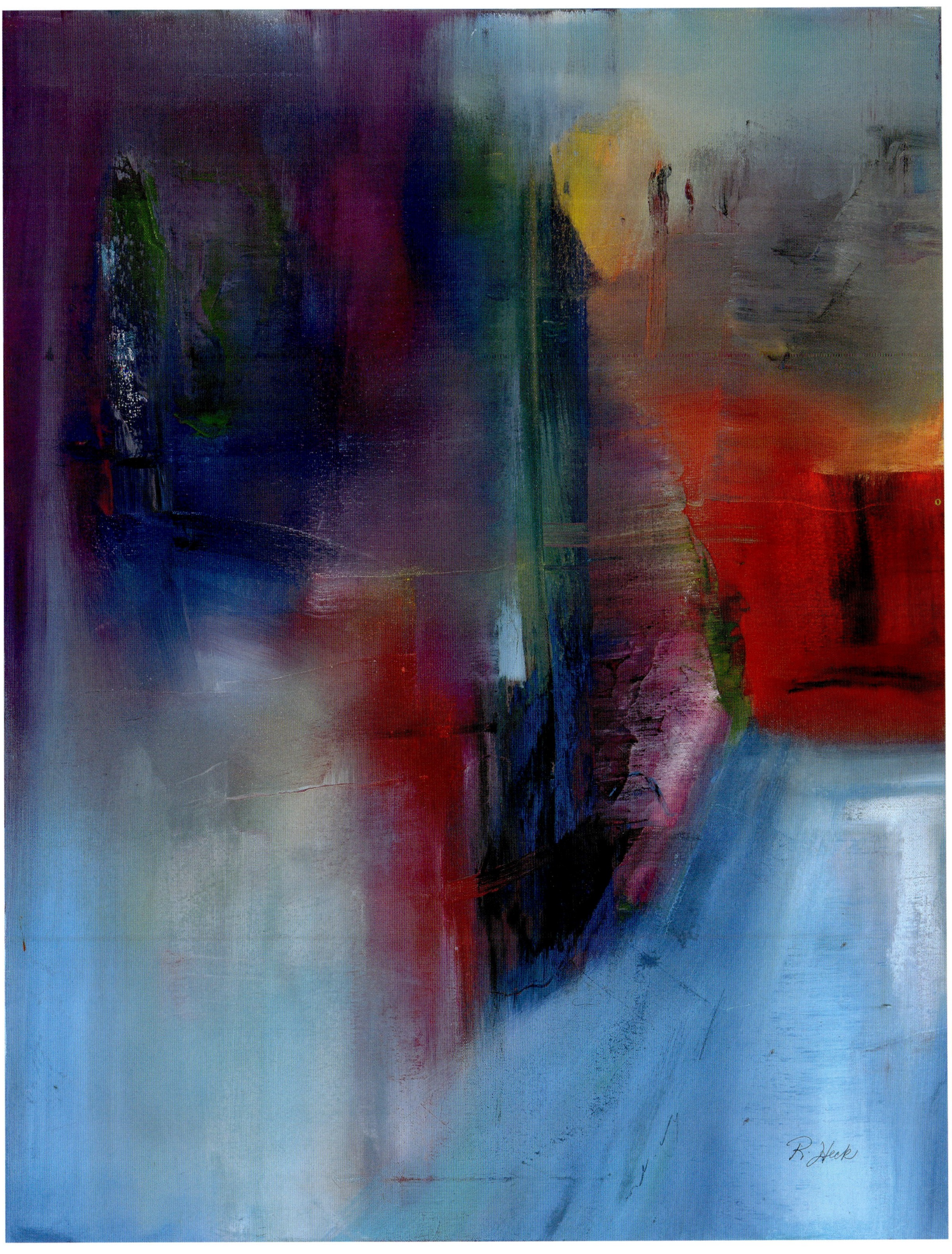

▼ WATERGARDEN | Mariko Hibbett
Acrylic on canvas, 24" × 48" (61cm × 122cm)

This painting is one of a series inspired by a trip to Bali I took a few years ago. There I became mesmerized by the beautiful lotus ponds filled with golden fish and found in the temple gardens. I took many photographs, and after returning home began to paint. At first the paintings were more realistic renderings of the fish, but over time they became more abstract, eventually becoming less about the fish and more about the water. In this painting I poured the paint over a textured surface to create random patterns similar to those found in water. I then went over the painting with thin layers of translucent washes to give it the depth and mystery of those Balinese gardens.

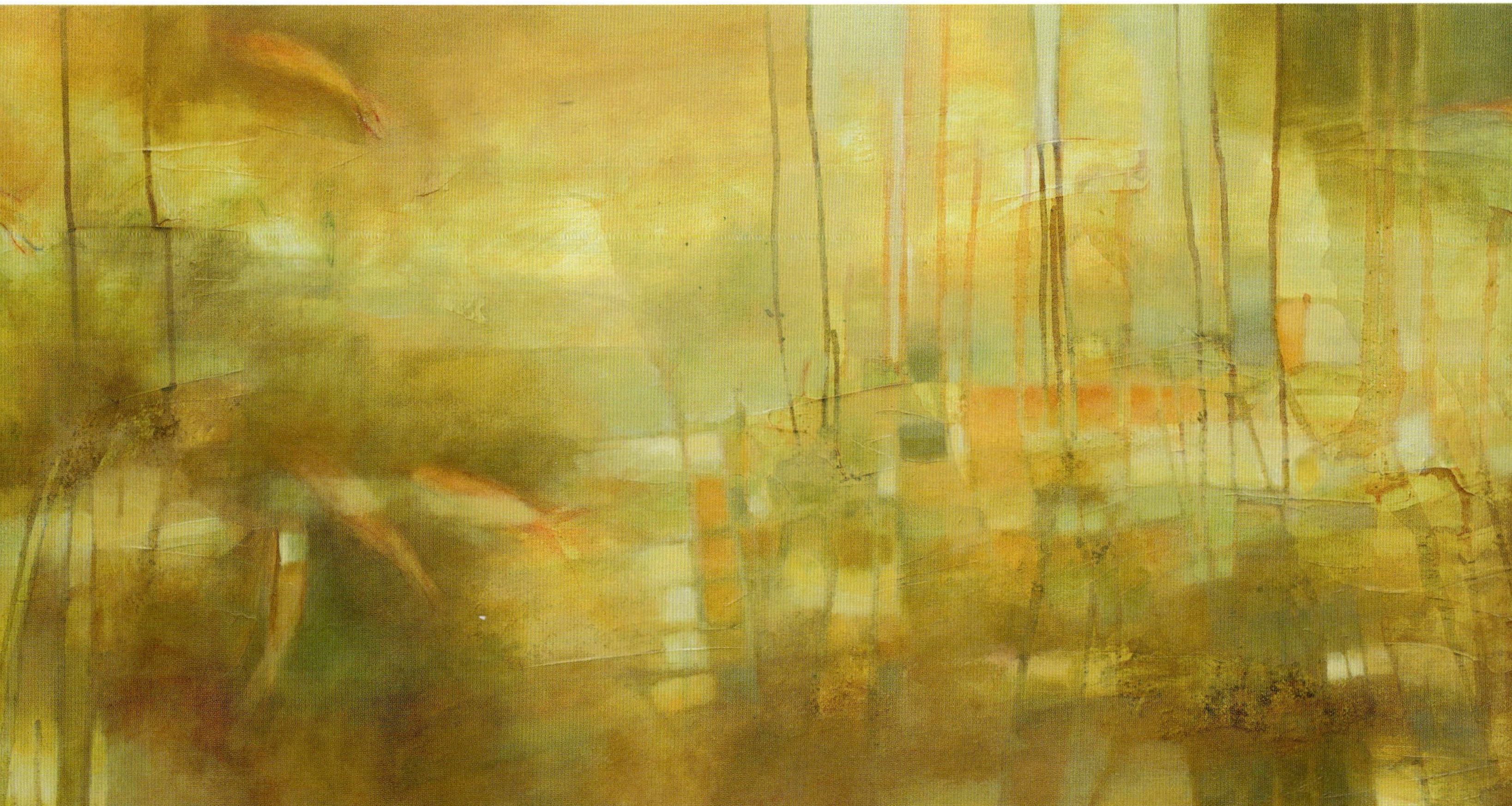

◄ FOOLISH DREAMS | Rick Heck
Acrylic on stretched gallery-wrapped canvas, 30" × 24" (76cm × 61cm)

This painting was created on a gallery-wrapped canvas using primarily Cadmium Red, Cadmium Orange, Permanent Violet, Viridian Green, cyan, white and black. I have an intuitive approach to painting. Each stroke of the brush is a reaction to the previous stroke and takes me on a journey to find a way to convey my feelings about a subject. I contrasted hard edges with the soft blended passages for variety. I used brushes as well as trowels to move paint around to give the painting its texture, resulting in a dreamlike image.

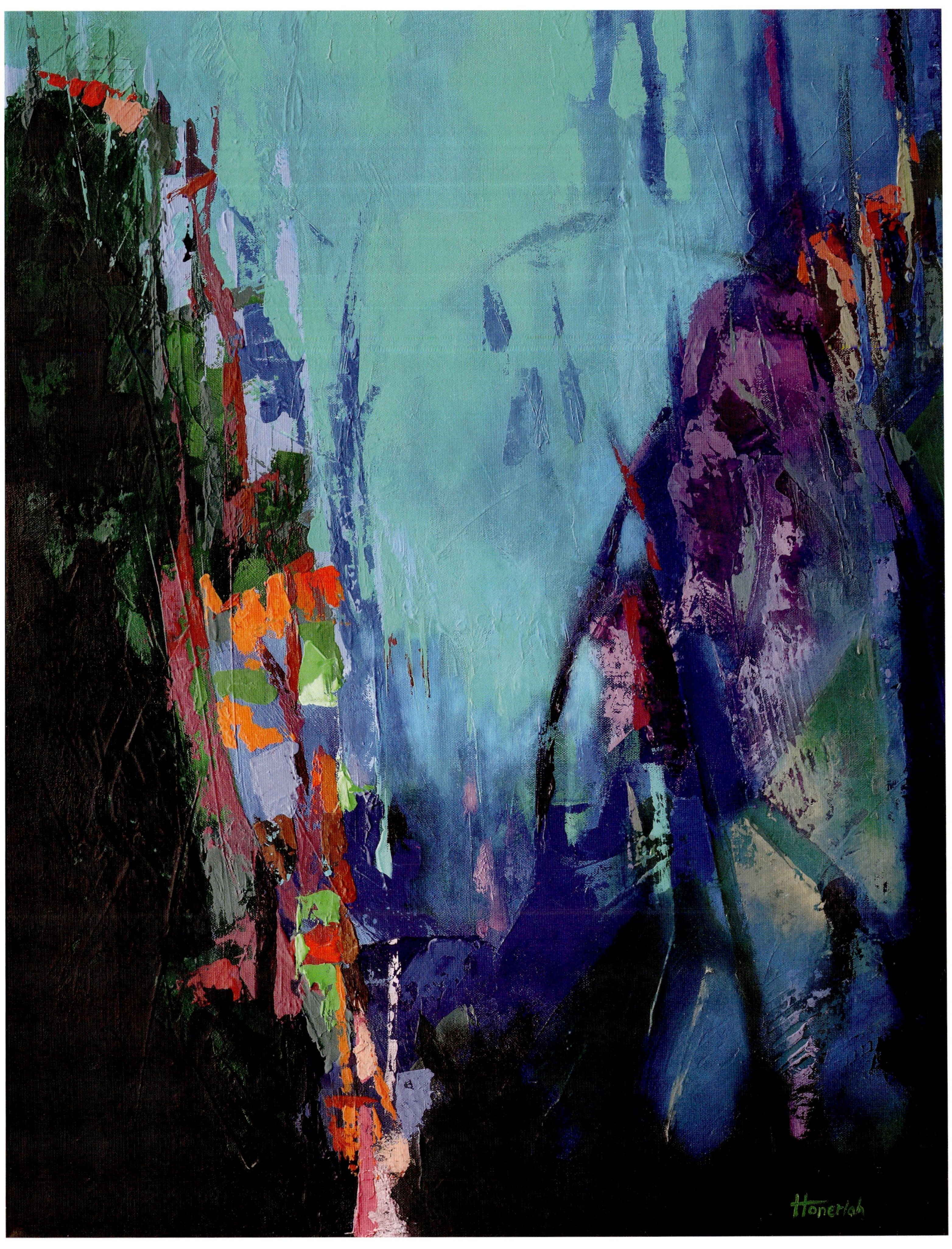
Honerlah

"Reality leaves a lot to the imagination."

—JOHN LENNON

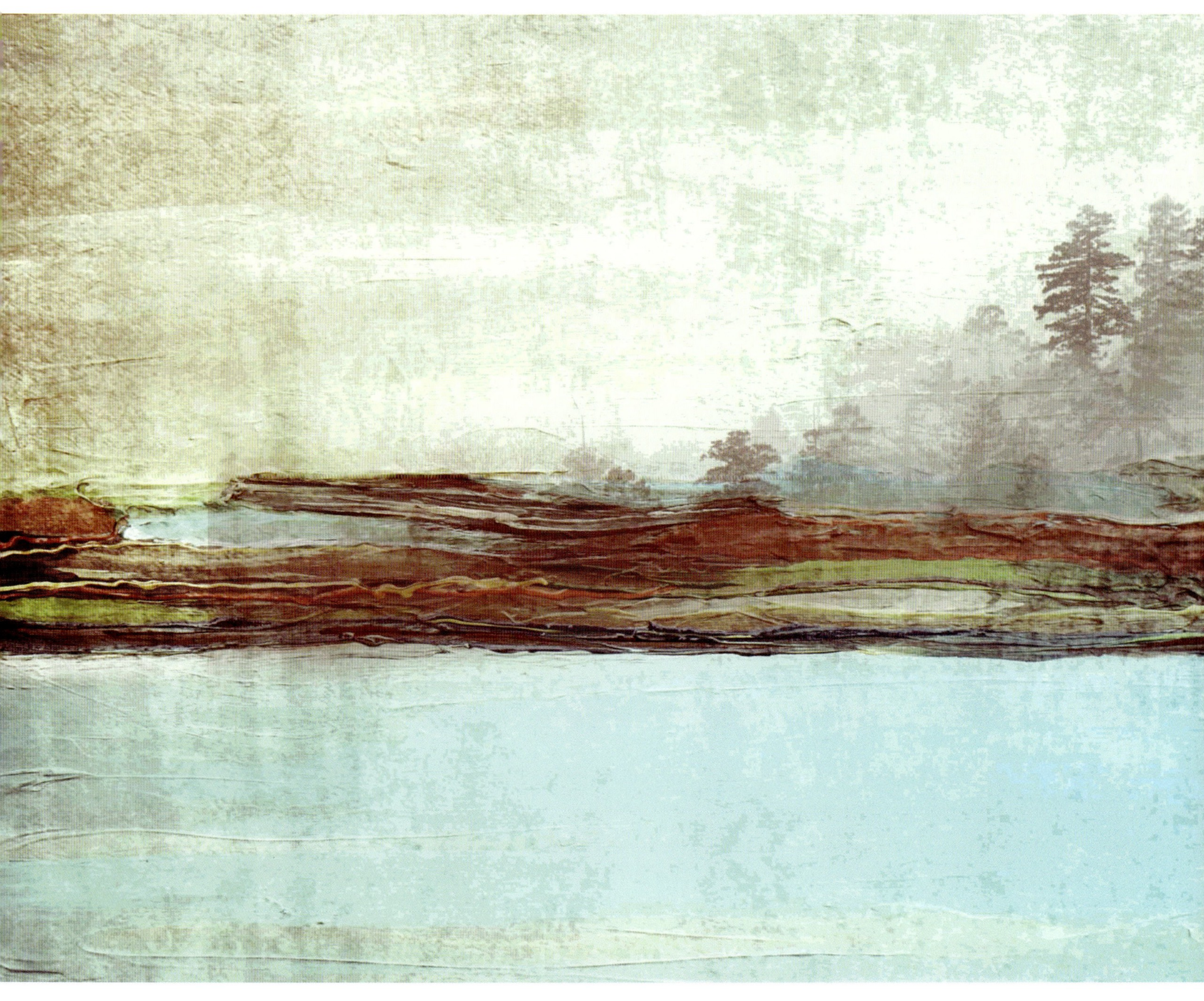

◀ THE GROTTO | Randy Honerlah
Acrylic on cotton duck canvas, 36" × 24" (91cm × 61cm)

The Grotto was painted from a vision I had after visiting Kauai and other islands many times. I love the tropics and the vibrant colors and deep valleys found there. The Grotto is not an actual place except in my mind and now on canvas. I usually start by painting a brief composition in a thin mixture of the dominant color, in this case Cobalt Blue and Teal. The painting builds from back to front and over again until I feel the right depth has been achieved. The sunset colors projected onto the mountainsides are an inspiring sight.

▲ BLUE LANDSCAPE | Irena Orlov
Acrylic with pastel accents on canvas, 30" × 40" (76cm × 102cm)

My art is a response of my soul to the reality. I create an emotional space through visual abstract images. I'm curious about everything where I see energy of life. I see boundless and unforgettable opportunities of conveying real space for imagination and creating a new one. I try to develop an emotional and visual horizon of perception through my artwork as much as I constantly search for images that appeal to participation and emotional experience. This is an improvisation of reflections, feelings as well as definite and indefinite actions, during the process of creation. Each of the improvisations merges into a specific form of art at a specific period of time.

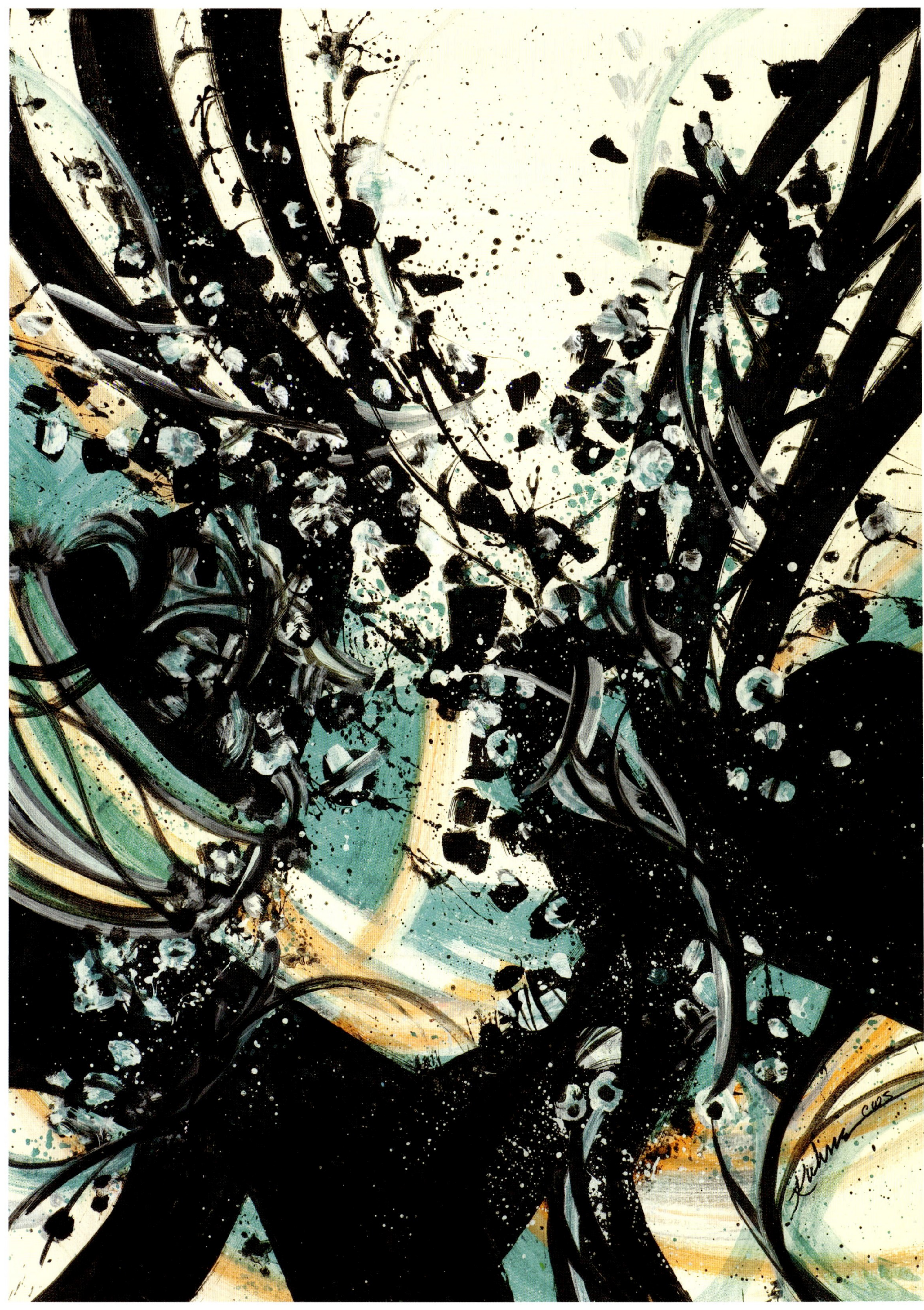

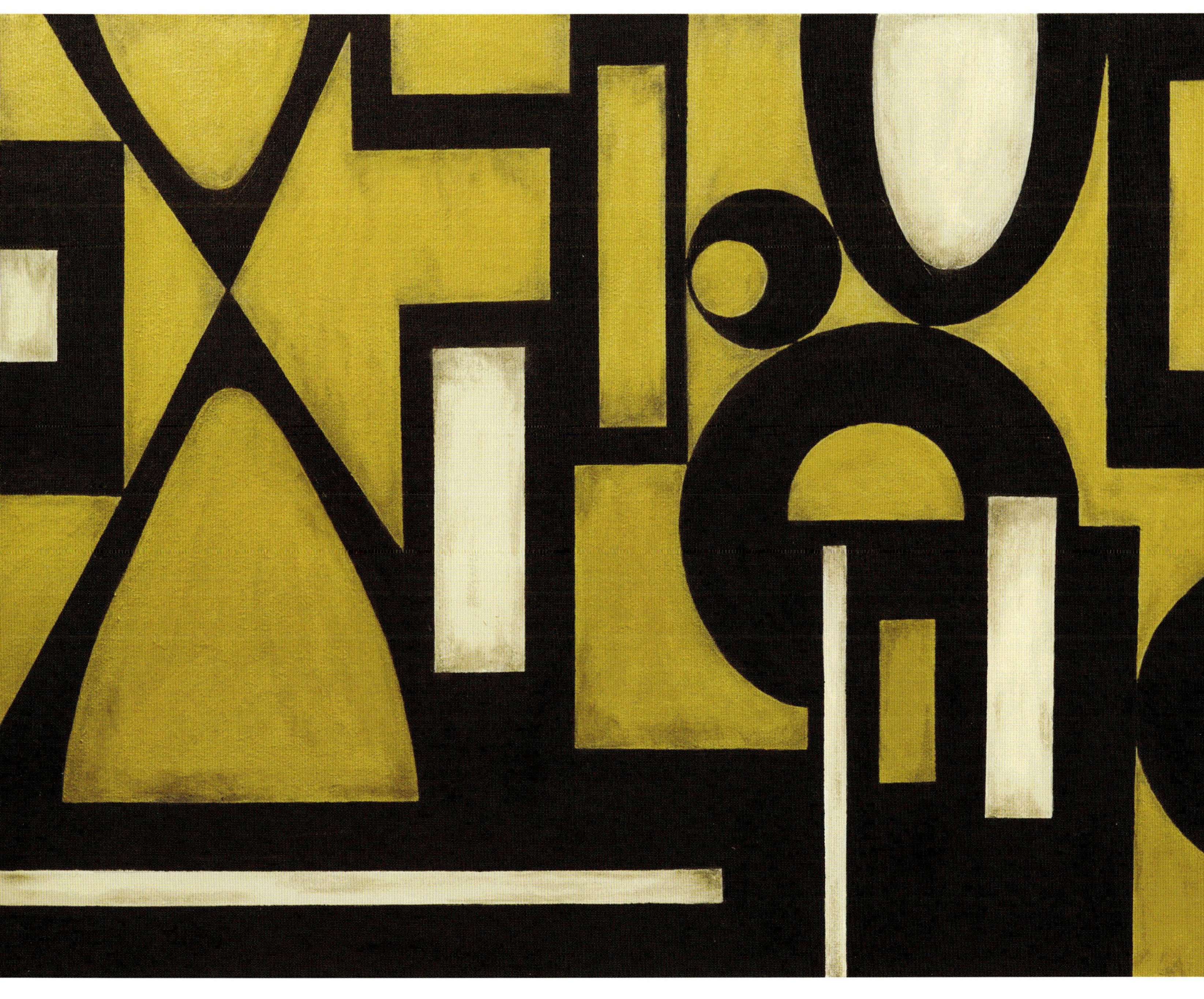

◄ EMERGING SPRING | Darlene Kuhne
Acrylic on 300-lb. (640gsm) cold-pressed Arches
30" × 22" (76cm × 56cm)

I work mainly in my studio where I have all of my supplies, books, etc. I use acrylic in all of my art—with pastels, mixed media, acrylic monoprints, figure drawings/paintings, even on the Plexiglas base of my neon light art. Acrylic is brighter, the colors deeper and more dynamic. I use it as a wash and thicken it sometimes with texture mediums added. Many times my technique starts with shapes, texture and directional lines leading the eye around the painting. I work my paintings in series, ten to twelve at a time, spread out on my tables. The varied colored schemes and collage parts give the paintings a different look. This painting started with abstract shapes—and colors developing into tree shapes—both controlled and by accident. My experience is to add new ideas and techniques and to try everything!

▲ GOLDEN MEANS | Janet Mangione
Acrylic on canvas, 30" × 40" (76cm × 102cm)

To me, a good design should make the viewer want to keep looking, perusing the canvas many times over. The Eiffel Tower, pier pylons, clock parts and the contrivances of steampunk—I am fascinated by the architecture of each of them. Although I enjoy working in other mediums, I find acrylics to be the perfect vehicle for my geometric concepts. The versatility of both thick and thin paint that dries quickly makes acrylic my best choice for precision painting. I also like the use of patina paint like Micaceous Iron Oxide for making a surface seem worn by time. It's exciting to build contrasts of light and dark values that weigh against each other. But like a Jenga game, if you take out one puzzle piece, the design falls apart and loses its high-strung elegance.

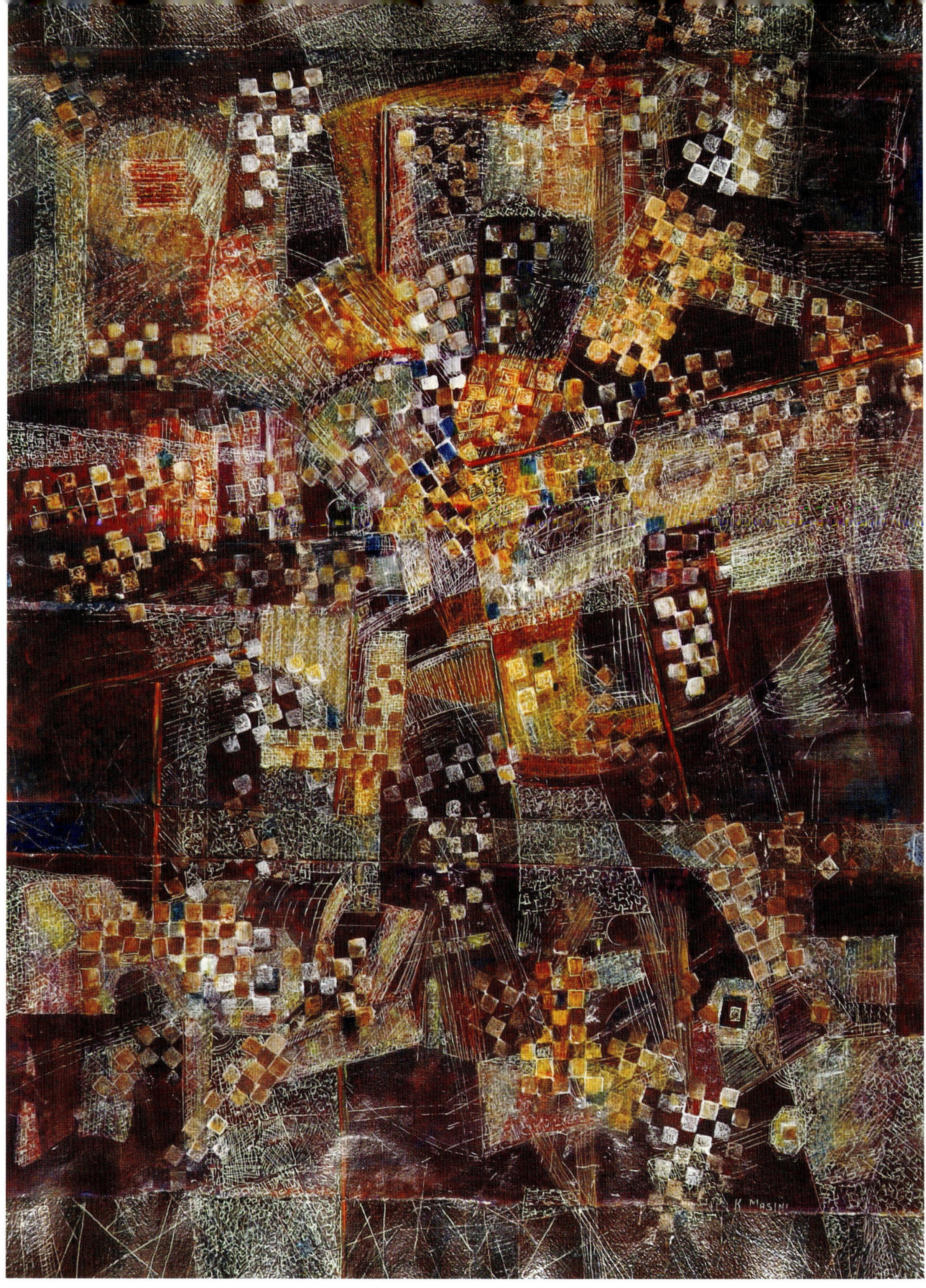

PLANNING THE GAME | Kay Masini
Acrylic, gloss medium, stamping with gesso, alcohol and acrylic ink on 140-lb. (300gsm) hot-pressed Arches
29½" × 21½" (75cm × 55cm)

When ideas pass from the artist's brain to the brush, the ideas may develop from words as well as images. I find the transition from the abstract to a tactile surface an exciting challenge when aided by multiple base layers of paint and mediums. Take the idea of chessboards stretched out to create a pattern, even with whole boards, broken boards, twisted boards, some on top of others, representing plans that may not have gone well. Not all random, not all simple, but all part of a life. Layers and the gloss medium create a surface like leather while the paper is composed of wide strips. I used stamps—purchased, antique and handmade—along with white acrylic ink to draw structure for *Planning the Game*.

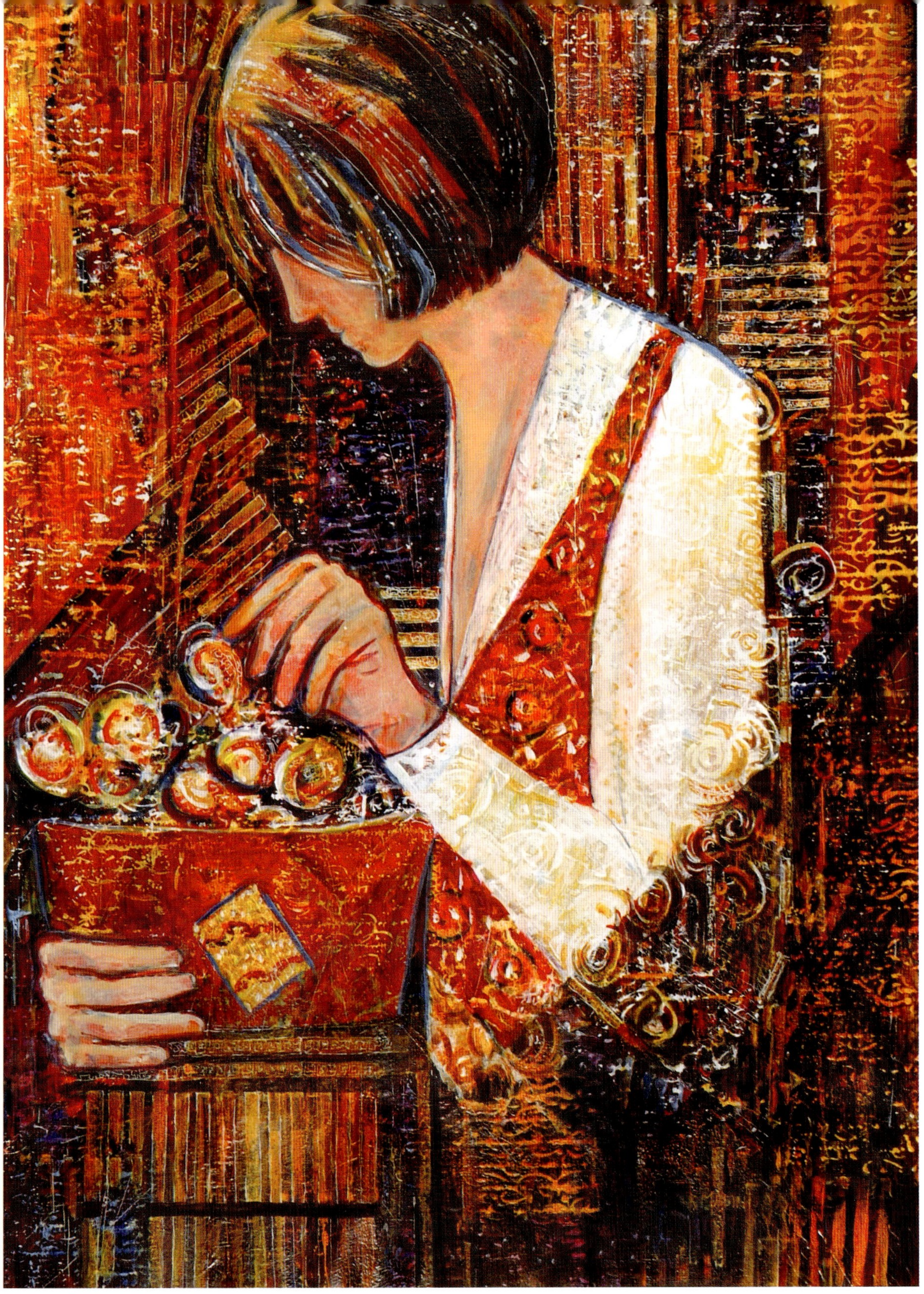

MATERIAL GIRL | Kay Masini
Acrylic, gloss medium, stamping with gesso, alcohol and acrylic ink on 140-lb. (300gsm) hot-pressed Arches, 29½" × 21½" (75cm × 55cm)

After we learn the rules of surfaces, paints, mediums, brushstrokes and design we learn the personal secrets of the things that light up our brains, which may be sights, feelings, memories or ideas. These are the switches that make us want to paint. I like to illustrate the abstract as it affects our realistic world. While *Planning the Game* holds minimal visual realism, *Material Girl* stands bravely among the pieces of life she will encounter. She has a base of painted layers in her background, but she has yet to identify her structures and future lines of direction. She has little texture in her skin, just delicate color. This contrast and the simple patterns enhance her story in both abstraction and realism in layers of our art world.

"With art we touch each other across time, countries and beliefs."

—KAY MASINI

"Paint to make yourself happy and everything else will fall into place."

—VICKY MCLAIN

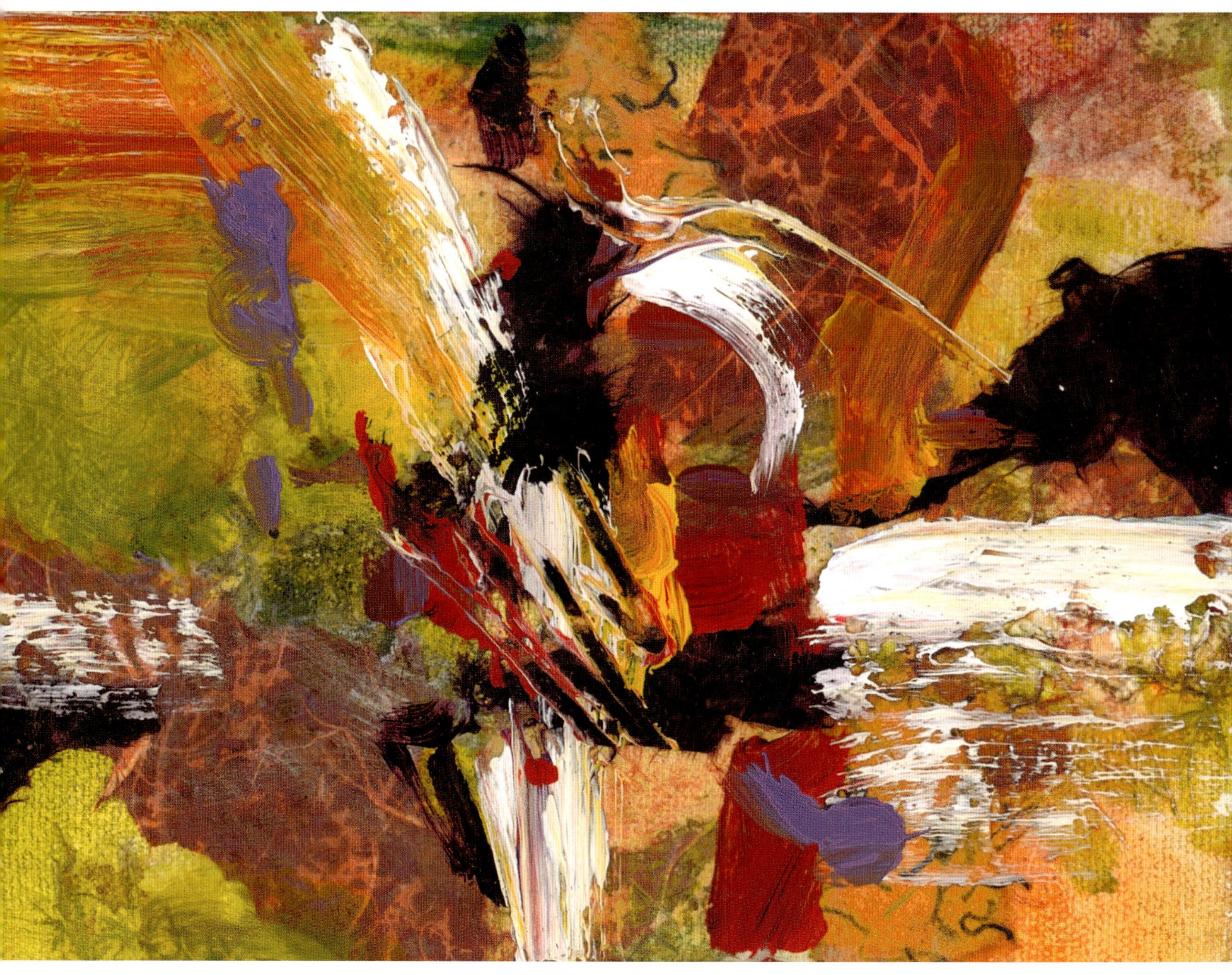

▲ ALLURING | Suzanne McCourt
Acrylic and mixed media on canvas, 5" × 7" (13cm × 18cm)

My usual size of canvas is 48" × 36" (122cm × 91cm) or 60" × 48" (152cm × 122cm). My unique style of "painterly storytelling" involves many layers, lots of planning and intricate design. One painting may take a few weeks, another months to finish. Many times after creating a series of work, I just cut loose, forget about the rules and play! *Alluring* is one such creation of abstracts of fun. And it is one of my smallest paintings. Good design can be created in all sizes.

▶ PASSION | Vicky McLain
Acrylic with textures of recycled dryer sheets, coffee filters and clear acrylic gesso on canvas, 40" × 30" (102cm × 76cm)

Passion was so named because it was several years in the making. I was inspired by colors I had felt while watching the movie *Passion of the Christ*. I normally don't paint abstracts, and I did not know what to do with the colors. Yet for several years these colors haunted me. After taking a class in composition, I felt for the first time that I had the knowledge to do something with the colors.

My technique involved clear gesso, recycled dryer sheets and coffee filters. I laid out my design with the textures. Cadmium Red, Cadmium Red Light and Cadmium Yellow Light dominated the painting. The stray drips were touches of green that I allowed to form. The final result of the painting was more than I had hoped for. It brought closure to the painting harbored in my mind for so many years and also set me free from the constraints of realism.

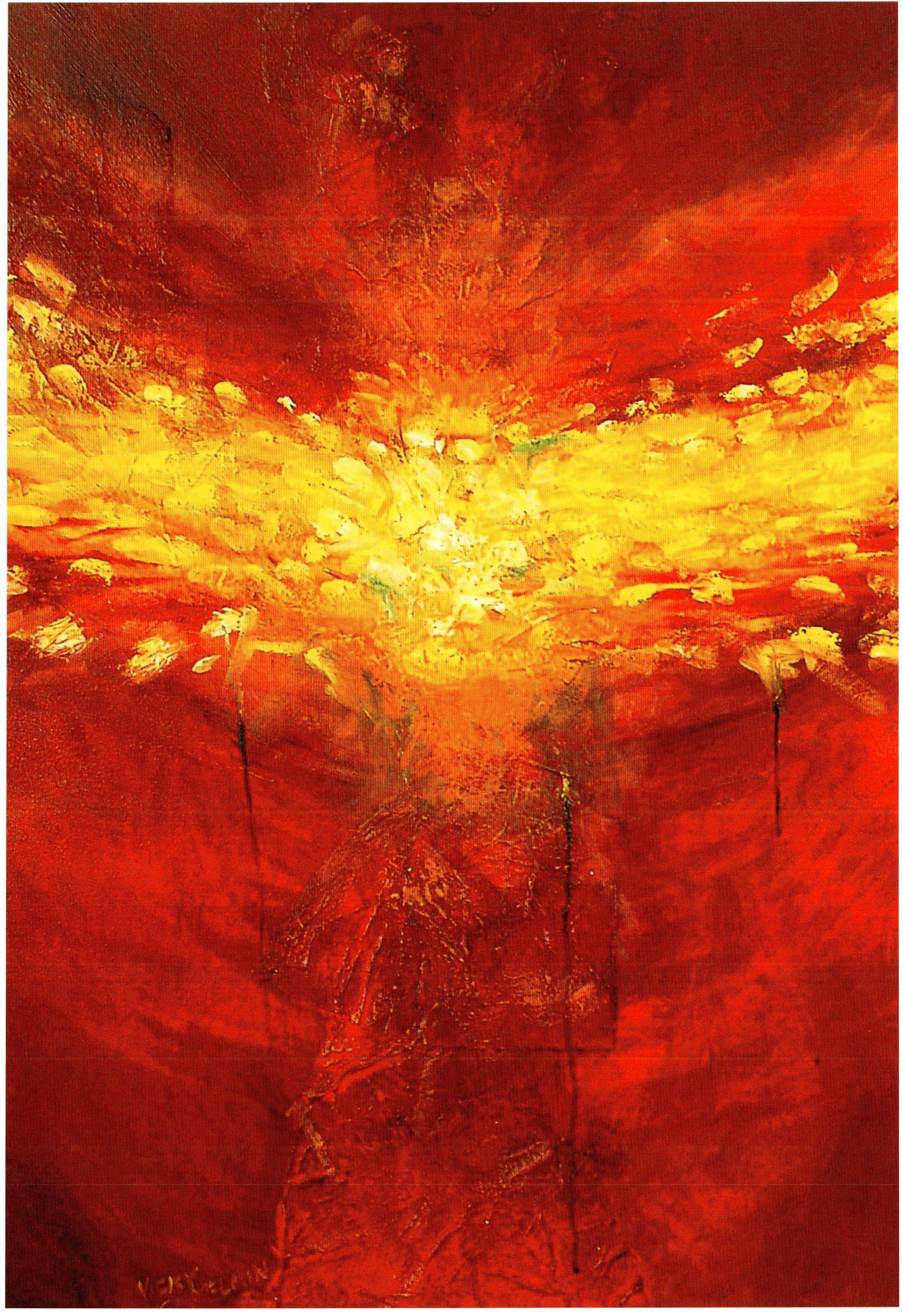

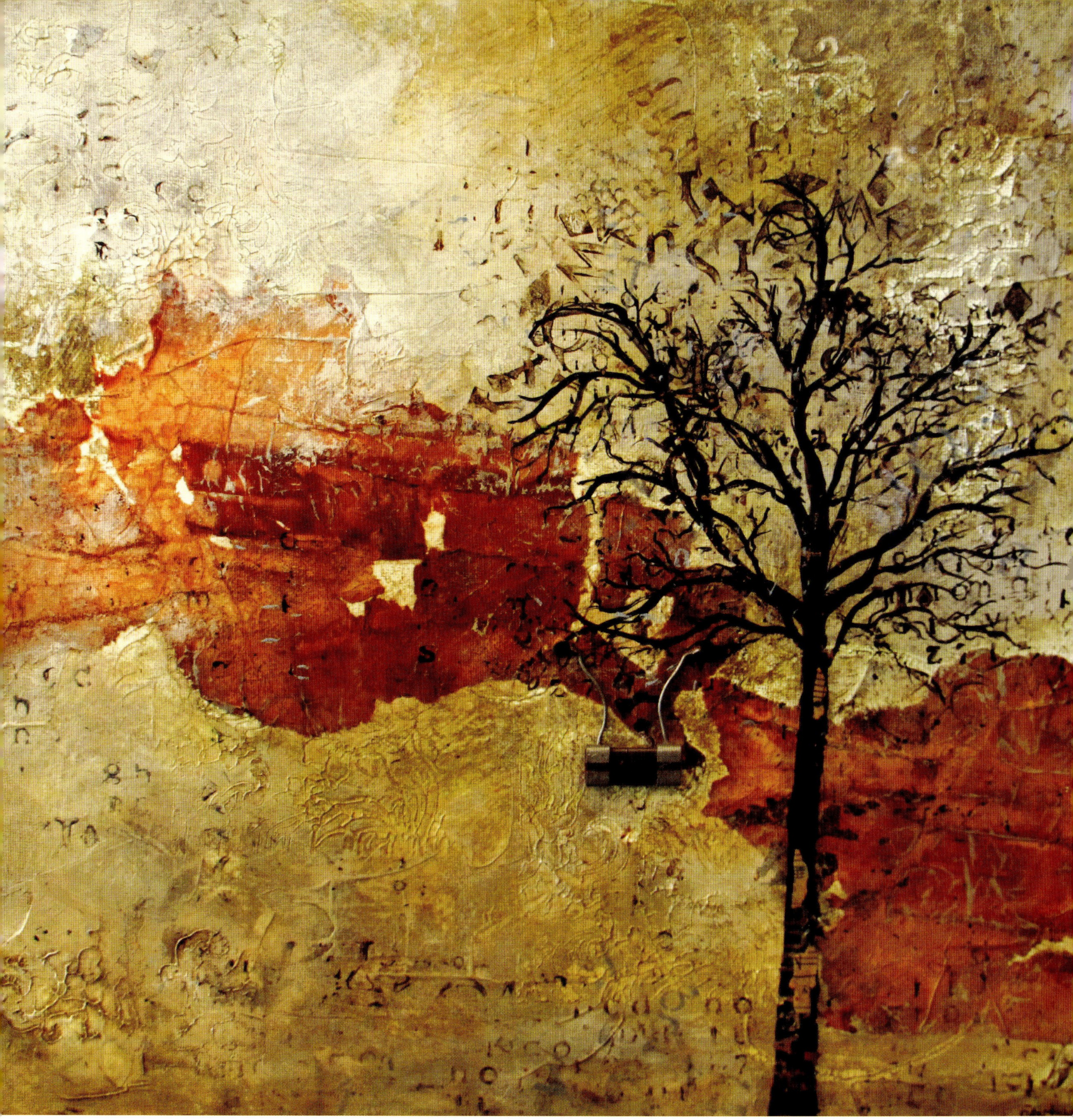

TREE OF KNOWLEDGE | Pamela Peterson
Mixed media with acrylic paint, molding paste, rusted tissue paper and metal object on canvas
12" × 12" (30cm × 30cm)

Nature has always been my source for inspiration and connection, so it was fitting that this work was born under a tree in the backyard. I began with molding paste to create texture and applied it randomly with a palette knife. Adding rusted tissue paper continued the organic feeling of the piece. Usually preferring to keep it simple, my palette consisted of Quinacridone Nickel Azo Gold, Cobalt Blue, Titanium White and Carbon Black. And like a tree, which grows without limits or boundaries but is guided by the unseen, I found the piece almost created itself.

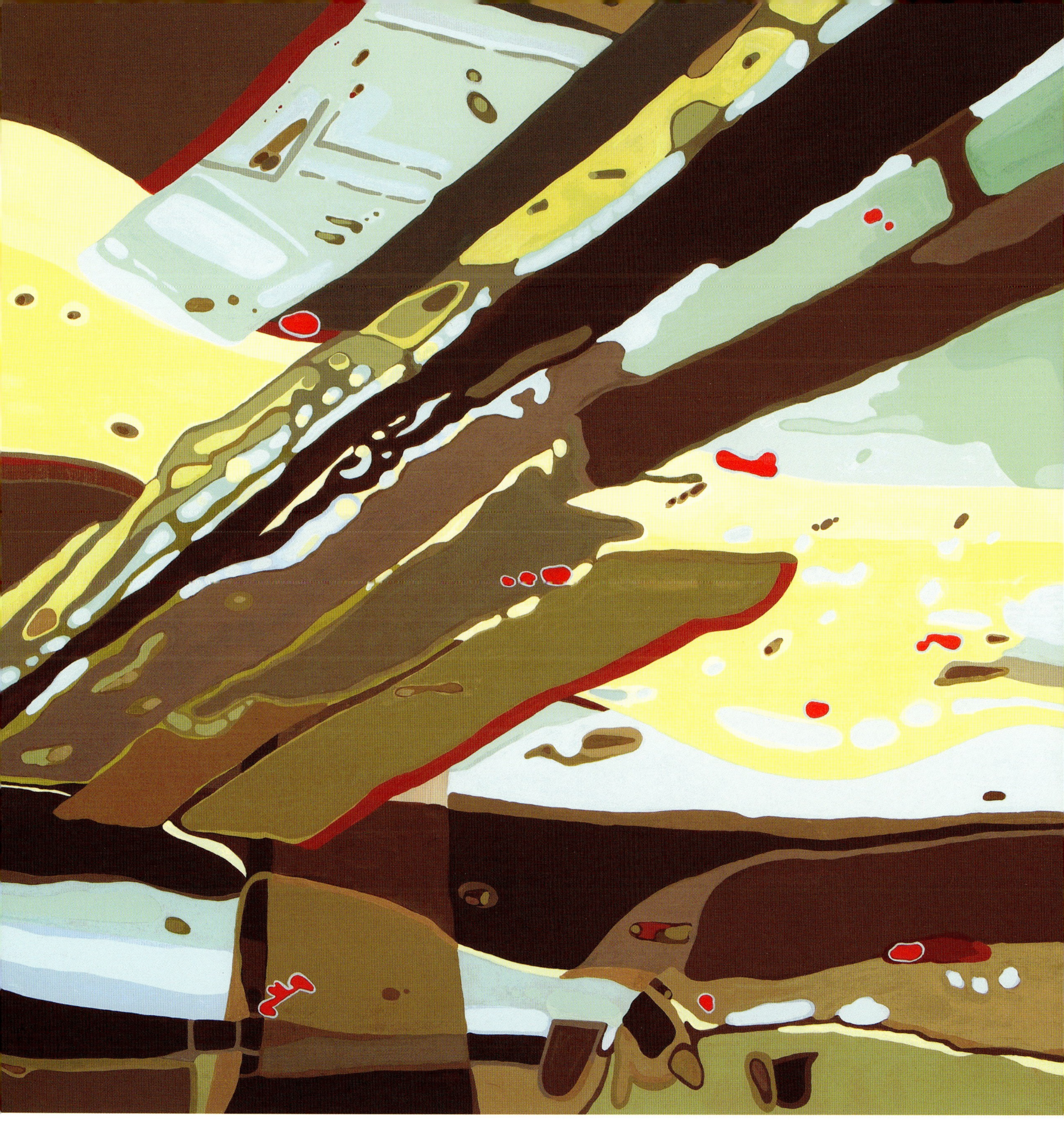

EGRESS | Jan Filarski
Acrylics on canvas, 36" × 36" (91cm × 91cm)

See a pattern of steps and puddles upside down in a photograph, and there's the idea for a painting. Buy new paint to try such as Golden Matte Fluid Acrylics and your favorite size in gallery-wrapped canvas, and you are ready. The paint has a rich velvet look to it when dry. Working on the painting in my living room at home, I viewed it from all directions making changes when needed. I worked with puddles of paint and added a little more blue or green or brown to the puddle to get my current color so the colors relate to each other well. Red is my favorite color, so I used some Pyrrole Red for the finishing touches.

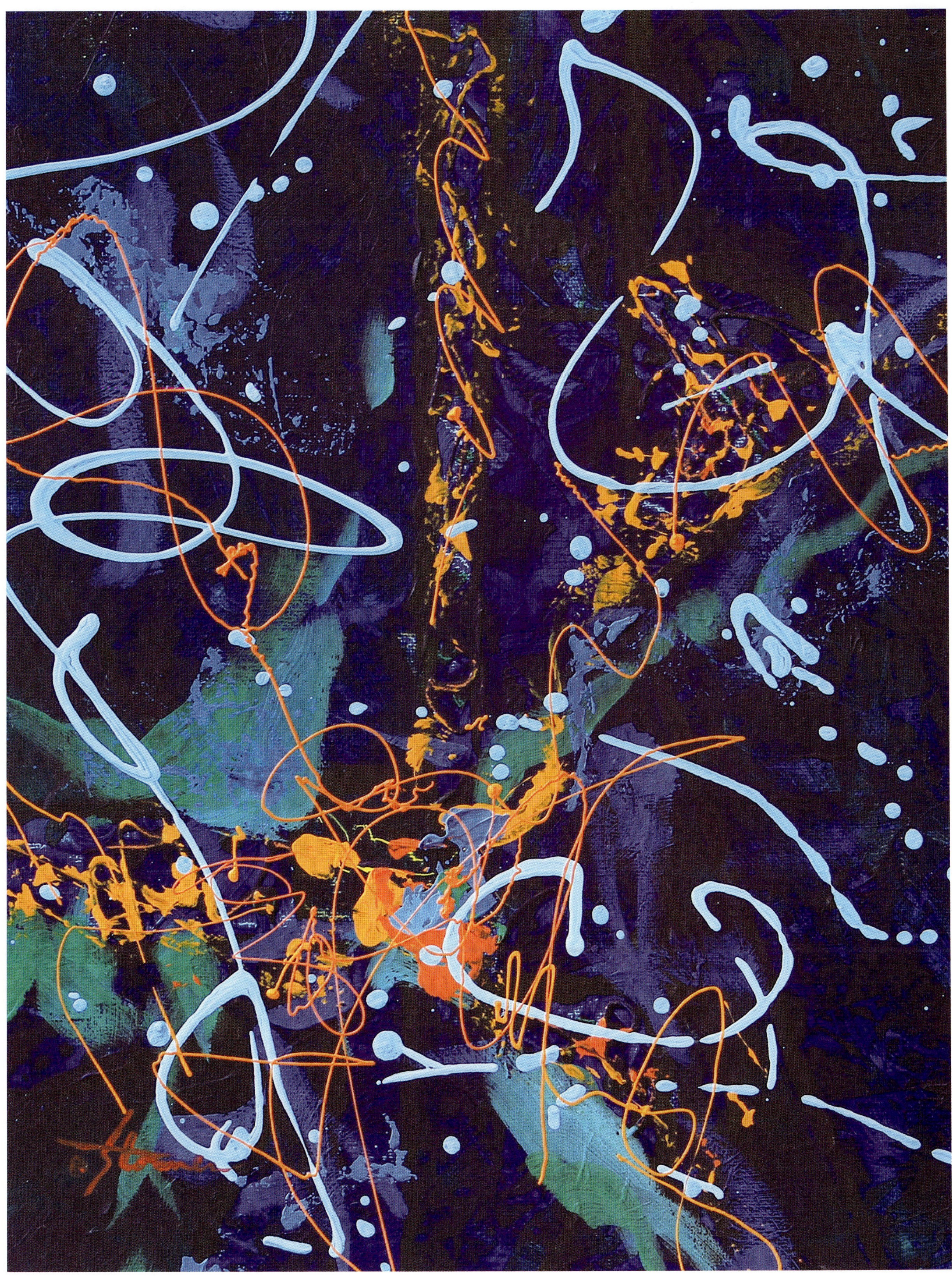

"Think big and bold—big canvas and bold color."

—DOROTHY STONELY

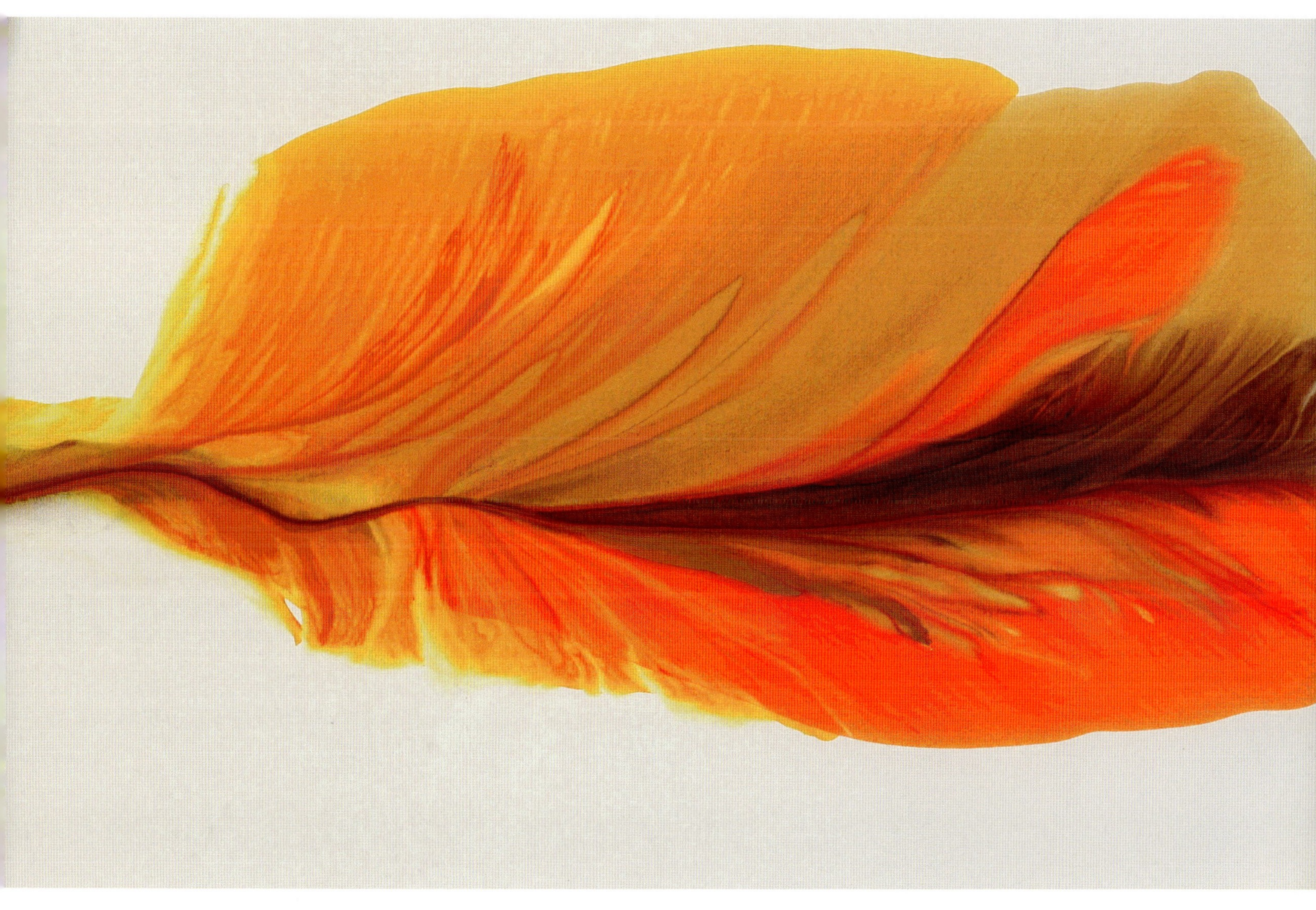

◀ HAPPY | Jan Stommes
Acrylic on stretched canvas, 14" × 11" (36cm × 28cm)

Having painted representational work for almost thirty years, I added abstract painting to my repertoire about a year ago. My style is eclectic, yet the underlying connection to all of my styles of painting is color. As a colorist, I allow my feelings to guide me when I paint an abstract. Brushing and blending color onto the canvas was the foundation in this studio piece. Cutting a small hole in a plastic bag allowed me to let the acrylic paint dance across the piece. As in my representational pieces, I lead your eye to the center of interest by the colors that I use.

▲ GIFT FROM THE GOLDEN EAGLE | Dorothy Stonely
Acrylic on canvas, 35½" × 58" (90cm × 147cm)

I use acrylic paint exclusively and enjoy the challenge of controlling the flow of liquid acrylic. My work begins with acrylic thinned to a milky consistency, which I pour onto unstretched canvas. The canvas is tacked to four supports of varying heights and positioned to form hills and valleys in the canvas. After the first pour is dry, I turn the canvas to a new position and pour another layer, continuing until the composition is complete. The canvas is then stretched and protected with varnish. Using this technique requires a lot of paint as much of it runs off during the process, but the amazing colors that often result from the spontaneous mixing of paint are delightful.

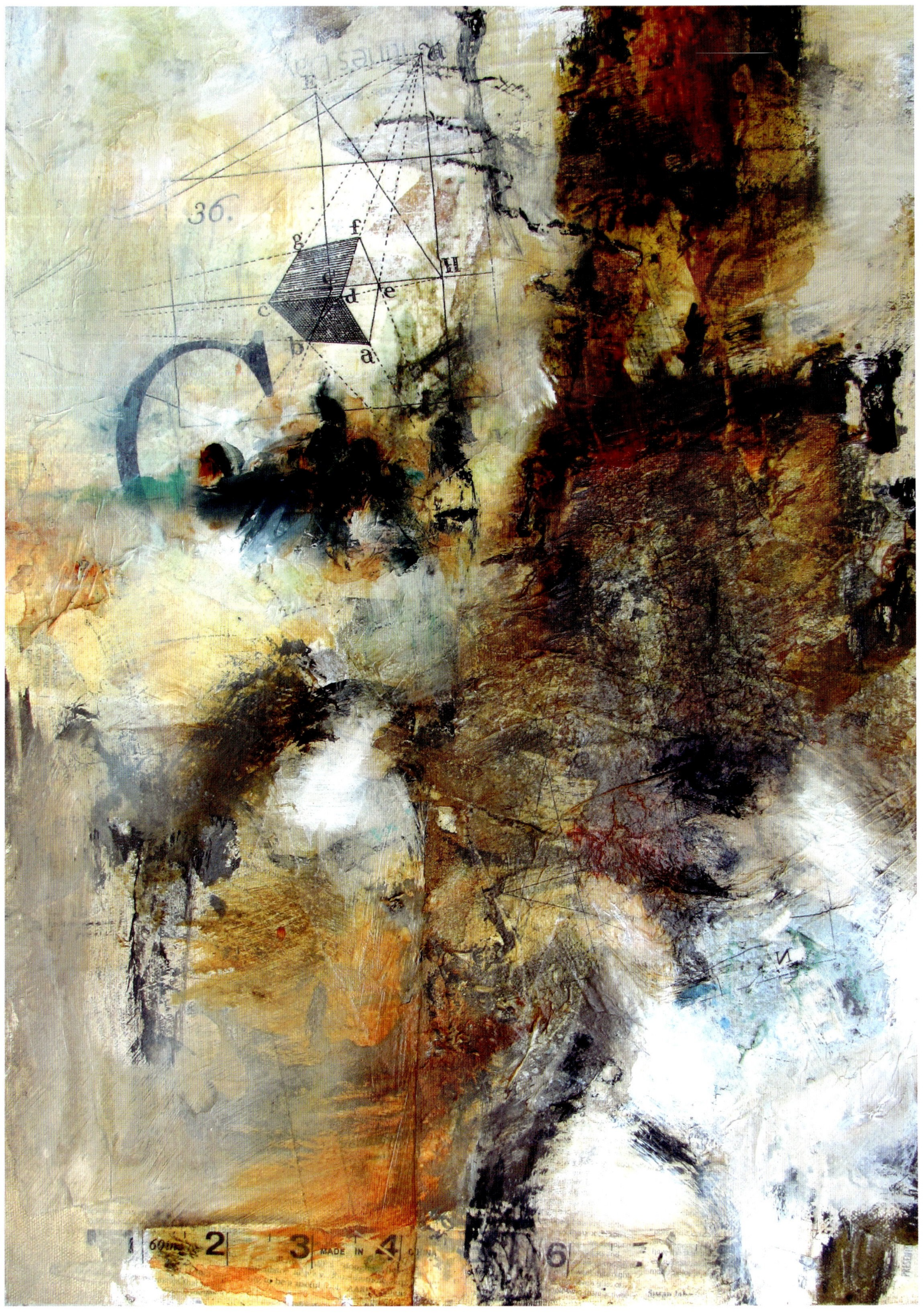

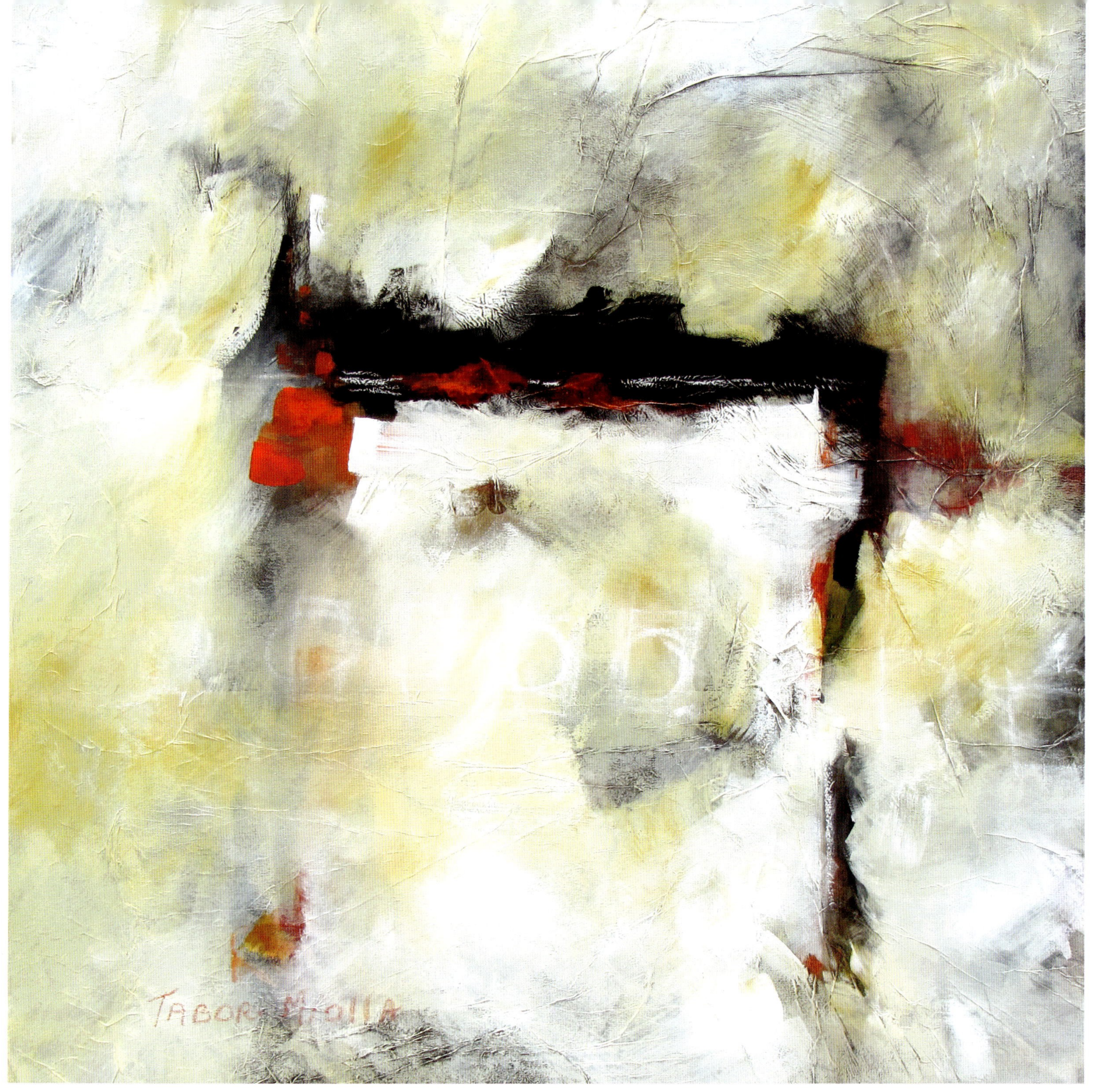

◄ IT'S ALL RELATIVE | Francesca Tabor-Miolla
Acrylic with collage on canvas, 20" × 16" (51cm × 41cm)

▲ LISTEN TO THE SILENCE | Francesca Tabor-Miolla
Acrylic with charcoal and pastel on canvas, 36" × 36" (91cm × 91cm)

Taking risks, breaking rules and making mistakes (for me) is the exciting part of creating—and working in acrylic easily affords me that luxury. My working process involves overlapping fields of color, creating and applying surface texture, often adding collage, objects and other mediums … concealing, revealing, adding and subtracting until the desired result emerges from the layers creating control and balance out of chaos. An intuitive painter, I work at a fast pace and usually have four or five pieces in progress at a time. However, due to contemplation and hard self-critique each piece may take weeks to complete.

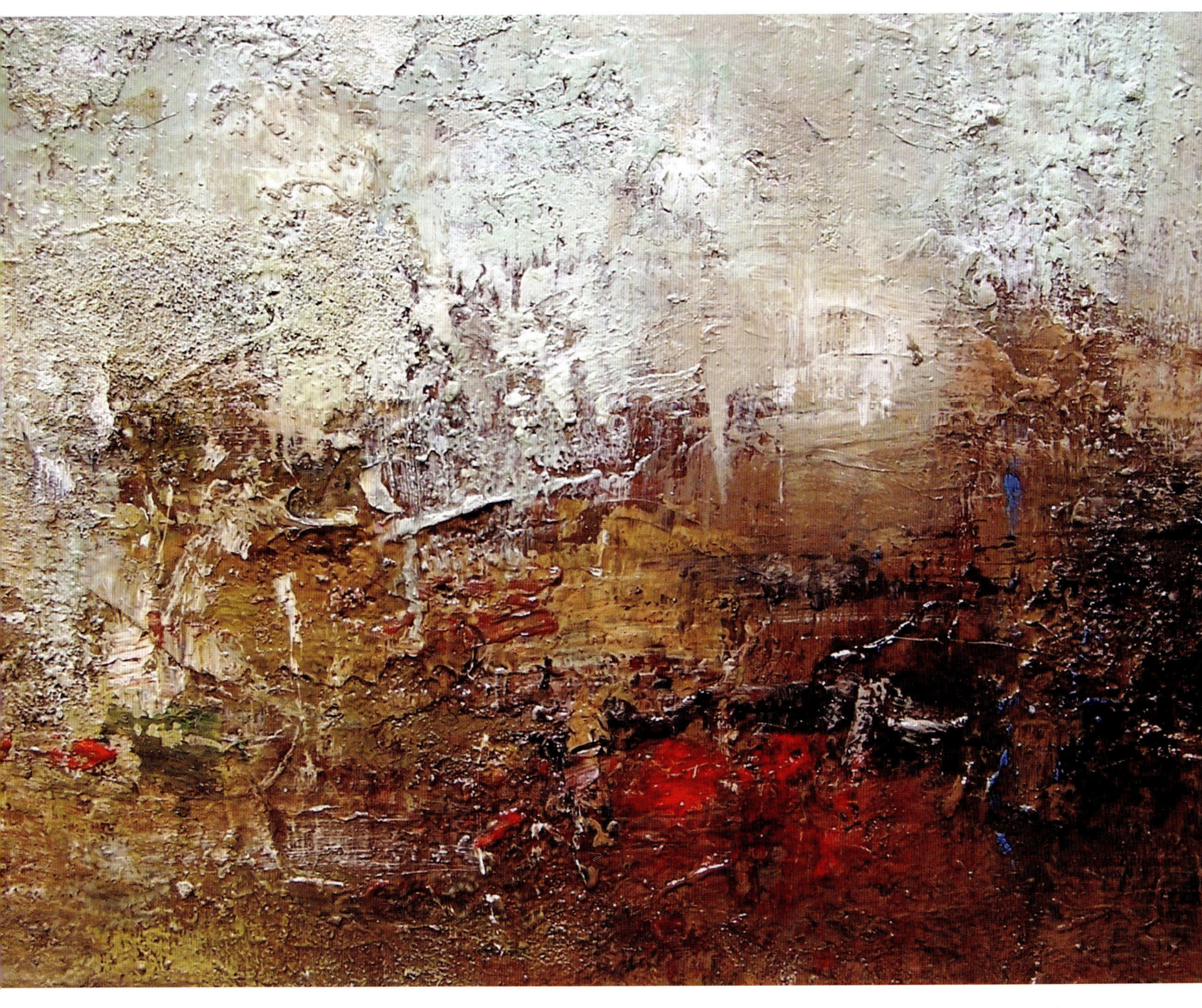

UNTITLED 1 | Yah-Hann (Erric) Yang
Mixed media and acrylic, 12" ×16" (30cm × 41cm)

I am interested in expressing on the canvas the inner spirit of myself influenced by nature. My deeply-felt, personal emotions allow me to explore a wide range of mediums, materials, texture, color and surfaces in an entirely abstract format. I enjoy using the process of painting as a tool to create texture and color, using layers to build up the surfaces or to scrape back. My goal is to allow my emotions to release on the canvas and become a language to communicate with people.

UNTITLED 2 | Yah-Hann (Erric) Yang
Mixed media and acrylic, 20" × 24" (51cm × 61cm)

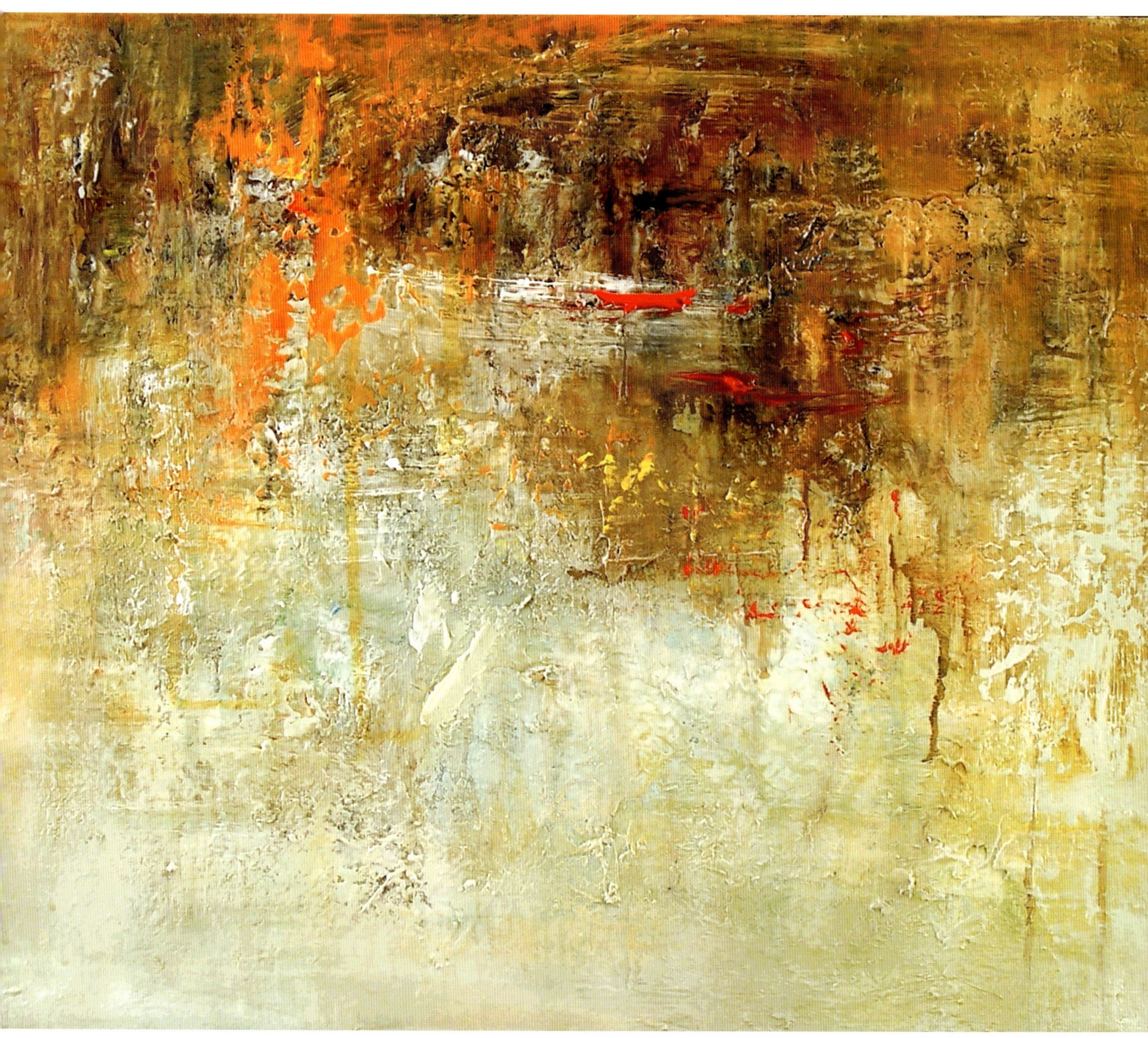

CROCODILE KING | Jacqui Beck
Acrylic and watercolor crayon on canvas, 25" × 31" (64cm × 79cm)

Crocodile King is part of a series of animal totem protectors. These represent the fierce strength we need in our lives for ourselves and those who love us. This strength, ideally, is tempered by a sense of paradox, irony and humor. You can't always tell who the strong ones are by their appearance. The best protectors have an understanding of and compassion for our uniqueness and fallibility. *Crocodile King* is a wonderful toothless protector. In *Crocodile King* I used high key color and strong values to create a bold design. I also used watercolor crayons with acrylic paint to outline shapes and create pattern and detail.

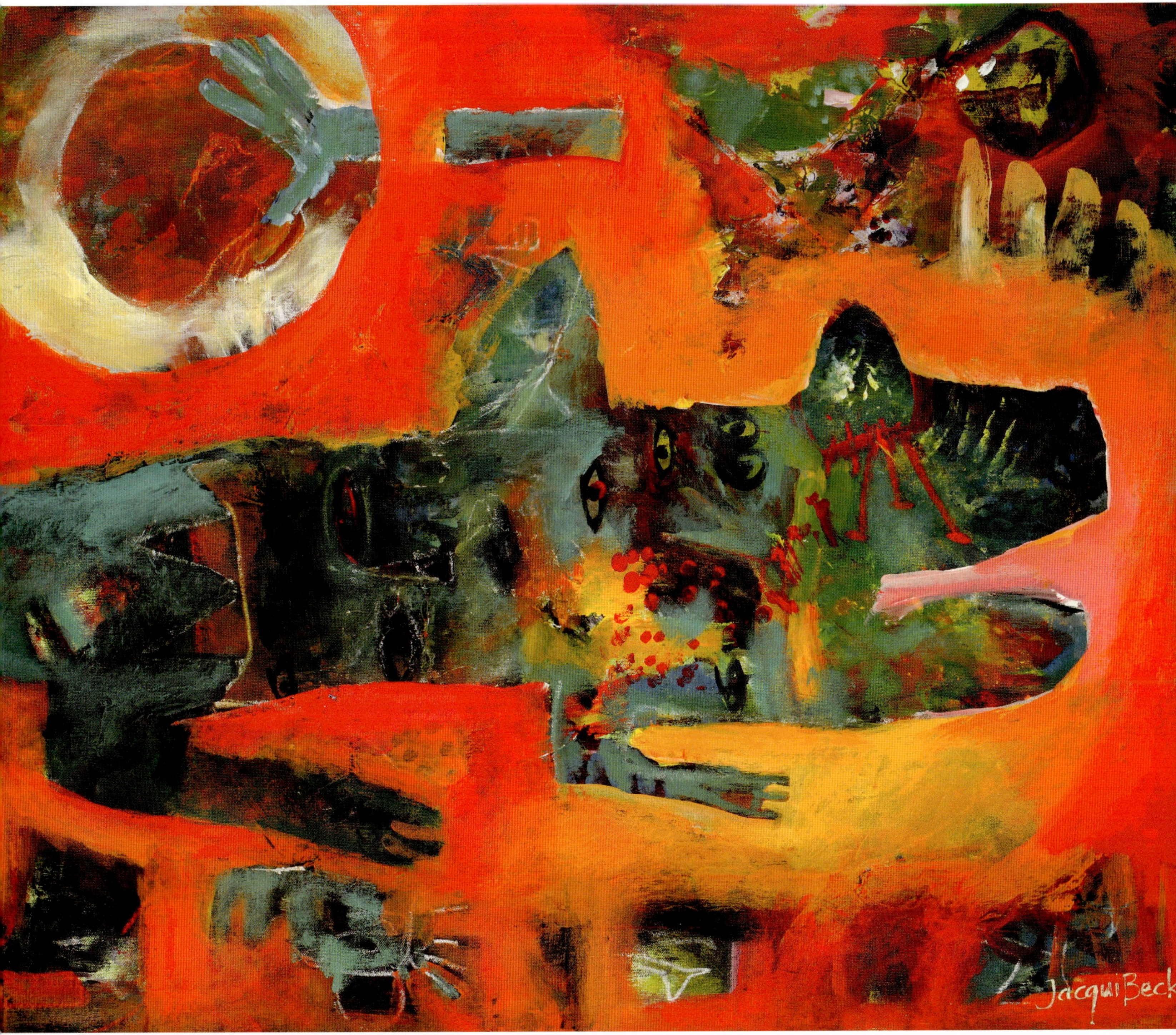

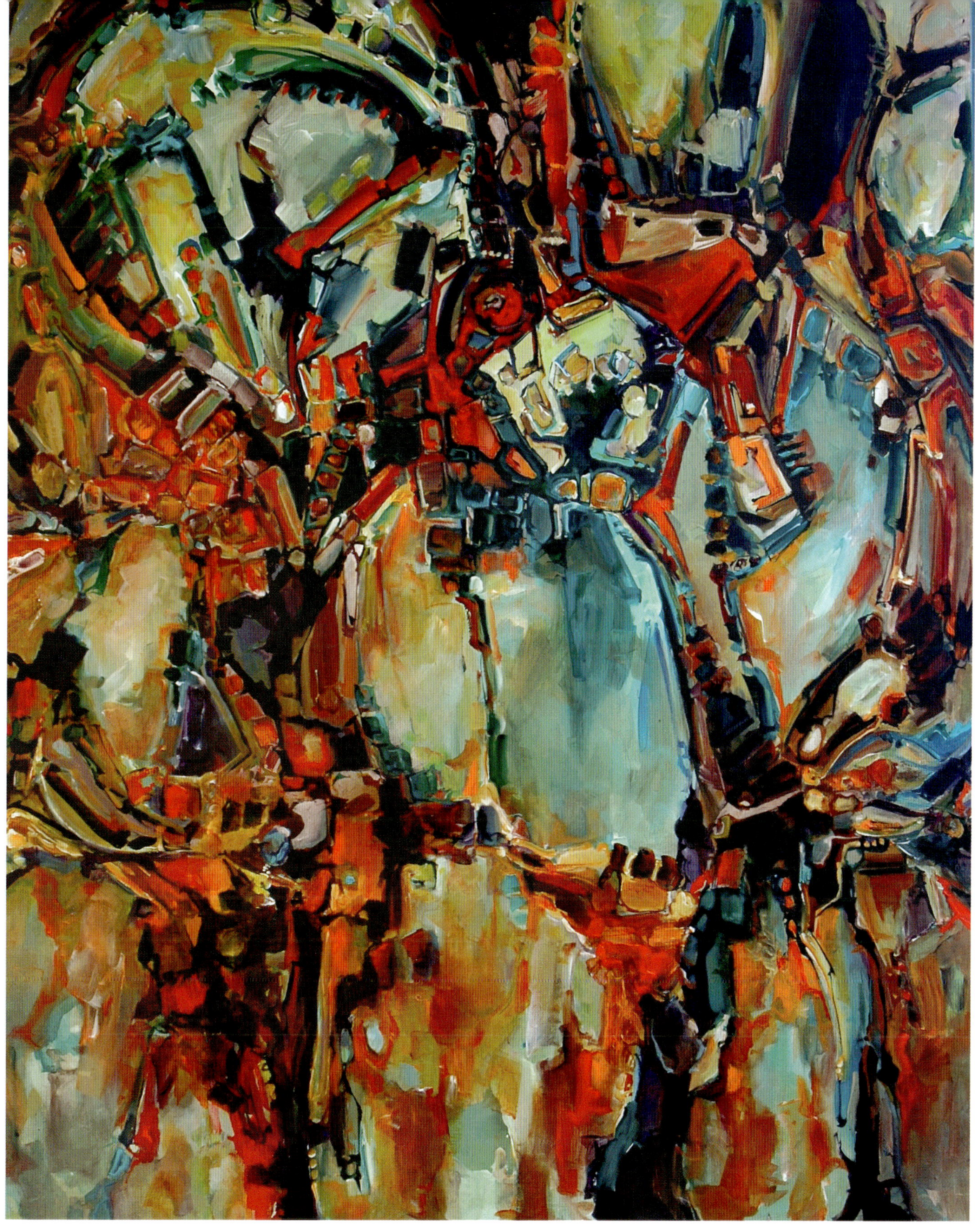

THREE'S COMPANY | Jane Tracy
Acrylic on board, 60" × 48" (152cm × 122cm)

I began painting less than a decade ago and as I'm approaching my mid-seventies, I've found that I paint best with a sense of urgency ... to be fearless, fast and fluid when I develop a painting. Fluid acrylic paints work best for me because they flow easily and dry quickly. Because I work quickly, most often on many pieces at a time, the spontaneous paint applications often require readdressing. Some areas need to be resolved, but the surprises always stimulate, the colors usually seduce and the process is always of the utmost importance. I often paint small study pieces but prefer larger formats for my abstract, nonrepresentational paintings. *Three's Company* is an example of the acrylic work I do, how I embrace and appreciate the qualities of the only medium I use ... acrylic.

CONTRIBUTORS

ABZHANOVA ANARA
ARCLA, Artists Union of the Republic of Kazakhstan
Chernova 10, Almaty, 050042, Kazakhstan
8702.756.8671
anara.artist@yahoo.com
anarabzhanovafineart.kz/en
p 54 *Autumn Reflection in Water*
p 55 *Mountain Flowers*
p 56 *Fall*

MARCO ANTONIO AGUILAR
Ocean Artists Society
661.675.6817
marcozart@gmail.com
marcozart.com
p 8 *Honu's Dance*
p 74 *Endless Journey*

DENISE ATHANAS
AWS, WHS, ISEA-NF
843.388.1839
deniseathenas@comcast.net
deniseathenas.com
p 106 *Burst of Color*

ANGELA BANDURKA
ISAP/S
P.O. Box 1972
Lynnwood, WA 98037
206.852.2391
abandurkaart@gmail.com
angelabandurka.com
p 11 *Don't Be Afraid to Take Chances*

JACQUI BECK
Seattle, WA
jacquibeck.com
p 84 *Decorating the Ordinary*
p 124 *Crocodile King*

RICHARD BELANGER
Societe Canadienne de L'Aquarelle
783 Route Missisquoi, East Bolton
QC, Canada J0E 1G0
richardbelangersca@hotmail.com
richardbelanger.ca
p 12 *Back Home*

LIANA BENNETT
liana@arts-umbrella.com
lianabennett.com
arts-umbrella.com
p 58 *Shadows*

PAUL BENNETT
49 Cedarwood Crescent, Robina
Queensland, Australia 4226
61 0755789235
paulbennett@acrylicartist.com
paulbennettfineart.com
p 10 *Outside Looking In*

JOE BERGHOLM
joebergholm@me.com
joebergholm.com
p 49 *Empire State Building*

CARA BEVAN
4857 Hoover Hill Rd., Trinity, NC 27370
336.861.6363
nobled9c@aol.com
carabevan.com
p 14 *The Grand Cayman Blue Iguanas*
p 15 *Ivy*

DONNE BITNER
NWS, FWS, WHS
Orlando, FL
donneart@aol.com
donnebitner.com
p 87 *Distant Shores*

FILOMENA DE ANDRADE BOOTH
ISEA
2235 Austin Hines Dr., China Spring, TX 76633
254.836.4518
fil@filomenabooth.com
filomenabooth.com
p 109 *A Matter to Consider*

CAROL BORRETT
1162 Maple Bay Rd., Duncan
BC, Canada V9L 5X1
250.748.5224
cborrett@shaw.ca
westcoastwatercolour.com
p 9 *Meeting Place*

URSULA J. BRENNER
Cincinnati Art Club
948 Butterfly Ct., Cincinnati, OH 45231
513.300.9997
ujbrenner@fuse.net
ursulajbrenner.com
p 110 *Dancing*
p 111 *Moment in Time*

JAN BROWN
Detroit Society of Women Painters and Sculptors
24725 Bashian, Novi, MI 48375
248.476.9164
jbrown12@twmi.rr.com
janbrownart.com
p 112 *Pierian Springs*

HANK BUFFINGTON
1303 Hillside Dr., Lancaster, PA 17603
717.391.2652
hank27@hotmail.com
hankbuffington.com
p 16 *Basement De Stijl*

HARRY BURMAN
Society of Creative Arts of Newton, PSA
201 Autumn Lane, Brewster, NY 10509
845.279.5388
burmanarts@gmail.com
harryburman.com
p 17 *Me*

DOTTI BURTON
NWWS (signature member), EAFA, SCA
29 Vista Del Mar St., Camano Island, WA 98282
206.714.3647
dottiburton18@msn.com
dottiburton.com
p 99 *Threesome*

DEREK CAMERON
NSPCA, Pastel Society of New Jersey
djcam@ptd.net
artderek.com
p 33 *Snow Business*

DIANE CANNON
PWCS, PWS, BWS
23 Tullamore Dr., West Chester, PA 19382
610.793.0881
diane7337@aol.com
dianecannonart.com
p *59 Ascending*

BRUNO CAPOLONGO
AOCA, MFA-V, OSA
10 Craig Blvd., Grimsby
ON, Canada L3M 4C1
289.235.9678
bc@brunocapolongo.com
brunocapolongo.com
p *23 The Dynasty Vase*

BARBARA L. CLARK
5809 Pine Ridge Circle, Vero Beach, FL 32967
772.633.0238
me@barbaralclark.com
barbaralclark.com
p *27 Eden Road #1*

RAY-MEL CORNELIUS
1526 Elmwood Blvd., Dallas, TX 75224
214.226.2576
ray-mel@raymelcornelius.com
raymelcornelius.com
p *70 A Magpie This Fall*

PATRICIA COULTER
1702 7 St., Cold Lake
AB, Canada T9M 1M7
780.813.4660
pcoulter08@gmail.com
patriciacoulter.com
p *101 Winter Sentinels*

LAURA CRABTREE-HOLLENBECK
1175 Braebury Way, Traverse City, MI 49686
616.719.8455
lauracrabtreeart@gmail.com
crabtreeart.org
p *31 How Do You Like Them*

PRESTON CRAIG
ISAP, SILA, NOAPS
7451 Ostrom Ave., Lake Balboa, CA 91406
818.609.1945
prestonc.net
p *63 Napa Red*

RON CRAIG
Valley Springs, CA
925.457.3419
roncraig@me.com
roncraigart.com
p *28 25 Gets You 15*

JAN CROOKER
Rehoboth Art League, Mid-Atlantic Plein Air Painters, New Arts Program
463 W. Main St., Kutztown, PA 19530
610.504.0819
jancrooker@hotmail.com
jancrooker.com
p *62 Morning Coffee*

NANCY CURRY
Lake Saint Louis, MO
nancycurry1@gmail.com
nancycurry.com
p *61 Open House*

PAM DITTLOFF
1704 Live Oak Park
Seabrook Island, SC 29455
704.342.0505 (home), 704.575.8505 (cell)
pamelad@carolina.rr.com
pamdittloff.com
p *35 Mountain Reflections*

ANN TRAINOR DOMINGUE
Copley Society of Art, New England Watercolor Society, New Hampshire Art Association
39 High St., Goffstown, NH 03045
603.497.8080
domingue@comcast.net
anntrainordomingue.com
p *96 Working Docks Lineup (aka Lined Up in Blues)*

SY ELLENS
NWS, MOWS, TWS-PS
326 W. Kalamazoo Ave., Suite 321
Kalamazoo, MI 49007
269.342.6326
syellens@sbcglobal.net
syellens.com
p *52 Summer Shimmers*

PHILIPPE FERNANDEZ
philippesarts@yahoo.com
fairytalebuzz.com
p *64 Witch Island*

JAN FILARSKI
ISAP, NCS
16740 Apple Lane S., Ray, MI 48096
586.781.5270
jfilarski@comcast.net
janfilarski.com
p *127 Egress*

KYLE FISHER
147 Brown Street, Philadelphia, PA 19123
609.977.1341
kyle@kylefisher.com
kylefisher.com
p *65 What to Do With It?*

CAROL A. GATCHEL
115 Arbon Lane, New Bern, NC 28562
252.637.1666 (home), 252.670.7637 (cell)
cagatchel@suddenlink.net
carolgatchel.com
p *108 Blocking Color*

SCOTT GLASER
scott@blazingglasers.com
blazingglasers.com
p *67 Withdrawal Symptoms*
p *66 Prairie Dog*

SHAWN GOULD
SAA
shawn@shawngould.com
shawngould.com
p *29 Chihuly's Garden*

PRISCILLA GREENBAUM
SWS
14800 Parisian Ct., Reno, NV 89511
775.384.6514
prisgreenbaum@gmail.com
p *115 Mirage*

PATRICIA GUZMÁN
Nicolás San Juan S20 – 404, México, D.F.
patriciafineart@gmail.com
patriciaguzman.blogspot.mx
p *13 Purificación*

TRIPP HARRISON
22 Cathedral Place, St. Augustine, FL 32084
904.824.3662
info@trippharrisongallery.com
trippharrisongallery.com
p 25 *Adirondack Chairs*

RICK HECK
Gilbert, AZ
rick@flowingpaint.com
flowingpaint.com
p 116 *Foolish Dreams*

ALICE S HELWIG
258 Dalhurst Way NW, Calgary, Alberta
Canada T3A 1P5
ashelwig@shaw.ca
p 90 *Breezes Through the Cottonwoods*

MARIKO HIBBETT
Oakland, CA
marikohibbett@gmail.com
marikohibbett.com
p 117 *Watergarden*

RAY HILL
2005 Greenbrier Lane, Clemmons, NC 27012
336.766.7864
artbyray@aol.com
p 22 *Along Fairway 1 – Salem Glen, NC*

SHEILA HOGGE
Birmingham Watercolour Society
Apartado 259, 18690 Almunécar
Granada, Spain
sheila@sheilahogge.com
sheilahogge.com
p 26 *Mother and Son*

RANDY HONERLAH
PAA, FAA, EDAC
randy@honerlahfineart.com
honerlahfineart.com
p 118 *The Grotto*

BERNIE HUBERT
5 Hawthorne Ct., Morristown, NJ 07960
973.879.8892
bhube3331@aol.com
berniehubert.com
p 68 *NJ Beach Umbrella*
p 69 *Seaside Heights, NJ, Beach and Casino Pier*

SHERYL HUGHES
Lighthouse Art Center, Sacramento Fine Arts, Blue Line Arts
artist@dashpast.com
sherylhughes.com
p 21 *Standing Egret*

STEVEN E. HUGHES
primaryhughes.com
p 75 *Cecropia Bot*

SHIRLEY JEANE
NVWS, WFWS
P.O. Box 371360, Las Vegas, NV 89137
702.645.0999
shirleyj@artbyjeane.com
artbyjeane.com
p 57 *Reading Railroad*

BEV JOZWIAK
AWS/S, NWS/S, TWSA/S
315 W. 23rd St., Vancouver, WA 98660
360.694.9262
paintingjoz@hotmail.com
bevjozwiak.com
p 30 *Universal Canvas*
p 72 *Brown Leather, Green Olives*

VANESSA KATZ
760.469.2356
artsy59@gmail.com
vanessakatzart.com
p 71 *Is It Cloudy or Bright?*

GARRY KAYE
300 Reynolds Rd., Saltspring Island
BC, Canada
250.653.4453
gbkaye@gmail.com
garrykaye.com
p 19 *First Ice*

PAUL KINSLOW
Sonoran Arts
pquinslo@cox.net
worldleftwild.com
p 78 *Under the Rim*

LOREN KOVICH
AWS, TWSA, MTWS
2225 Alpine Dr., 1A, Helena, MT 59601
406.495.9203
lorenkovich@yahoo.com
lorenkovich.com
p 113 *Green Frenzy*

KRISTIN KRIMMEL
Fort Gallery Artists Cooperative, Federation of Canadian Artists, CARFAC
Maple Ridge, BC Canada
kkrimmel@shaw.ca
kristinkrimmel.com
p 32 *Connections 1*

DARLENE KUHNE
Arvada & Denver, CO
303.642.3125 (home), 720.935.2596 (cell)
darlenekuhne@gmail.com
p 120 *Emerging Spring*

AILI KURTIS
ailikurtis@hotmail.com
ailikurtis.com
p 45 *White Lake*

RON LACE
NOAPS, AIS, MGAL
1550 Stonegate Pass, Germantown, TN 38138
901.619.8728
rflace@yahoo.com
rlacestudio.com
p 18 *The Prophet*

MARISSA MADONNA
20 October Hill Rd., Oak Ridge, NJ 07438
973.896.0398
marissamadonna@gmail.com
marissamadonna.com
p 39 *Ballerina in Blue*

PATRICIA MAGUIRE
Boca Raton Museum of Art Artists' Guild (signature member), American Impressionist Society, Delray Art League
929 Fern Dr., Delray Beach, FL 33483
561.716.5686
patimaguire@aol.com
patimaguire.com
p 92 *Morning Clouds*
p 93 *Early Morning Light*

MAC MAK
California Art Club, Mode of Design Alliance, Asia International Contemporary Arts Promotion Association
L7-18 JCCAC, 30 Paktin St., Shekkipmei, Kowloon, Hong Kong
852.6255.6526
mac@am-artworkshop.com
am-artworkshop.com
p 88 *Red Taxi*

JANET MANGIONE
P.O. Box 12729, Rochester, NY 14612-0729
janetmangione9@gmail.com
p *121 Golden Means*

Kay Masini
ISEA, Three Cities Art Club, Internationale Vriendenkring (Belgium)
13629 Westbrook Rd., Plymouth, MI 48170
734.207.1556
kaydonmasini@aol.com
p *122 Planning the Game*
p *123 Material Girl*

SUZANNE MCCOURT
ISAP
Aptos, CA
831.246.3004
paint4me@gmail.com
suzannemccourt.com
p *95 Guitar Man: Blues Guitar*
p *124 Alluring*

VICKY MCLAIN
Cheraw Arts Commission, Chesterfield Visual Arts Alliance, South Carolina Arts Commission
vicky@drivenbyart.com
drivenbyart.com
p *125 Passion*

MARK E. MEHAFFEY
5440 Zimmer Rd., Williamston, MI 48895
mark@mehaffeygallery.com
mehaffeygallery.com
p *91 So True*

SYNDI MICHAEL
4510 Mapleton Dr., West Linn, OR 97068
503.358.2348
feathers97@comcast.net
p *38 His Royal Highness*

TRACY MILLER
National Society of Painters in Casein & Acrylic, International Equine Artists
16 Ruxton Ave., Manitou Springs, CO 80829
719.650.0827
tracymillerfineart@gmail.com
tracymillerfineart.com
p *79 Passive Agreement*

BILLY-JACK MILLIGAN
1948 Hald-Dunn TW1 Rd., Canfield
ON, Canada N0A 1C0
905.701.4783
billyjacksfineart@gmail.com
billyjacksfineart.com
p *37 Spanish Symphony*

JOHN MULLANE
49-A Edgewater Park, Bronx, NY 10465
917.330.2382
johnmullaneart@gmail.com
johnmullane.blogspot.com
p *37 Siberian Summer*

LINDA S. OLMSTEAD
Colorado Watercolor Society (signature member)
2757 E. Jamison Ave., Centennial, CO 80122
303.771.4564 (home); 303.916.5396 (cell)
p *94 Sitting on the Catbird Seat*

IRENA ORLOV
ISAP, NAIA, AWA
irenaorlov@att.net
irenaorlov.com
p *119 Blue Landscape*

MELINDA PATRICK
Artists of Texas
Magnolia, TX
832.413.1142
melindapatrick@gmail.com
melindapatrick.com
p *76 Hey Cupcake!*

PAMELA PETERSON
MCS, LGAL, EAG
LaGrange, IL
pam.peterson@artpastiche.com
artpastiche.com
p *126 Tree of Knowledge*

BOB PETILLO
Petillo Arts, Art Educators of New Jersey, National Art Educators of America
P.O. Box 98, Lafayette, NJ 07848
973.903.1099
bpetillo@embarqmail.com
bobpetillo.com
angelfire.com/nj/Petillo
p *40 Nautical Still Life*
p *41 Tenement*

IGOR RAIKHLINE
2635 Delridge Dr. SW, Lilburn, GA 30047
770.573.4558
iraikhline@aol.com
igor-raikhline.com
p *60 Birthday Girl With Yesterday's Balloon*

MARC REMUS
Affentorplatz 18, 60594 Frankfurt, Germany
0049.69.628101
info@remus.biz
marcremus.com
p *98 Expressions of Cologne*

DANIELLE RICHARD
PSA, PSEC, MBA
danielle@daniellerichard.com
daniellerichard.com
p *6 Forever Here*
p *24 His Blue Shirt*

MICHAEL JAMES RIDDET
SAA
20158 Chamberlain Lane, Gays Mills, WI 54631
608.872.2429
riddetstudio@mwt.net
riddetstudio.com
p *34 Knowledge Is Power*
p *141 A Brief History of Flight in America*

MARY K. ROHDE
Phoenix, AZ
totallyart.rohde@gmail.com
p *80 Gayla*

JOANNE BEAULE RUGGLES
724 Patricia Dr., San Luis Obispo, CA 93405
805.543.5968
jruggles@charter.net
beaulerugglesgraphics.com
p *89 In Matters of the Heart*

TOM SACHADE
503 Martha St., Burlington
ON, Canada L7R 2R1
905.466.7384
tsachade@cogeco.ca
facebook.com/sachadeart
p *73 A Tuscan View*

NANCY SEILER
Missoula, MT
406.370.1254
nancy@nancyseiler.com
nancyseiler.com
p *100 Aspens XX*

DIANNA SHYNE
359 Hill Park Ct., Camano Island, WA 98282
360.387.4950 (home), 425.387.4859 (cell)
gotzshyne@hotmail.com
diannashyne.com
p *103 Americana*

JAN STOMMES
OPA, AIS, The International Guild of Realism
112 Altenburg Ave., Owen, WI 54460
715.229.2904 (home), 715.613.7513 (cell)
janstommes@gmail.com
janstommesart.com
p *128 Happy*

DOROTHY STONELY
ISAP/S, Central Coast Art Association
P.O. Box 798, Moss Landing, CA 95039
831.633.3006
dstonely@sbcglobal.net
stonely.artspan.com
p *129 Gift From the Golden Eagle*

ANDA J. STYLER
143 West St., Unit 123C
New Milford, CT 06776
860.355.2556
andastylerfineart.com
p *43 August*

FRANCESCA TABOR-MIOLLA
100 Lamplighter Lane, Ponte Vedra, FL 32082
904.273.0448
sassyandtwisted@bellsouth.net
sassyandtwisted.com
p *130 It's All Relative*
p *131 Listen to the Silence*

YELENA YORK TONOYAN
yelenayork.com
p *81 Luck*

JANE TRACY
203.915.7702
janetracy@gmail.com
janetracyartist.com
p *135 Three's Company*

ROSA VERA
118 Via Finita St., San Antonio, TX 78229
210.451.8041
rositavera@aol.com
rosavera.com
p *82 Jazz Horns*

MYRNA WACKNOV
NWS, CWA, SDWS
675 Matsonia Dr., Foster City, CA 94404
650.574.3192
myrnawack@prodigy.net
myrnawacknov.com
myrnawacknov.blogspot.com
p *102 When in Doubt*

JOHN WALKER
Downers Grove, IL
info@walkerbrushworks.com
walkerbrushworks.com
p *44 VooDoo Steps Out*

SHARYNE E. WALKER
ISAP/S, AOI, Society for Art of Imagination
2575 #14 S. Willow Ave., Fresno, CA 93725
sharyne@sharyne.com
sharyne.com
p *104 The Tattooed Angel*

DEB WARD
Georgia Watercolor Society, Ohio Watercolor Society
1165 Chapelow Ridge Rd., W. Harrison, IN 47060
812.637.3090
debwardart@gmail.com
debwardart.blogspot.com
debwardart.com
p *46 Oriental Roses*

HANK WASHINGTON
California Art Education Association
Bakersfield CA
661.332.1258
imhankypanky@yahoo.com
p *83 OPW*

LINDSAY WATSON
PMAA, AFAA, FCA
lindsayj3@shaw.ca
lindsayj3.shawwebspace.ca
p *47 Karyn and Kayo*

DAVID WICKS
CWS, WFWS
Morrison, CO
artopia@comcast.net
wicksart.com
p *48 Duesy*

STEVE WILDA
NSPCA, Allied Artists of America, Academic Artists Association
53 Rocky Hill Rd., Hadley, MA 01035
413.584.8482
artofsw3@gmail.com
stevewilda.com
p *20 Coffee Break*

KEITH WILKIE
McLean, VA & Surfside Beach, SC
703.869.4754
keithwilke.art@verizon.net
keithwilkieart.com
p *42 Surfside*

APRIL WILLY
Indiana Artists Club, Hoosier Salon, Indiana Design Center
1870 E. 106th St., Carmel, IN 46032
317.362.9656
aprilwilly@aprilwilly.com
aprilwilly.com
p *86 Relative Distance*

NANCY YAKI
ISAP, NOAP
P.O. Box 98, Los Olivos, CA 93441
805.245.4353
boandero@gmail.com
nancyaki.com
p *50 Moss Cove*

YAH-HANN (ERRIC) YANG
kyoco722@gmail.com
kyoco722.wix.com/erric
p *132 Untitled 1*
p *133 Untitled 2*

HAL YASKULKA
LAA, Tirage Art Gallery, Film Art LA
16514 Simonds St., Granada Hills, CA 91344
818.94.8621
halvador@yahoo.com
halyaskulka.com
p *51 Mediation, Ashley*

KATHLEEN L. YOKOUCHI
PAH, HWS, WAG
15 Craigside Pl., Honolulu, Hawaii 96817
808.550.3054
nuyolks@gmail.com
p *105 Good Luck and Prosperity!*

BRENDA HOPE ZAPPITELL
200 NE 2nd Ave. #103, Delray Beach, FL 33444
561.886.8611
artisthope@aol.com
zappitellstudio.com
p *114 Celebrating Yin*

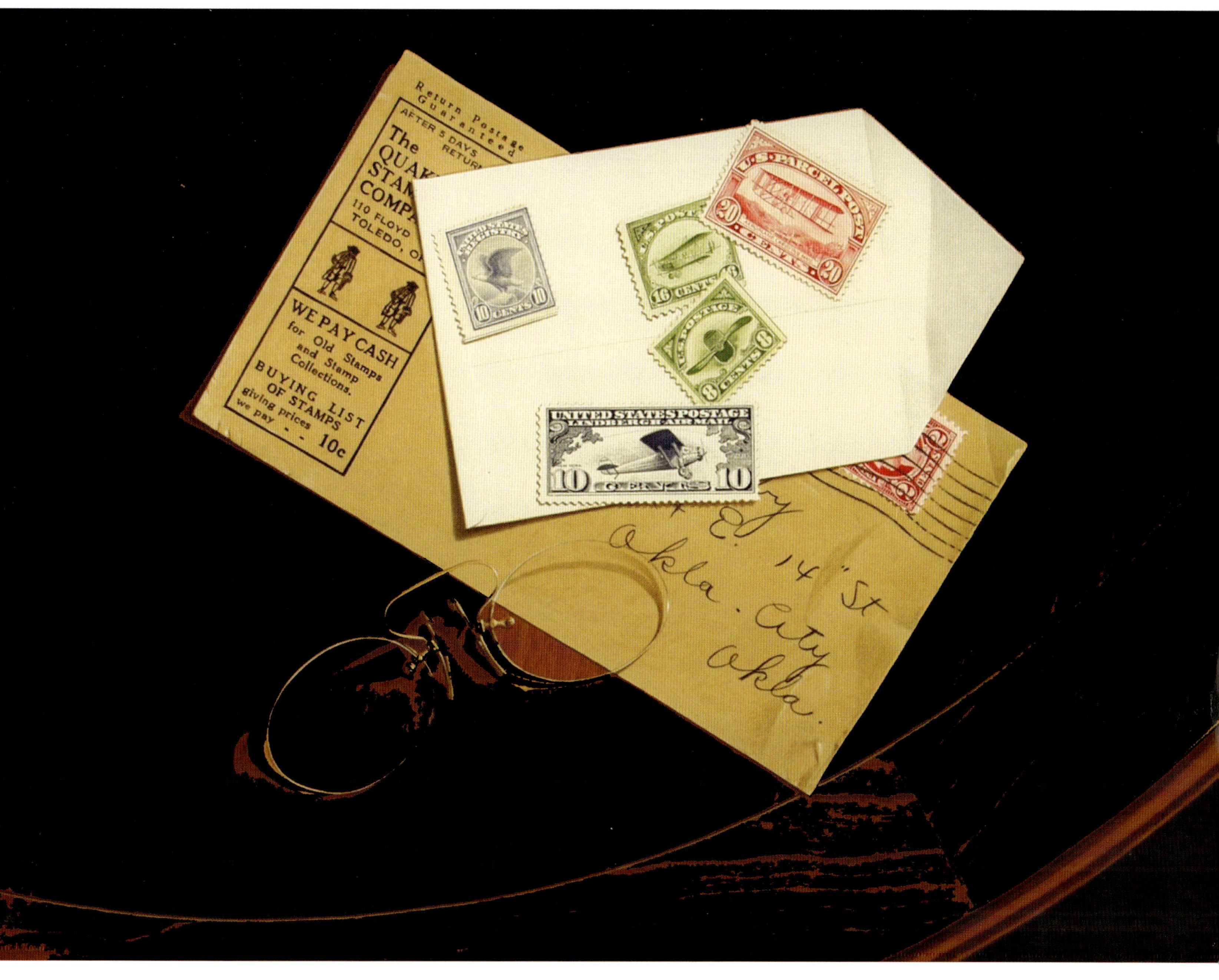

A BRIEF HISTORY OF FLIGHT IN AMERICA | Michael James Riddet
Acrylic on hardboard, 9" × 12" (23cm × 30cm)

The original intent of this piece was simply to challenge my ability to paint the Spirit of St. Louis stamp life size. Five stamps, two envelopes, pince-nez spectacles and a library table later, I had completed one of the most time-consuming little paintings of my career. Whenever I tackle a trompe l'oeil painting with historic content, I insist on having the actual objects in hand. Stamp detail is a challenge. I work with three forms of magnification in tandem: my bifocals, jeweler's head piece and an old handheld 80mm medium-format camera lens. This combination allows me to subtract tiny bits of acrylic pigment with a needle in order to simulate the original engraved surface of a stamp. Confronted by a stamp collector, I was asked why I had glued the stamps to the painting. The illusion was complete.

INDEX

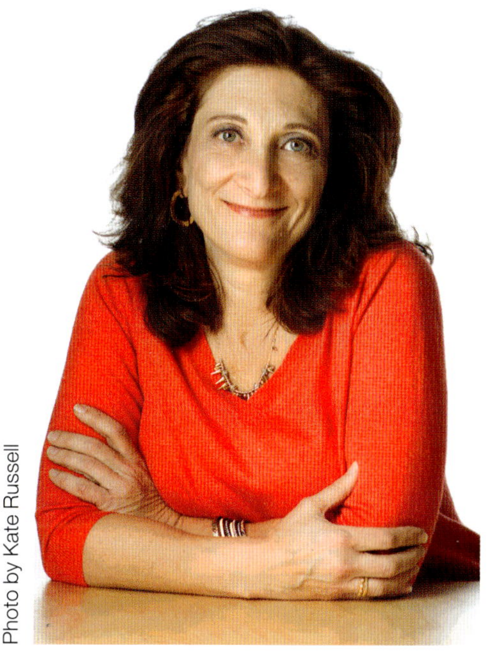

Photo by Kate Russell

ABOUT THE EDITOR

Born and raised on the east coast in the United States, Nancy received a BFA from the Rhode Island School of Design and an MFA from Columbia University. From creating costumes and sets for theater and film to coordinating public arts programs for the state of New York, she has had a wide-ranging career in the arts, all of which inform her work. She now lives in Santa Fe, New Mexico, and has been painting for more than thirty years, exhibiting and teaching both nationally and internationally. Her previous books, *Acrylic Revolution*, *Acrylic Innovation* and *Acrylic Illuminations* offer a multitude of techniques and ideas with the intent to add inspiration to artists everywhere. Please visit her website **nancyreyner.com** for current work, her painting blog, workshops and gallery representation.

Cover image: *HOW DO YOU LIKE THEM*, Laura Crabtree-Hollenbeck, p31

Back cover image: *BLOCKING COLOR*, Carol A. Gatchel, p108

 Published by North Light Books, an imprint of F+W Media, Inc., 10151 Carver Road, Suite 200, Cincinnati, Ohio, 45242. (800) 289-0963. First Edition.

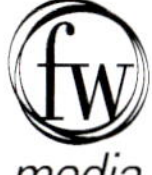

Other fine North Light Books are available from your favorite bookstore, art supply store or online supplier. Visit our website at fwmedia.com.

18 17 16 15 14 5 4 3 2 1

DISTRIBUTED IN CANADA BY FRASER DIRECT
100 Armstrong Avenue
Georgetown, ON, Canada L7G 5S4
Tel: (905) 877-4411

DISTRIBUTED IN THE U.K. AND EUROPE BY F&W MEDIA INTERNATIONAL
Brunel House, Newton Abbot, Devon, TQ12 4PU, England
Tel: (+44) 1626 323200, Fax: (+44) 1626 323319
Email: postmaster@davidandcharles.co.uk

DISTRIBUTED IN AUSTRALIA BY CAPRICORN LINK
P.O. Box 704, S. Windsor NSW, 2756 Australia
Tel: (02) 4560-1600, Fax: (02) 4577 5288
Email: books@capricornlink.com.au

ISBN-13: 978-1-4403-2886-2
SRN: U2633

Edited by Sarah Laichas
Designed by Clare Finney
Production coordinated by Mark Griffin

METRIC CONVERSION CHART

TO CONVERT	TO	MULTIPLY BY
Inches	Centimeters	2.54
Centimeters	Inches	0.4
Feet	Centimeters	30.5
Centimeters	Feet	0.03
Yards	Meters	0.9
Meters	Yards	1.1